TRACES OF J. B. JACKSON

Midcentury: Architecture, Landscape, Urbanism, and Design
Richard Longstreth, Editor

TRACES OF J. B. JACKSON

The Man Who Taught Us to See Everyday America

Helen Lefkowitz Horowitz

University of Virginia Press

CHARLOTTESVILLE AND LONDON

University of Virginia Press
© 2020 Helen Lefkowitz. Horowitz
All rights reserved
Printed in the United States of America on acid-free paper

First published 2020

9 8 7 6 5 4 3 2 1

Library of Congress Cataloging-in-Publication Data

Names: Horowitz, Helen Lefkowitz, author.
Title: Traces of J.B. Jackson : the man who taught us to see everyday America / Helen Lefkowitz Horowitz.
Description: Charlottesville : University of Virginia Press, 2019. | Series: Midcentury : architecture, landscape, urbanism, and design | Includes bibliographical references and index.
Identifiers: LCCN 2019036774 (print) | LCCN 2019036775 (ebook) | ISBN 9780813943343 (cloth) | ISBN 9780813943350 (ebook)
Subjects: LCSH: Jackson, John Brinckerhoff, 1909–1996. | Authors, American—Biography. | Cultural landscapes—United States.
Classification: LCC PS3560.A2159 H67 2019 (print) | LCC PS3560.A2159 (ebook) | DDC 813/.52—dc23
LC record available at https://lccn.loc.gov/2019036774
LC ebook record available at https://lccn.loc.gov/2019036775

Furthermore:
a program of the J. M. Kaplan Fund

Publication of this volume was assisted by a grant from Furthermore: a program of the J. M. Kaplan Fund.

Cover art: J. B. Jackson (photograph by Peter Brown)

For Sarah Horowitz and Ben Horowitz, who knew Mr. Jackson well
and for
Lucie Fielding
and for
Judy Liebman, Aaron Horowitz, and Adam Liebman
and, as always, for
Dan

CONTENTS

ILLUSTRATIONS

Black-and-White Figures

Color Plates (following page 178)

ACKNOWLEDGMENTS

Getting to know J. B. Jackson enriched my life in many ways, and important among them was the contact it gave me with the larger world of those in my generation who learned from Jackson and became his friends. I first had the pleasure of meeting Paul Groth. A friend and mainstay ever since, Paul has led me to sources, shared material, and answered every question. During my long journey to understand Jackson and write about him, I've come to know others and, along with Paul, I regard Doug Adams, Vince Healy, Janet Mendelsohn, Barton Phelps, Elizabeth Barlow Rogers, Ted Rogers, John Sinton, Paul Starrs, Marc Treib, and Chris Wilson as companions in arms. They have taught me about Jackson in their works and conversations. I cherish their friendship and am deeply thankful for all they have given me over the years.

Following Jackson's death in 1996, numerous opportunities arose to speak and write in ways that stimulated my own awareness of Jackson's contributions. And more recently, several important invitations in 2015 allowed me to think more broadly about Jackson and realize it was time to write this book. Each occasion brought an engaged audience who asked good questions and made thoughtful comments. The 2015 events also led to meeting or reconnecting with others who knew Jackson, including Bob Calo, Tim Davis, Randy Hill, and Richard Longstreth. When teaching at Smith College, I came to know Jeffrey D. Blankenship, who was researching Jackson for his dissertation, and I have recently read his articles in drafts. I am especially grateful to Chris Wilson, Jordi Ballestra, and all the participants of *PhotoPaysage/LandscapeRepresentation,* the 2015 conference at the University of New Mexico, for insights and comments. In giving presentations about this evolving manuscript since that time, I've received good critiques from colleagues at the Radcliffe Institute and the Spring Seminar held at the Huntington Library.

At the Center for Southwest Research, the repository of the J. B. Jackson Papers, Audra Bellmore, curator of the John Gaw Meem Archives of Southwestern Architecture, has generously given of her time to offer indispensible help to this project. I also wish to thank Erin Fussell, Karen Mazur, and Robin Moses for their careful and timely assistance at the CSWR.

Soon after Jackson's death, the late Grady Clay solicited for my use copies of Jackson's letters from many recipients—David Crane, Patrick Horsbrugh, among others. John K. Notz Jr. became my enthusiastic guide to the Deerfield Academy, cheering me on and aiding access to its archives, where I benefited from Ann Lozier's gracious help. More recently, John Sinton, himself a writer on the landscape, sent me copies of Jackson's letters to his mother, Nell Sinton, her portrait of Jackson sketching, and a Jackson sketch for illustration. Jeffrey Flemming, Donlyn Lyndon, William H. Tishler, and Howard D. Weinbrot are among those who extended specific help. To all, I offer thanks.

Archives provide lifeblood for historical research. In addition to that of the Deerfield Academy, among the institutions whose holdings made this work possible are those of Harvard and Columbia Universities. I also wish to thank W. W. Norton & Company for access to Jackson's file. Phillip Campanile ably assisted me with materials at the University of California, Berkeley.

Friends gave me important help. Bettina Friedl and Sandra Rebok carefully translated German words. John Demos offered continual encouragement; and his eagle eye spotted a large lot of early *Landscape* volumes for sale. Many family members, friends, and colleagues listened to me talk of Jackson over the years and offered support and advice. I particularly remember the push Susan Ware gave me to think of my work as biography and lively conversations with Kathleen Dalton. For illustrations, I am grateful to Paul Starrs, John Sinton, and Marc Treib.

Valued institutional support came from Smith College, whose emeriti research grants stand as a model for other colleges and universities. Smith staff from many areas—including faculty, information technology, and library—gave needed assistance. Special thanks goes to Floyd Cheung, Dominique Tremblay, and Lisa DeCarolis-Osepowicz.

I am also grateful to Furthermore: a program of the J. M. Kaplan Fund and to the Foundation for Landscape Studies for supporting the publication of this book.

Access to the rich resources of Widener Library is one of the benefits of a Harvard graduate degree. Summer residency at the Radcliffe Institute in 2016 allowed me the company of gifted colleagues and the able research assistance of Adrian Horton, then a rising Harvard senior. I wish to thank the Harvard University Archives for promptly attending to my many requests and for permission to quote material from their collections.

It has been an extraordinary privilege to be a Reader at the Huntington Library in San Marino, California, during almost all of my adult life. The community of scholars who today gather there stimulate my thinking and enrich my life in immeasurable ways.

Readers helped to turn the raw into the cooked. Dan Horowitz, always my first and last reader, gave his usual wise counsel and encouragement at every stage. In addition, I had extraordinary help from Chris Wilson, Ben Looker, and Brian Goldstein; their careful readings of the manuscript and candid comments pushed me in varied ways to improve the work.

I have been fortunate in having the University of Virginia Press as the publisher of this work. At the outset, anonymous readers for the press offered important insights and saved me from errors. Richard Longstreth gave early encouragement and, as editor of the series Midcentury: Architecture, Landscape, Urbanism, and Design, chose to include this book. At the press, senior editor Boyd Zenner first encouraged submission and then shepherded and carefully edited the manuscript, finding myriad ways to improve it. As computer files became book pages at the University of Virginia Press, I wish to thank Mark Mones, assistant managing editor, who oversaw production; Cecilia Sorochin, art director; and copyeditor Jane Curran. To all at the press, known and unknown, I am deeply grateful.

INTRODUCTION

I see things very clearly, and I rely on what I see. . . . And I see things that other people don't see, and I call their attention to it.
— J. B. Jackson, interview with Bob Calo, c. 1988

For more than four decades, beginning in the mid-twentieth century, John Brinckerhoff Jackson was a perceptive and insightful interpreter of the cultural forces shaping the natural world. He wrote, illustrated, published, taught, and lectured about what he named "landscape," and through a steady flow of vivid and elegant essays, he enabled Americans to see everyday America through its places and spaces as they evolved over time.

Jackson gave the common word *landscape* his own definition. Detaching the term from its connection to oil paintings and formal gardens, Jackson's "landscape" encompassed the full imprint of human societies on the land. What humans shape, he argued, is not random, but ordered, and each landscape is the "expression of a culture, of a way of life."[1] Most concisely, Jackson called landscape "history made visible"—visible through the materiality of structures, developed or preserved land, and transportation systems.[2]

Jackson's principal subjects were houses, roads, fields, towns and cities, buildings and signs, and the imagined lives lived in and around them. He led readers down paths that brought them in touch with both the familiar and the lesser-known and gave meaning to the places and spaces they lived within, observed, or perhaps just read about. He placed landscapes within the fourth dimension of time and demonstrated ways that cultural forces—including but not limited to religious, economic, political, and technological ones—gave shape to terrain and structures. In prose notable for its clarity and wit, he conveyed how human desires and tastes came into play. Jackson saw it all, with a special gift for seeing beyond what was immediately before his eyes.

In 1951 he created the magazine *Landscape,* wrote for it, designed it, drew many of its illustrations, and edited and published it for its first seventeen years. Through *Landscape,* his university teaching, and his presence at conferences he built a network of thinkers and doers. He had a captivating personality on the podium. His lectures drew large audiences to his classes in the 1960s and 1970s at Berkeley and Harvard, and at his public lectures across the continent—lectures that preceded his teaching and continued long after it. Jackson wrote essays until his death in 1996, and his work was published in a wide variety of periodicals and anthologized in important books. With his manifold efforts, Jackson laid the foundation for the field of landscape studies.

I have researched his published writings and his archived papers at the Center for Southwest Research at the University of New Mexico (CSWR). In addition, I have been privileged to transcribe many of his handwritten words currently in my possession (but soon to deposited with his other papers). I have also been able to find elements of his background story through traditional research methods in libraries and archives and via the more recent resource of the Web. Although I came to face the reality that, given the incomplete record of Jackson's life, I could not develop a full biography, I could write a biographical study based on many of the traces that exist.

To convey the life, work, and varied gifts of this exceptional person, I have sought to develop a method that captures Jackson's complexity and allows insight into the different paths he took over time. To do so, I have relied as much as possible on his own words, using the bounty of sources he left behind to write a series of essays on his life and writings. The open format of the essay allows me, as someone who knew Jackson from 1973 until his death in 1996, to react in my own voice. These essays are my version of what the traces of J. B. Jackson—the body of found materials on his life and thought—reveal. As the essays grew in number and I ordered them in rough chronological order, they began to take shape as a biography of J. B. Jackson. My hope is that this work will lead to a fuller appreciation both of J. B. Jackson's contributions to the study of landscape and to a greater understanding of the complex person behind his printed words. I offer *Traces of J. B. Jackson* to inform and extend his legacy.

J. B. Jackson was a person who drew others to him, and I was fortunate enough to be one of them. I was his literary executor, and thus many of the papers left at his death passed through my hands before they were deposited at the CSWR. Other papers he entrusted to me during his lifetime. In 1994, returning from an errand to his house, I found him in the yard outside his kitchen burning his papers in a large oil drum. I yelled for him to stop. He answered, "The past is too much with me." He was in despair, feeling that he was weighed down by his work of the past, and he wanted to rid himself of its remains. I called out that there was another solution—I could take the papers he didn't want and send them to my house for safekeeping. He agreed, and we carried what survived the bonfire to my rental car and put them in its trunk. I left immediately to mail them off. These papers are the basis for many of the traces in this volume.[3]

We had an important personal correspondence, one I find redolent of nineteenth-century exchanges. Through visits and letters, I and my husband came to know him well—at least those parts of him he chose to reveal to us. Although for quite some time mourning his loss kept me from working with the materials at the CSWR and in my possession, I have nonetheless long felt the need and obligation to write from them.

On one level, I wish I could write a full biography of J. B. Jackson; however, I can't. I am a historian who writes only from materials that exist. In Jackson's case, there are gaps in the record of his life I cannot find ways to fill. For example, little evidence of him exists before he was in his teens, and even less of his relationship with his absent father; and I have only his own testimony and his 1940 enlistment record to substantiate his residence in New Mexico from 1938 to 1940. Awareness of what I could not learn held me back from this project for many years; but recently I realized that I could write from what the record does reveal and what I know at first hand—his traces.

Jackson's traces are indeed significant. They bring to light important elements of an extraordinary person. They demonstrate the recognition of his gifts when he was still in his teens; his early intention to be a writer and his sustained efforts to be a novelist; his courage during World War II; his fascination with travel and his many observations in travel journals; his solitary creation of *Landscape* magazine and its development under his leadership; his personal growth in midlife and engagement with lecturing and teaching; and his search, as he aged, for connection to others and acceptance of ways of life different from his own.

Others have contributed to Jackson's legacy in important ways I do not presume to duplicate. Although sketching was a meaningful part of Jackson's life from his early years until his death, it is mentioned here in passing. I cannot add to, but only learn from, Douglas Adams's discussion and presentation of Jackson's sketches in *Drawn to Landscape*. This most recent book on Jackson also contains—in addition to the two fascinating and informative DVDs that served to inspire the volume— valuable treatments that include Jackson's slide collection by Paul Groth, the history of *Landscape* magazine during and after Jackson's time at its helm by Paul Starrs and Peter Goin, and the subsequent directions of the field of landscape studies by Tim Davis. Earlier volumes, edited by Jackson's contemporaries and younger colleagues, remain key to understanding Jackson and his legacy.[4]

What I can do, as a historian, is interrogate the documents Jackson left behind: those entrusted to me in his lifetime, those offered to me after his death, and those found in institutional archives. The collection of papers at the CSWR is vast, but I have selected from them only those elements that allow me to make some fresh contribution. The Center holds many papers, drawings, and photographs awaiting future Jackson researchers. I was able to find extraordinary material in the archives at Deerfield Academy and Harvard University. The W. W. Norton Papers held by Columbia University's Rare Book & Manuscript Library contained unexpected treasures. I also benefited from the generosity of a number of Jackson's friends, who sent or let me see his letters and sketches in their possession. Finally, at the point when I thought my research had come to an end, two boxes of material arrived at the CSWR, and I was given permission to review and cite their contents.

I have long committed myself to writing all I know and can learn, even when this means focusing on words intended to be private or ones that display a revered person's bigotry. Born in 1909 into a family with elite aspirations, Jackson inherited many of the narrow-minded views of the white Anglo-Saxon Protestant establishment of his day, an aspect of himself he later rejected and worked hard to outgrow. Jackson wanted nothing in his personal life to be revealed, and he made this demand of me in his lifetime. I refused to accede to it at the time; now, as it hovers over me these many years after his death, I refuse once again. Jackson helped create and promote a new way of thinking about the shaping of the physical world by human endeavor; it is important to understand the inner sources and conflicts that made his work possible and sustained it for over four decades.

And for that same reason, I include in these pages a record of our correspondence. It tells of certain aspects of Jackson's life and thought from 1974 until 1996. Those who knew Jackson well are aware that to each friend he revealed only the piece of himself he wanted that person to know. There is much about him that I do not know, but I present his side of our correspondence to illustrate what he allowed me to see of him. I was, and remain, grateful for his accepting me as one of his many younger friends and ultimately entrusting me toward the end of his life with some of the materials from which these traces have been drawn.

I came to know J. B. Jackson in 1973. My husband, Daniel Horowitz, and I were then young historians on fellowships in Washington, D.C., researching separate projects in the Library of Congress. We saw an advertisement for a new book—*American Space: The Centennial Years* by John Brinckerhoff Jackson. Sight unseen, we agreed to review it for a historical journal. The book proved fascinating and evoked the kinds of spatial explorations and conversations that began in Dan's and my undergraduate years, when we were courting. With all the presumption of our relative youth, we assumed Jackson's fresh prose and engaging ideas came from a person at the outset of a career. Just to check, however, we looked up the author in the great library's card catalog. To our surprise, we learned that Jackson was no longer young, and that from 1951 to 1968 he had edited and published *Landscape,* a magazine with which we were then unfamiliar. We also learned Jackson was currently teaching at Harvard in the fall and at Berkeley in the spring.

After I located *Landscape* in the library, I sat on the floor of its vast stacks, open in those years, to read through many of the magazine's issues. I found *Landscape* a delight. It told me about what I wanted at that time to know—houses, fields, roads, front yards, garages—all vividly described and interpreted. Dan and I wrote our review, the only published collaboration we have ever undertaken, and it came out in the *Journal of Interdisciplinary History* in 1974.[5]

In that same period we secured a shared position to teach at Scripps College in Claremont, California. As we began to prepare for our move to a place that then seemed very far away, we chose to travel to Cambridge, Massachusetts, to say goodbye to friends and to the university where we had both gone to graduate school. As we walked across the Harvard Yard, pushing our two-year-old son in a stroller, Dan asked, "Do you think we could meet Mr. Jackson?" We headed to the building where he was likely to be and located his office. After our knock on the door, a resonant voice said, "Come in." A small man came to greet us and welcomed us into a large room where a seminar table served for a desk. After sitting around it briefly,

Jackson suggested we go to a café to have coffee and talk. He grabbed his leather jacket and checked for cigarettes.

When seated, Jackson did not seem small. His baritone voice was beautiful, and as he spoke, it expanded to fill the space. I remember noting the way he used the words "we" and "us." He learned of my work, then on the history of American zoos, and conveyed to me that I was engaged in his enterprise. He charged me with carrying landscape studies to the West. I felt elected by him, and yet I was quite conscious he assumed I knew many things I actually knew nothing about. I remember trying to be clear with him that I was a historian of more limited scope, a novice, but he either wanted to have none of it or pretended so.

What about our two-year-old son, never one to let others forget his needs? Somehow he was mesmerized by this man. Jackson didn't ignore him—he easily interrupted whatever he was saying to focus on that young child for a moment, just enough, before taking up his line of thought again.

It was a long visit in the café, and we walked back to Jackson's office in the late afternoon half-light. He gave me handouts that included copies of material on the balloon frame house and the grid.

Once settled in California, I began writing to him. Receiving his first letter in return and those that followed were memorable events. A letter from him was heavy—it weighed in the hand. My name was large in black ink on the envelope. And inside was his voice—interested, kind, and encouraging. Our correspondence, begun in spring 1974, continued until his death.

The next time we saw him was when he taught a brief course at UCLA in 1978. He came to Claremont twice to lecture in the early 1980s. Now accompanied by two children, Dan and I began to visit him in his home outside of Santa Fe, staying for significant periods in the 1980s and 1990s. In those years we met his friends from his varied circles and got a sense of the richness of his world in New Mexico. In 1994, I traveled alone to tape a set of conversations with him and later to prepare the collection of his essays, *Landscape in Sight: J. B. Jackson's America*. It came out in 1997, one year after his death.

For that book I wrote an introduction based on a full reading of Jackson's published writings, library research, and the recorded conversations of 1994. In many ways, *Traces of J. B. Jackson* is an extension of that work, enlarging upon and, at times, correcting the narrative I presented in 1997.

A brief account of Jackson's life provides context for the essays that follow. John

Brinckerhoff Jackson was born in 1909 in Dinard, France, of American parents, William Brinckerhoff Jackson and Alice Richardson Jackson. The household, which included a half brother and half sister from his mother's previous marriage, settled for a time outside of Washington, D.C., but returned to Europe at the outset of World War I, when Brinck was four. At that point his parents separated, and he was never to see his father again.

After returning to the United States, the boy lived with his mother and siblings in New York City. There his formal education began at the Riverdale School, a private day school. At age eleven he entered Le Rosey, the famed international boarding school in Switzerland, remaining there for two years. After that, he had one year at Eaglebrook Lodge in Deerfield, Massachusetts, followed by a year of study in France. Returning to the United States, he entered preparatory school, initially at Choate and then at Deerfield Academy, from which he graduated in 1928.

Jackson attended the Experimental College at the University of Wisconsin for a single year, 1928–29, and entered Harvard as a sophomore the following year. He graduated as a member of the class of 1932 with a major in history and literature, and courses in German, French, English, and geography. Irving Babbitt, a leading literary scholar and conservative critic, greatly influenced Jackson's thinking. Active in extracurricular life, he wrote for the *Harvard Advocate,* a storied literary magazine, and served on its editorial board. In his senior year he presided over the Cercle Français and acted in one of its plays; he also wrote the book for the 1932 spring musical of the Hasty Pudding, a Harvard social club famous for its comic theatricals.

Jackson's life immediately after Harvard is a bit harder to track. In the year that followed his last as an undergraduate, it is likely he traveled extensively in Europe, spending significant time in Austria. In the fall of 1933 he entered the architecture school at the Massachusetts Institute of Technology, remaining at least technically for the academic year. "Technically" because, living very near Harvard in Cambridge, Jackson seems mainly to have pursued writing. He had some success: under the name Brinckerhoff Jackson, he published "Prussianism or Hitlerism" in the *American Review* in 1934; and in 1935 he placed a fictional piece, "A Führer Comes to Liechtenstein," in *Harper's Magazine.* During this time he also traveled widely in Europe.[6]

In 1935, he briefly held a job as a proofreader at the *New Bedford Mercury,* a daily newspaper. He worked as a volunteer for the Harvard Bicentennial in 1936 but also spent much time in that and the year following in Austria, where he was likely researching or writing his 1938 novel, *Saints in Summertime,* set in a fictionalized Central European nation. During this period, when not abroad, he resided in Cambridge and Boston. In 1937, he traveled to the Yucatan; in 1938, to Cuba.

After the publication of his novel, Jackson ventured to New Mexico. Breaking with his social class, he got a job as a working cowboy on a large ranch in Cimarron, near the Colorado border.[7] It was while there, in early October 1940, that Jackson enlisted in the army and moved to Fort Bliss, Texas, to begin training for the cavalry. Shifting to military intelligence, he moved on to Camp Richie, Maryland, to receive instruction in preparation for service as an intelligence officer.

By 1943 Jackson was in North Africa, where he served with the Ninth Infantry Division as part of the military intelligence staff known as G-2. He was assigned to the division's combat unit, with interrogation of German prisoners as one of his principal tasks. He was wounded in battle, and after recovering, he advanced with his unit first to Sicily and Italy and then to England in preparation for D-Day. He landed on the beaches of Normandy on June 8, 1944—D-Day plus two. He then moved eastward with the Ninth through the Ardennes and saw combat as a staff officer at the Battle of the Bulge.

Jackson wrote of spending the winter in the Hürtgen Forest with his division. To help him understand his surroundings, he bought guidebooks, postcards, maps, and elementary school geography texts; and through them he began to learn about the landscape. His immediate goal was military: to protect his division as it moved east. He interrogated German prisoners to get more information about the land, and he learned to read and interpret aerial photographs.

During Jackson's long military service, he rose to the rank of major and received the Purple Heart, as one "wounded by an instrument of war in the hands of the enemy"; the Bronze Star "for meritorious service"; and the Silver Star granted for "conspicuous gallantry and intrepidity at the risk of life above and beyond the call of duty."[8] With the cessation of hostilities in Europe in May 1945, Jackson (by his own telling) searched out the popular geography books in Paris that had impressed him during the war—a Gallimard series, edited in the 1930s by Pierre Deffontaines. Jackson also reported that, still in uniform, he wrote guidebooks for the use of American soldiers in Europe.

Once he had his discharge papers from the army, Jackson returned to New Mexico. He leased a ranch in Clines Corners, about fifty-five miles east of Albuquerque. His work ended abruptly, however, when he was thrown from a horse, shattering the bones of his leg. Recovery took eighteen months and involved surgery in New York. According to his own account, during his long convalescence in New Mexico he began to think of developing a magazine of geography along the lines of the French publications he admired. The appearance in 1948 of *La Revue de géographie humaine et d'ethnologie,* edited by Pierre Deffontaines, provided an additional stimulus.

Jackson launched *Landscape* in spring 1951. In the previous year he published two articles in *Southwest Review,* "The Spanish Pueblo Fallacy" and "The Pueblo as a Farm." Jackson was obviously situating himself in New Mexico, and he initially focused his magazine on the "Human Geography of the Southwest." In addition to editing and publishing *Landscape,* Jackson wrote almost everything in the first three issues, under his own name or initials or various pseudonyms. By its second year of publication, *Landscape* had broadened its range beyond the region. As the magazine began to gain a small audience, it attracted important writers, such as Christopher Tunnard, Paul Shepard, and Edgar Anderson. Jackson remained one of *Landscape*'s principal writers and published in it some of his most eloquent and informative essays and book reviews.

One source of *Landscape*'s growing reach came with Jackson's connection to the geographers at the University of California at Berkeley. After visiting there in 1957, he returned frequently, initially to learn and later to instruct. Gradually a brilliant group of writers affiliated with Berkeley and beyond chose to try out their ideas in *Landscape* prior to the publication of their own influential books. They include Carl Sauer, Wilbur Zelinsky, Fred Kniffen, Grady Clay, and Edward Hall.

Jackson was now developing a reputation within the university world, initially at Berkeley, where, by 1967, he was teaching for a quarter each year, developing courses on the history of the European and American landscapes. He gave over ownership of *Landscape* in 1968, and by the fall of 1969, he also began teaching at Harvard, where he served both as lecturer in the Department of Visual and Environmental Studies and as visiting professor in the Department of Landscape Architecture. With these teaching opportunities his life changed markedly, and for about a decade he divided his life between a Cambridge autumn, a Berkeley winter, and a Santa Fe spring and summer.

All the while he was writing and lecturing, and new publication opportunities emerged. In 1970, Ervin H. Zube edited *Landscapes: Selected Writings of J. B. Jackson,* the first compilation of Jackson's essays. It would be followed by three more during his lifetime, all of which Jackson himself edited. In addition, several other books featured one or more of his essays. In 1972, Jackson published the full-length study *American Space: The Centennial Years.*

After withdrawing from formal classroom teaching in the late 1970s, Jackson began to lecture widely. He continued to write and publish essays in periodicals and books, to increasing acclaim. With rather less publicity, he also began to work as an ordinary manual laborer. His final job was cleaning up after workers at an auto repair shop. On one of the last days of his life, he rejoiced to a friend that he had learned to steam-clean a car.

Landscape in Sight: J. B. Jackson's America was the final book of Jackson's essays. It was conceived with Jackson's permission, and its introductory essays were fully drafted during his lifetime. Appearing in the year following his 1996 death, it is an abundant collection of his essays—both those best loved and those representing many sides of his thinking and writing. *Traces of J. B. Jackson* is my attempt—as the editor of that 1997 volume and the writer of its introductions—to bring what can be known of Jackson's complicated and rich life into clearer focus. He was a brilliant man who brought new ways of thinking and seeing to Americans. J. B. Jackson was a marvel, and so he remains in memory.

1

EARLY TRACES

First Traces

John Brinckerhoff Jackson was born on September 25, 1909. His birth certificate, registered in Dinard, France, provides the first trace of his life: "Le vingt-cinq septembre mil neuf cent neuf, à six heures du matin, est né, Roche Fontaine en cette commune, John Brinckerhoff JACKSON, du sexe masculin, de William BRINCKER-HOFF, et de Alice RICHARDSON."[1]

At the time of his birth, his parents had been married for roughly a year and a half, and if the data on the wedding certificate is correct, his father was in his early fifties, his mother in her early thirties.[2]

Two photographs of J. B. Jackson, dated 1910 and 1913, show him to be a beautiful child.[3] Both were likely taken outside of the family house in Maryland where, after the family's return from France, he spent his first years.

The next written traces are travel documents from 1914, when Brinck, as he was called, was four. These give the simple facts of his family as it prepared to leave for Europe. William B. Jackson, his father, was born in 1859, in Newark, New Jersey. His height was five foot seven, his eyes gray, and his complexion swarthy. His occupation was listed as "retired."[4] Jackson's mother, Alice Richardson Jackson, was born in St. Louis, Missouri, in 1879 in this telling, although her gravestone gives the year as 1876. Along with J. B. Jackson's correct year and place of birth, one learns that

Figures 1 and 2
(*left/right*): John Brinckerhoff Jackson, 1910 and 1913

Figures 3 and 4
(*left/right*): Alice Richardson Jackson, n.d., and William Brinckerhoff Jackson, 1920

his two half siblings were also born abroad: Betty in Lucerne, Switzerland, in 1901, and Wayne in Weisbaden, Germany, in 1905. All five members of the household lived in Glen Court, Silver Spring, in Montgomery County, Maryland. They left the United States for Europe on July 18, 1914,[5] just ten days before Austria declared war on Serbia, igniting World War I.

When the Jackson family returned to the United States, sailing from Naples on September 10, 1914, it consisted of Alice Jackson and her three children.[6] Young Brinck, by his own account, never saw his father again. The four resettled in New York City. The 1920 census located them in a rented apartment at 1142 Madison Avenue, with Alice as the household's head.[7] Remaining in Europe, William served during the war with the Red Cross as a lieutenant colonel. In 1920, he became the Red Cross's commissioner to Albania.[8] A letter of appointment and a 1920 photograph of a dapperly dressed William Jackson, standing under ancient arches in Tirania, Albania — sent to his brother, not to his son — is one of the few bits of evidence of Brinck's father's existence after World War I.[9]

While such information is useful background, the kind of evidence that enables a richer understanding of J. B. Jackson's life and mentality derives from later in his childhood.

School

First the facts, and a bit of visual evidence. Brinck Jackson received his earliest formal education at New York's Riverdale School, then for boys only. It was followed by two years at Institut Le Rosey in Switzerland, a boarding school famous for educating children of the international elite. A photograph of Jackson during these years shows him on skates, although, by his report, skiing was his favored activity.

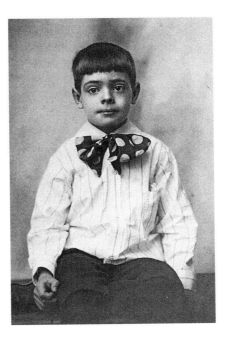

Figure 5. J. B. Jackson, boyhood, studio photograph

Figure 6. J. B. Jackson, Le Rosey, third from left

When Brinck was fourteen, his mother attempted to enter him in Deerfield Academy in western Massachusetts. However, he was determined unqualified for admittance and placed at Eaglebrook Lodge, a new boarding school for younger students, created as a feeder school for the academy. Because of the connection between Deerfield and Eaglebrook, most correspondence regarding Jackson between 1924 and his graduation from preparatory school in 1928 resides in the Deerfield archives. These letters reveal that although the young Jackson was shaped significantly by his mother and the schools he attended, early on he demonstrated the independence of mind, rebellious streak, brilliance, and personal charm that later defined him.

In March 1924, Frank Boyden, Deerfield's headmaster, received a strong complaint from Alice Jackson, who suggested she might place her son in another school. Boyden turned to Wilmot V. Trevoy, a fellow Amherst alumnus in the class of 1902, then living in New York City and working with youth, asking him to serve as an intermediary to ascertain Alice Jackson's specific concerns.[10]

Trevoy reported in early April that Mrs. Jackson was "still on the rampage about Eaglebrook." In his view, the problem was that "she has kept Brinck with her so much and has talked to him in such grown-up fashion that she has partially spoiled [him] for contact with boys of his own age." Brinck was thus unable to deal with the normal talk of schoolboys, "their various 'kicks' which do not really mean a thing," and interpreted their complaints "as having a basis," which he conveyed to his mother. Trevoy advised Boyden simply to respond courteously and let Trevoy take on, if necessary, "the role of the Dutch uncle and give the Dutch uncle's talk," meaning he planned to speak frankly, even harshly, to Mrs. Jackson. In the meantime, he did not think Boyden should seek another school for Mrs. Jackson's son.[11]

Alice Jackson clearly thought differently, because at the end of the academic year she took Brinck abroad, where he studied at Institut Carrial in France.[12] Upon their return the following year, 1925, she enrolled him at Choate, a preparatory school then known for its hold on the upper-class Eastern establishment. And it is at Choate that an early intimate trace of Jackson himself emerges. In a box of Jackson materials delivered to the CSWR in the summer of 2017 is a letter Brinck wrote in early spring 1926 to his mother.[13] Behind it must have been a letter from the headmaster of Choate to Alice Jackson regarding her son—one that, in turn, provoked a letter from her to Brinck urging him to behave in a more disciplined fashion. Her words elicited a reply that tells a great deal about the sixteen-year-old's sense of independent judgment and his effort to disentangle himself from part of his heritage.

To his "Darling Mother," he wrote that he had just received her letter "exhorting" him "to discipline." With this he firmly disagreed. What he needed was not discipline, which implied "conflict that must be put down." Rather, he needed to be convinced to do the right thing for its own sake. Neither a "10 year old [n]or a criminal" should be forced to obey either his teachers or the law. They should be "persuaded that what they are doing is right. Then they can be loyal to the idea." The school authorities or possibly Alice herself had proposed he go "without tea for a month." He countered that "total abstinence from lying, for a day would be better."

Brinck interlarded his statements with conciliatory terms of address—"sweetness" and "darling"—but concluded with a sharp rebuke: "don[']t ever tell me I have puritan blood or that either you or father have it. It[']s a thing to be ashamed of not to be proud of. They may have had a lot to do with founding of America but not otherwise than materially. It[']s just what they stood for intolerance, selfrightousness that everyone is fighting against now[.] Besides ancestors don[']t t[h]rill me." To a mother who treasured her lineage and valued the name "Brinckerhoff," this reproach must have seemed like a personal insult. In his teen years Brinck's rebellious streak led him to question his heritage.

Figure 7. J. B. Jackson with his dog

Brinck also then understood the social and cultural context of forces attempting to control him, as conveyed in this letter by his sendup of the way that Choate sought to train its students in proper behavior in assemblies. The headmaster directs the chorus of teachers. "When he is officially humorous the satellites rock with mirth, and when he is in a denouncing mood they frown and pouch their lower lip." The oldest boys then imitate their teachers to the audience of the younger students under their domain.

The headmaster and his assistant had their own perspectives on Brinck Jackson, however, as can be seen from their letters in the archives of Deerfield Academy, where Alice Jackson was once again attempting to place her son. "Brincky is an attractive boy, a brilliant conversationalist, the kind of person you would like to have with you on a camping trip," wrote C. Wardell St. John (assistant to his father, Choate's headmaster) to Frank Boyden. He added discreetly, however, that "the boy's education has been interrupted too frequently, and his Mother does seem to change her plans pretty often." With this, he forwarded Brinck's transcript with the comment, "It's not very good, as you can see."[14]

Headmaster George C. St. John offered Boyden a more detailed report: "Brincky is a very exceptional case: he is

Figure 8. J. B. Jackson, early teen years

a boy whom we should gladly keep here and gladly recommend to you, though he has made a very poor record in his work and shows no sign of any promise of doing better." The boy is, he added, "an intellectual and an individualist" who "believes that he can guide his own education better than any school or college can, and calmly buries himself in Machiavelli's 'Florence' when he should be preparing an Algebra lesson or doing required exercise." Young Jackson was capable but had "never trained himself—or been trained—to do a task that didn't interest him, or to conquer a lesson of which he personally couldn't see the value." On the other hand, the headmaster continued, he is "charming, lovable, interesting and responsive," though "as obstinate as an allegory on the banks of the Nile when it comes to having his own way."[15] Then again, "he is

Figure 9. J. B. Jackson, midteen years

the best educated boy we have in School! He provides a really intellectual stimulus to table conversation, does unusual work for the Literary Magazine, is a wholly congenial companion for the Masters—and seems to earn a place for himself on those grounds." In conclusion, St. John wrote to Boyden, "If you succeed in making the boy see the value of routine and the daily task, I think you may be helping in the creation of a great man!"[16]

Clearly, Choate's headmaster perceived Boyden of Deerfield Academy as a magician who could turn stubborn or recalcitrant boys into good students. During his long administration (1902–66), Boyden reshaped a coeducational academy on the Connecticut River in central Massachusetts into a well-regarded preparatory school. By the late 1920s, it accepted boys as boarding students.[17] For these male students, Boyden was no ordinary school head. He was everywhere in the school, attempting to know and shape each of his boys. In *The Headmaster: Frank L. Boyden of Deerfield,* John McPhee wrote that, rather than receiving a report card, each

Deerfield boy met privately with Boyden "six times a year and was told where he stood. In these talks, the Headmaster drew the boys out, getting their reactions to their courses." McPhee was relying on his memory of his one Deerfield year, likely in the late 1940s; but even if this was a practice only then, Boyden nonetheless was known throughout his tenure to be omnipresent at Deerfield, with his office at the entrance to the academic building. He was at all the students' sports events and often served as coach. He spoke often to them about the world and their responsibilities on entering it, giving lessons on patriotism, loyalty, and discipline. He was known to have a special genius that enabled him to find a way to reach boys under his care, even recalcitrant ones.[18]

Not knowing of Boyden's earlier difficulties with Alice Jackson, the senior St. John warned Deerfield's headmaster: "His Mother is, I think, at the root of the trouble; she believes him a genius, and feels that rules are beneath him, and that any insistence on standards proves an incapacity to appreciate her boy. He has won his way so far through charm; but I like him too well to let him continue in that path without a struggle."[19]

Boyden understood from his earlier experience that when he accepted Brinck Jackson, he inherited his mother. He replied to St. John that he was only admitting the son because of Trevoy's pressure. Boyden continued, "I told him last night I would accept Brincky on his account, with the distinct understanding that he was to write Mrs. Jackson that she must 'keep her hands off', that if he was coming to us for more education . . . he was to have the same routine of work as the other boys."[20]

The conditions must have been accepted, for Brinck Jackson boarded at Deerfield for the two academic years between fall 1926 and his graduation in spring 1928.

Boyden's early communications with Mrs. Jackson began politely. In early fall 1926, he apologized for missing her attempts to see him, but he was happy to report, "We have been very much pleased with Brinck so far. His main difficulty is, of course, to adapt himself to regular, organized work. He has a single room, which I think will be conducive to study, and I think he intends to be successful in his scholastic work this year. I assure you I shall be glad to cooperate with you at any time." After stating that their past communications regarding Brinck had previously been indirect through Trevoy, he now wanted to affirm directly regarding her son, "I am very glad to have him here."[21]

In late December, Boyden sent her news that Brinck was doing "satisfactory" work. For the mother of a genius, that might not have been praise enough. Boyden clarified, "His work is continually improving and at the present time he has a B, or 88%, average."[22]

Mrs. Jackson paid the bill for the semester's tuition, but in a manner that probably troubled Boyden. Likely seeking to get around a restriction that money for Brinck's education from his father or a trust fund was limited to paying his tuition bills, she rounded the number to $700, putting in an extra $62.50 as money her son might draw on "so that he may always have sufficient [funds if] he wishes to purchase various things for himself."[23] This sum, equal to over $920 in today's dollars, may have seemed an extravagant amount to the headmaster.

In that first school year, Mrs. Jackson's plans became an issue. In January 1927, Boyden learned that she had booked passage to Europe on a date that would require her son to miss the final week of the term. Bowing to the inevitable, Boyden wrote that although he thought "Brincky was a little premature in stating that school closed on the 8th of June as we are not through until the 15th," he would allow him this time to "go early" if it proved impossible for Mrs. Jackson "to change the date of passage." Shifting gears, he added that Brincky "has done excellent work so far this year and it has been a real pleasure to have him here."[24]

By February, Mrs. Jackson's ambitions for her son were soaring. Perhaps in anticipation of the trip abroad, she was thinking of a personal visit in England, or perhaps her plans involved only correspondence, to "discuss with the authorities at Oxford University the possibility of . . . Brinckerhoff's entrance into one of the colleges there." Receiving this news, Boyden cautioned her that "you will probably need a statement regarding his school life with us here at Deerfield Academy."

Nevertheless, he did not discourage her, but rather offered a positive assessment of the boy, emphasizing his literary skills: "The English department especially has found him a student with the finest appreciation of the best in literature, and with very marked possibilities in writing. He is the type of student who would profit greatly from a literary course at Oxford; and there is no doubt in our minds that he would make the right contribution to the life there, for he is in every way a boy of finest character."[25]

During that summer abroad, Brinck, approaching the age of eighteen, corresponded with the Deerfield staff member assigning housing for the coming academic year. Since he would still be too far away to fill out the necessary slip, he wrote, he hoped his letter to her would serve. Having lost his place in Davenport House, he reminded her that he wanted a single room and then suggested the houses supervised by masters that would suit him. He went on to tell her of his travels, adding in an effort to charm: "I have had a wonderful summer, motored from Nice through Switzerland up here; we are going to Berlin day after tomorrow. What may I bring you back from Paris?"[26]

By October 1927, however, Alice Jackson, was proving not so charming. The tone of a letter she sent to Boyden set the master's teeth on edge. Her stationery now pronounced her "Mrs. Brinckerhoff Jackson," although her husband, absent from the household for over thirteen years, had normally used only the first of his given names. She may have resorted to this bit of pretension as a sort of armor, for although her son by Jackson likely had a trust fund that supported his education, she was a working woman, an antiques buyer for Lord & Taylor. In the two years of Deerfield correspondence, she lived at three different New York addresses— perhaps an indication of something other than prosperous stability.

The occasion for the October letter was her displeasure at the living conditions her son was facing. The background that can be gleaned from Boyden's reply reveals that, in order for Brinck to have the single room he requested, he had been placed in the house of history teacher William Avirett. Because the lease for the house came only as the term began, its renovation produced difficulties, especially a lack of heat and hot water. Nonetheless, all the boys placed in the house determined to stay there. Brinck's living situation, however, provoked Mrs. Jackson to write, "If I felt there was any good reason why the boys should undergo certain discomforts, if it was for their souls' good I would not write to you—but I can see really *no* reason & it is hard to imagine an excuse for the fact that *no* heat & *no* hot water is installed in the house where Brincky is. I really feel a sense of it not being altogether just to parents or boys but perhaps there is some reason I do not understand. If so I shall be glad to know and hope you are doing your best as no doubt you are—to remedy this condition."[27]

By his telling, Boyden wrote her two replies, but he thought the better of them and didn't send either. In letting her know this in the third one actually sent, he wrote that "perhaps they [his initial responses] were too strong."[28] What she received was a condensation of a much longer letter that left out the full explanation of the situation in the house and merely dressed her down. Boyden had let Brinck do most of the work of explaining the situation to her along with his and the other boys' decision not to move to another house. "Frankly," Boyden wrote sternly, "I am not in the habit of getting such letters and do not care to receive any more. I assure you we are doing everything possible for the comfort and training of our boys. Any time parents are not satisfied, I shall be glad to arrange for a removal." Mrs. Jackson apparently sent no more letters of complaint.

Although I do not know the specifics of how Deerfield's headmaster intervened in young Jackson's life, what has been written about Boyden elsewhere conveys the larger influence of his leadership, and evidence from the academy's archives give something of his sense of the boy then called Brincky. The headmaster became known for creating "Boyden boys," those imperfect lads in whom he saw talent or some special spark and, by reaching out to them, helped give them direction. Boyden must have seen possibility in young Jackson. In recommending him for college, his knowledge of Brinck was accurate, and his statements generous. In later correspondence, Boyden often referred to Jackson's special gifts, recalling a speech Brinck gave as an academy senior. To a fatherless boy, Boyden's daily presence and his attentiveness must have had a profound impact.[29]

Brinck Jackson changed at Deerfield. Boyden believed in the all-round student, and the young Jackson became that to a degree. Never in the first rank of athletes in the school, he nonetheless participated in school sports. In his first year, he played league soccer; in his second year, league baseball and track. His literary interests got full play. He served on the boards of the school newspaper and literary magazine, and he acted in the senior play.

Brinck experienced care and attention not only from Boyden but also from Deerfield teachers. One reads this in the long memorandum of William Avirett, both his history teacher and the master of the house in which he lived his second year. Avirett's words were written to Boyden and dealt with Brinck's next step. Both he and his wife had grown fond of the student, Avirett wrote. "He makes a delightful boy in the house, and his natural charm and personality have added a great deal to the pleasure we have found this fall." In regard to the quality of Brinck's work, however, the report was mixed. As a history student, Brinck's "mind is quick but undisciplined. He receives ideas readily and interprets them understandingly. In other words, he shows a marked capacity for absorbing knowledge through reading and discussion. On the other hand, he shows incapacity for orderly, systematic, careful work. In History, the mechanics of making an outline and analyzing text come hard for him."

At this juncture of Brinck's schooling, this posed a problem. The history exam for the College Board, required for admission to many colleges, called on exactly the

skills he did not possess, putting him "at a very real disadvantage," despite his deep understanding of the subject. The solution Avirett strongly suggested was the Experimental College within the University of Wisconsin, created and headed by Alexander Meiklejohn, president of Amherst from 1913 to 1923.

After his departure from Amherst College, Meiklejohn brought its alumni to Wisconsin as members of the faculty of this new branch of the university. Links between Deerfield and Amherst College ran deep. Boyden, an alumnus, regularly hired other Amherst graduates as his teachers. Thus, the instructors at the Experimental College were familiar figures to Boyden and to many of his teachers, and the new school's approach seemed well suited to young Jackson.

Avirett wrote, "I know the majority of the faculty intimately and would regard them as an outstanding group of men. Their major interest is in knowing and understanding, so that Brinckerhoff would find himself very much at home. He would undoubtedly have to work harder than ever before but would work in a congenial atmosphere under conditions favorable to rapid and worthwhile growth. . . . In recommending consideration of Wisconsin, I am not doing so as a second choice, forced by the elimination of other first choice universities. I am regarding it as the best thing of its kind in existence and as am [an] institution ideal to meet the needs of this student. It is possible that in such an environment he would develop his potential capacity into truly high records of accomplishment."[30]

Soon after, Boyden wrote to Meiklejohn, "I should like very much to send you a boy next year and hope he can be admitted to your college. He is a very unusual boy, of very keen intellect and real genius. I am sure you would find him a very desirable student and one who would greatly appreciate the courses which you are offering. His name is Brinckerhoff Jackson. He received part of his education in Europe but for the past three years has been with us."[31]

Experimental College, University of Wisconsin

J. B. Jackson's next step was indeed the Experimental College of the University of Wisconsin. The school came into being when, three years after leaving Amherst, Alexander Meiklejohn joined the faculty of the University of Wisconsin and began to lay the foundation within its governance of a new school for first- and second-year students. Within the coeducational university, the Experimental College followed Amherst in that it was for men only, and six of the ten members of the initial faculty came from there, including several who served as Jackson's advisers and final graders.[32]

Meiklejohn wrote in 1932 that the goal of the new college was the development of "intelligence"—that is, the curriculum was focused on general education, rather than on preparing students for professional life.[33] Professors were called "advisers"; teaching was by tutorial. The college received its first class in the autumn of 1927. In the single year Jackson attended, 1928–29, the curriculum focused on ancient Athens in reading, discussion, and writing. The broad cultural approach of Lewis Mumford, a friend of Meiklejohn, served as an important influence.[34]

The extant papers from Jackson's Wisconsin year—on Greek education, the conflict between education and religion in ancient Greece, and middlemen between producers and consumers in the United States—give little sense of the play of Jackson's mind at work. The writing seems dutiful, unlike the more imaginative pieces he had written for the literary magazines of Choate and Deerfield. In November 1928, Jackson's adviser reported his work "Satisfactory" and described the young man as "artistic" and "rather quiet," adding that he "has a good many ideas & tastes of his own regarding what is worth studying." The January report by a different adviser, however, contained these words: "Jackson has been one of the delights of my life. . . . He has done fairly conscientious work in subjects that don't interest him particularly, and is always alert in conversation or discussion." Jackson had also taken part in a production of *Lysistrata* and helped another student in making frescos.

Grades normally were not given until the end of the second and final year, but because Jackson was transferring, something had to appear at the end of his first year. He received an A-.[35] As the academic year closed, a letter to Jackson's mother expressed the deep regret of his advisers at losing him to another university. "He has of course done very good work, and quite apart from that his own spontaneous activities were finely directed and very well carried on. He has very great promise for the future, both in the fields of thinking and of appreciation."[36]

In Jackson's later judgment, what proved important at Wisconsin was less the curriculum and the evaluations he received than a book he read during that college year, the first volume of Oswald Spengler's *Decline of the West.* As he recalled over six decades later, "It transformed me. . . . It is a fascinating, obsessive book." Jackson was entranced by the way Spengler put together elements of a culture.

Spengler argued that civilizations rose and fell by biological rules, going through the seasons of the year. The West, which Spengler defined as Faustian (in contrast to calm, balanced Apollonian), was restless, urged on toward a goal. It had its spring-time in the Gothic, its high summer from the Renaissance to the eighteenth century, and began its autumn with the Romantics. To understand the present, Spengler urged his contemporaries to forget about current art and music and look at engineering and technology. Spengler sparked Jackson's imagination in ways that would remain with him for the rest of his long life.

Jackson later explained his departure from Wisconsin by emphasizing the discomfort he felt with the student body of the Experimental College. Most other young men at the college were farm boys from the Midwest or Jews from New York—people with whom Jackson was socially unfamiliar and may have disdained.[37] It was an easy explanation, but clearly only part of the story. Jackson sought to transfer to Harvard from the moment of his arrival in Wisconsin.[38]

Harvard—Before, During, and After

Harvard loomed large in Jackson's life. What it meant to him I do not fully know, but it is clear that Brinck longed for it during his freshman year at the University of Wisconsin, and after transferring as a sophomore, he experienced Harvard's undergraduate life to the full. After graduation, he lived in Harvard's shadow in Cambridge as he struggled to become a published writer. In his sixties, he returned to teach there, residing for at least some semesters in Eliot House, the undergraduate residence of his senior year.

In late September 1928, soon after arriving at Wisconsin, Jackson wrote to Harvard's dean of the freshman class to announce, "I want very much to go to Harvard," and to ask whether he could be admitted as a junior after a two-year stint at Wisconsin, or whether he was going to need supplemental work.[39] An "Assistant" at Harvard replied tactfully, but clearly, in ways that might have felt intimidating to a less determined young man: "No promise can be held forth that your application for admission will be accepted after two years at Professor Meiklejohn's Experimental College." Jackson was, however, welcome to apply.[40]

A month or so later, Jackson wrote again, this time to the Committee on Admissions. He alluded to the earlier exchange of letters but altered the content of the reply he had received. "I was informed by you two months ago in reply to an inquiry I made, that I would be admitted to Harvard from the Experimental College of Wisconsin if at the end of the two years course I was recommended by Professor Meiklejohn as satisfactory." Audaciously, he now proposed coming to Harvard after a single year, either as a sophomore or, if necessary, as a freshman.[41] A sharp rebuke from Harvard informed him that the earlier letter had offered no promise of acceptance and that he would have to submit his record for approval. Further, "In order to be admitted to Harvard by transfer, you must present evidence of at least one full year of work completed in a regularly organized college of liberal arts."[42]

Jackson was undeterred. "I understand without agreeing with you, your decision concerning the value of one year in Professor Meiklejohn[']s College," he replied. Since in order to be admitted to Wisconsin he had been "obliged to fulfill the regular scholastic obligations which are required by Harvard," why should a single year at an "unrecognized college" now disqualify him for entering the freshman class?[43]

In return came a stern letter from Henry Pennypacker, the chairman of Harvard's Committee on Admissions. "We do not accept candidates for admission by transfer from any year of that Experimental College either to our Freshman Class or to any other class in our undergraduate body." What emerged as the issue in Jackson's case was the exam by the College Entrance Examination Board. To enter Harvard, Jackson had to submit proof of passing it, a feat his Deerfield history instructor had deemed unlikely. In fact, the school's headmaster had steered him to the Experimental College in large part because it did not require the exam.[44]

Switching tactics, Jackson wrote back a thank-you note on his mother's "Mrs. Brinckerhoff Jackson" stationery with the tony address of Ardlea Court, 170 East 51st Street: "I am much obliged to you for your kindness." Then, perhaps to protect another summer abroad, Jackson asked when and where he might take the examination before June, noting it was scheduled for June 17–22. To this came the curt reply that there were no earlier opportunities; the examination would be held only during the week beginning June 17. However, a further round of missives clarified it would be possible for Jackson to take the examination in Cambridge in September.[45]

In March, Jackson wrote—with what was now coming to look very much like typical presumptuousness—that he had been "informed by a good authority" that he would be admitted to Harvard as a sophomore, but this was not official, and he now wanted some "authentication," because his plans were dependent upon it. Also, he wanted to secure a room in a sophomore dormitory.[46]

Actually, Jackson presumed correctly. On March 13, a Harvard official wrote, "By a recent special vote of the Committee on Admission you will be allowed to enter Harvard next fall as a provisional Sophomore," provided that preparatory school work met Harvard's standards for freshmen, and work at Wisconsin at the end of the academic year was of "honor grade." The College Board examination requirement was not mentioned.[47] Clearly someone, or perhaps several persons, with standing at Harvard had intervened between December and March. The record does not offer further information on this point—only that Jackson applied and entered Harvard in the fall of 1929.

Many years later, Brinck once boasted to me that he had received letters of invitation from the presidents of both Harvard and Yale with the words "Just come!" Obviously, this was not so. However, equally obviously, he did receive favored treatment.

Jackson's Harvard application contains a few interesting facts. His address on applying was 315 E. 51st Street in New York, a different home address from that appearing on his mother's stationery on which he had written to Harvard a few months earlier. He reported that his father, a Yale graduate and a lawyer, was dead—a statement of which William Jackson's profession was likely the only accurate element.[48] He listed, prior to prepping at Choate, attendance at Institut Carrial in 1924.[49] He declared his interests lay in history, English, and architecture, and expressed the hope of specializing in English and history (appropriate for Harvard's oldest concentration, history and literature). He wished to come to Harvard, he wrote, "Because I have always considered Harvard the finest educational institution in the country, and because its history and background are those of the best of America. Because of its proximity to Boston and its facilities for research." On the application page is a photograph of a very handsome young man, then almost twenty, looking highly respectable in a tweed jacket and tie.[50]

There are several ways to look at J. B. Jackson's college career. The first is to see how he performed academically. If I put on my college professor's cap, I look at his grades and see him as a frivolous young man, hardly serious about his work. His November report listed his grades as 1 B, 2 Cs, and an E (meaning unsatisfactory and no credit given). This report led to a conference with the assistant dean and a letter from him to Jackson's mother (who once again had moved, this time to 210 E. 73rd Street). Jackson's grades at the end of the semester were "Unsatisfactory"—because in addition to two Cs, there were two Ds. No disciplinary action was taken, however. Jackson did better in his second semester, and he was promoted to the junior class. He fulfilled part of his science requirement by a half-course in geography, in which he got a C.[51]

At Harvard, Jackson followed his Deerfield-era practice of stretching the limits of the academic schedule to maximize time in Europe. In August 1931, he

Figure 11. J. B. Jackson, Harvard college application photograph, 1929

wrote to tell the dean of his class that he had unintentionally booked a passage that would cause him to arrive after the registration period for classes was closed. The following month, he sent a telegram announcing "LATE FOR REGISTRATION REGRET BUT UNAVOIDABLE." The note accompanying it, written by an unknown hand, waived a fine and gave the explanation, "delayed by customs." Below Jackson's message on the telegram is the handwritten note by the receiving office, "booked passage in Feb."[52]

A review of Jackson's academic record from his junior and senior years shows him to have gotten by in college with a "gentleman's C." (It should be noted that during this era, a C was a respectable grade, likely comparable to today's B, following the grade inflation that began in the 1960s.) In the fall semester of Jackson's junior year, he took three history courses, with grades of C, B+, and C+; his fine arts grade was C; and his German grade, C-. Spring semester saw no improvement, although he did manage to get an A in his history course (though a C once again in geography). In his senior year, his grades were mainly Cs with a slight sprinkling of Bs.

Jackson's lowest grades in all three years were in German, which is rather interesting, because he used his German effectively as an army intelligence officer to interrogate prisoners during World War II. Perhaps an explanation for his low marks

EARLY TRACES

27

Figure 12. J. B. Jackson in his twenties

was not a lack of knowledge but of attendance: his many cuts were noted on grade cards. Fortunately, his Cs in geography and fine arts proved to be no prediction of his future interests and attainments (see color plate 1).[53]

In 1994, Jackson told me that the eminent literary scholar F. O. Matthiessen, his adviser and tutor at Harvard, did not think highly of him. "I would not say that he was contemptuous of me, but he said after a while, 'Well, there's no use your pretending that you're going to go into graduate work because that's not your field. Just write about Charles Lamb.'" Matthiessen was probably the author of a handwritten note accompanying an official report during Jackson's sophomore year that described him as an "earnest and probably hard-working, although rather half-baked intellectual." It's thus unsurprising that Jackson never put forward Matthiessen's name in later years when he was in need of a recommendation.

There is a second way to look at Jackson's Harvard years—as an expression of the particular notion of college life that held sway at the time. Although he attended Harvard during the Great Depression, extracurricular life in that period—at least among those of Jackson's background—continued more or less as before. In January 1931, when Jackson applied for a room in the newly opened Eliot House for his senior year, he was already very busy with the three organizations that were to engage most of his attention for the rest of his college career: the *Harvard Advocate,* the Dramatic Club, and the Cercle Français.[54] This is where Jackson put in his primary effort in college.

Jackson's engagement in extracurricular life, however, requires a closer look. Although it may have been pleasurable, what was involved here was not really fun and games. It was in Harvard's extracurriculum that Jackson found outlets for creative expression. The *Harvard Advocate* gave him opportunity to publish his fiction and his understanding of architecture and culture. As an editor of its literary board, he joined a group of like-minded undergraduates who met and decided on works to include in their periodical. The French club enabled him to act on stage in the French language and exercise leadership as its president in his senior year. For the Hasty Pudding, he wrote the book and lyrics for the 1932 club's famed comic annual spring musical. Part of its fun was that, in typical undergraduate fashion, female characters were played by the club's male members in drag. Jackson's *Pudding on the Ritz* played to audiences beyond Cambridge, including "close to 3,000" in a theater in New York City, as reported in the *New York Times*.[55] These undergraduate activities gave Jackson a realm in which he could exercise his varied creative talents. His contributions to the *Advocate,* dealt with separately in the section that follows, give the most solid evidence of Jackson's presence at Harvard.

I know almost nothing about Jackson's social ties at Harvard. Membership in the Hasty Pudding meant he was socially acceptable, but there is no evidence he was a member of one of the prestigious "final clubs"—the venerable Harvard societies, such as the Porcellian, comparable to fraternities. What friendships Jackson may have made in college did not last beyond the decade after his graduation. In 1935, needing to supply recommendations as he sought employment, he listed Gale Noyes, an assistant professor in English, who in his time at Harvard participated in many undergraduate dramatic and literary activities overlapping with those of Jackson; and J. M. Potter, a member of the class of 1926, who had likely been a graduate student or junior professor affiliated with Eliot House in Jackson's final undergraduate year.[56] In 1938, as he sought to publicize the novel he had written, he suggested that his publisher call on Robert Hillyer, a Pulitzer Prize–winning poet, who was an assistant professor of English during Jackson's years. In addition, he named Paul Hoffman, a Harvard classmate whose own novel had been published by Harpers in 1933.[57]

Figure 13. J. B. Jackson, Harvard senior, 1932

One other detail to add to these traces is that Jackson did not pay his final bill of $120.72 (roughly $2,261 in today's dollars) in time to graduate with his class in 1932. On several occasions during his lifetime, Brinck mentioned to me that he had inherited a trust fund from his paternal grandfather. This probably supported his education and, later in life, enabled him to live and write without having to work for pay. My suspicion is that Jackson exceeded the fund's allowance at Harvard, causing the delay in his getting his degree. Though always counted as a member of the class of 1932, Jackson received his diploma in early 1933.[58]

Jackson spent the summer following his departure from Harvard in Europe. Here chronology becomes a bit murky, for his recollection is at odds with some hard evidence. A year intervened between the end of Jackson's undergraduate career and his entrance into MIT to study architecture in the fall of 1933, and he stayed on MIT's books though the academic year that ended in late spring 1934.[59] Jackson's residence during this time is unknown, but from his dated drawings, it appears that although much of the winter he was enrolled at MIT, he was actually riding a motorcycle through Central and Eastern Europe. By March 1934, however, aspiring to be a published writer, he was living close to "Mother Harvard," on Linden Street, between the Harvard Yard, the center of Harvard's academic campus, and its residence halls.[60] After a brief stint on the *New Bedford Mercury* as a proofreader, he left to work for the Harvard tercentenary, placing him back on the Yard, if only for volunteer work.[61] Jackson moved to Boston's Beacon Hill by February 1937, and there he remained, except for travel, until the fall of 1938, when he left for New Mexico.[62]

Jackson did not return to Harvard until 1969. After over seventeen years as editor and publisher of *Landscape* magazine, he began to teach at the university, and he lived, at least for some of that time, once again in Eliot House. While much of the setting remained the same, by the late 1960s the university offered very different educational possibilities, allowing Jackson to give courses to students that mattered to him and to them.

2

EARLY WRITINGS

From an early age, Jackson was, first and foremost, a writer. Today he is remembered primarily for work beginning in 1951 — his essays, *Landscape* magazine, and his contribution to the field of landscape studies. But his first published writing appeared in 1926, when he was a boy of sixteen. As a young man, his goal was to be a novelist, and he published a novel in 1938. For many years afterward he continued to write novels, but none of them found their way into print.

Brinck's literary efforts began in childhood with a handwritten humor newspaper and continued into his prep school years. Examined today, these early attempts convey, along with his cleverness, certain of his boyhood interests and attitudes. Jackson's writing began to take a more serious turn in college. His correspondence with publisher William Warder Norton regarding the 1938 publication of *Saints in Summertime* is suggestive, revealing his ambition and hopes. These, however, were dashed in 1940, when Norton rejected the manuscript of a second novel, ending the fiction phase of Jackson's publishing career.

Youthful Writings

"EUREKA"

In the bundle of materials entrusted to me by Jackson rests a fragile compilation of brown paper sheets held together by a pin. These pages form the newspaper of a made-up town called Eureka and feature short articles and ads, largely written by hand, along with drawings and small pasted photographs. "Eureka" was a youthful creation, and my guess is Brinck Jackson was its author. Admittedly almost all the pieces are written in the small, tight cursive writing in ink of an adult hand, but possibly Jackson's mother or adult half sister Betty (who was living at home with him at the time) served as transcriber.

"Eureka" can be approximately dated because one piece mocks President Calvin Coolidge, who took office in August 1923, when Brinck was turning fourteen.[1] The paper shows familiarity with small-town newspapers and their advertisements as it playfully mocks them. "AGED INVENTOR OF TOMATO SKINNER, DIES AT 89" proclaims one "obituary." "Jacob T Hinimus 89 inventor of the famous Himinator, gently passed away last night. Mr Hinimus was born in Angel county Kentucky and while yet a child his parents remarked on his wonderful inventive genious [genius] at the age of thirteen he devised an elaborate apparatus by which he closed and opened his window from his bed (for further information apply higgins memorial ass.)."

An ad for a lady's comb is written in pencil in a different hand that could be Brinck's. The tone is comically grandiose. Under a pasted image of a small-waisted and highly coiffed lady brandishing a comb, the caption identifies "Phyllia Flunk—the incomparably beautiful heroine of 'Ladia's Lament', the new Croation [Croatian] play, who moved vast audiences to laughter & tears by her winsome ways, & who had established herself permanently in the hearts of all those who have been fortunate enough to see her & feel her charm, uses Bloom's Guaranteed Rubber Combs."

"Eureka" is, of course, nothing more than a clever fourteen-year-old's idea of satire. What makes it seem significant is that, three decades later, writing in *Landscape*, Jackson would engage in similar-style wordplay, employing newspaper lingo and advertising hype to spoof elements of American life in the 1950s.

CHOATE

Brinck's first published writing appeared in February 1926, when he was sixteen. The *Choate Literary Magazine* featured his story "Blacksome & Veepings," an amusing morality tale of commerce. The title carries the name of the cloth and tailoring establishment that the two central characters jointly own in a New England town. Blacksome, the elder of the two, was one of the original pair who founded the store in 1884 and is beloved by all. At the story's opening, he is partnered by Herbert Veepings, the heir to his father's share of the business. The young Veepings held social aspirations. Brinck wrote, "It must be thoroughly understood, therefore, that Herbert was a gentleman, otherwise his conduct might be construed as that of a conceited young snob, instead of an exemplary effort on the part of a gentleman of twenty-five to assume his rightful position in the sun."[2] He desired a more gentlemanly occupation, such as that of bookseller, one that could be construed as a hobby and was embarrassed by Blacksome's affable manner.

Herbert sought to train his elder partner to become more genteel, but rather than comply, Blacksome decided he needed to hire another young man in his place. Thus appeared Wilbur Scroop, a slick fellow who had worked in an automobile agency. The new employee changed the nature of the store in ways that created heavy debt for the owners. On discovery of this, Blackstone fired Scroop, bought out Herbert Veepings, and attempted to return his shop to solvency. What is noteworthy about this story is both its Dickensian overtones and its author's own perspective. Asked in 1991 about the five works or authors that had most influenced him, Jackson named Dickens as one, and the affinity is apparent here in details such as the characters' names.[3] "Blacksome & Veepings" is a morality tale centered around the old-fashioned ways of an imagined New England past. Brinck consistently opposes the newer order in the character and practices of the aspiring (and ultimately mendacious) young "gentleman" and the rather crass new employee. The story opens a window onto the mind of an intelligent and conservative boy, an adored son of a mother who dealt in antiques, and a student at a New England prep school known for fostering traditional values.

His next contribution to the magazine was an essay, "A Plea for a Little Less Wisdom," exploring the tension between science on the one hand and mythology, religion, and poetry on the other. It is a piece filled with humor and contradiction. Until the final sentence, it is difficult to pin down Brinck's own perspective.

The work begins with the way science "destroys harmful and binding superstitions," and then turns to its destructive side. "Only two weeks ago," he writes, "a scientist announced in the papers that birds do not sing; they merely utter challenges to other thrushes and robins and canaries to engage in mortal combat." This example is part of a larger scientific development in which "plants, animals, even human passions and motives have been dissected and found to be composed of the roughest materials. We are invited by these implacable pursuers of Fact to regard poetry as the result of complexes and instincts, distorted and suppressed; and not as a product of a poet's mind." Mythology is destroyed by scientific discovery of the "gases and flames" of the solar system. Geography turns from being "an exploration of exotic countries and peoples and becomes a study of economic problems and exploitation possibilities." Jackson concludes, rather grandiosely, "It is a precise world and I think William J. Bryan, Conan Doyle, and myself are out of place in it."[4]

Reading this piece makes it is difficult not to see continuities between Jackson's thinking in 1926 and in 1996. Though still a boy in his teens, Brinck displays love of poetry and mythology and demonstrates remarkable erudition, from scientific discoveries to an understanding of the academic discipline of geography. The tension between scientific fact and religious and artistic impulses was something Jackson would wrestle with throughout his long life. However, once he found his calling—in landscape writing, lecturing, and teaching—he was able to reconcile the two and thereby find his place in the world.

DEERFIELD

Almost immediately upon entering Deerfield Academy Brinck submitted work to *Pocumtuck,* Deerfield's literary magazine. His first piece, "The Heirs of Simon Legree," appeared in the November 1926 issue. The essay takes on the contemporary glorification of the white "Nordic" hero who protects Americans from all foreigners. In place of Simon Legree, villain of Harriet Beecher Stowe's novel *Uncle Tom's Cabin,* Brinck contended that 1920s magazines and movies offered evildoers from Italy ("a little count with a goatee" or "a fierce man with stupendous earrings"), Spain ("tricky, cruel, jealous"), Russia ("a perambulating beard and bomb"), among others. At seventeen, he already understood the power of media to shape public awareness, causing readers and moviegoers to "unconsciously" adopt the attitudes being put forth. "What are the efforts of the Klan and the [isolationist] one hundred per centers," Jackson asked, "compared to the efforts of Hollywood, the Saturday Evening Post, and the railroad station school of literature? What are the efforts of a few hundred fanatics to act intolerance when publishers and producers have millions thinking intolerance?"[5]

Brinck realized that the United States was hardly unique in its domestic heroes and foreign villains, citing also the English and the French, with their stereotypes deriding Americans. He argued that international efforts, such as the League of

Nations and treaties, could mean little when such mass imagery incited the belief that "everybody else [is] the epitome of everything vicious and dishonorable. While there is such poison in the world's blood, no counsel of doctors at Geneva can help us." The only cure, Brinck posited, was to recognize the nationalistic intolerance being portrayed, thereby rendering it powerless.[6]

By the March 1927 issue of *Pocumtuck,* Brinck Jackson was on its board of editors, where he served for a single term. In its March number he presented "A Cynic," a piece of fictional reportage that seems straight out of his "Eureka" mock newspaper.

Brinck's final contribution to *Pocumtuck* came in May 1927, near the close of his junior year at Deerfield. "A Thibetan Idyll" takes as its principal character Spoomi, a sacred bull descended from the original white bull "who arrived in Thibet upon a flaming comet." Spoomi lived in a jewel-encrusted stall in the grandest temple in Thibet, where he was pampered by priests, who fed him delicacies and offered him honey and wine to drink. But Spoomi was unhappy and began to waste away. Near death, he broke free and, after sacrilegiously drinking the holy water and eating the altar flowers, went to the doorway of the temple. There "he smelt the fresh earth and grass, and saw the tops of the hills opposite red in the early sunlight, and the pasture slopes bright green."

The temptations of "the Evil One" overwhelmed Spoomi, and he lit out for the pastures. He ate its delicious grass, made friends (after rolling in the mud to hide his decorated horns and hoofs), and began to think of travel. But with evening came the high priest, who spoke to Spoomi of his necessary role in the country's religion, where his moves were interpreted as prophecies, and where the priests' very existence was dependent upon serving him. The happiness of the people of Thibet fell on his bovine shoulders. Other priests must never discover "their idol to be a mere animal, subject to animal temptations."

Thus reminded of his responsibility, Spoomi agreed to return to the temple. The high priest denied his request for one more roll in the mud but acceded to the more modest "mouthful of beautiful young grass." Spoomi lived out his venerated and long life, "a little melancholy perhaps but always courteous and patient." When he occasionally dreamed of the fresh grass and woke up "restless and troubled," he was calmed by the high priest. Spoomi would then say, "Enough I am an animal agin."[7]

This story is hard to interpret nine decades after it was written by a youth whom I only knew much later as an adult. Nevertheless, I'll give it a try. "A Thibetan Idyll" seems to me a parable about growing up with privilege linked with sacrifice. The context in which one lives, whether one is a sacred bull or an adolescent boy, requires living out a role and denying certain pleasures. This leads me to wonder: What were the unwanted privileges the youthful Jackson wished to shirk, and what were his desires in 1927, the roll in the mud and taste of fresh grass that he felt duty-bound to suppress?

Harvard

Brinck Jackson must have had his eyes set on the *Harvard Advocate* from the moment he arrived on campus in September 1929, for his first piece appeared in the December issue. "The Nightmare before Christmas" is a story of Christmas woes, exemplified by the Briskets, a family of modest means living in the Bronx. As the holidays come to the city, the elder Briskets feel compelled, as do many of their peers, to spend money on gifts for their children. "To these harassed individuals each wreath is a noose, each sprig of holly a martyr's palm." As shopping continues, the parents' agony increases. The tree is decorated, the Christmas dinner is laid and eaten. After one of the Brisket children insists that the only thing he wants from Santa is an electric train, his angry father falls asleep in the living room. Awakened by a noise and imagining a burglar, Mr. Brisket gets his revolver, only to find Santa Claus in the living room, "complacent and florid and fat." Confronting him, Brisket shouts, "You're the one whose responsible for all this Hell; well, you're going to get what's coming to you!" After his fired bullets reduce Santa to a puddle of water, Brisket goes lightheartedly to bed.[8]

The next morning, Brisket declares to the children that Santa does not exist and all their presents come from their mother and father. With that, Christmas turns into a delight. The children's appreciation of their presents warms their parents' hearts. The reindeer on the roof get sent to the zoo, and the citizens of the Bronx erect a gold statue of Brisket to honor his deed.

A clever tale, but wrapped into this story is a great deal of snobbery regarding parents of modest means, living on a careful budget squeezed each year by the desire to give Christmas gifts to their children. For almost all of the story, their circumstances and life are treated unkindly. Brisket himself was "a very unimportant little man." He worked long hours as a clerk in an office in lower Manhattan, six days a week. He, his wife, and three children lived in the Bronx "in a big apartment house on a noisy street, and pretended they were happy." A certain mockery attended all his wife's and his own efforts. "When Spring came light clothes were exhumed that smelled atrociously of moth balls. Brisket got out his straw hat and wore it down town in the subway crowds, satisfied that he was welcoming the season in his way as well as the Hellenes did with song and festival."⁹ The author, a college sophomore—looking down from the clouds at the little people who did the work of the world—was clearly establishing his own superior social standing.

In the October 1930 issue came a story of heroism, this time displaying different gifts of its author. "M'man Potiron" relates the story of a lower-class Frenchwoman by that name during the Franco-Prussian War and its aftermath, as told by an aristocrat to the narrator. The work's primary interest lies in its detailed depiction of a village in Normandy and its many plot twists. Potiron is a young woman of low reputation who cleans in the village hotel. She steals papers off the desk of one of the billeting German officers and, assuming they hold military secrets, walks to the French military headquarters, some distance away, where she is promised a reward from the French Ministry of War. Her courageous act evokes admiration by the villagers, gifts, and even a cottage in which to live. As years pass and no reward from the nation comes, Potiron takes herself to Paris and the ministry. There she learns that the seemingly important papers held nothing of military value, only the beginnings of the German officer's novel and personal mail. Never revealing this to the villagers, she lives out her life in their esteem.

At the end of her story, the aristocrat asks, "was that not bravery?" The narrator responds, "It was something much rarer than that . . . it was good common sense."[10] Such moral relativism may have been held by Jackson at the time or, possibly, served him only as a literary device. Jackson's aim seemed to be entertainment, and also perhaps the desire to exercise his talents and display his knowledge of history and France.

"Strohmeyer," appearing in the *Advocate* in April 1931, shows Jackson again peering at the lower classes from a superior perspective.[11] In this case, the story is told by a lone traveler staying at a small hotel for an idle month, observing those who serve him. He introduces Strohmeyer, the hotel's owner, a man filled with ambitious plans to turn his modest hotel into an attraction for a "cosmopolitan clientele." Strohmeyer has a staff of three: Joseph, a young and inept man of work; Emma, a beautiful housemaid and server; and, in the background, an unnamed older woman who cooks the meals served to guests. The story contains little narrative, but what there is revolves around the romantic interplay between Joseph and Emma and Emma's efforts to discourage Strohmeyer's persistent advances.

Late in the story, a family of four arrives from Prague and seems to fulfill Strohmeyer's vision of a great future for his modest establishment. Their complaints and demands change the rhythm of the hotel's days and set its staff on edge. After observing the gentleman from Prague give Emma a tip and receive a kiss from her in return, Strohmeyer first upbraids Emma and then issues a surprisingly stern correction to the offending man. Hearing this, Emma first teases her employer but then goes over to the guest to inform him that, though he made no motion to depart, his bill will be ready in the morning and his baggage delivered to the train station. As the man protests and inquires why she works in such a place, Emma tells him she does so to be near Joseph. With the departure of the Czech family, the regular disorder and banter of the small hotel returns.

On taking his own leave, the narrator learns to his surprise that the old woman in the kitchen is Strohmeyer's wife, and it is her presence that allows him to employ Emma: "You don't suppose that a nice girl like Emma would consent to live in the house of an unmarried man, or that I would like a girl who would!"[12]

One final look at Strohmeyer, his wife, and Emma ends the tale. Sitting in a café, the lone traveler sees them in a row boat on the lake listening to music coming from an orchestra on the shore and reflects that they were "as near as they ever got to the cosmopolitan world."[13]

Each of these stories in the *Advocate,* with their settings in the Bronx, a village in Normandy, and a resort area by an Austrian lake, makes good use of Jackson's observations from his home base in New York and his travels in Europe. Although Jackson's elitism is most evident in the story of Brisket, in the two that follow he continues his bemused delight in the foibles of the lower classes. Both reveal some insight into the motivations, feelings, and illusions of an imaginary Frenchwoman and an Austrian man, but their two narrators, nonetheless, remain on Olympus looking down with an amused wink on the underlings beneath them.

Something new, however, does appear in Jackson's third story: a foreshadowing of his later evocative descriptions of natural landscapes. "The mountains are not high," he writes, "and although at their base near the water's edge they are dark-green and cheerless, as they rise they recede like the top of the forehead, and at the summit the curve is so gradual that it is hard to say where the highest spot is." Of the human scene, he merely notes, "Up there the sun stays longest, and there are fields and a few houses," before turning his eye back to the natural world.[14] In mid-life and after, Jackson would continue to appreciate natural beauty—as his journals and sketches attest—but in his published writings his attention turned increasingly to those fields and houses.

As he was composing these stories, Jackson ascended to the *Advocate*'s editorial board, his election announced in February of his junior year.[15] He served on a board of seven (later expanded to nine) literary editors and six officers. James Agee, later a renowned novelist and poet, was president, one among a number of writers and board members during Jackson's time who went on to have distinguished writing careers. (Jackson, however, never mentioned any of them in any known context.)

The *Advocate* offered an undergraduate's eye on literature and the arts outside college gates. In Jackson's era, artistic innovation was in the wind, and the literary magazine's table of contents lists reviews of the works of Ernest Hemingway and D. H. Lawrence, among others, as well as considerations of French cinema and discussions of the art of Henri Matisse and Pablo Picasso. Jackson was thus fully exposed to the currents of modernism. How he responded in a broader sense is unknown, but in one arena he definitely resisted—architecture. In the May 1931 issue, Jackson offered "Our Architects Discover Rousseau," a full-throated critique of architectural modernism. It is a long piece that displays its author's strong opinions and wit, as well as his wide reading of architectural criticism.[16]

Jackson's take-off point was an article in the *Harkness Hoot,* a newly launched iconoclastic publication by Yale undergraduates. One of its articles, critical of Yale's Gothic buildings under construction, lambasted the use of their historical style, contending that Yale had "fallen back, slavishly and ignobly, into the past. It has forgotten art and become obsessed with archeology." Jackson disagreed profoundly, using the Baroque to do so. He proclaimed, "Baroque was a magnificent style because it typified a magnificent age." It was the "last vital style which fulfilled its function of interpreting an age." For Jackson, the era of Baroque was one in which style depended "on man for its growth, and not material or method."[17]

Near the end of his junior year at Harvard—just before he again took off to Europe for the summer—culture was what Jackson valued. As he thought about architecture, he wrote, "our attempts to glorify our prosaic edifices may not always be happy, but anything is better than revealing their true nature. Such frankness means that a home is an animal's den, that a railroad station is the assembly place for dirty engines and hurried people, that a dinner is stuffing food into the mouth; whereas it has been the constant endeavor of humanity to dignify itself by dignifying its functions and habitats, making a home the image of the owner's taste, a station a public monument, a dinner a ceremony."[18]

By contrast those committed to modernism in architecture describe its exemplary buildings as "frank, original, modern, free, democratic, untutored," and thus appropriate for the present age.[19] Against this, Jackson wrote, "those Modernists who have gone native in the jungle of Machinery. . . . Condemn all art which is not the product of technology (or as they call it science) and since human art is deadly to them there remains none but the utilitarian-romantic. Add therefore to the Trinity of Business, Technology, the Machine, a sort of Brahma or Oversoul: Utility (that being the glorious concept which directs all activities), and you have the four elements of Modern Architecture."[20]

Jackson drew on the opposition to Romanticism and Rousseau learned in an English class from Irving Babbitt, Harvard's leading conservative critic. Jackson found a way to oppose architectural modernism by linking its justifications to the spirit of Rousseau. Jackson connected celebrators of the modern movement, such as the Yale men in the *Hoot,* to the romantic insistence on nature and nakedness. Offering this rebuttal, Jackson states, "Perhaps we are too remote from Nature, but it is hard to understand what is so vile about pretense as long as it represents a sincere effort to be better, and even harder to understand what is so edifying about nakedness."[21]

With this, Jackson turned to the symbol of modernity, the skyscraper, and scorned its celebration, holding up for mockery words written by modernist architects and advocates, such as Frank Lloyd Wright.[22] Jackson condemned all the structures he despised—works that included Wright's "dreary monkey houses and mausoleums," the buildings of the 1933 World's Fair, Le Corbusier's structures, and the "siedlungen [working-class housing estates] of Amsterdam, Berlin, Leipzig," all of them "callous to the needs and desires of the individual man, but gushing with humanitarianism for the mob."[23]

Jackson ended with an indictment of the contemporary world mirrored by modernism. The architects of such abhorrent buildings are simply "enthusiastic exponents of a submission to the present chaos." Condemning their work as "nothing but the exaltation of things essentially ugly and miserable and senseless," he continued with the judgment that modernist architecture's "utilitarianism is cynicism, its adaptability is fatalism, its frankness is impotence and the failure of the creative instinct. It is the glorification of our mediocre social theories, already half repudiated; it is the denial of everything that art has been and must be to civilized mankind." Linking modernists to romantics, he concluded, "the world is heartily sick of romantics, and their end cannot come too soon."[24] Reading this tirade, I wonder if Jackson, at the end of his junior year in college, was caught in his own rhetoric or if he fully believed what he was writing.

Any narrative of Jackson's time at Harvard is bound to be incomplete, for there exist only a few traces of it, including these pieces from the *Harvard Advocate*. Jackson's collegiate writings, however, are telling. In addition to exemplifying his way with words, his three pieces of fiction clearly demonstrate his desire to place himself within Harvard's social world as a member of the American upper class. At the same time, his vigorous defense of Baroque and rejection of modernism in "Our Architects Discover Rousseau," if written from the heart, offers evidence that, when he was an undergraduate, J. B. Jackson was a cultural conservative of the deepest dye.

The Young Man as Writer and Novelist

In our conversations Jackson obscured some of his past from the period before the beginning of *Landscape* magazine. As a result, my 1997 essay on his life and work was informed by both what he stated *and* what he concealed. He chose to emphasize his years of indecision and wanderlust that followed his graduation from Harvard, and then the rough life he led as a ranch hand in the late 1930s. What he never spoke about was his dream to be a man of letters—both a novelist and a nonfiction commentator on the world's scene. Looking back over the traces Jackson left behind, especially the handwritten newspaper he created as a child and his early published stories, I believe being a writer had been in his mind from very early on.

In our taped interviews of 1994, Brinck made much of his varied activities after Harvard. He told me that entered MIT briefly to study architecture but left after his first year to become a reporter for a New Bedford newspaper. Then he went abroad, first taking a course in commercial art in Vienna, followed by a motorcycle trip through central Europe. Returning to the United States, he took a job in the president's office of Harvard to work for the university's 1936 tercentenary. I assumed this covered the full span of the four years, 1932–36.

However, the *Harvard Crimson* and dated drawings that Jackson gathered in a scrapbook created for his mother in 1946 belie certain aspects of this narrative, particularly its chronology. Though a member of the class of 1932, he actually received his degree in March 1933. This may have meant nothing to him, as his sketches document that the summer of 1932 found him in Innsbruck, Austria (see color plate 2). In the autumn months that followed, he took a bicycle trip that included Liechtenstein and Bavaria. Jackson seemed to have skipped his graduation ceremony in the winter of 1933, as he was then in Rome.[25]

Motorcycle travel through Central Europe is illustrated in his sketches: in spring 1933, he rode around Vienna and to Nuremberg and Munich, ending in Passau;

during 1933 he also went to Poland and Czechoslovakia; in June he was in the Tyrol and Zell-am-See. (Interestingly, in such places he didn't draw the glorious mountain scenery that attracted most tourists, but rather buildings and monuments.)

His stint in the architecture program at MIT came during the academic year 1933–34. His true work, however, lay elsewhere. On March 9, 1934, he sent a telegram to William Warder Norton, head of the publishing company W. W. Norton, asking if he could come to see him in New York. Jackson was then living almost adjacent to the Harvard Yard, and he was writing.[26]

His purpose in visiting Norton was to ask for help in publishing a magazine piece he had written, an essay analyzing the philosophical underpinnings of the Third Reich, ultimately titled "Prussianism or Hitlerism." After the trip to New York, Jackson did some rewriting and then, on March 30, sent the draft to Norton. "I hope you will make your criticism of it as valuable as it was last time by telling me plainly what you think of it, and of my attempts to clarify the issue," he wrote. "I know that it is not very clear, even consistent, but that is because it is a subject which is actually too much for me."[27] Within a week Norton replied with some suggestions, such as the need for Jackson to state his position in his opening paragraph. If Jackson agreed, he would then send the revised piece to the editor of *Atlantic Monthly* "with an urgent recommendation that he read it himself, and after doing so get you in to have a talk about it, whether he accepts it or not." Norton recommended that Jackson take this path, and if the *Atlantic* rejected the work, that he move on to "Harpers, and The New Republic."[28]

I am struck by the level of chumminess and access that this correspondence reveals. I don't know how Jackson got to Norton, but the initial telegram was signed "Brinck"; as time went on, Jackson called Norton by his middle name, Warder, and twice referred to "Boo," the family nickname for Wayne Gridley Jackson, his older half brother, a lawyer then working in New York City.[29] Was Wayne the connection between writer and publisher, or was it Alice Jackson? In the publisher's correspondence, mixed with letters to and from "Brinck" or "Brincky," is one from Mrs. Jackson, bringing to Norton's attention a female author hoping to change her publisher. In his letters, Brinck frequently sent his regards to "Polly," the nickname of Norton's wife, Margaret Dows Herter Norton. In a letter from Warder Norton to Edward Weeks, a member of the *Atlantic* staff, inquiring on Jackson's behalf about the whereabouts of the magazine's editor, Norton began, "I have a young friend in Boston."[30] All of this speaks of relationships forged long before the March 1934 telegram, and of Jackson's powerful connection to the publishing world.

Norton put a great deal of effort into helping his "young friend," as an April 28 letter to Jackson detailed. "On the day your revised manuscript arrived I received a call from Dr. Werner Hegemann, a distinguished German exile attached to the New School. You may know his book, HISTORY UN-MASKED, in the German. I thought it would be a very good stunt to ask him to read your paper and I found that it was. It made him perfectly furious, really got under his skin, and he went so far as to insist that Max Ascoli, who I feel is the most brilliant of the exiles (he is an Italian not a German) read it." Both Hegemann and Ascoli were anti-fascists. The complexity of Jackson's

Figure 14. Wayne Gridley Jackson

piece appealed to Ascoli, who praised it highly despite the need for further revision. Norton reported, "I am really not pulling your leg when I tell you that he says he wishes he might have written it himself."[31]

"Prussianism and Hitlerism" did not appear in any of Norton's favored publications, but rather in the *American Review,* a relatively new periodical known for its radical conservatism. Here also Jackson published a book review that gave him an opportunity to continue his opposition to architectural modernism. In the summer of 1934, Jackson spent time in Liechtenstein and, in February 1935, published "A Führer Comes to Liechtenstein," in *Harper's Magazine.* In this fictional piece, Jackson began his exploration of fascism's attraction to young men, a depiction that three years later was to resurface in his published novel.[32]

These publications netted him $240.[33] Finding himself in need of a steadier source of income, in January 1935, Jackson turned to the Harvard Alumni Placement Office. From its records we can trace his residence to 5 Linden Street, essentially across the street from the Harvard Yard. The report of his personal interview at the placement office described Jackson as "a modest, convincing, and cultured young man who believes he can write and wants a chance to prove it." The interviewer noted that Jackson might be a good fit for Condé Nast in New York. On

January 21, Jackson called to report he had gotten "a proof reading job on the New Bedford Mercury (morning paper) [but] wants to go ahead with Condé Nast. Available for N.Y. interviews any Saturday."[34]

The office's assistant director promptly wrote a long letter to Condé Nast, presenting Jackson as he had presented himself. Along with his Harvard credentials came the information that Jackson was a Unitarian and his father (with no hint of the latter's separation from the household or the earlier stated "fact" that he was deceased) worked for the Red Cross. Jackson's published pieces were enclosed. Mindful of protecting future efforts of the placement office for other job seekers, the assistant director stated that he submitted these materials "with a large question mark and hope I am not presumptuous in approaching you with them."[35] A response from the woman who served as the initial contact between "college candidates" and Condé Nast indicated that she would be happy to hear from the applicant. The placement officer let Jackson know this, but here the thread was dropped. Jackson never made it to New York, and his writings were returned. On March 1, 1935, the final entry in his Harvard placement file declared it "inactive."[36]

Whatever the state of his finances during these years of the Great Depression, Jackson somehow managed to continue traveling abroad, now with the purpose of finding information and local color for his writing. By the mid-1930s, he began to turn his knowledge of Austria into prose. On May 18, 1937, Alice Jackson announced to Warder Norton that "Young Brinck is writing a book—did Boo tell you?"[37] "I hope you and Boo will be over to see us before we sail on the twelfth," replied Norton. "As for Brinck's book, if he doesn't let Polly and me have a look at it before anyone else we most certainly will bring down the house over his head when he comes to see us!"[38] The book that emerged was the novel *Saints in Summertime*, published by Norton in summer 1938.[39]

Traces of the book's journey to publication begin November 9, 1937, when the manuscript appeared in three volumes at the Norton office. Following a hiatus of many months, on February 27, 1938, Jackson wrote to Norton, "Wayne tells me that the manuscript is in the hands of some reader and that I should hear from you in the course of a week." Using the excuse that he was about to travel to Cuba, Jackson continued, "I am anxious to have the matter settled one way or another. I can understand how busy you may be, and any doubts you may have developed as to the worth of the book, but as I am about to go away for a month I am anxious to have the matter settled one way or another." If the manuscript was rejected, he would immediately send it to another publisher. If accepted, he would make suggested changes, "provided they are not too drastic, I could perhaps do them before leaving and again avoid a long delay. . . . You know, I'm sure how willing I am to follow your suggestions when I can."[40]

Norton did accept the manuscript, and on April 9, Jackson returned the signed contract, adding that he looked forward to seeing him and Polly "again" in New York. In what would become a topic raised repeatedly over the next months, Jackson brought attention to the misspelling of "Brinckerhoff" in the document. "Incidentally my name has 2 Fs at the end," he noted. "Phonetically the second one doesn't help much, but it belongs there." In June, right before publication, another mistake reappeared in final proofs. "I was horrified to discover that my name on the title page was spelled without a *c,* a letter that I am determined to keep in my name until death," Jackson wrote, adding, "You won't let them cheat me out of it, will you?"[41]

As the book went through the process of publication, three topics animated what seems a fairly straightforward correspondence between author and publishing house. Since neither had a clear take on the title, Norton paid writer Paul Hoffman, a friend and Harvard classmate of Jackson (who serendipitously lived in Utica, New York, at "1104 Brinckerhoff Avenue") the sum of ten dollars for title suggestions. By early May, one stuck—*Saints in Summertime*—although it engendered little enthusiasm from Jackson.[42]

A more serious source of concern was how to describe the novel's contents. In early November 1937, when the manuscript appeared at the publisher's office, Jackson explained in an accompanying letter to Warder Norton, "You'll find it to be a political melodrama, laid in present-day Ruritania [a fictionalized Austria], involving much action in the way of kidnapping, electioneering strategems [stratagems], gun play, and adultery. It is conventional in plot and form, and if it amuses whoever reads it, it will have served its purpose." However, when the book was about to appear, Jackson objected to the initial publicity copy that portrayed the novel in just that fashion.[43]

On June 16, 1938, Jackson wrote, "The Rudisches are not the theme of S in S; politics is. And as I told Mr. Norton, every character in the story has to my mind a definite symbolic value and the situations between them are dramatizations of recent political events in Central Europe. Rudisches are padding to make the allegory a little less obvious." Jackson continued, "I don't for one instant believe that the novel represents a contribution to political thought, but I am equally sure it is not a particularly entertaining one, i.e., comic novel. and I'd rather be abused for what few ideas I express than be damned for writing a flat farce."[44]

The third concern was payment for *Saints in Summertime*'s promotion. Jackson agreed to a contract limiting his royalties to 7½ percent for the first two thousand copies sold rather than the usual 10 percent. He gave up 2½ percent for publicity by the press with the understanding that the publisher would spend the entire $50 to promote the book.[45] Jackson himself worked his modest Harvard network on his book's behalf, bringing in Paul Hoffman, who suggested the book's title, and Robert Hillyer, who wrote a blurb.

Saints in Summertime garnered excellent early attention. On the book's publication date—Thursday, July 21, 1938—it received a featured "Books of the Times" review in the *New York Times;* staff reviewer Ralph Thompson called it "a remarkable work, crafty, witty, and original." The review paid some attention to the plot, but more to the ideas behind it. It raised the question of Jackson's "black pessimism," as expressed at the end by one of the central characters in the novel, but declared the author was less a pessimist than "a mourner of the recent failure of democracy in Austria."[46]

The review Jackson clearly treasured above all was in the *Saturday Review of Literature,* dated July 23, 1938, for he kept a copy of the entire issue in his papers. His photograph takes up much of the cover, portraying a handsome young man in jacket and tie, his face turned slightly to the side, unsmiling, eyes looking intently at the camera. Underneath his name is a quote from the review "A genuine novel of ideas . . . is curiously rare in an age overshadowed by ideas and their consequences." The review by Elmer Davis went on to praise the book as a "dramatization—highly intelligent, and spiced with ironic comedy—of the great conflict of our times." Inside the issue was a large ad, perhaps using some of $50 setback, praising the book and offering Jackson's language to describe its contents.

By the time the reviews began to appear, Jackson had been writing a second fictional work for several months. He had produced enough by May 13, 1938, to inquire of Norton, "Do you think 50,000 words is too short, or can I aspire to a novella or novelette? I should like to know your opinion before I go too far." Norton responded immediately to quell Jackson's impulse to write shorter fiction: "50,000 words is too short and we would much rather have one novel than two novelettes."[47]

By October, reviews of *Saints in Summertime* were in, as were the book's modest sales of something over a thousand copies. Jackson had decided to move to New

Figure 15. *Saturday Review* cover, 1938

The Saturday Review

of LITERATURE

VOL. XVIII No. 13   NEW YORK, SATURDAY, JULY 23, 1938   TEN CENTS A COPY

LYTTON STRACHEY *By George Dangerfield*

IN THIS ISSUE

ELMER DAVIS
*Reviews "Saints in Summertime"
by Brinckerhoff Jackson*

ROBERT M. HUTCHINS
*Reviews "What a University President Has Learned"
by A. Laurence Lowell*

STEPHEN VINCENT BENÉT
Reviews "A Day of Battle" by Vincent Sheean

AMY LOVEMAN
Reviews "My Sister Eileen" by Ruth McKenney

CRANE BRINTON
Reviews "Persons and Periods" by G. D. H. Cole

EDITH HAMILTON
Reviews "The Complete Greek Drama"

CHRISTOPHER MORLEY
Translations from the Chinese

Other Reviews by ROBERT DISRAELI,
LOUIS UNTERMEYER, N. L. ROTHMAN

BRINCKERHOFF JACKSON

"A genuine novel of ideas . . . is curiously rare in an age
overshadowed by ideas and their consequences" . . .
(See page 5)

BOOK PREVIEW: THE HORSE AND BUGGY DOCTOR
By Arthur E. Hertzler

Mexico. Although his motivation is unknown, the western state held for him a special appeal. He had a wealthy New York uncle, Percy Jackson, who, in addition to his legal work in the insurance field in New York and his leadership in the Boy Scout movement, owned a ranch in Wagon Mound, New Mexico, and was actively involved with the American School of Research (now the School for Advanced Research) in Santa Fe. Percy's mentorship of his fatherless nephew cannot be fully known, but by his later account, Jackson visited his uncle on the New Mexico ranch during several summers when he was a child. The combination of memory and Percy Jackson's wealth and influence must have exerted a strong pull. Writing was nonetheless very much on the author's mind. In a business-like fashion, he wrote to Norton before going west to say that "the second book is underway: it has not progressed very far, and I hope perhaps to finish it this winter. If it is of the same literary quality as Sts in Summertime, and equally remote from current American problems—would you find it acceptable?" Understandingly, he continued, "You may well have hesitations about accepting another book of the same restricted appeal. If so I hope you will tell me frankly so that while I am still East I can make or start to make other arrangements." He also asked to be paid the royalties owed him, writing that the money was not only due him but was needed to finance the trip west. "I've received nothing for the work of a year and a half," he pointed out.[48]

With extreme kindness, Norton immediately sent a reassuring reply. He was happy to learn Jackson was going to New Mexico to work on his next book. Although the sales of his first one had not been large, they were "sufficiently encouraging . . . to make us want very seriously to consider what you will write next." Emphasizing that the excellent reviews led him to want another novel from Jackson, Norton mentioned specifically that of Ralph Thompson in the *Yale Quarterly*, "Statements such as his back our own views, and I hope will encourage you too, Brinck." Offering further reassurance, Norton wrote, "So, do feel that you have, in addition to a friend of a good many years standing, a publisher who is genuinely interested in the sort of writing you are up to."[49]

Something other than writing was likely driving Jackson. For this we only have his word late in his life, for the written record has a gap of two years. To me and to others Brinck spoke of his work as a ranch hand and the pleasure he took in relishing the rough life. He also, he said, had been rodeo rider, was injured, and spent time recuperating in a hotel run by Will Haegler, a man from Switzerland, who, along with his family, remained important to Jackson in the years that followed.

The next trace of Jackson the writer comes in a letter to his Deerfield headmaster,

Frank Boyden. On October 16, 1940, Jackson wrote Boyden he had enlisted in the army, adding, "I have a book coming out next spring."[50] In point of fact, Jackson had not yet submitted his work to a publisher. On army stationery eleven days later, Jackson wrote Warder Norton: "The manuscript of a novel of mine will (I hope) shortly arrive at your office." Norton immediately replied, expressing surprise and delight. Jackson's letter "was a knockout which was exactly as if both barrels of a shotgun had been fired in our office." Out of one was the "manuscript which we had almost given up hope of receiving. (There is a great temptation here to bring the word *phoenix* into this picture but we will let the ashes rest.) And out of the other, the news of your joining with the 7th Cavalry. Polly still can't picture you in your leggings!"[51]

Norton's next letter, written on November 6, 1940, however, must have delivered a crushing blow. With the utmost tact, he let Jackson know that he would have to "turn elsewhere for publication." Jackson had written that his second novel, set in Boston, should appear for "purely personal reasons" under the pseudonym "Sullivan Ames." That led Norton to write, "honest to God, Brin[c]k, we neither of us feel that this is a book by Brincky Jackson, the author of SAINTS IN SUMMERTIME." It lacked his "characteristic ironic way of dealing with a serious problem." Though it had good characterizations and Jackson's "good clean writing," the manuscript was written with a heavy hand. "It is though what you wanted to say had remained in a rather commonplace state, and had not really passed through the fire of your own philosophical and thoughtful self." "We do assure you," he concluded, "that this book seems to have been written by Sullivan Ames, and that when Brinckerhoff Jackson writes his next novel we will want to publish it."[52]

And that was that. J. B. Jackson trained for the cavalry, transferred to army intelligence, and served in North Africa and Europe for the full term of America's engagement in World War II. His longing, however, for a future as a novelist did not die, nor did his fiction writing. No manuscript has ever surfaced, but a trace of his efforts remains in his private writings. Traveling in Europe sixteen years later — after publishing *Landscape* for almost five years — Jackson confided to his travel journal that he still had a novel in the works.

Jackson's Published Writings in the 1930s

The content of Jackson's published writings in the years between his departure from Harvard in 1932 and his move to New Mexico in 1938 pose complex issues not easily resolved. Where was he politically? To what degree did he bend his positions to accommodate his publishers and audience? How did his class position—both real and assumed—limit his vision?

Jackson continued his sustained attack on architectural modernism in 1935, with a scathing review of Charles Harris Whitaker's *From Rameses to Rockefeller* in the *American Review*, but employing the language of this politically conservative journal, he shifted to a new enemy. In contrast to his 1931 *Harvard Advocate* piece in which he castigated Big Business, Jackson turned against the Left to berate the book's author as one who "now flirts with Union Square," the Manhattan location that served in the 1930s as the site of many radical protests. The writings of Lewis Mumford, once admired, Jackson now labeled "Kulturbolschewismus," or cultural Bolshevism.[53]

Jackson's primary attention in these years, however, was focused on Central Europe. As his sketches and travel journals reveal, both Germany and Austria were important destinations for him as a young man. In this he may have been influenced by his mother, for she accompanied him on many of his trips abroad, even as an adult. On a sketch Jackson made in 1929, the summer before entering Harvard as a sophomore, he later wrote that he drew it at a place from which "we all left on a day's notice to go to Vienna and celebrate Mother's birthday." In the scrapbook of sixty-eight sketches Jackson put together for his mother, eleven were drawn in or near Vienna. Austria had served as the setting for his 1931 short story "Strohmeyer." In the years between finishing at Harvard and moving to New Mexico, he was often in Austria and Germany.

The essay "Prussianism or Hitlerism" offers an analysis of what Jackson perceived in Germany in 1934. For me, as a Jew and as a historian with a full understanding of Nazism's consequences, it is a difficult read. It likely posed difficulties at the time as well, appearing as it did in the *American Review*.[54] This short-lived magazine was published by Seward Collins, an admirer of both Mussolini and Hitler. On the far right, Collins solicited articles from New Humanists and Agrarians as well as pro-fascists. One can only hope that, in 1934, Collins misunderstood Jackson's complex work.

In this piece, Jackson attempted to separate, at least intellectually, what Hitler appeared to be putting together: Nazism and Prussianism. In 1934, after dividing into four parts the former state (within Germany) of Prussia, Hitler claimed that the Third Reich was Prussia's reincarnation and the upholder of its spirit. In explaining differences between Prussianism and Hitlerism, Jackson tried first to distinguish between the methods of Prussia, which he understood as admirable efficiency and discipline, and Prussia's selfish and brutal ends in foreign policy. He argued that Prussia, unlike Hitler's regime, had been a tolerant state, accepting of a range of peoples as long as they served the state. "Prussia is not, and never was, nationalistic," wrote Jackson. "She never pursued a domestic or a foreign policy the end of which was to achieve ethnic or linguistic or religious unity." By contrast, Jackson viewed Hitlerism as a nationalism born in the Romantic Movement of the early nineteenth century, one linking "race unity" with the barbaric worship of nature.[55] Given Jackson's well-established aversion to Rousseau and Romanticism, this is for him strong condemnation.

The editor of the *American Review* typically commissioned articles, including those favorable to Mussolini and Hitler. Jackson's disavowal of Hitlerism is clear, but what may have appealed to Collins at the time is the essay's profound social and political conservatism. Jackson portrayed the rise of Hitler as democracy in action: "Admitted that Hitler's Democracy is not what Democracy should be; it bears, nevertheless, a startling resemblance to what Democracy is: the tyranny of popular ignorance, of popular heroes, and a general lowering of the cultural level to suit the capacities of the Common Man."[56]

In light of this, what is odd is the way Jackson pulled back near the end of the piece, suggesting that perhaps Germany could benefit from a dose of true Prussianism: "Prussia has ever been sceptical of Democratic judgment, . . . and now is the time that this scepticism can stand Germany in good stead." In the meantime, "We want to know what Germany has to say; we cannot forever condemn the Third Reich without a hearing." There is a chance for "art and philosophy and religion. They are struggling now in Germany to acquire form. . . . It is possible that German blindness will make her pass this chance by; but if it does—then, and not before, will be the time to talk about reaction and disillusionment."[57]

Writing over eighty years later and with full knowledge of the Holocaust, I find this position very hard to take. True, Jackson wrote this in 1934—not after September 15, 1935, when the Nuremberg Laws were enacted; but already in 1933 Hitler had declared a boycott of Jewish businesses and, by law, forced Jews out of civil service and the legal profession. By the time of Jackson's writing, naturalized German Jews were stripped of their citizenship, book burnings had occurred, and violence against Jews was steadily increasing.

One cannot argue that in 1934 Jackson was uninformed. The scrapbook of his drawings places him in Munich in 1932, where he wrote in a note, "I attended a

Nazi rally in a beer hall," and in southern Bavaria where he stated, "caught my only glimpse of Hitler . . . in an open car" following a rally. In 1933, as Jackson was riding a motorcycle over a wide swath of Germany and Austria, he "had to be pushed down this street on my motorcycle by four stormtroopers" in Nuremberg.[58] Jackson would later draw on these experiences in another magazine piece and for a 1938 novel.

In this essay, Jackson's *only* mention of Jews or anti-Semitism came not in reference to discriminatory or violent acts but to what he claimed was the nation's aesthetic incapacity: Germany is unable to "express herself, no matter how hard she tries. She either makes a fetish of the forms of expression or else denies them completely; she is either intensely idealistic or intensely materialistic, but never is she the mistress of the forms." Having put forth this highly questionable premise, he continued, "This trait offers perhaps some clue to the German hostility to the Jews, who as a race are materialistic and are also past masters of expression, bankers and 'intellectuals.'"[59] Latent in this backward compliment is Jackson's stereotyping of Jews, reflective of his social class in his era. More distressing is his willful blindness to the evil before his eyes.

His story "A Führer Comes to Liechtenstein" appeared in *Harper's Magazine* in 1935 and located the driving forces of fascist appeal in the person of Schaan, a young photographer in that tiny principality.[60] The piece is written from the perspective of an art historian or connoisseur seeking permission to photograph works of art in a prince's palace. As the art lover waits, he gets to know both the town and Schaan, who becomes his guide through the web of officialdom. Returning the following year, the author finds a changed Schaan. The photographer has now become political, having discovered identity and power in the uniform, songs, and ideology of a "German leader." He takes the author to a secret meeting, a rather pathetic gathering but one that reveals the hold fascism has on young men. Those attending sing "German Nazi" songs. Schaan observes that "the Movement" enables him to enter what "the Leader calls the Heroic Life." The two men part on civil terms, but with an awareness of the chasm that has opened between them.[61]

In *Saints in Summertime* Jackson continued his fictional engagement with youth and fascism.[62] A complex and multifaceted work, it is in many ways a reframing of the Liechtenstein piece in the form of an extended novel of ideas. Set in Ruritania (a fictionalized Austria) in 1937, it contains, as did "Strohmeyer," fine landscape descriptions capturing scenes with great economy. The action of the novel pits a range of characters against each other. Sophie Westerling has a choice between her husband Anton Westerling, urbane editor of the *People's Voice* and a social progressive, and Florian, her brother's friend, a village mechanic who is an enthusiastic member of the local fascist group.

Sophia and Anton spend a summer in the village of Sophie's youth, surrounded by her somewhat eccentric and disorderly family. The local election for Provincial Assembly is being waged, and the owner of the hardware store is running as a social progressive. Around him congregate a number of characters who, in interacting, debate the issues igniting Central Europe. The problem for Sophie is that Anton, who stands for reason and humane values, is a self-centered, emotionless cad. By contrast, Florian, a young man drawn to right-wing violence, is handsome, passionate, and impulsive. Ultimately Sophie chooses the attractive youth, although not for his politics.

It is hard to read the work now with a young Brinckerhoff Jackson in mind rather than the older Brinck Jackson I knew. The novel does clarify some aspects of the younger man. It confirms what he himself affirmed, his long-lived hatred of a liberalism based on human goodness. Although Jackson frequently characterized himself as a hopeless reactionary, his statements in later life, in *Landscape* and elsewhere, present a more mixed picture. It is clear, however, that, beginning with his exposure to Irving Babbitt at Harvard, Jackson rejected Romanticism and its belief in man's perfectibility. Perhaps this was the reason he gave his principal female character in his 1938 novel the name Sophie, Rousseau's consort for Emile. While many of Anton's judgments may sound reasonable, what complicates the novel is that Jackson put them in the mouth of a man utterly lacking in feeling and human sympathy.

Florian, by contrast is handsome, direct, and clear in his desire for Sophie. Until his death, all of his misdeeds take place off stage. The reader only learns he is a "Smith," one of the anonymous members of a gang who wear Black Front badges and beat up an illiterate peasant. Florian is useful in demonstrating the sense of power that belonging to a fascist paramilitary group extends to a young man. Without analyzing the theories of "the Smiths" or what their actions portend, he basks in the new-found importance bestowed upon him by the collectivity. If in Florian readers are not introduced to the banality of evil, they are enabled to see its ordinariness.

In 1938, one might usefully have read the novel to understand the events of Eastern Europe. In that context it is insightful. I, however, read it to understand the younger J. B. Jackson and find it fascinating, baffling, and repellent by turns. Over time Jackson's views of religion changed, for many of his beliefs in later life can be found spoken by Sophie's ridiculous mother. When I began to read the novel, after first acquainting myself with its contemporary reviews, I feared I would find Florian appealing—to the author as well as to Sophie. I did not. Jackson's Florian is comely but also immature and brash; never charming or wise or even kind.

While certain others of Jackson's class were drawn to fascism's energy, Jackson seems to have resisted its calls to action. Although anti-Semitism may have blinded him in 1934, it did not lead to Nazism's toxic hatred. Other than Sophie, who is vague and impulsive, no character in the novel escapes the author's satiric jabs. Politics forms much of the matter of the book; a deep pessimism about human nature informs it.

With the publication of *Saints in Summertime,* traces of Jackson's writing life and many of his attitudes go cold for many years. It is only in the 1950s, after World War II and Jackson's long military service, that—with *Landscape* and his travel journals—the trail picks up again.

The Writer as Traveler

In the two slight travel journals that recorded his trips to Mexico and Cuba (in 1937 and 1938, respectively), Jackson revealed intriguing aspects of himself during the time he was writing and seeing *Saints in Summertime* through publication.[63] He was a curious, resourceful, and energetic traveler. He sketched, looked at buildings and neighborhoods. He had an unusual eye for detail, accompanied by a memory that allowed him to write precise descriptions of what he had seen and experienced well after the moment. His observations convey something of the potential that he realized later in his landscape writings. Inevitably, certain of his observations also reveal the elitism of his youth and early manhood.

These travel journals stand in sharp contrast to those Jackson produced in the 1950s. The later ones are richer and understandably convey a more mature sensibility. By then Jackson was no longer a mere observer but an intellectual in an increasingly public realm, a man growing into a new professional role. At midlife he was substantially more self-aware and was struggling, although not always successfully, against his privileged background and its biases as he sought to become more open and humane.

MEXICO

In 1937, Jackson traveled to the Yucatan with two other men on a quest to view Mayan ruins. I've not been able to find out any information on these companions, but I presume they were roughly Jackson's age. The journal tells me only that Robert Chamberlain, the likely organizer of the trip, was given to sulks, and that Jackson was closer to him than to Carl Ruppert. The trio had good connections with the high-placed, cosmopolitan society living in Carmen (likely Playa del Carmen), Mexico, the town where they began and ended their trip. The travelers thus had access to a bit of special treatment and some luxuries; but once out of the urban area, they roughed it.

After a flight on a small plane from Merida to Carmen, the three men were met by the manager of the Phoebe Hearst estate and taken to their hotel. Jackson's first impression of Carmen: "Pretty town, tiled roofs blue & pink & yellow walls. fine laurel trees & palms." A Mr. Moore, estate manager, served as host, and likely escorted the trio as they "called on chief of Customs, Mayor, Assyrian storekeeper." Later, the three men went to Moore's office, where he gave them "maps, etc." In this initial period, they saw an archeologist and visited in the homes of Moore's sister and secretary, whose house Jackson snobbishly described: "Room like bad French stage set—tall vases with artificial roses, bad furniture . . . and chromos." None of the meals on his first day proved to his liking, either. Lunch at the hotel featured "flies, dirty dogs, travelling salesmen—only pork, beans & eggs & beer." Supper was "dreadful . . . badly and dirtily served."

The three travelers gathered supplies necessary for outdoor living in the rough— including a machete, hammocks, blankets, and a file—and mysterious items that Jackson called "alligator boxes." Before walking around the town, they went to see the boat that would take them to the Candelaria River and into the interior. On the following day, they bought food, met the cook, and started their journey.

Transcribing this 1937 journal proved very difficult for me, for its words, written in pencil, were hard to read. Persevering, though, I learned a good deal about Jackson in his late twenties. Beyond the presumptions of this relatively privileged young man whose way in Mexico was eased by good connections, the journal showed his willingness to travel under arduous conditions and his resilience. Moreover, I perceived not only his extraordinary recall and his capacity for observation, but something new—his interest in those he met along the way.

Ruppert was seldom mentioned in the journal; Chamberlain was often described as being low in spirits. Jackson (at least as he presented himself) took in stride most of whatever came. While the two others sulked, he went swimming. He was curious about the life around him. He walked, seemingly alone, around the settlements and

Figure 16. J. B.
Jackson, Yucatan, at
left, 1937

towns along the way, and he sketched. Writing one Sunday, Jackson noted, "Made
friends with Indian who showed me his house and introduced me to his wife. Later
swam across river."

Much of the trip, however, was under unpleasant conditions and yielded sight
of very few of the legendary ruins of the Mayans. Jackson described the first he
saw. After a failure to get horses, the three went on foot through a jungle, taking
a "prehistoric road 1 meter wide—finally arrived at pyramid—30 feet high much
overgrown and delapidated [dilapidated,] climbed it. could make out nothing—
immense skin of snake lying on top[,] tried to get to another pyramid but jungle
too thick."

The travelers were left by their boat at a place called Refugio to await another ves-
sel that would take them further along the river. One night when it rained and the
three were suffering under an awning, Jackson wrote, "Smoke horrible and Chamberlain worse than ever." As he was to do at other points of frustration on the trip,
he turned to the literary companion he had selected to accompany him: Samuel
Boswell's *Life of Samuel Johnson*. (Late in life, Jackson cited Johnson's *Journey to the*

Western Islands of Scotland as one of the five books that had most influenced his landscape writing.)

As the trip along the river progressed and certain hopes of the travelers didn't materialize, Jackson noted in his diary that Chamberlain had made their arrangements. When a hired guide said he knew of no ruins nearby, Jackson wrote, "Consternation Chamberlain in charge. at loss to know what to do & say." At one point, after five members of a family boarded the boat the trio had booked for themselves alone, Jackson had "words with Chamberlain about their presence."

By the ninth and last day of their journey by boat, the search for Mayan ruins had proved nearly fruitless. Jackson reported, "Got up at 6. Tiger had eaten dog. no breakfast. ½ can of corn beef in middle of morning. Waited for barges to arrive. 3 from San Rafael came with 100 passengers—dogs, chairs, babies, parrots, pigs, chickens, food, baggage. They sat on barge all morning. . . . Went with small boy, ½ miles into woods. Nothing but overgrown mounds, very disappointing."

Once back to Carmen and civilization, with Chamberlain still sulky, Jackson's bad mood lifted, and his report took on a positive glow. The meals were good. Jackson went to a café whose cook was "an authoress. bought first book with autograph. . . . Promised to bring her Larousse," a promise he later kept. In the plaza he observed what would long remain an interest—the Corso, the daily social promenade, generally occurring late in the day along a main street. Although he didn't name it at the time, he offered this description: "Men counter clockwise, women clockwise." Jackson had an astute eye for class distinctions, recording "Humbler classes inner track, Spanish etc outer." In this period of his life, Jackson relished certain social privileges. When he went to a movie with "Mrs Moore & Mrs Ayer in box," he noted, "Very gala affair. always same boxes for gentry."

As his two companions peeled off in the time that followed, Jackson was entertained during the day by the same two women and enjoyed vermouth, a good meal, and a drive through coconut plantations. For the two nights without Ruppert and Chamberlain, he picked up two strangers—a Mexican engineer and a Mr. Herrle from New Orleans, a "mahogany expert"—to share his room, perhaps to defray expenses. No details of these encounters exist beyond Jackson's abrupt and puzzling end to the journal: "spent night in same room with Herrle. He gave me vile drink— Fruit, milk, lemon[,] sugar and ice."

The many pages that follow are left blank, but at the very back, a penciled note suggests an entry a writer might make, anticipating a future use: "10 houses, in the fields: pigs, pigs, and a man playing the harmonica."

Jackson's second extant travel journal covers a trip to Cuba he began in late winter 1938, immediately after signing the contract to publish *Saints in Summertime*.[64] Like the back page of his Candelaria journal of the year before, this one suggests Jackson was using it as a notebook to write down impressions for use in future fiction.

Jackson arrived in Havana by boat on March 12, 1938, traveling with a person only identified by the initials V.P., a married man in the social world Jackson's family shared with W. W. Norton.[65] Unlike Robert Chamberlain and Carl Ruppert, V.P. remains in the background here; Jackson never reported comments from him. He merely accompanies Jackson, adjusting to his choices, allowing him to sketch whenever he wants and certainly to write in the notebook I now hold in my hand.

Correa, their driver, met the two men in a Dodge sedan upholstered in red leather. One of Jackson's first acts was to buy a newspaper and "read about Austria." The news was important and terrible—it was the day of the Anschluss, when Hitler announced the annexation of Austria to Germany. It harmed the lives of persons Jackson knew well. It potentially would affect the reception of his forthcoming novel. Still, Jackson's focus remained on Havana. He wrote that Correa took them "through narrow crowded noisy streets, like the worst part of downtown Paris." The passengers stopped at a bank, using it much as a later generation did an American Express office, and Jackson found a letter from his mother awaiting him. The bank manager suggested sights for them to see. In offering "a list of sugar plantations to visit," he made it apparent they were perceived as upper-class visitors, to be directed only to a preselected slice of Cuba.

After lunch and a walk-around, the men began their journey. In describing what he observed from the car window, the twenty-eight-year-old Jackson clearly wanted to see beyond travel brochures and the banker's suggestions. In doing so, however, he often took a disdainful tone. Havana's sidewalks, he wrote, "were narrow & crowded. Dirty long windowed houses without art or substance, full of women nursing babies & expecting more. Negroes coatless men, cantinas, grocery stores, all open onto the street." The road took them "through a zone of shacks—the worst I have ever seen, made [of] palm bark and rubbish. Thickly inhabited—filthy, crowded, with no care on the part of the city. After that came a hideous 3 or 4 miles of junk shops, empty lots, filling stations etc. like a Southern City in the U.S.A."

As the two men and their driver traveled through Cuba, much of the journal continues in this vein. Jackson typically didn't like what he saw, and he had little curiosity about life behind building facades. About the countryside outside the car window, he commented, "The country was rolling, open and fine: but uninteresting & unstimulating—entirely too vegetable. . . . A dejected landscape."

Once he had arrived in a place and walked, however, he observed churches and houses with an eye attuned to architecture and construction. In one smaller town, he noted, "The more pretentious houses—those of brick, have the eternal 4 corinthian columns, the others of wood have struts." In another area, he was struck by the oddity of a cathedral having "the strange but somewhat frequent motif of the middle door being less imposing than the two flanking ones," and he accompanied these words with a small sketch.

He looked for oddities, finding in them sources of amusement, such as several statues, including "one to the man who had been on the school committee for several years & had organized the Fiesta of Flowers of the Liceo." In a park, he noticed among a group of boys playing nearby that "one of them wore a bright blue sweater with a red insignia stating that he was Campeon de Yoyo, 1938."

Though Jackson was a close observer with an eye for whimsy, much of what he saw and recorded was shaped by the casual racism of his time and background. Of a crowd going by, he observed, "Hundreds of young men & women in their best clothes. The women in imitation silk or cotton prints with plenty of make-up[,] tightly curled hair and pink—nigger pink—nails. They look like mill-hands, but are well behaved and pay little attention to passersby except when they are friends." He described in great detail the attire of the men in their "shiny white suits, with broad shoulders & small waists," and generalized, "No one is handsome or well built, and often their faces are cruel; but in spite of the negro blood no faces are brutal, only the complexion & not the features show the infusion. . . . The women's skin is usually sallow, but much makeup, and bleached hair makes it unattractive. . . . Few older women are ever seen, and those are almost always old hags with dark faces & white hair, begging or selling lottery tickets." In conclusion, he remarked, "Negroes have the same beautiful voices; they are by no means as numerous in the towns as statistic[s] led me to believe—less of them than in any Southern city."

Reading this passage, I note Jackson's interest in fashion and style, but I also am aware of the deep racial prejudice he exhibited as a young man. He used the word "nigger" casually and revealed his expectation that mixed-race Cubans who carried "Negro blood" would have "brutal" faces. He is callous about the appearance of older women. One needs to remember this passage. It is a way of marking where Jackson began in early manhood, not where he ended up.

As the day proceeded, the two men attended a vaudeville show, and by 10 PM went to bed. With a hint of an appreciation that would emerge in the 1950s, Jackson wrote that above his bed he saw the "reflection of the neon light—red & blue—on ceiling very beautiful."

Seeing himself as a novelist, Jackson used this journal to discipline himself to observe closely and make careful note of what he saw. Interestingly, as he wrote on the next leg of the trip to the Cuban town of Trinidad, Jackson changed his style. He began writing in a terse mode suggestive of Ernest Hemingway, or perhaps of his era's writers of hard-boiled detective fiction: "Children followed us. There was an old theater. I bought a pair of white trousers at an Empire store. 2 women begged from me all the time. I had a shave that lasted 20 minutes. V.P. was sitting on the upstairs porch of the hotel looking at the Square. I made a sketch. We had a greasy lunch served in a hurry. Noisy men all around us."

With the words, "After lunch went out to sketch," the 1938 travel journal abruptly ends.

3

WARTIME SERVICE

J. B. Jackson had a long war. He volunteered in early October 1940 and served until summer 1945, remaining in the army reserves until 1951. Military service in World War II was a pivotal experience in Jackson's life. It tested his mettle, and he was not found wanting. It served as a lodestar. On his gravestone, aside from the dates of his birth and death, are only these words: MAJ US ARMY, WORLD WAR II, PURPLE HEART, SILVER STAR.

In reexamining the transcripts of my 1994 conversations with Brinck, I find that the incidents from the war he recalled half a century later were, with two exceptions, amusing ones. He told me one hilarious story of making himself so sick on French pastries bought in Algiers that he landed in a hospital. He also chuckled a good deal as he recalled the military order he was given to set up a house of prostitution for the troops in Sicily.[1]

The first exception came when Brinck spoke of the public's disrespect for soldiers during his early cavalry training at Fort Bliss. It was a shock, after his privileged life, to be barred from a restaurant by a sign on the door proclaiming "No enlisted men" and mocked on a commercial airline—with the words, "There's a cavalry man on board"—for smelling of horses.[2]

The second exception involved crossing from Wales to France on a freighter, when he, as Captain Jackson, was the officer in charge of two thousand men onboard a ship intended to land immediately after D-Day. The crossing ended in a terrifying

manner when the freighter's captain mistakenly attempted to land on the wrong beach, with "German planes . . . flying around trying to get at us." After watching the "fireworks" all night, the next morning Jackson and his men were conveyed to Utah Beach, where they landed and disembarked safely.[3]

Brinck outlined for me his military experiences prior to going abroad. Following a stint at Fort Bliss, where he took some sort of correspondence course that led him to become a second lieutenant, he was sent to Fort Riley, Kansas, where for about six months he trained soldiers for the cavalry.

After Pearl Harbor, Jackson was posted in Washington, D.C., where he was one of three or four lieutenants in the Munitions Building whose job was to read dispatches coming in and convey their essential information to the generals and their staffs. He then trained at Camp Richie in Maryland for intelligence work before being sent on active service to North Africa and Europe.[4]

Jackson wrote eloquently regarding the important meaning of World War II to his understanding of the landscape.[5] His sketches of that time not only help one visualize the relationship of his wartime endeavors to his later work; as organized by Doug Adams, they also contribute to a chronology of his wartime movements.[6] He drew a landscape of Dakar while he was in Senegal in 1943; one of Winchester, England, places him there in preparation for the American invasion of the Continent on and after D-Day, June 6, 1944. Soon after arriving in Normandy, he drew a church in Verneuil-sur-Avre; and in Autumn 1944, the place where he was billeted, near Malmedy, Belgium. Jackson made field reconnaissance sketches in Belgium and Germany in 1944, and in March 1945, one at Remagen, Germany. Two nonmilitary drawings place Jackson in southern France on May 8, the day after the German surrender, and at Hettange, France, just south of Luxembourg, on August 8, shortly before his return to the United States.[7] On September 12, 1945, he was discharged from active service.

I have been fortunate to find additional traces of Jackson's wartime service, beginning with his enlistment record, which follows. The Deerfield Academy archives contain Jackson's letters to Frank Boyden, narrating significant wartime experiences and perceptions. Wartime held one surprise, found in the *New York Times,* and two pieces written by newsmen on the scene convey one of Jackson's brave deeds.

Jackson's Army Enlistment Record

Name:	John B. Jackson
Birth Year:	1911
Race:	White, citizen
Nativity State or Country:	Massachusetts
State of Residence:	New Mexico
County or City:	Colfax
Enlistment Date:	8 Oct 1940
Enlistment State:	New Mexico
Enlistment City:	Santa Fe
Branch:	Cavalry
Branch Code:	Cavalry
Grade:	Private
Grade Code:	Private
Term of Enlistment:	Enlistment for the Philippine Department
Component:	Regular Army (including Officers, Nurses, Warrant Officers, and Enlisted Men)
Source:	Civil Life
Education:	4 years of college
Civil Occupation:	Farm hands, animal and livestock
Marital Status	Single, without dependents
Height	68
Weight	140[8]

Deerfield as Home

When J. B. Jackson entered the army in 1940, he declared his place of birth was Deerfield, Massachusetts. He wrote to Frank Boyden, Deerfield's headmaster, to let him know that he had done so "as a means of avoiding complications, as I was born in France as a matter of fact."[9] But there was something deeper behind Jackson's declaration. At a critical period in his life, Brinck received from Boyden the attention he gave to all the boys under his care. This likely meant a great deal to an adolescent whose father deserted him at age four. Brinck thus found in Boyden a surrogate father. In joining the army, Jackson was attempting to live out the ideals Boyden preached.

On entering Deerfield, Jackson learned the story of Tom Ashley from Boyden. Tom was a local farm boy whom Boyden persuaded to attend the academy. Returning to Deerfield as a teacher after graduating from Amherst College, he urged that the academy follow the model of elite prep schools and become a boarding school. With the entry of the United States in World War I, Tom volunteered for the marines. Leading a battalion, he was killed in action, June 6, 1918. Boyden kept his memory alive at Deerfield, each year telling incoming students Tom Ashley's heroic story. As represented by the headmaster, Tom embodied the character traits — loyalty, patriotism, discipline, and determination — Boyden sought to instill in "his boys."

In a 1940 letter from Fort Bliss telling Boyden of his decision to suspend his literary career and put aside his hopes for a ranch in New Mexico, Jackson made it clear that he had learned the lesson of Tom Ashley. "I still believe," Jackson wrote, "that educated men have just as much of a duty to perform in national defense as have other classes." Then, in a more light-hearted vein, he continued, "You will perhaps not believe me (of all people) when I say that boarding school discipline makes army discipline easier to take; but such is the case. Once the urge to answer back is overcome (and common sense tells me that is necessary) the orders are easy to follow and in some cases to foresee."

In this early report, Jackson praised all aspects of Fort Bliss, describing it as "a very handsome place, like a mid-western college in appearance, with its own movies and churches and stores etc, as well as airport and armory." The barracks were "new and luxurious" and the food "excellent." Jackson had been a ranch hand, living fairly rough, so the stability of Fort Bliss may have been a welcome change. Knowing of Boyden's love of horses, Jackson emphasized the fact that he had joined the cavalry, and that the past three years in New Mexico had turned him into a "competent horseman."[10]

Boyden responded to every nuance. He promised his full cooperation in case Jackson's designation of Deerfield as his birthplace should somehow raise suspicions. Writing back, Jackson said, "It was smart of me to remember the county but

I told the authorities not to look for a record of my birthday in the town-records (if Deerfield has any such) for they would merely be disappointed."[11] To this Boyden agreed to cooperate, and wrote, "I know that the Town of Deerfield would be glad to claim you as a son." Pleased with Jackson's sense of duty and patriotism, Boyden added words of his own about the responsibilities of educated men. He recalled his memory of Jackson's able "senior talk," adding the hope that one day he would speak to a large gathering of Deerfield alumni. In a lighter vein, he turned to his own love of horses and applauded Jackson's choice of the cavalry.[12]

In midsummer of 1943, Boyden received a handwritten note from Jackson, written two months earlier, with this news: "I've been over here in North Africa for the past 3 months and can[']t complain of a dull time. At present I am resting and trying to get rid of Tunisian fleas before preparing for the next episode when I return to the U.S. minus one leg. I will tell you about my activities some Sunday evening, but at present I cant. Will you ask the local Red Cross to send me some fudge? Other men receive presents from their home towns, but unfortunately I have none."[13]

Boyden successfully accomplished his mission, and a large box of fudge, accompanied by another holding a fruitcake, reached Jackson in late October. The food parcels found him no longer in North Africa, but in Sicily. The day after he received them, Jackson wrote Boyden a long letter that began with thanks for the treats and continued with an evocative and occasionally witty description of his life and work in the army. Boyden would long remember its specificity and its references to Jackson's training in German at Deerfield. Because of the unique trace it provides of Jackson's military experience, the letter follows in its entirety.[14]

> Some[w]here in Sicily
> APO 9, G-2 section
> Postmaster, NYC
> Oct. 17, 1943 [Typewritten]
> Rec. Oct. 28 [Handwritten]

Dear Mr. Boyden

My foolish and presumptuous request for fudge from the Deerfield Red Cross has been answered, and far more generously than I deserved. A large box of fudge and another of fruit cake arrived yesterday, and already it has done a great deal to raise morale in this unit. I hope you will tell those who were responsible for this kindness that I am most grateful for their thought and effort, and embarrassed that I can do nothing to repay them. Perhaps the circumstance that the gift is being shared will justify, partly at least, the trouble taken by the Red Cross, and my own tactlessness in asking for a present.

I imagine the box has been pursuing me around the Mediterranean theater for some time, for I haven[']t stayed in the same spot for more than ten days at a time since last March. I wrote you, I think, sometime during the engagement at Sedjenane — not far from Bizerte and Tunis. The first of these cities I saw a few days after it had fallen, the second only a month ago. For almost immediately after the end of the campaign I was ordered to a city in the Western part of North Africa, and there and nearby I spent some time. Spring in North Africa is a beautiful time of the year, as beautiful as it is in California, and as deceptive; for what comes afterwards is not Summer as we understand it, but drought, and along with the drought come most of the Seven plagues of Egypt: flies, locusts, dust, and (not to speak disrespectfully of our allies) frogs as well. So we were all very glad to leave North Africa after a prolonged dose of of it, and of course it was very pleasant to find ourselves taking part in a Mediterranean cruise.

This division has received so little publicity, not that I for one care, that no one seems to realize that we took part in the Sicilian campaign. But we did, though we arrived several days after the initial landings, disembarking in the cust[o]mary manner. Not, however, without having been present at a very sensational technicolor airraid the moment we reached port; an occasion more like Hollywood's idea of war than war itself: flames, smoke screens, explosions, and a great deal of noise. I had never been to Sicily before, and was glad of an opportunity to see something of it. In parts there has been a great deal of destruction of a very regrettable sort; old towns and villages laid low, and nothing spared within them. It can[']t be helped, and will continue to happen throughout this war; but we should think twice before making accusations ag[a]inst the enemy of wanton misbehavior. In the part of Sicily where we were, the people were comparatively prosperous, and we saw no evidences of starvation or of any other misery than that occasioned by the actual warfare raging in the neighborhood, though that was more than enough. But apart from a great many public works we saw no very striking evidence of Mussolini's attempts to reform the Italians; they are still dirty and undisciplined and incompetent; still quite unable to act like soldiers, for all the training they have had as children, and which so shocked the world when it was first started. They were moderately glad to see us, partly because of the inevitable cousins they had in Brooklyn, and partly because we were kind to them and gave them food and cigarettes out of our rations; but most of all because they thought our arrival meant the end of war and the return of their men, and so it did; the Italian army as you know made a miserable sort of showing and surrendered so fast in some instances that it clogged the roads. The Germans wwere quite another matter, and fought well and cleverly. I had the misfortune, along with a great many others, to be wounded; very slightly in my case, a mortar fragment in my left arm. It hurt not at all, and seemed unimportant, so that I was much surprised and disconcerted to find myself evacuated back to Africa, by every conceivable form of transportation: jeep, ambulance, truck, train, plane and hospital ship. There I stayed for a month, and now I am back again, hoping to stay. There was a chance of my being sent to Italy, but I'm glad to say it has not materialized. There will be quite enough action for me in the future, I have no doubt, and it would have meant my going among strangers and leaving my friends here. Yesterday I received the Silver Star, with which I am very pleased, so I have further reason for wishing to stay among the men I know and have worked with. At present we are bivouacked not far from the sea, in an olive grove; and all day long we do absolutely nothing. Now that the nights are shorter and cooler, and that the rains have begun life is not as carefree as it was a month ago, but still, we have every reason to be glad that we are where we are: in a part of the island where fruit and eggs and washerwomen abound, and where there are a great many fine buildings and cities to be seen. The next move will take place shortly.

My work, as perhaps I told you, has been that of interrogating German prisoners. It is strenuous and wearing when we are in combat, and because the prisoners are not very numerous at all times, and yet very valuable as sources of information, I have to run around a great deal to find them, and then see that the information they divulge reaches the proper place. When I see them—a few moments after they are captured—they are usually very docile, and frightened of what they fear is in store for them; and I've had no difficulty with them at all. For whatever proficiency I may have in the language Miss Hawkes may take much credit, but they are usually straightforward and respectful: not bad types of men or boys: intelligent, well-informed on military matters, and good soldiers. It is when they recover their self-confidence, which happens about twelve hours after capture, that they reveal themselves in their true colors then they become arrogant, know-it-all, and full of talk about their rights under international law; something that sounds particularly outrageous coming from them. It will be no easy job to reform them, and whoever thinks that kindness will do the trick is unfamiliar with the German mentality; a very fine and valuable mentality in its way, but a very dangerous one. I shall meet it again in the not distant future. From these men, along with military information I learn a great deal about internal conditions in Germany itself in the course of conversation, or while reading their letters—one of my less attractive duties; but such news does not directly concern me, or even interest me after the first.

I have little way of knowing how the American public is taking the war news or what it thinks of the prospects for a rapid end, except that I imagine it is running true to form and is too enthusiastic and too optimistic and too unwilling to face unpleasant facts, as usual. But no one here has many illusions at the moment about the crumbling of German morale, or the sudden occurrence of some miracle which will make war less costly and painful than it has previously been. We have seen two such long wished-for miracles take place in the last two months: Mussolini's downfall and the declaration of war by Italy against Germany; but the war still continues much as before. But perhaps it won[']t do us as a nation any harm to do something the hard way for a change.

It is time for me to apologize for this disgraceful typing and to end, with further thanks for your thoughtfulness. I think of Deerfield very often; I think of it as having been a much larger part of my boyhood than it actually was. But I am sure that it was a very important and profitable part of it. The lessons that our elders try to teach us are not always learned on the spot, as you must well know; they suddenly come to life many years later, when they remain permanent. What Deerfield stood for in my day, and what I hope it still stands for, seems to me to be the best and healthiest aspect of America. So much of the country is undisciplined and unbalanced, so many qualities and virtues we thought of as American are being repudiated, that the islands of sanity are all the more precious. I am grateful for my contact with such a place, and ashamed that a gift of fudge should be the occasion for my expressing what I have long felt on a topic very often in my mind. Many thanks again, and my best wishes to the family.

Sincerely,
Brinck Jackson [handwritten]

CAPT J. B. JACKSON 0–418193
APO 9., G-2 Section
Postmaster N.Y.C.

One question has long puzzled me. Why, in the years after World War II, did Jackson never come to visit Frank Boyden in Deerfield? He was often close by. In September 1945, awaiting discharge from the army, he was living in his mother's house in New Canaan, Connecticut, a distance of approximately 130 miles from the school. Nonetheless, Jackson wrote to Boyden that, although "a pilgrimage to Deerfield . . . was one of the things I most wanted to do while I was in this part of the country," he doubted he could make one.[15] In 1958, lecturing at Yale University, Jackson sent his regrets that though nearby—in this case roughly 100 miles away—he was not able to come. "Perhaps when work lets up in the Fall I can pay a sentimental visit to Deerfield—after 30 years!"[16] What he had once characterized as "a pilgrimage" had now become "a sentimental visit."

For many years Jackson contributed to the Alumni Fund, for which he was thanked and remembered by Boyden; and once, in 1964, he did pay the campus a visit. But he didn't stop. He reported to Boyden, "I had the pleasure of driving through it this September, and if it hadn't been Labor Day I would have paid a visit."[17]

In trying to understand why Jackson never managed to visit a man who had once been so important to him, I recall the deep grief Brinck expressed to me in 1995, when he spoke of his father's desertion not only of the family but of him: "He sent me only one post card, *one post card*."[18] In all the years of his father's life after 1914, he wrote only that single time and never came to see him. My sense is that during Brinck's two critical years at Deerfield, Boyden loomed very large in the fatherless boy's life, and Jackson implicitly understood that if he came to Deerfield he might find his illusions shattered. He might see qualities in Boyden he didn't like, sensing the headmaster's total immersion in his school at the expense of other attributes. More importantly, there would be all those other boys, whose presence was bound to remind Jackson that Boyden was a school head, not a father, and that Boyden's relationship with him was not unique. Worst of all, there might even be a vagueness about Boyden's memories of Brinck himself. Jackson was probably wise to stay away.

Wartime Surprise

I once asked Jackson if there had been anyone in his life with whom he had been especially close. I was hoping to learn of a relationship of some intimacy, male or female. He could only mention Will Haegler, the Swiss hotel keeper who had cared for Jackson after an injury during his prewar ranching days in New Mexico and had partnered with him in leasing a ranch right after World War II. Jackson made it clear that his friendship with Will extended to Will's family and remained unbroken right up to the time of our talk. This is why I was surprised during the course of my research, to find an announcement in the *New York Times* of March 8, 1943, headlined: "Mrs. B. W. Bellinger Engaged to Be Wed; Ex-Student at Masters Fiancee of Capt. J. B. Jackson, U.S.A." The prospective groom, I learned, was "Captain John Brinckerhoff Jackson, U.S.A., son of Mrs. William Brinckerhoff Jackson of New Canaan, Conn., and the late Mr. Jackson."[19]

At the time of Barbara Wood Bellinger's engagement announcement, Jackson was overseas. In a May 1943 letter to Frank Boyden, Brinck wrote that he had been in North Africa for "the past 3 months." So when did the couple meet? Was it while Jackson was working in the Munitions Building in Washington, D.C.? Were they corresponding during the time Jackson was serving abroad? Was the engagement by mail? A good many courtships and engagements did happen by correspondence during World War II: some led to marriage, some did not.[20] At any rate, I could learn nothing more about the specifics of this wartime engagement—only that no marriage between J. B. Jackson and Mrs. Bellinger ever took place.

Another Brave Man

Two printed pieces, both originally newspaper reports, tell a bit more of Brinck Jackson's military service in World War II. The first is by the renowned war correspondent Ernie Pyle and—republished in book form—conveys how he saw Jackson in the field. The second is a straightforward news article from the *Springfield Republican*.

Ernie Pyle wrote a syndicated column on World War II in which he tried to capture the experience of common soldiers. After D-Day, as the American forces made their way over land from the beaches of Normandy, Pyle moved with the U.S. army's Ninth Division and met Jackson, an officer serving with the Intelligence Unit in the Ninth. Pyle's columns on the army's advance were collected in the volume *Brave Men,* published in 1944. Of Jackson, he wrote:

> Captain John Jackson was an unusual fellow with an unusual job. It fell to his lot to be the guy who went in and brought out German generals who thought maybe they would like to surrender. This happened because he spoke German, and because he was on the staff of the Ninth Division which captured the German generals commanding the Cherbourg area.
>
> Captain Jackson went by the nickname of "Brinck." He was a bachelor, thirty-two years old.[21] It was quite a coincidence that he was born in the town of Dinard, about thirty miles from Cherbourg, but he was straight American, for generations back. His folks just happened to be traveling over there at the time he showed up. Captain Jackson's mother lived in New Canaan, Connecticut, but he liked to think of New Mexico as home. For several years he had been a rancher out there, and he loved it. His place was near Wagon Mound and Klines Corners, about forty miles east of Santa Fe. The war played hob with his business. Both he and his partner were overseas, and there was nobody left to look after it. They had lost money last year for the first time.[22]
>
> Captain Jackson was a short, dark man with a thin face. He wore a long trench coat with pack harness, and his helmet came down over his ears, giving him the appearance of a Russian soldier rather than an American. He spoke perfect French, but he said his German was only so-so. It was actually better in his job not to speak German too flawlessly, for then the captured officers might have thought he was a German turned American and been so contemptuous they wouldn't have talked to him.[23]

On June 30, 1944, the *Springfield Republican,* a leading Massachusetts newspaper, also reported on the Ninth Division's actions in Cherbourg and offered an example of when Jackson's German—less-than-perfect or not—proved important:

> In contrast to the capture of Gen Von Schlieben was the taking of Brig-Gen Sattler, commander of the fortress of Cherbourg, whose fall sealed the fate of the town. A colonel, commanding an infantry regiment, accompanied by Capt John B. Jackson, staff German interpreter, was told that what appeared

Figure 18. Photo of J. B. Jackson, on left, 1944

On reverse: Getting the Dope from Nazis

Capt. *John Jackson*, (left), of New Canaan, Conn., and Lt. Col. *Robert Robb*, of San Francisco, Calif., examine German maps and corps orders captured during the fighting along the Cherbourg Pennisula. These documents contained vital information, which helped the Allies to plan future operations. (Passed by censors). Credit line (Acme Photo by Bert Brandt for War Picture Pool) 6-21-44

to be a white flag had been seen. Without seeing the flag themselves, they went boldly into the fort over a wide moat full of water.

They first encountered a machine gunner, who promptly surrendered. They made him carry his handkerchief, tied to a stick, and accompany them to Sattler. The fort is essentially a long street on a high hillside. On one side are earthworks; on the other barracks.

Capt Jackson went along the street yelling: "All Germans come out and surrender." Scores did. The machine gunner with the handkerchief disappeared around a corner. Jackson attached his handkerchief to a broom stick, and proceeded to the main bunker, calling for officers to surrender.

Suddenly there appeared a big man with bright red coat lapels and a gun who commanded: "Halt! Send one man to parley."

Jackson went forward. "My colonel demands your surrender. Your situation is hopeless," he said.

"What do I get in return?" asked Sattler. Jackson replied, "Only honorable captivity."

Sattler refused to believe that Von Schlieben had surrendered, and ordered all his men to man their guns. It was a frightful moment for Jackson and the colonel.

"But," said Jackson later, "I thought he was awful dumb. He had a long parley with his staff and said he would surrender if the Americans had tanks. I assured him that we did. Then he demanded the right of officers to take orderlies. We refused. Then we gave him all the old platitudes about saving life. At last he said he would surrender, but that he was talking only for the men in his own bunker. It might be against the consciences of the others."

"I told him that most of them had surrendered already."

"That doesn't concern me," he said. Sattler wept as he left the fortress, and the Russian workers performing forced labor inside the stronghold hooted him and sang the red "Internationale."[24]

Postscript

Unquestionably these traces offer only small glimpses of Jackson's long war. They are, however, all I could find. What they don't convey is the profound impact his wartime experiences had on him. One important element we know from Jackson himself, is that his intelligence work in World War II gave him a new understanding of the landscape.[25] Only implicitly, however, can we approach the broader impact of war service on the man who signed up in 1940.

Remember that this was the person who had published in Seward Collins's *American Review* a piece expressing his unwillingness to "condemn the Third Reich without a hearing." This was the traveler who four years later wrote so disparagingly and even cruelly about persons he saw in Cuba. The Jackson we encounter after the war, however, is a substantially different human being. He still has prejudices and blind spots, but he has become more open to the world and less judgmental. While such changes can happen by slow evolution, my belief is that in J. B. Jackson's case, they emerged from the crucible of war.

4

LANDSCAPE YEARS

The Founding of *Landscape* Magazine

Jackson's published statements have provided, up until now, the only source for the 1951 founding of *Landscape* magazine. In these narratives and in conversations repeated by those (including me) who have written about his work, Jackson linked its creation to his war service.[1] From these sources we know that, as an intelligence officer in World War II, he used the knowledge he had gleaned from his education, years abroad, and military training in map reading to help guide his infantry division first in North Africa and then in Sicily. In the "dry and relatively empty landscape" of North Africa and Sicily, the map training helped, but after D-Day it offered little of value. After landing on the beaches of Normandy in June 1944, Jackson found more than maps were needed in the more complex landscape of western France. "It was when the division headquarters was billeted in a Norman chateau that I discovered a sizeable library devoted to the bocage country—something I had never heard of before, though we were in the midst of it and having trouble getting out of it."[2]

With his division, he spent the winter in the Hürtgen Forest.[3] To comprehend his surroundings, he bought guidebooks, postcards, maps, and elementary school geography texts. His immediate goal was military: to learn the lay of the land in order to better fight the Germans. He wrote, "If the farmers raised wheat (as some of them did), would our half-tracks bog down in the naked winter fields?

Were there roads in the valleys, where there was a problem of bridges, or on the hilltops, where there was a problem of visibility? And the house types had to be identified . . . to know if the barns were large enough to accommodate trucks and whether there were orchards where guns could be concealed."[4] As he interrogated German prisoners, Jackson was able to get more information about the land, and he learned to read and interpret aerial photographs. Popular and inexpensive French books on geography—works by Pierre Deffontaines, Vidal de La Blache, and Albert Demangeon—caught his interest, and with the end of combat, Jackson got in touch with some of the book editors in Paris with the idea of starting a magazine.

But between the time Jackson mustered out of the army and the launch of *Landscape* lay almost six years. He has written that his first move, once out of uniform, was to buy a jeep and head west in an attempt to take up the life he had left before the war. He returned to New Mexico and reconnected with Will Haegler. The two leased a cattle ranch, but an accident upended their plans. Jackson was alone on the ranch during a snow storm, and his horse threw and then dragged him, severely breaking his leg. When the break failed to heal after six months in a cast, he traveled to New York for surgery. During the long convalescence that followed, Jackson returned to the plan he had begun to develop at the war's close: to create a magazine of geography comparable to the French publications he had admired.

While there is no reason to doubt Jackson, documentary evidence exists complicating his story. As the above discussion of Jackson's early writings makes clear, from childhood to his service in World War II, Jackson was a writer. It is thus fair to assume that much of his postwar life was spent in writing. And in late winter of 1951, Jackson, now forty-one, had completed another book manuscript, this one focusing on Native Americans in New Mexico, and hoped to get it between two covers. In mid-March he wrote, "the magazine will perhaps give me some publicity with publishers."[5]

Jackson wrote these words in the first week of February 1951, and they rest in the bundle of papers I prevented Brinck from burning in 1994. Beginning with a few journal-type entries from February 5 to February 10, the materials include carbon copies of typed letters, from early February through March 1951, addressed primarily to Jackson's mother and brother.

Jackson destroyed most of his personal correspondence, but, perhaps because the two months were special, he had long saved these pages. It was in these months that he created *Landscape*. During February and March 1951, Jackson wrote almost all of the text, acquired the photographs, drew the headings, and made all practical arrangements for printing the first issue. His journal and letters of February and March 1951 reveal how Jackson went about his work—researching and writing to deadline—and they provide some details about production. Perhaps more importantly, they convey Jackson's initial hopes for his new enterprise.[6]

On Wednesday, February 7, 1951, Jackson indicated he had a magazine in the works. He had just received the new winter issue of the *New Mexico Quarterly* containing his own review of what he labeled "unimportant books on the West." In a journal entry, he deemed his piece to be "well written, alert and fair," but he added that "it touched upon nothing of interest to me or to the average reader." He went on to make this judgment: the quarterly "has ceased to represent the Southwest in any real sense; all that it does is say We too have read books, we too are civilized, in just the same manner as you Easterners."

In his journal, he worried that the magazine he was now developing might not appeal to his intended audience. He was trying to reach "the modern Southwesterner" but feared that he, "like all modern men, immediately plunges into the abstractions and generalities behind the scene in order to understand it, and thereby sees none of it at all." Thus, in a backhanded way, Jackson stated his intention: to teach his magazine's readers to *see*.

During the months of February and March, creating the magazine required a great deal, perhaps all, of Jackson's writing time. In early March, he twice mentioned to his mother and brother the piece he was then working on, "Chihuahua; As We Might Have Been."[7] At that point he was close to the finish line, seeking to fill out *Landscape*'s first issue. "I enjoy this piecemeal writing on the magazine," he acknowledged, "not weeks and months of worrying about one topic, but the feeling that there is a little variety." What follows is something that is known, but it is good to hear it from Jackson himself at the time: "But as I told you, I am having to write most of it myself, and that means I have to attempt a variety of points of view if not of style."

How long had Jackson been contemplating the creation of *Landscape*? There is one hint it had been on his mind for at least a year. In a letter to his brother Wayne, probably written on March 15, 1951, he mentions returning home from the library to "rewrite an article Adlai Feather had written for me a year ago." Apparently, he was far enough in his thinking about the magazine in spring 1950 to solicit a piece from Feather, a former academic and then nurseryman in Messila known regionally for his knowledge of local history and folklore.[8] Jackson added that Feather's work was intelligent and well informed, but "quite without shape or style," confiding that "at the risk of offending him I have changed it a great deal."

Other than Feather's contribution, Jackson wrote everything in the first issue of *Landscape*. Searching for material, he tried some field research. Perhaps in February, he wrote to tell Alice and Wayne that he was planning to go to Tucumcari, "a town of little or no charm, but a bustling place where a new irrigation system is being put in. . . . I may find something to write about there, and I will get away from old world charm for a little while." When he traveled to Farmington for a trip of about two days, he found the experience "very pleasant and stimulating." He ventured to the Chamber of Commerce, where he "asked all sorts of questions about Farmington and the Mormons and oil and gas wells, and was given a great deal of information."

He visited the nearby small Mormon settlement of Kirtland, New Mexico, and found it "very like a New York State town with pretty brick houses and enormous trees," and also "very democratic, very well behaved, because of the Mormons, and very enterprising." There he spoke with "two very nice and intelligent Mormon women about how the town was laid out, and they in turn passed me on to two others in Farmington." He was particularly taken by the words of one of the women, who told him that in earlier days "they had all meals together, 20 or 30 families at one table, and said that until she was fifteen she never saw a coin or a dollar bill in her house; they did everything on barter among themselves." The trouble of the present day, she said was "too much money, . . . we are no longer dependent on each other." Brinck liked these people, finding them "very reminiscent of the best of New England; very idealistic but also very hard-working and shrewd . . . admirable . . . and extremely well-informed about their past and the Church."

Later that day, Jackson went to see a gas compressor. "It was beyond words refreshing and heartening to come in contact with such good people, not only the Mormons but all the men working on the gas and oil wells." It has been suggested by Doug Adams that Jackson's intelligence work in the army taught him to ask questions to elicit information.[9] Perhaps this is so, but here one also sees his curiosity about the world and its peoples that made asking the right questions an important step to understanding. Although there were slight glimpses of this possibility in his 1937 travel journal, fully realized here in 1951 is Jackson's appreciation of others who led different ways of life.

During this period, Jackson was reading a number of books to help fill the magazine with reviews. In early March, he reported to his mother and brother that he was working on a review of *Masked Gods: Navaho and Pueblo Ceremonialism,* by Frank Waters.[10] This book was particularly important to Jackson because it was closely related to his own full-length manuscript, currently awaiting revision. Waters, he wrote, "has been reading Jung and Campbell and Northrup and has made something of a mess as a result; but a very earnest and important book nevertheless, and I enjoy writing on that subject." To Wayne, he observed that Waters "touched on many of the things I had been writing on. . . . I think I did a better job, but seeing his work made me realize the shortcomings of some ideas." Jackson now believed his own revision would have to be "a very drastic job, and take a long time in consequence." His last sentence to Wayne, however, was key: "I am now as you know more interested in the magazine."

Creating *Landscape* allowed play to Jackson's many facets. One was his acute visual awareness, and in early March he began a search for photographs. He wrote to his mother and brother, "I stopped by . . . to see Laura Gilpin the photographer, to buy if possible an aerial photograph for the magazine. She had a very handsome one of the Rio Grande Valley north of Espanola which she will let me have for twenty dollars, though her usual price is 50." He went on to comment that "she considers her pictures works of art, which is perhaps the case, though I wouldn't have thought so myself." Jackson noted Gilpin showed some concern about whether the photograph was to be "cut or altered in any way." He couldn't promise, but she let him have the photograph anyway. "She is a very pleasant and intelligent woman, busy at present on a book of pictures of the Navaho," but he added, "If she would only let me take the pictures for her she would be finished in two weeks or less; as it is she has been working for more than a year."

Later in the month, he found more aerial views, this time from a supplier more to his taste. In Albuquerque, he visited the Soil Conservation Service, where he was able to obtain several photographs for free. "Had I known," he wrote to his mother, "I never would have had to pay 20 for a Laura Gilpin picture." He had also found a commercial photographic outlet where he met "two young men who fly a great deal and got two aerial views for the magazine. I am very enthusiastic about aerial views; they show the pattern better than anything else can, and they are not much used in this sort of writing. If I could I would have nothing but them." He also liked the price, six dollars, rather than Gilpin's larger fee.

In addition, Jackson drew headings for the magazine's articles. On a Saturday in mid-March, as he listened to *La Boheme* on the radio, he designed "lettering for the heads of the article. . . . It is hard to know how they will reproduce, but otherwise

I would not have headings of any style at all." A few days later, he had Miranda Masocco over for supper, and "while she talked I drew some more lettering for the headings."

Jackson was well aware that creating *Landscape* magazine required more than just words and images. Dorothy Stewart, an older, well-established printer in Santa Fe, offered guidance as Jackson faced certain practical issues of publishing. He did not approve of Stewart's printing style, however, writing to his mother that on her pages, "the letters are upside down or badly printed. Great fun, but not what I want."

As he wrote to his mother and brother, sending along a sample of the type, Jackson explained that his options at his Santa Fe printer were limited: "I don't think the type is exciting, and I would have preferred a larger page; but neither can be changed, and it's not too bad." He was, however, pleased when he got the later proofs. Although both the modern sans serif type and the small size of the pages were dictated by the printer, "They were clear and well printed, and though I don't find this type at all exciting it is nevertheless quite professional looking and more and more things seem to use that face."

When the printing process began, Jackson had not finished writing—he clearly worked best under deadlines. Awaiting proofs, he confided to Wayne that he was seeking to fill out the magazine with more material. On Thursday March 15, he wrote that he hoped over the weekend "to complete almost all the text for the first issue. It will be almost entirely of my composition, though signed with other names to give it that much variety at least." As he listed what he had completed, he essentially gave the contents of the first issue: "The Need of Being Versed in Country Things, "Southwestern Colonial Farms" (using a photograph taken by Wayne), "Chihuahua; As We Might Have Been," and the rewritten "Desert Harvest," by Feather. Jackson planned to include book reviews and short notices of articles dealing with the Southwest. He likely included a draft of a critique of maps of the Southwest in his letter to Wayne, for a carbon copy of "Maps" rests in this saved batch of papers.

As late as March 20, however, Jackson was still writing for the first issue. Meanwhile, his book project remained on his mind. On March 21, he went to Albuquerque to have lunch with a person identified only as Alice (likely Alice Lee Marriott), hoping for her reactions regarding his manuscript. Perhaps influenced by his piece on Chihuahua and the American Southwest, Jackson wrote to his mother in anticipation of the meeting, "it happens that my ideas on it are totally changed; it is not enough to deal only with [the] Indian, but I would also like to include our

Figure 19. Cover of first issue of *Landscape*, 1951

LANDSCAPE

Human Geography of the Southwest

VOLUME 1
NUMBER 1

SPRING 1951
Fifty Cents a Copy

own agricultural landscape and architecture as a basis of comparison, and perhaps classical Europe of two or three hundred years ago, say Tuscany. So it is more than a job of rewriting; it is one of entirely new writing. But we'll see how the magazine works out."

Jackson anticipated *Landscape* would come out "in the first week or so of April," with a print run of a thousand copies. He would "circulate some of them by hand from book store to bookstore, and give some to a regional periodical distributor." In the final letter in this set, Jackson reported to his mother, "I wrote the last items for the magazine, but the printer can only promise it for the fifteenth or so of April." Always the writer, he ended, "So I shall start on something else for a while."

So much for the process of bringing forth the first issue of *Landscape.* What of J. B. Jackson the visionary? In this saved correspondence, Jackson's larger aims took a backseat to production, but at one moment they broke through. In the March 15 letter to his mother and brother, Jackson set out what he desired for the inaugural issue of *Landscape.* "I hope that this first issue will at least show what I want for future editions. . . . I don't want any articles on other parts of the world, or on geographical problems in particular if I can help it; there is a great deal of world literature on that, and it serves rather to inform people about parts of the world they know nothing about; my idea is to tell them about the world they DO know."

Here I'm struck by a certain continuity. Forty-four years later, in what was probably his last public utterance—his acceptance of the 1995 PEN award for the Art of the Essay—Jackson spoke movingly about the meaning of landscape. In the classroom, he said, he told his students that he wanted "to remind them that each of them had his or her own landscape which was part of the way they related to the wider world." Landscape, he continued, was a felt experience, "a place with which we have daily contact," and forms one of "the oldest and most universal of our collective memories. It is where we live and work and celebrate together. . . . Where we evolve as social, territorial beings."[11] At that moment in 1995, Jackson reaffirmed the purpose that had been driving him since he composed the first issue of *Landscape* in 1951: to open people's eyes to the everyday landscape; to probe its meanings—to tell his audience "about the world they DO know."

The First Issue of *Landscape*

Holding in my hand the first issue of *Landscape* magazine—which Jackson kept alongside the journal entries and letters chronicling its creation—I feel its physical slightness. It is thin and almost pamphlet size. But I remember, in 1973, what it felt like to encounter it for the first time. It packed a powerful punch. As I read its pages, I was filled with a growing sense of excitement: in my mind's eye, I see my then-self with my jaw open in amazement. Intrigued since my freshman year in college by the physical world around me, I had as a graduate student begun a serious study of places and spaces and their broader cultural and historical meanings. *Landscape* offered me language and insights to see more clearly and inquire more deeply.

Writing in 1997 about the contents of this inaugural issue in *Landscape in Sight,* I focused on two of Jackson's major essays: "The Need of Being Versed in Country Things" and "Chihuahua; As We Might Have Been." Here, I have a different purpose, to convey what I learned from rereading the entire first issue after having absorbed what these Jackson letters told regarding what was on his mind in early 1951 as he launched *Landscape.* I now see more fully how the magazine revealed his interests and his special gifts.

I can't ignore those primary two essays, for they remain important in revealing Jackson's particular understanding of landscape and offering a vivid example of the approach he would take in future issues. "The Need of Being Versed in Country Things" celebrates the view from an airplane window that enabled travelers to discover "the beauty and excitement of the rural landscape." Jackson wrote: "It is from the air that the true relationship between the natural and the human landscape is first clearly revealed. The peaks and canyons lose much of their impressiveness when seen from above. . . . What catches our eye and arouses our interest is not the sandy washes and the naked rocks, but the evidences of man." When he turned to inquire into the meaning of the view, Jackson paid tribute to the human geographer who observed as did a naturalist: "the whole world of beasts and plants is worth studying. The common and familiar specimens are no less instructive than the rare." With that, Jackson exclaimed, "How much more rewarding is the world which we ourselves have helped to make!" Although the city was part of the design, "beyond the last street light, out where the familiar asphalt ends, a whole country waits to be discovered: villages, farmsteads and highways, half-hidden valleys of irrigated gardens, and wide landscapes reaching to the horizon. A rich and beautiful book is always open before us. We have but to learn to read it."[12]

"Chihuahua; As We Might Have Been" offers a vivid example of this reading. In this illustrated piece, Jackson focused on the border in the southwestern desert between Mexico and the United States that revealed the force not of nature but of human history. In a land unified by climate, topography, and vegetation, he wrote, "an abstraction, a Euclidean line drawn across the desert, has created two distinct human landscapes where there was only on[e] before." As he described the Mexican side of the border, Jackson explained that while the poor in cities build adobe houses in the manner of farmers, those who can afford it discard these rural ways. Houses of the wealthy tend "to repudiate every local tradition of plan and material and ornamentation." In an earlier time, the ideal was a house that was "ornate, formal, and reminiscent of a European social order—Paris or Madrid at two removes." After this gentle opening, Jackson abruptly switched into a verbal explosion that remains, for me, unforgettable: "What is the ideal now? Something not easy to define, but easy enough to recognize: a blend of Hollywood and Tel-Aviv and Frank Lloyd Wright; wrought iron and plate glass and tapestry brick and bougainvillea and Kubla Khan's pleasure dome, conspicuously, not to say defiantly located in the midst of an English lawn. If as someone once incautiously remarked, architecture is frozen music, this is Spike Jones straight from the deep freeze."[13]

Exploring an unassuming piece beyond these two dazzling ones gives early evidence of the approach that would later become important in Jackson's work: the firsthand exploration of building types and settlement patterns set within an understanding of their cultural context, practical origins, and continuing uses.[14] Writing "Southwestern Colonial Farms," under the pseudonym A. W. Conway, Jackson described "the so-called 'casa-corral' unit," lauding it as "one of the last and most picturesque reminders of the old Spanish Mexican rural economy in this region" (see color plate 3). What was the purpose of this single-story adobe house with adjoining adobe-walled corral for livestock? Jackson offered two quite practical answers: first, the unit's walls protected isolated ranches from Apache raids; second, combining house and corral kept the animals close by and extended to them the warmth of the house. Wayne's photograph and a map locating casa-corral units in the Southwest accompanied the article.[15]

Since these three essays were not enough to fill a full issue, Jackson went in search of more material in the library. He found "something on . . . producing artificial rain sixty years ago."[16] This developed into "Warning to Rainmakers," a short acerbic tale of the failure of an Australian rainmaker working in Colorado in 1892. "Before enough rain fell to quench the thirst of a grasshopper," it was reported at the time, "the rain ceased." The fellow was found two years later in a hotel room—"His death was attributed to suicide." With this squib, Jackson gave a signal that readers of the new journal should anticipate playfulness, one occasionally expressing Jackson's mordant sense of humor.

By contrast, Jackson's piece on the origin of place-names in New Mexico, eruditely titled "Toponymics," referenced scholarly publications, demonstrating Jackson's serious side, and "Maps" compared roadmaps produced by the state of New Mexico with the better ones made available by service stations. Here, Jackson vented his frustration with the state's map: "At last report Abiquiu was still on the west bank of the Chama, and not on the east." In asking the question, "Why is it that distances between two points cannot be established once and for all?" Jackson suggested he was an experienced traveler by car.[17]

The issue was rounded out by several book reviews, accounting for nearly a quarter of the magazine's pages. They point to many of the most significant and lasting concerns of Jackson's subsequent career. In their language, subjects, and awareness of the needs of ordinary people, these reviews also measure the personal as well as the intellectual distance Jackson had traveled since the 1930s.

Jackson headed the "Books" section with a long review of *Masked Gods* by Frank Waters, published in 1950. Writing under the initials "P.G.A.," representing the pseudonym of P. G. Anson, one of the voices Jackson was later to use to criticize modern architecture, Jackson began his erudite three-and-a-half-page review of the book with an implied question: why another book, especially one with no new material that also failed to synthesize all that was available? The answer he offered was the importance of changing perspectives on religious ceremonies. In an earlier period, the anthropological one ruled "that religious forms . . . were related to social or cultural forms." But more recently the work of Freud and Jung had led to reinterpretation, and in the case of *Masked Gods,* Jung had provided Waters with the notion of the "collective unconscious."[18]

Intended for the general reader, the book evoked effectively the "Indian Southwest" but failed to make "more use of the material accumulated by several generations of ethnologists," whose work would have allowed Waters to portray "a past far more complex" and more ancient than the one presented. Within a long and complicated critique, what stands out is Jackson's opposition to Waters's dependence on Jung and the "collective unconscious." This was a deep objection, revealing the importance religion was now playing in Jackson's consciousness. In a March 15 letter to the anthropologist Vera Laski, Jackson discussed Jung's approach: "I found Jung's ideas in quantities of books in France, but I must say I prefer when possible a more frankly religious point of view; too much is ascribed to the collective unconscious without anyone bothering or daring to define it. Nevertheless anthropology is much benefitted by a few of his theories."[19]

In the review, Jackson specifically argued against Walters's saddling of Jung's collective unconscious with all of evolution, thereby making it "a biological as well as a spiritual development." Jackson offered his own perspective: "Intuitive religion, one may almost say any religion, explains Man's development in a far different manner. It does not hold that he evolved from a lower form of life and that he will in time evolve into something higher; it holds that he was created a perfect and Godlike being. . . . That he fell from his divine estate, and that the world of matter is an illusion which will vanish when he is restored to his true identity."[20]

Under his own initials and in a different tone, Jackson reviewed a book of sketches of Santa Fe life, *No High Adobe* by a reporter for the *Christian Science Monitor,* Dorothy L. Pillsbury. He first displayed the velvet glove, praising her for offering the perspective of "the sensitive newcomer to these parts, enchanted with the uneven lines of adobe, the lard-cans of geraniums in the windows, the smell of pinon smoke on a winter's evening." Quickly, however, came the iron fist. Pillsbury displayed no awareness of "pot-holed streets, droughts, slums, and Los Alamos." Moreover, although once a social worker, she failed to treat the deeper side of her Spanish American neighbors: "what we have to learn to understand and love are a class of uprooted country people and a generation made restless by the war. . . . The efforts . . . of a large group attempting to maintain its dignity in a bewildering world." In this context, Jackson criticized Pillsbury for failing to mention "the church and the role it continues to play" in the lives of Spanish American women. With that, Jackson turned to irony, putting on the glove again to recommend the book to "anyone wishing to relive the first weeks of discovery in Santa Fe."[21]

In the next review, written under the initials of A.W.C.—corresponding to A. W. Conway, one of his pseudonymous *Landscape* voices—Jackson took on *The Architecture of the Southwest* by Trent E. Sanford. Jackson had found Stanford's earlier book on the architecture of Mexico "very readable and informative."[22] It displayed his "Beaux Arts training or its American equivalent," as he considered the important monuments of Mexico, a nation whose unified traditions allowed this approach. It was not, however, useful in a book on the Southwest, a vast region made of diverse groups with their own building traditions. Moreover, "the history of the Southwest was chiefly made by anonymous men—by settlers, explorers, pioneers, farmers and ranchers," and their "indigenous" dwellings express "the true architecture of the region."[23] Suggesting his own fascination with what he would later call the "vernacular," Jackson then cited the "modest and prosaic" dog-run house, the one-story adobe dwelling, and the bungalow. Jackson asserted that architectural study should broaden its scope by turning analysis away from formal aesthetics to look "sociologically" at these "indigenous . . . forms," thereby serving as inspiration to contemporary southwestern architects.[24]

Jackson should have read the book more carefully, for although it offered much attention to missions, it treated many of these very subjects. Sanford's work was also attentive to class, including the pretensions that came with the growth of wealth. Some of the book's photographs, although perhaps too few, departed from monuments to give variant house types and even motor courts. My own guess is Jackson was using the book as a whipping boy to buttress themes he hoped to develop further in *Landscape*.

Worrying he didn't have enough material for the inaugural issue of *Landscape*, Jackson wrote as late as March 20 that he had bought another book to review. What emerged was an interesting double review revealing Jackson's political convictions. Discussing Albert N. Williams's *The Water and the Power*, Jackson opposed the book's advocacy of vast irrigation and hydroelectric projects on five western rivers to be controlled by the federal government along the lines of the Tennessee Valley Authority. Jackson bristled at the author's language, believing it showed a disregard for the human beings living on the land. If such an authority came to the Rio Grande, it would allow efficient governance by Washington and might "create a rich and industrialized valley"; but at what cost? Such a project would "destroy most of the living remains of Pueblo Indian culture, force whole populations to move, and force many others, notably the Spanish American, to adopt a social and economic program for which they have no liking." The result would be destructive both nationally and morally. "Mercy killing has not yet been sanctioned in the law courts, but as a social philosophy, as a way of liquidating inconvenient cultures, it enjoys enormous prestige."[25] Jackson reviewed the human costs of the TVA—the seventy thousand forced to move, the loss of twenty thousand acres of land cultivated by as many as twelve generations of the same family. Although Williams imagined opposition to his proposals to come from reactionary big business and utilities protecting vested interests, he ignored those "more numerous and far more respectable . . . those who have a personal attachment to the land."[26] This is where Jackson took his stand.

With this stated, Jackson introduced a second book, *Water, Land, and People* by Bernard Frank and Anthony Netboy, offering softer solutions to the problems of soil depletion and water waste. Jackson found practical their proposals to zone agricultural areas in ways supporting conservation, with leases for tenant farmers requiring standards for land maintenance and credit expansion to enable tenants to own the land they worked. Jackson ended the review of both books with a question neither raised: "What is the trouble with us Americans that we treat the land so badly?"[27]

Jackson claimed the utility of these reviews in filling out the first issue of his magazine, but looking at them as a whole, I see something else at work. In them he expressed themes that mattered to him deeply and form much of the spine of his work until the end of his life. A learned man who read widely in many fields, including anthropological studies, Jackson wrestled with contemporary thought coming from abroad and held religious beliefs in line with basic Christian tenets. He had little respect for gilded writing aimed at tourists, believing deeply in seeing and reporting the potholes in the streets. Even more important to him was respect for the traditions, practices, and experiences of the varied peoples and cultures around him, especially those struggling to make ends meet. He disapproved of mainstream architectural history and criticism for its exclusive emphasis on monuments and architects and its failure to treat the "indigenous" structures of regions in their varied traditions. He conveyed his opposition to federal power, typically a conservative position, but, in his case, linked to sensitivity to the lives and desires of vulnerable people. In 1951, Jackson is difficult to place on a typical political spectrum; this problem only increases in the years that followed.

Fittingly, Jackson chose to close *Landscape*'s first issue by giving a look to the future, a nod to education, and a statement of respect for his neighbors. He offered a high school student's pride of place in this first issue with the boy's appreciation, in Spanish, to the town he loved: Truchas, New Mexico, located on the High Road to Taos.

From "Human Geography of the Southwest" to "Magazine of Human Geography"

Jackson's claim on our attention originates with *Landscape* magazine—how it shaped his work after 1951 and how it inspired the work of others. It was a bold venture to bring *Landscape* singlehandedly into being, and an even bolder one to continue it. Jackson's bet paid off. Within three years *Landscape* had begun to emerge as a periodical commanding the attention of readers and writers. It developed steadily during Jackson's seventeen years as its editor and publisher and led to his productive life beyond as a sought-after essayist, teacher, and lecturer.

Knowing *Landscape* started as a solo effort, reading its early issues is a little like watching a high wire act. One admires the moves, all the time aware of the audacity of the performer. I have sought to learn from the magazine's initial volumes how a novelist then working on a book on Native Americans of the Southwest became the creator of landscape as a field of study. How did *Landscape* attract readers and contributors in its early years? To what degree were Jackson's abiding concerns apparent in his early expressions, approaches, and ideas?

I remain fascinated by the essays that Jackson wrote in these early issues. He offered close observation wedded to vivid description and deep erudition. With an outsider's eye and a unique vision, he looked carefully to see, think, and write on places and spaces. As a writer of fiction, he had the power to dramatize what he saw in a range of voices. As a reader with penetrating intelligence, he drew from a deep well of learning. And finally, as a man with a sense of humor and a mischievous side, he was capable of writings that sparkled with clever wit.

"Ghosts at the Door," appearing in the second issue of *Landscape,* conveys many of Jackson's special gifts. In this essay Jackson developed what became one of his best-known themes, the American vernacular with its origins in the remote past of Europe. His opening evocation allows us to see the importance of his work as a novelist in his landscape writing. He began, "THE HOUSE STANDS BY ITSELF, lost somewhere in the enormous plain. Next to it is a windmill, to the rear a scattering of barns and shelters and sheds. In every direction range and empty fields reach to a horizon unbroken by a hill or the roof of another dwelling or even a tree. The wind blows incessantly; it raises a spiral of dust in the corral. The sun beats down on the house day after day." At this point readers might anticipate that the author is about to introduce his main character, and he does—only his protagonist is the American front yard.[28]

Jackson argued that although lawns require much care, those in the West are not useful in any usual sense. On ranches, they are normally out-of-bounds, something like the unused front parlor of an earlier time. Lawns exist as testimony to an earlier, distant landscape's beauty. "In essence the front yard is a landscape in miniature. . . . a much reduced version, as if seen through the wrong end of a pair of field glasses, of a spacious countryside of woods and hedgerows and meadow."[29]

He then reviewed the long history of the European landscape, revealing his bent of mind. In one of our taped conversations, Brinck acknowledged his fondness for looking at things "in terms of dichotomies." He said it is "the way I think—the rich versus the poor, the field versus the forest, the city versus the country." At that point

I mentioned the vernacular, and he immediately supplied "the establishment," adding it was the way his "nineteenth-century mind" worked.[30] The creative tensions produced by such dichotomies give drama to his writing and offer polarities easy to grasp.

For Jackson, American lawns—his "ghosts at the door"—were the descendants of the European meadow, standing in opposition to the forest. Meadows were safe pastures for cattle and sheep, a contrast to forest danger. Transferred to North America, grazing lands became the commons of the New England village and, in time, emerged as places of leisure and play, devoted to baseball and other sports. When "the private dwelling took over the lawn," it inherited aspects of the commons and became the location of new games, parties, and rituals such as weddings. This made the lawn part of the civilizing process—as Jackson put it, "schools where certain standards of conduct and even certain standards of dress were formed." Through this succession, Jackson transformed a patch of grass into an emblem of civilization.[31]

In writing on places and spaces, Jackson looked for common elements. Whereas his training in architectural history focused on the unique creative masterpiece, Jackson normally took as his subject the fundamental type. The "ghost" is not a specific example of landscape architecture, it is *any* front lawn. In addition, Jackson imbued the type with meaning. He linked it to a history of its origins and development in ways that carried important values into the present.

In "The Almost Perfect Town," the lead essay in the first issue of *Landscape*'s second year, Jackson offered as an object lesson the fictional "Optimo," a small western city with certain salient characteristics.[32] Defying topography, Optimo was laid out in a grid of streets running north to south, east to west. At its center was the grid-breaking square, taking up two blocks in both directions and housing the courthouse, a large and ugly edifice. South Main Street plunged down to the river, where in early days warehouses and stores were located near riverboat transportation. These were eventually supplanted by a railroad depot, grain elevators, and stockyards. What little manufacturing Optimo attracted was situated there as well, along with the flimsy houses of Latino wage earners. Unsurprisingly, South Main was also the locus for the town's unrespectable amusements.

By contrast, as Main Street climbed the hill north of the courthouse, it offered sites for the large, handsome houses of the wealthy. In the present day, most of these once-dignified homes serve as funeral parlors or offices for Optimo's physicians, dentists, and lawyers. On both sides of the courthouse, east and west, lay the town's

Figure 20. J. B.
Jackson sketch,
"The Almost Perfect
Town," 1952

commercial district, and beyond that, the modest homes of Optimo. If one looked
at the edges of this residential area, one could see tractors on properties, a positive
sign of the easy transition in this place from urban to rural and the likely harmony
of town and farm.

Jackson loved towns such as this. He also saw them as threatened by contemporary planners, urging—in the case of fictional Optimo—that the courthouse
be torn down to facilitate travel and provide parking. The Chamber of Commerce
sided with the planners, insisting that Optimo could only grow if it modernized in
ways that attracted industry and tourism. Jackson refuted this contention with a
concise history of the courthouse that underscored its importance. When the open
place at the town center became the site of the courthouse, its construction offered

a "frame . . . for all activity of a communal sort." The courthouse building therefore served as the symbol of local representative government.[33] As had the front lawn, the courthouse square emerged in Jackson's telling as the emblem of higher values. In this case, the square with its courthouse epitomized American civic life.

From its outset, *Landscape* opened up a varied world that included playful moments in the midst of serious discourse. The second issue of its inaugural volume marked the debut of a new author, "Ajax," the pseudonym Jackson chose for his comic pieces. "Storm Brewing," Ajax's initial contribution, consisted of a blizzard of short news articles set in the future, running chronologically from the near-present (1953) to the distant reaches of 1975. These imagined the many impacts of rain making and climate control. Jackson's humor in this case also had a serious side, showing his distrust of corporations, the tourist industry, and the federal government.[34]

Jackson frequently placed serious translated articles and essays from abroad in *Landscape* but could, as with "A Black Guide to Sinistria," offer one in fun. This takeoff on France's *Blue Guide,* written by Michel Perrin and translated by Jackson's friend Marie Armengaud, presented the itinerary of a group trip to an imagined land bordered by the Lugubrioso Range, the Plain of Gloom, and the Triste River. For example, on Tuesday, "At approximately 2 o'clock, accident at Hairpin Curve. The dead will be buried on the spot (or deposited at the Triste river): survivors will await the arrival of an emergency car."[35]

On occasion, as Jackson added light touches, he blurred the line between reporting and comedy. On the page immediately following the harrowing Sinistra journey appeared "A Brief Lexicon of Road Words" by S. C. Babb (probably Jackson himself). The lexicon delivered legitimate information, but in ways intended to amuse. The entry for "Advertising, Road-side," offers a good example: "Let's be reasonable, out-door advertising is merely one way by which people take advantage of the existence of a highway to make money. (see ACCESS, RIBBON DEVELOPMENT, PARKING). Do you want to outlaw ALL roadside advertising, or do you distinguish between national advertising serving no local interest, and local advertising including signs indicating off-the-road hotels etc? . . . (See MAINTENANCE, SIGHT, ACCESS, RIBBON DEVELOPMENT). Or do you consider it primarily an aesthetic offence? (see ROADSIDE IMPROVEMENT)."[36]

As I reread early issues of *Landscape* through the lens of time and with knowledge of Jackson's full career, what I have found particularly interesting are hints of key themes Jackson developed over the next decades. Jackson grew with his magazine in many ways. It connected him with a world of contemporary thinkers and writers who shared his interests and opened him up to many ideas and approaches. It brought him into the creative orbit of Berkeley and led him into teaching. Yet certain deeply rooted judgments, beliefs, and attitudes remained constant.

One can see early statements of important positions best in his early book reviews, where Jackson the intellectual came to the fore. Knowledge that he wrote almost everything in *Landscape*'s first three issues allows his authorship of reviews to extend beyond his own initials and include the pseudonyms (and their initials) he employed. For example, writing as P.K. in a long review of Kenneth Clark's *Landscape Painting,* Jackson offered an extended précis of the book, filled with praise. Yet at its close, he took issue with Clark's single explanation that technology and scientific understandings of nature led to the decline of the landscape genre. Giving voice to his deep opposition to Romanticism, Jackson wrote, "The death sentence of the landscape as an art form was therefore not pronounced by modern science alone. The rise in the importance of the artist's personality is also responsible."[37]

It was in book reviews, too, that Jackson articulated his growing understanding of the study of landscape. In his Autumn 1951 review of Laura Thompson's *Culture in Crisis: A Study of the Hopi Indians,* Jackson took issue with the author's approach, which imagined human societies as part of ecological systems. While plants adapt to conditions of soil and climate, he commented, persons are actors. They encourage the growth of some plants and discourage that of others, kill animals, enrich or harm the soil, and cut trees. In contrast to Thompson's ecological approach, Jackson supported a human geography that was "sceptical of 'scientific' laws, aware of the enormous diversity among human groups, and disdained no discipline in its effort to understand the man-made environment."[38] Over time, as the environmental movement grew in strength, Jackson's expression of opposition to ecological approaches—what he often called "environmentalism"—was to become stronger and more controversial.

Had Jackson continued *Landscape* as he began it, with himself as essentially its sole author, it would have remained an interesting but idiosyncratic magazine. Instead, by volume 2, important authors began to place their articles there. I've now identified three contributors to volume 1: Wayne G. Jackson and Adlai Feather wrote essays; Alice Marriott, a book review—one family member and two friends. By contrast, the first issue of volume 2 contained a piece by the British landscape architect Christopher Tunnard, who was then an associate professor of city planning at Yale. Jackson had reviewed his *Gardens in the Modern Landscape* in the Autumn 1951 issue. Perhaps that brought *Landscape* to Tunnard's attention, for in Spring 1952, he contributed a substantive piece, "Fire on the Prairie," excerpted from his forthcoming book, *City of Man.* In the same issue, Geoffrey Baker and Bruno Funaro, future writers of the book *Shopping Centers,* discussed this topic in "New Towns, New Centers." These two articles signaled an important moment—*Landscape*'s move out from its regional world and beyond Jackson's personal contacts.[39]

Jackson's own contributions, under his own name or pseudonyms, nonetheless remained plentiful, as they would throughout most of the years of his editorship. After "The Almost Perfect Town," Jackson wrote (as "A. W. C."), "Village Types in the Southwest," illustrated with photos, aerial views, and maps. As Ajax, he offered "A Golden Treasury of Western Prose and Song." This piece played comically with the varied voices of a western writer, Hank Strong (born Fauntleroy Riemenschneider); an academic, Melissa Popkin, Ph.D., professor of humanics; a writer on Latin ways famous for her recipe for sopa de chili, Lois Lurge (the pseudonym of Mrs. Wesley Snodgrass); and a poet of the Voiceless Generation, Peter Goldfish. This was J. B. Jackson at his zaniest.[40]

Jackson's "Notes and Comments" section, on the other hand, was serious and became increasingly bold. It first appeared in the second number as a modest feature, a roundup of what Jackson considered worthy articles from other publications. With the first issue of volume 2, Jackson started using "Notes and Comments" to address topics that concerned him. Here, along with information about a new magazine and praise for a town giving up its parking meters, he discussed the serious threat posed by pumice mining. At the end of this section, however, his mischievousness could not be contained, and he wrote, "LANDSCAPE has long pondered the wisdom of offering a prize to the juvenile delinquent who would discover a method of knocking parking meters permanently out of commission."[41] In the next issue, Jackson moved "Notes and Comments" to the very front of the magazine and over time developed it into his editorial page and the place of some of his most memorable writing.

Jackson continued to use book reviews to set down his strongly held convictions about architecture. In a Spring 1952 review of *Baroque and Rococo in Latin America* by Pal Kelemen, Jackson (writing as H. G. W., the initials of his pseudonym H. G. West), Jackson argued that illustrations ought to show more than the faces of buildings. Architecture, he proclaimed, exists "not merely in terms of façade treatment: but in terms of plan and location, of the organization of space, of perspective and drama. . . . [It is] a three dimensional art, and no collection of photographs of façades can replace the plan, or in the case of a whole city, the map."[42]

In Jackson's third issue, Winter 1952, he reaffirmed his understanding of what it meant to read the landscape. In "What We Want," he wrote: "The cultural history of America is just as legible in the appearance of our landscape (for those who know how to read it) as it is in the monuments and institutions of our cities. The layout of fields and houses and towns, the variety in the types of rural dwellings, the countrysides produced by different economies, different ethnic groups, different topographies—these are some of the things which we must learn to see even before we can understand them."[43]

The Autumn issue of 1952 marked a shift in *Landscape*'s focus from the American Southwest to the wider world. It was now, as its contents page announced, a "Magazine of Human Geography." In Jackson's lead essay, "Human All Too Human Geography," he declared he intended to widen the scope of *Landscape*: its "only editorial policy . . . [would be] the welcoming of any idea which can enlighten us as to the true nature of Man's place in the world."[44] Implicitly, he now aspired to cover the international scene, as illustrated by the piece "State versus Nature in Soviet Russia."[45]

"Human, All Too Human, Geography" offered its author's version of the history of geography in the past century. It had, Jackson argued, taken two successive wrong turns. First, out of Darwinism came environmental determinism, essentially the ecological approach his previously published book review faulted. The second deviation was economic determinism, connected in his mind with Marxism—given his politics, a bête noire. Jackson and *Landscape* stood for a third approach, a geography based on an understanding of "Man the creator of dwellings and landscapes; the creator of his own habitat, his microcosm." At its center Jackson placed the house and declared it to be the primary "object of the human geographer's study." "Is there not a deep connection between our attitude toward our dwelling and our attitude toward the man-made environment?" he asked rhetorically. "Is not one microcosm the prototype of the other? Does not the ordering of Man's most intimate world, the domestic scene, suggest to him how to order the larger landscape?"[46]

To these questions, Jackson had provided the answer in an earlier paragraph: "The dwelling is to be regarded as the microcosm, as the prime example of Man the Inhabitant's effort to re-create Heaven on earth." When I first read these words, I imagined them metaphorically. To Jackson, however, they were no metaphor—they were expressions of his life-long, deeply rooted religious belief, perhaps the clearest statement of his faith in print. He wrote, "We must not be afraid to rediscover and reassert a neglected truth: that Man is the Product, the Child of God and that his works must therefore always betray, even in a distorted form, that identity." Further

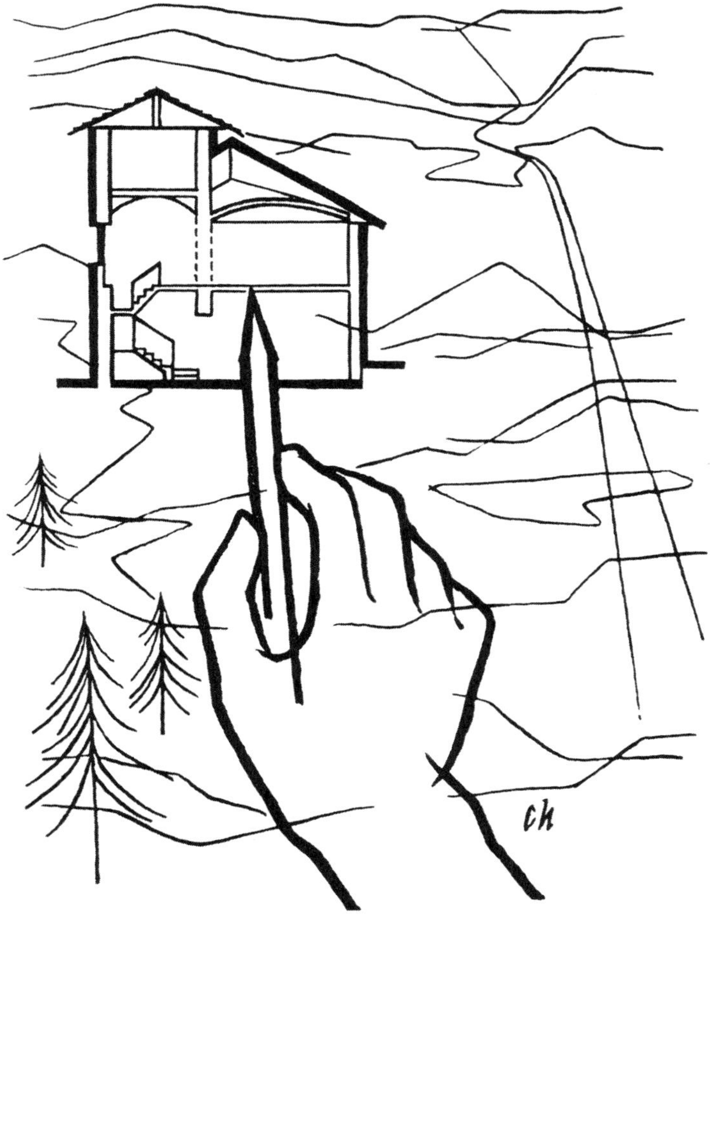

Figure 21. J. B.
Jackson illustration,
"Hand Drawing
House," 1957–58

along in the essay, he added, "To reaffirm the unity of Man and of his world, his Divine origin and his ceaseless efforts to re-create here on earth a dimly perceived Divine order, is the only way to establish on a firm footing the study of Man's modification of his environment."[47]

Jackson's religious conviction, generally hidden in his writing, was not expressed in any known formal practice until late in his life. In his conversations with me in 1994, he made it clear that as a youth he had disdained the chapels he was forced to attend in prep school and did not attend in college, remarking of his time at Harvard, "But then I didn't have any religious experience."[48] His travel journals of the 1950s establish that he went to Baroque churches not to partake in worship but to sketch. In the United States and abroad at midcentury, recountings of his Sundays suggest they were no different from any other days of the week. Jackson operated in a secular world and in most of his essays spoke its language. But it would be a mistake to ignore this testament of his underlying faith.

Jackson included in this Autumn 1952 issue a long translated excerpt from *Géographie et Religions* (1948) by Pierre Deffontaines that proclaimed, "The primordial imprint made by Man on the earth's surface is the dwelling." Its purpose was not only shelter from the elements, a place for storage, and areas for work: "it also accommodates a peculiar spiritual ingredient . . . notably the religious myth. It serves as a background for religious activities and in so doing takes on a character which sets it entirely apart from the lair or nest of an animal."[49]

One of Jackson's best-known early pieces, "The Westward-Moving House," appeared in the same issue of *Landscape* as this extract.[50] Possibly the words and ideas of Deffontaines were percolating in Jackson's mind as he imagined the different generations of Tinkhams who moved from east to west and built three successive houses over the course of three eras. Each expressed a world view, two confirming a religious orientation. The Tinkhams of the late seventeenth century lived in an ordered village in rural New England with lives centered around the meetinghouse, the focus for worship and community. The meetinghouse was their super-parlor, where the super-family of the village met to pray. It was also their forum, barracks, and place for celebration. For these Tinkhams, nature constituted danger: Nehemiah's well-made, unadorned house—built the traditional way—turned its back on the woods.

By contrast, his mid-nineteenth-century descendant, Pliny Tinkham, chose land isolated from other settlers when he moved his family to Illinois. He wanted not only fertile land but also freedom from the constraining presence of parents and village. Placing his house in the center of his land, he used the new technique of his day, balloon-frame construction. Such a house was both quickly built and flexible, allowing for additions that responded to change. Light-filled, spacious, and practical, the house was not for show but designed to meet the needs of the family. Pliny was a commercial farmer, and his farm was a place of work, but he and his family had a love of Nature, and his wife embellished the land around the house with trees and an ornamental garden. Religious but not church-going, Pliny saw the outdoors as his place of worship and his homestead as "the source of every virtue." Ultimately he chose to be buried on his own land, "a final planting."[51]

Nothing lasts forever, not even the often-celebrated family farm in the Midwest. Later generations of Tinkhams in the twentieth century took to the range in Texas. Jackson turned to the present tense to explore the world of Ray, Pliny's current descendant. Ray is building a house in town, close to his children's school and to the shops that Shirley, his wife, will frequent to supply the family with food for the table. Educated at the agricultural college, Ray applies all the latest methods to his farm twelve miles away. It operates factory style, using the labor of a paid workforce, as well as irrigation and chemicals, to achieve the highest yield. Ray transforms the land, and Jackson labels his house a "transformer," for it is designed to catch the forces of nature—sun, air, light, distance—and transform them for the family's use. The kitchen will turn raw materials into food; the living room will convert "electronic impulses into entertainment"; and Ray's separate dressing room off the garage, where he will clean up before entering the back door, will allow him to shed his work life and become "a different person."

The family life of Ray's ancestor Pliny on his midwestern farm, filled with "reading out loud together, Bible instruction, games, large holiday dinners, winter evenings in the sitting room" is gone. Ray's wife Shirley understands that "the only time her family spends its leisure together—except for rapid meals—is when they are out in the car." Labeling Ray's house "a transformer," Jackson explains, is meant to signify that "it imposes no distinct code of behavior or set of standards; it demands no loyalty which might be in conflict with loyalty to the outside world. . . . It filters the crudities of nature, the lawlessness of society and produces an atmosphere of temporary well-being where vigor can be renewed for contact with the outside." Not a lofty goal, to be sure, but one Jackson saw as fitting U.S. households in the early 1950s.[52]

Connected to the depiction of Ray's house in Texas is a key issue—Jackson's long-held hostility to architectural modernism. In an earlier H. G. West piece in the Winter 1952 issue, "A Change in Plans: Is the Modern House a Victorian Invention?" Jackson had complained that the postwar American house "has broken with every tradition, social and esthetic; it recognizes the authority of no other period or class or place. More than any other specimen of the Modern style it has repudiated ancient conventions and comes close to being what its designers wanted it to be: a shelter, informal and free and hospitable; youthful and capable of taking on any character given it." By the time "The Westward-Moving House" appeared, however, it was clear to Jackson that the typical dwelling being built in his day did not really belong in the Modernist movement.[53]

Writing again as H. G. West, Jackson reviewed two books: *A Decade of New Architecture,* a collection edited by Siegfried Giedion, the important Zurich writer on modern architecture; and *Early American Architecture* by Hugh Morrison. Jackson/West lambasted modernism for its emphasis on houses of the rich and overly intellectualized and antiseptic public buildings. Structures designed in the International Style were beautiful, but that was their problem. Rather than aiming "to improve the lot of Man," their goal was "to create pure geometrical forms, an autonomous art of cubes and cylinders and two dimensional planes; independent of the past, independent of the earth and of life."[54]

Jackson reflected that those within an architectural movement were unable to perceive their enemies. He used Morrison's book to relate the history of the rapid fall of eighteenth-century classicism, with its established and clear standards, to the "eclecticism and functionalism" of the early nineteenth century. This trajectory offered the possibility that advocates of the International Style, currently at work on restating their principles and simplifying house design, will find that "all the while there enters through the back door of the modern dwelling a troop of interior decorators, landscape architects, home consultants, psychologists, appliance and television salesmen, each of them bent on making the modern home as complex and irrational and individual as possible." While European architects could look to the state as builder, in the United States business holds the reins. "One need not admire flimsy construction, the short-sighted planning, the over-dramatized, over-colored, pseudo-modern ranch houses which are rising all over the country; but one ought to be able to recognize them for what they are: the first grass-roots indication of the dwelling of the future."[55]

What this early statement makes clear is that Jackson did not celebrate trends he saw in the present; he simply recognized them and attempted to understand the forces creating them. Rather than decrying the ugliness of houses being built in countless subdivisions in the 1950s, he focused on their social and cultural functions. They served the needs of families as places of renewal. They, too, were "transformers."

By the first issue of volume 3, Summer 1953, there are indications that *Landscape* was a success. Along with "Notes and Comments," a serious essay, reviews, and perhaps a comic piece—all under Jackson's name or pseudonyms—now came regular contributions of botanist Edgar Anderson, along with offerings, gradually growing, of new work by other writers. *Landscape* was off and running.

In volume 6 (Autumn 1956), Jackson took the measure of how far *Landscape* had come in its initial five years. After revisiting the decision to move its subject matter beyond the Southwest to the broader field of human geography, he wrote, "If we are really to understand a landscape, we must look upon it in wider human terms: as the expression of a culture, of a way of life." He suggested seeing landscape as "we have learned to see certain cities: as a complex and moving work of art, the transcript of a significant collective experience." This statement opened the door to the new work on urbanism as a key domain of *Landscape*.[56]

Jackson now made it clear that landscape understanding could be laden with judgments. While agreeing with professional geographers that all landscapes were interesting, he declared his belief that some offered more to their inhabitants, or as he put it, "the more functions a landscape serves the more productive it is in terms of human values." A one-function town, such as a coal-mining village, gave less to its residents than did the poorest of Hopi villages. Here he called on planners to help develop or restore additional functions to towns and cities, such as places for leisure, recreation, sport, and appreciation of nature. It was important to place new government offices and institutions, colleges, and museums in locations where they added new life to a town. Planners "versed in architecture and urbanism with an awareness of social and geographical factors whose work it is to restore order and beauty in our surroundings" hold the promise of curing the "ills" of the present "human landscape."[57]

Jackson committed *Landscape* to reminding its readers of the interesting and varied nature of the field. No single profession or discipline held answers, rather thinking must come from the wide range of design professions as well as those in geography, anthropology, and urban studies, and wise citizens. He looked to the opportunity to learn and draw information from other magazines. *Landscape*'s goal was to remain "a publication which attempts to experience the landscape in terms of its inhabitants, so that others may learn to do the same."[58] And he was making it clear he intended *Landscape* to serve as a forum for broad discussion of the future, as well as the past and present.

Life in Santa Fe in the *Landscape* Years

Jackson's ties to Santa Fe were strong. He told me that in the summer of 1945, he drove there from his mother's home in Connecticut after receiving his army discharge papers. By February 1946, in a long letter in the *Santa Fe New Mexican* he was already letting others know his strong opinions about the city. Santa Fe, he wrote, was a unique place as "the only stronghold of Latin and native Indian influence left in the United States . . . [the nation's single] center of American (as distinct from Anglo Saxon) civilization." Was Santa Fe to go the way of Bridgeport or Des Moines, and become just like any other city? Was it to be a tourist trap, complete with "a highway lined with chicken dinners, filling stations, tourist accommodations, fortunes told, chiliburgers, bingo"?

After asserting that Santa Fe had no chance of developing into an agricultural or industrial center, Jackson advocated that the city's true destiny lay in the arts. Santa Fe was a center of skilled craftsmen expressing local Indian and Spanish influences, and of artists "whose taste and imagination is a great stimulus to the handicrafts." Santa Fe must cherish its "unrivaled combination of setting, of indigenous architecture, and of an atmosphere part Spanish, part Indian, part American." Jackson wanted its street names, now under consideration, to foster this destiny.[59]

This letter suggests Jackson was, at that moment, casting his lot with Amelia Elizabeth White, wealthy patron of the arts, hostess, and close friend of his late uncle, Percy Jackson. "Miss White" was the woman whose Santa Fe home had served as his refuge when he had furloughs during his time at Fort Bliss; according to Brinck's statement to me, she even came to that Texas military base to visit him.[60] In later years, Jackson chose to live outside the city and question many of his 1946 letter's assumptions. But his judgment recognizing the importance of its peoples remained.

Sometime after arriving in New Mexico in 1945, Jackson leased a ranch east of Albuquerque. It was there he suffered the serious break in his leg that required surgery and a long recuperation. His ranching days over, he bought a house in Pojoaque, approximately sixteen miles north of Santa Fe. Then, at the beginning of February 1951, Jackson sold the Pojoaque house and leased one at 634 Garcia Street in Santa Fe, placing him in a residential area roughly one mile south of the Plaza on the east side of the city. This was a sector favored by members of the art colony and close to El Delirio, the Santa Fe home of Miss White and her companion Catherine Rayne.[61]

Why did Jackson move? Two reasons, I think, the first being money. Selling his Pojoaque dwelling gave him an infusion of capital. Much has been made of Jackson's wealth, which enabled him to live his adult life without remunerative employment; but during this period he had responsibilities. He was sending his mother money for her support and also hoped to help his older brother, Wayne, who was then suffering from tuberculosis. (Although Wayne carried the Jackson name, he was not favored by the wealth of his stepfather's line.) Moreover, Jackson was not only writing for his magazine; he had to spend money for its practical aspects, including printing. In selling his property, he received not only a down payment, likely a mentioned $4,000, but also a monthly payment of $100 a month.

Regarding the sale of the house, Jackson wrote to his mother and brother, "I am more grateful that I sold when I did; the people who have bought the Bouquet Ranch . . . are very ordinary country jews, running chickens all over the place, and the neighbors are beside themselves, and are trying to sell as fast as they can." While I cannot know whether the neighbors' discontent was caused by the chickens or the Jewishness of their neighbors, or if Jackson's was thinking only that he might have gotten less money if he had waited to sell, nonetheless, it was painful to read his casual anti-Semitism and learn that, even after the war, he retained the bigotry of his past.

In March 1951, a time when he was deep into designing lettering for articles in *Landscape*'s first issue, Jackson wrote to his mother, expressing a desire to work in the Texas Panhandle. A job there would offer both income and knowledge: "It would be a wonderful opportunity not only to make about two hundred a month all clear but to know the farming and country side of that part of the country; and I am most interested in that for the magazine." This was an odd statement, given its timing; perhaps it simply expressed a longing.

Jackson's move to Santa Fe must have been related to *Landscape* in another way. The city offered him resources and an encouraging community as he pursued the ambitious endeavor of launching a magazine. Being in town put advisers, a library, and a commercial printer nearby. Jackson moved in, however, with views about the architecture of Santa Fe quite in contrast to those expressed in his 1946 letter to the *Santa Fe New Mexican*. In Winter 1950, he published an article in the *Southwest Review* called "The Spanish Pueblo Fallacy." Here he decried the popular confusion of Pueblo Indian and Spanish American building, blending two quite distinct traditions, leading to the architectural style Jackson derided as "Santa Fake."[62]

Jackson's journal of 1951 begins with his move to the house on Garcia Street. The first entry is rather curious. On Monday, February 5, 1951, after a bit of whimsy, Jackson turned to his gloomy state of mind. "I called Mother at 12 today: having nothing much to say except that I was disheartened with the house and wanted to get out of it. Poor mother, who has heard the same sort of complaint from me for 40 years, was sympathetic as always." (Then age forty-one, Jackson was exaggerating a bit.) From this point on, running throughout the journal entries and letters was Jackson's hope that the house he rented might be sold out from under him, thus freeing him from its lease. He also imagined escape through travel. He had recently returned from France (and possibly Florence) and planned to go to Paris in September. But in the meantime there was the work of making his new dwelling habitable, moving in the furniture, and unpacking the books.

Books were very much on Jackson's mind. Looking at his unsettled objects, he wrote in his journal, "I glanced through some of the stack of French books—too lazy, too apprehensive of new ideas to cut the pages." Two days later, as he discarded many of his possessions, he connected thinning them out with his writing. "A florid or even a well nourished style in writing is not my vain; I am better for little food and very plain food as well."

Jackson's twenty-four carbon copies of letters to his mother and brother, written in the early months of 1951, accompany these journal entries. In addition to giving information on the founding of *Landscape* and his social milieu in Santa Fe, these letters also focus on Wayne's illness. Alice Jackson was attending him, first in Washington, D.C., and then in Wallingford, Connecticut, where he recovered at Gaylord, a sanatorium.

Jackson's letters frequently commiserate with his mother's troubles—first the tedium of her life in Washington, later her multiple tasks in returning to her Connecticut home, and then her regular drive of approximately sixty miles to Gaylord. Jackson had much sympathy for Wayne's boredom during convalescence under quarantine. Whether specifically to amuse his mother and brother or simply to continue his usual pattern of correspondence, Jackson told them a great deal about his daily life and thoughts.

Both his letters and journals chronicle Jackson's intense intellectual interests. Despite what he had written in his journal, he thought about what might lie in the books he had not yet read, ideas then stirring European intellectuals. By the second day of journal entries, Jackson had his courage back. He noted in his journal, "I read more in Psychoanalysis et Sociology—a treatise on the Freudian approach to society. The fault of Freudianism (according to Bastide) is the emphasis on the biological origins of social & personal traits. Whereas he believes they have a social or economic basis. During the night I finished *Le Crepuscule de l'image,* an intelligent book on modern French art, spoiled by a silly racism [clearly recognized better in others than in himself] and a narrow belief that only France has produced any art in the last century."

Once settled on Garcia Street, Jackson engaged in an active social life, occupying many of his evenings and some of his days. He was connected to the younger set of artists and writers, as well as the older society represented by Miss White. He went to parties and at one point even gave one. He dined out frequently in others' homes and at restaurants, and he had guests for dinner. There were concerts and picnics. The telephone rang repeatedly, and often at the other end was Catherine Rayne, then the primary resident in Miss White's house.

In his letters and journal entries, Jackson used harsh words about some of those around him, conveying their insularity and gossipy talk. On one occasion he was insulted at a reception in the library of El Delirio. A woman he knew said to him, "I saw you doing your business at the tea party the other day." When Jackson asked her what she meant, she told him it was "being agreeable to people . . . [he] didn't like." No further words illuminate what Jackson thought the woman was insinuating, only his prickly remark, "I objected to her watching me and commenting on it to me."

There were certain women whose company Jackson enjoyed and about whom he wrote warmly, including Dorothy Stewart. In his journal he described attending one of her parties. Stewart was "so much at ease with everyone, and . . . makes everyone at ease with her." While Jackson liked her very much, he didn't appreciate her aesthetic stance or worldview. She typically invited guests for a purpose, in this case to look at a new book of cave paintings. He saw her enthusiasm for the work as "part of the anti-cultural, anti-European state of mind which pervades so many intelligent Americans." For them Europe held "nothing to offer, while Mexico is the land of promise."

Jackson seemed to spend the most time with Miranda Masocco. She was younger than he, and he consoled her in her unhappy relationship with a boyfriend whom Jackson regarded as "a selfish and self-centered young man." Jackson also enjoyed the company of the French-born Marie Armengaud, a woman in her early fifties, known to history as one of the lovers of poet and writer May Sarton. It is worth noting that none of these women posed any possibility—or threat—of romantic attachment. Whatever his wartime engagement had once meant to him, no words of his I have ever read suggest a possible courtship. When alone, Jackson enjoyed classical music on the radio and operatic arias on the record player Wayne sent him. He did not, however, enjoy twentieth-century music. Igor Stravinsky spent time in Santa Fe and was Miranda Masocco's friend. Around March 12, Jackson was invited to have a meal with Stravinsky and his wife at Masocco's home. He begged off and later remarked that he was glad he had, "especially after hearing Petruska [Stravinsky's piece of ballet music] yesterday."

During these months, Jackson referred several times to a woman named "Faith." In his first journal entry he mentioned she had gone to Tucson, "smiling and optimistic and happy"; in a letter likely written in early March, he wrote that her mother had died; and on March 17, he stated that once he was free of his lease he might rent her apartment. During March 1951, Jackson gave a party for Fritz Peters, the nom de plume of novelist Arthur Anderson Peters. Writing to his mother, he remarked that Peters had been "Faith's husband for two or three weeks." Peters had recently published the novel *Finistère* and had come to Santa Fe; but, Jackson wrote, "Santa Fe is paying no attention to him at all; his book isn't even for sale here."[63]

On one of his trips to Albuquerque before the party, Jackson bought *Finistère*. The novel has remained a noted work for its treatment of an adolescent's discovery of his homosexuality. In regard to Peters, Jackson related, "He was apparently brought up for 16 years in France, and spent as a result of the war some six months in a mental hospital which gave him the material for his first book. Evidently his bringing up was supervised to a great extent by Gourdieff [the Russian mystic] at Fontainebleau. His collapse wouldn't seem to be the best recommendation, nor his having been married three times for a few months or weeks each time. Still, I'm told he is a very agreeable and sensitive person. We'll see."

The day before the party for Peters, Jackson finished *Finistère* and wrote he "disliked it very much; not only the subject, but the presentation; it is not a theme which can be handled like any other, and calls either for a sensational book or one with great psychological insight, and Peters doesn't seem to have either." Jackson's negative appraisal of the book proved to be no impediment to the evening, however. The following night he reported, "The party has come and gone, and was highly successful." He added, that because he was busy serving drinks to the twenty guests, he never got to talk to his guest of honor.

Several statements about the older generation of civic leaders in Santa Fe during this period show that Jackson was a man caught between worlds. He didn't then have the words he used later in life—"establishment" versus "vernacular"—but they describe an element of the conflict he felt in 1951. On the one hand, there was the world created by older women in the city. "Santa Fe is dominated by a half dozen intelligent, prosperous, elderly women," he wrote in his journal, "each with a cause like an invisible child which they are resolved to forward and see admired." He pointed to the three institutions on Museum Hill. He regarded the Laboratory of Anthropology as Miss White's "backward and somewhat delinquent offspring." (Percy Jackson, his uncle, had fostered this organization.) The Folk Art museum he termed "Miss Bartlett's abortion." Dismissing the third institution, dedicated to the arts of Native Americans, as "Miss Wheelright's Hogan," he described it as failing. (All three remain today as among the revered cultural resources of Santa Fe.) Jackson also heaped scorn on the efforts of Mrs. Dietrich, which contributed to the establishment of the Indian Market. To Jackson, all of these institutions were "concerned with worthwhile enterprises, but financed by capital from elsewhere, disdainful of local interests & prejudices, and none with a man in a position of any importance or authority. As a resort they become more & more remote and even hostile to the community, and more defiant in their determination to 'stand for' something presumably superior to the environment, and finally reactionary." Harsh, nasty, misogynist words.

By moving to Garcia Street in 1951, Jackson was linked to many of these women. Writing of his mother's support for distancing himself from them, Jackson noted, "She was sincere . . . in her desire to see me get away from this atmosphere of old women, and the old women of Santa Fe cannot easily be avoided." His mother's words may have been motivated by hope to have him closer at hand. Jackson had earlier written of her letters in which "she couldn't understand my love of the Southwest. I shall not try to make it clear; she has seen this country and has found no charm in it."

Jackson then described what had just pleased him, a visit earlier that day to his old neighborhood in Pojoaque, where "I saw something of it again this evening that made me love it more than ever. What was it? Merely a glimpse of Procopio [one of his former Hispanic neighbors] reading the Country Gentleman at the bare table; he is fasting for Lent. His hands are almost deformed from work; bent, fingers cut, the nails almost gone; and he himself is getting to be an old man." Jackson admired Procopio's home life with a "gentle and beautiful wife" whom he saw cooking tortillas "for the boys." The house that had been Jackson's was now "smelly and dirty and full of broken toys and unused electric bulbs; but far more genuine and part of the landscape than it was in my occupancy. None of these things," he summarized, "were to fall in love with; but it was the world of simple men and simple lives, and I shall miss even the briefest contact with it."

Beyond this singular group of personal writings from 1951, it is difficult to find information about Jackson's inner life in Santa Fe. My guess is Jackson kept these papers because they recorded the important time when he created *Landscape* magazine. With more words unavailable, what exists is the clear statement of Jackson's subsequent action. In the early 1950s, he moved to a rural settlement, La Cienega, approximately twelve miles south of the city. He first rented and then, in 1954, bought the land on which he would build the house that remained his home until his death.

Whether living in Pojoaque, Santa Fe proper, or La Cienega, Jackson sustained a public life in the city, one that changed with the creation of *Landscape.* Through his writing, editing, and publishing of the magazine, Jackson's reputation began to grow, and he became a public presence called on to speak on a wide range of matters. From Santa Fe, his prominence gradually moved out into the wider world. Two newspapers, the *Albuquerque Journal* and the *Santa Fe New Mexican,* offer the traces.

While still in Pojoaque, Jackson established a set of annual awards for the best Spanish- language students in the Santa Fe County schools, later amended to those writing the best essays in Spanish. He continued giving these monetary prizes for many years. Once living in Santa Fe proper, Jackson acted a good citizen, despite his distaste for the society of women who seemed to rule the city. He became a member of the board of the International Folk Art Foundation, addressed the New Mexico Foundation on Indian Affairs, and regularly attended artists' exhibits.

Although in his February 1951 journal Jackson had expressed disdain for the "enlightened humanism Quakerism" around him, in 1952 he participated in a conference organized by the American Friends Service Committee of Santa Fe. He served as one of three panelists at a World Affairs Forum on "The Future of Europe," held in October. Described in some detail in both newspapers, the event conveys something of the political culture in Santa Fe during the era of the Cold War and the Korean conflict. Jackson's contribution followed a speech on the evening of October 17 by Milton Mayer, an American journalist identified as having just returned from Germany, where he had been a professor of social research at the University of Frankfurt.[64] The other panelist was Howard J. MacMurray, "the head of the government department at UNM and state chairman of the United World Federalists." In the Albuquerque paper Jackson was only identified by the statement that "he has also returned from Europe recently."[65] Coverage in the *Santa Fe New Mexican* placed Jackson also at a roundtable with the topic "Whither Germany?" On the day following the forum, the city's chapter of the American Association of University Women announced Jackson as one of the speakers for United Nations Day.

Many of Jackson's activities related to his regular travels to Europe, typically taken twice a year. On May 27, 1953, for example, Jackson spoke at the Garcia Street Club on "Impressions of Yugoslavia," formed "during an extensive trip abroad recently." The following year he donated a pair of "heavy knit socks from Yugoslavia" to the Museum of International Folk Art."

Jackson's move to La Cienega did not seem to alter his civic involvement. The Albuquerque newspaper reported on May 22, 1955, that Jackson—now identified as "the editor of 'Landscape' magazine"—was to lecture the following evening at the Museum of International Folk Art in Santa Fe: "Mr. Jackson, who has returned recently after a three months' tour in several European countries, will discuss the forms of popular and folk art of today which he observed during his travels. . . . On display in the auditorium will be sketches and drawings which Mr. Jackson made in Europe."[66]

Ultimately Jackson's internationalism provoked a reaction that remained perhaps unknown to him. The news report of this 1955 lecture triggered the opening of his FBI file. During the Cold War era, foreign travels of Americans could provoke intense scrutiny. A redacted copy of an October 26, 1955, memorandum recently furnished by the FBI carries the information that "a highly confidential source who has furnished reliable info in the past, and whose identity cannot be revealed, (documentation—anonymous) advised on 10/25/55 that JOHN B. JACKSON, Box 215, Rt. 2, Santa Fe, N. M. [redacted words] The subject advised that he was a native born American and [redacted words] WFO [likely Washington Field Office] indices contain no identifiable info concerning this subject." The memorandum advised "an immediate investigation to determine the employment and citizenship of this subject" and emphasized the need for "immediate, preferred and continuous investigative and administrative handling."[67]

The investigation that followed uncovered newspaper records revealing Jackson's international interests and his lecture in 1953 discussing Yugoslavia. It established his address as Box 215, Rt. 2, La Cienega, and the facts of his birth and parentage.

It brought out his past engagement in the 1952 World Affairs Conference sponsored by the American Friends Service Committee and what emerged as a suspicious speech by Mayer. It led to one investigator to read *Landscape* in the library, "without discerning any information of pertinence to this investigation." Records of Dun and Bradstreet gave a mélange of accurate and inaccurate information regarding Jackson's background and finances. The 1955 report concluded Jackson did not pose a security risk at present, but if the Washington Field Office learned of "actual travel performed by JACKSON in one of the satellite countries," he should be interviewed and observed in case he was later "approached by Soviet or satellite personnel in the United States."

Thus in December 1955, when Jackson "indicated a desire to travel to the USSR," the State Department made his file available for review. Jackson was then planning a four-month trip through Yugoslavia, Rumania, Russia, and Poland, as well as his usual travel sites in Western Europe. On December 20, his movements in Washington, D.C., were tracked as he went to the Rumanian and Hungarian Legations and the Czechoslovakian Embassy.

What the FBI apparently failed to discover was that J. B. Jackson had served with distinction in military intelligence during World War II, as well as the fact that his brother was in a high position at the CIA. During the war Wayne Jackson had left his law practice to enter government service and by 1951 was special assistant to Allen Dulles.[68]

In his travel journals, Jackson occasionally linked what he was seeing abroad with Santa Fe's cultural institutions, and not in flattering ways. In spring 1956, as he traveled in Austria, a visit to the Heimatmuseum in Braunau am Inn led him to think of Santa Fe's Folk Art Museum, by contrast: "The more I see of these small heimatmuseum, the less I think of the Folk Art museum in Santa Fe—not only as to contents but as to presentation." In 1958, again traveling abroad, he explored a history museum intended largely for children and wondered "what Santa Fe could & should do with its museum."

Jackson's interest in public education was not limited to the arts. In 1956, after visiting with Adlai Feather, Jackson drove on to view an exhibit of high school science projects. In 1957, he became one of the early board members of Science Comes to You, Inc., an effort to establish a science museum in Albuquerque or Santa Fe.[69]

Aside from speaking at and participating in the life of the cultural institutions of Santa Fe, Jackson was exhibiting his sketches. The Albuquerque paper reported in October 1958 a second exhibition in Santa Fe of Jackson's work, this time as one of a group of four, in a show at the Museum of New Mexico.[70] His drawings were singled out and reviewed favorably by a critic in the *Santa Fe New Mexican*: "Impressionistic and sensitive, they are completely unpretentious and thoroughly charming, done with fine control and insight."[71]

Landscape's tenth year, celebrated in 1960, brought recognition in Santa Fe of Jackson's achievement. In the years that followed, he emerged in newspaper reports as a valued contributor to discussions of planning and development in the Southwest. In 1962, he was among the scholars, architects, planners, and government officials who gathered for a two-day seminar in Santa Fe under a Rockefeller-funded "Area Study Group" to consider design and development issues in northern New Mexico and southern Colorado.[72] The following year he was the luncheon speaker at the New Mexico Joint Development Conference and at the meeting of the New Mexico chapter of the American Institute of Architects.[73] In 1965, as "editor-publisher of Landscape Magazine," he was hailed as one of the "national figures" speaking at the six-state regional conference of the American Institute of Architects."[74] Although such events took place in Santa Fe, their scope was the broader region. And by then Jackson was giving more of his local civic self to the village of La Cienega.

La Cienega

La Cienega became central to Jackson's life, but he got there by accident. In the 1950s, he was on the board of the International Folk Art Foundation, serving with Yrjö (Y. A.) Paloheimo, the Finnish consul in Los Angeles, who, with his wife, Leonora Curtin, lived part of the year on the La Cienega ranch her family had owned since 1933.[75] Curtin was deeply involved with Native American culture and languages, and as a young adult in the 1930s, she had founded and supported Santa Fe's Native Market, focused on Hispanic crafts and art work.

According to Marc Treib, in the early 1950s, Paloheimo invited Jackson to dine at his La Cienega home. In an interview with Treib in the late 1980s, Jackson quipped that his was the "classic 'guest-who-came-to-dinner story.'" In a walk about the grounds, Paloheimo showed Jackson a small house on the property and offered to rent it to him. Given Jackson's many misgivings about living in Santa Fe, he welcomed this opportunity, and the four-room house became his home for many years.

Figure 22. Forecourt
of J. B. Jackson's
house, La Cienega,
New Mexico; photo-
graph by Marc Treib

Jackson clearly liked the La Cienega location. In 1954, he took legal action to clear the title of a farm property of twelve acres nearby. There he came to build the large house that was his home from 1965 until his death in 1996.[76]

By 1960, Jackson had chosen Berkeley architect Donlyn Lyndon to design his home. After Lyndon's plans proved to be beyond the ability of the local builder, Jackson worked closely with the latter to develop his own plans.[77] Jackson told Treib he'd had "something vaguely North African in mind."

Although New Mexico is typically thought of as a dry region, Jackson's property contained marsh land. The existence of water allowed the flourishing of trees, plants, and grass but required careful siting of the house and preliminary ground work (see color plate 4).

Jackson planned his home to be a grand house, and it was. He created a wing for his mother, then failing in health, and built a small house for her nurse close to the road. However, Alice Jackson's death in 1965 meant she never occupied her suite; and her bedroom and bath came to serve as generous guest quarters. Although Jackson later explained the house's entry porch with its large piers to Lyndon as intended for his "motorcycle club—once a month I have to have a place for them to park their motor cycles," newspaper reports and personal slides in Jackson's collection show its use for large neighborhood gatherings of a more festive sort.[78] Jackson regularly opened his home to his neighbors; it was the site for an annual party and, at least on one occasion, a wedding reception (see color plate 5).

Jackson's move to La Cienega refocused his attention, and he began to think of ways he might support its largely Hispanic community. He concentrated his first efforts on a swimming pool, built behind La Cienega's two-room schoolhouse. The *Santa Fe New Mexican* reported that the pool, named El Zambullo (The Plunge) La Cienega, boasted "diving boards, filtration system, showers, dressing rooms and all the trimmings" and was built "with public donations and local labor." At the dedication ceremony on August 29, 1959, Father John Hallinan blessed the pool, the Sociedad Folklorica organized music and dancing, and members of the community offered "Spanish food" as refreshments.[79] A later report identified Jackson as a giver of "major assistance in financing the pool." In the accompanying photograph, he was pictured with Mrs. M. A. Romero, president of the Sociedad Folklorica, and E. S. Chavez, president of the Zambullo Committee.[80] In 1963 it was revealed that Jackson's $25,000 donation (an amount that would be over $220,000 today) actually paid for the pool.[81]

When the pool was rededicated in early May 22, 1960, with Father Hallinan again giving the blessing, a flag bearing the crest of the de Baca family on a white field was presented, to be flown as a signal that the pool was open. Such festivities continued at least until 1964, when it was reported that a new flag, representing "the coat of arms . . . of long residents of Cienega," was donated by Wayne Jackson.[82]

In 1963, after the Santa Fe Board of Education announced the closing of La Cienega's elementary school, Jackson fought vigorously to keep it open. Although the tiny school had strong community support, it then served only fifteen students in three grades. Coming to a board meeting, Jackson "pointed out that he had retained an attorney to appear before the board and argue the community's case for keeping the school open," thereby forcing a review of the board's decision. Jackson and community supporters won that round, but in 1965, the school was closed. Its converted rooms became La Cienega's community center, which took responsibility for the pool.

In 1976, the center was the site of a dinner of traditional New Mexico dishes held in Jackson's honor. La Cienega residents publicly expressed their gratitude to Jackson not only for the swimming pool but also for being "instrumental in helping to acquire former school rooms for a center," continuing to support it, and teaching the community, as one woman stated, "how to read the instructions and how to get to the heart of the matter at hand." At this gathering, attended by more than sixty people, Jackson's neighbors wished him "Godspeed" before he departed on Amtrak for fall teaching duties at Harvard. "The children came as did the grandparents to wish Jackson well while he away from the village where he long has had a special place in the hearts of residents." It was reported that "some villagers referred to him" as "El Patron."[83]

Musings, 1959

In January 1959, Jackson cleaned his rented house and reorganized his possessions. In doing so, he discovered some empty pages in one of the large blank books that served as travel journals. He began using it for reflections.[84]

Over his evening meal, he started reading the first of the twelve volumes of John Ruskin's *The Seven Lamps of Architecture,* just purchased, and felt an urge to put an idea of Ruskin's down on paper. His musings offer an enlightening glimpse of how Jackson's mind worked as he confronted the ideas of another. In this conversation with himself, he not only wrote to understand Ruskin but also to refine that understanding. It was important to him to express what he was learning in a manner that satisfied his own literary sensibility.

Jackson wrote down Ruskin's idea that "sacrifice in the sense of offering is an essential ingredient in (ecclesiastical) architecture," and then he began to rework the passage. His initial try was "non utilitarian ornament, rich materials are an offering to God, and help sanctify the church, and also encourage art." He modified and simplified this statement several times, resulting in this sentence: "The willing offering of beauty and workmanship is the sacrifice which makes the church acceptable to God." Feeling that the wording still wasn't quite right, he rewrote once more, and then signaled his success by underlining the words: "The willing and selfless gift of ornament or workmanship is the sacrifice, due to God, which makes the church a work of art."

By late January, he had finished his cleanup. Or, as he put it, "almost finished— for like the Navaho weaver I'm fearful of perfection." He found himself appalled by all the possessions he had accumulated—chairs, sketches, unused drawing materials; but he was rather pleased at his "modest wardrobe." He felt satisfaction in discarding unwanted items and making his living space more habitable.

With his radio on during breakfast, he found "peculiar radio stations coming in strong—Shreveport, Salt Lake City, a Navaho announcer in Gallup advertising day old bread, and Nebraska." (Here, Shreveport, my childhood home, jumps off the page.) At the table he was reading a work by Benjamin Whorf, likely *Four Articles on Metalinguistics*. Whorf's ideas may or may not have precipitated the credo Jackson was then attempting to write. He worked at refining it, trying several phrasings of "We are all part of the life order of the world" before coming to his final version: "We belong to the Earth's life—From this (in time) I will deduce our attachments, loyalties, involvements, kinships. . . . *But* we also belong (or are part of) something else—and that is where the trouble—not only for me but for man begins."

I can only wish Jackson had played out this final thought to the end. But actually I believe he did so in 1952. The words he published then in *Landscape* are worth repeating: "Man is the Product, the Child of God and that his works must therefore always betray, even in a distorted form, that identity. . . . To reaffirm the unity of Man and of his world, his Divine origin and his ceaseless efforts to re-create here on earth a dimly perceived Divine order, is the only way to establish on a firm footing the study of Man's modification of his environment."[85]

5

FORAYS

Travel Journals, Home and Abroad, 1954–1960

Jackson's travel journals offer some of the most revealing traces from his *Landscape* years. They convey how he observed, inquired, and thought; created fieldnotes; and learned about places. They give insight into how he distilled this raw matter into his published writings. They also reveal Jackson's human side: his habits, emotions, and foibles; his bigotry and efforts to overcome it; his ambitions; his frustrations and his satisfactions. His midcentury travel journals provide abundant insights into the inner man.

I found it difficult to transcribe these densely packed pages and to extract their meaningful moments, but as I did so, my understanding of their importance evolved. These travel journals were produced by a writer, and they constitute his workbooks. As a historian, I take notes from written documents, such as letters, diaries, and books. Jackson took them from observation. I work from libraries and archives, including—in this case—these journals. Jackson read constantly and deeply in ways that shaped his writing, but he also worked from observation and reflections made during travel, as written down in these journals.

As I typed, I gradually came to understand something else. Jackson was a writer with a notebook. Its pages may have been meant for one purpose, but the notebook was open, the pen or pencil was in hand. Thus, while Jackson's journals may not have been intended for personal reflection or self-understanding, its blank pages were there. On occasions when he might have been troubled or tired, Jackson set down what he felt. Some of these journals have pages torn out, perhaps because he had second thoughts about a bit of writing. But there remain entries in which Jackson seems to have written his deepest feelings and let the words stand.

Also, for a writer such as Jackson, who was also a reader and an intellectual, a journal exists as a place for trying out ideas and, occasionally, writing drafts. At times, Jackson used his journals as the paper he had at hand on his travels, available for moments when thoughts occurred to him. These yield compelling moments and present surprises. Ideas that seem to come from observations made in the American heartland appear instead to have had origins in what Jackson saw as he walked in foreign places.

I don't know when Jackson began writing down his impressions during travel, but by the second extant journal in 1938 it was clearly an established practice. During his trip to Cuba, he mentioned times that he wrote in his journal and sketched. In certain instances, these two activities attracted attention. Jackson frequently noticed others gathering to watch him draw. His writing was also observed, once with consequences: during a 1958 trip to Eastern Europe, his notebook was seized by Customs as he left Bulgaria.

A word about Jackson's journalistic practices. He wrote as if he were describing something immediately in front of him. As he was often driving a car and alone, such cannot have been the case. On occasion he noted that he was writing days after an event took place or a particular observation occurred to him. Jackson's statements are generally so detailed and specific, however, that it is hard to believe he was not dictating as he walked or drove. Once, in Munich, following his report of returning to his hotel to sleep, he mused, "—or did I get something to eat? I can't remember: in any case it doesn[']t matter in the least, only indicating how speedily recollection fails." It seems, however, that in Jackson's case it seldom did.

He had an extraordinary memory. One can sense this in the way his published essays refer to a broad array of sources, many almost certainly read in years or decades past. His journals reveal even more—his amazing visual memory. Hours or days after a trip by car or train, he was able to recall with great specificity and in sequence countless details of the landscapes he had moved through. He described the way certain fields looked, identified trees, considered the qualities of light on hills or mountains, the shapes and colors of houses, barns, monuments, and urban squares. Reading his travel entries conveys the sense that as he wrote he relived a journey of one or several days as if he had a motion picture of it rolling in his mind.

It is not surprising that travel was important to Jackson, and that, as a writer, he chose to record his impressions, for travel consumed much of his life. Emblematically, he was born during a trip his parents had taken abroad. He once said his initial childhood memory of the landscape came in Switzerland when, age four, he first saw a meadow. Brinck had years of schooling in Europe, including two at Le Rosey in Switzerland and one at Institut Carrial in France. Many of his summers in preparatory school and college were spent abroad. Travel was frequently taken with his mother, who after the departure of her husband when Brinck was four, became an antiques buyer for Lord & Taylor and later for her own shop; thus, some of her travels likely held a business side. Nonetheless, Europe held a special aura for her. Jackson went abroad in his immediate postgraduate years and frequently journeyed there more than once a year in middle age. In one of my talks with him toward the end of his life, Jackson expressed a special wish to visit Switzerland again.

Travel in the United States served an additional purpose in the 1950s. With the founding of his magazine, he began to give serious thought to the wider American landscape, make contacts in universities, and develop methods for understanding the patterns he observed in American towns and cities. Some of these domestic explorations, too, he chronicled in his journals, occasionally adding field notes and quick sketches,

Jackson's extant journals cover only a small portion of his travels. Those documenting his trips to Mexico in 1937 and Cuba in 1938, I've have placed with his early writings. The section that follows begins with his travel in 1954 and ends in 1960. I don't know why there is a long hiatus between Jackson's early travel journals and those of the 1950s. In the intervening years that included his service in World War II, Jackson may not have written in this manner, or his journals may have been lost, regarded as not worth keeping, or even destroyed. I also have no knowledge of why there are no extant travel journals after 1960.

By 1954, except for trips he made with his mother, Jackson seems to have traveled alone, and the journal he carried became something of a companion. By the mid-1950s (when he was in his mid-forties) solitude was his established way of life, and as a writer it served him well. That is not to say, however, that he was content. Jackson was a restless man who was always trying to find himself.

His travel journals reveal a good deal about writing, personal relationships, and sense of self. In the decades after the 1938 publication of his novel, he continued to write fiction and dream of its finding its way into print. During his mother's lifetime, he wrestled with his conflicted feelings about her. Devoted to her as he was, he felt constrained by her expectations and longed to break free. Moreover, he had been raised without a father, and so a central question became that of his manliness. For those of us who knew him in his later years, the resolution of this issue shaped much of the persona we saw at first hand.

Although his journals normally were not diaries filled with self-examination, on occasion the open page served that purpose, and at these times he wrote his heart out. In most of the entries, however, Jackson attempted unvarnished descriptions only of the landscape—what he saw and the sense he was making of what was before his eyes. His journals thus offer his first efforts to describe places and spaces that, later distilled, became part of his published writing on the landscape.

In the Autumn 1956 issue of *Landscape,* under the pseudonym P. G. Anson, Jackson reviewed three contemporary travel guides by Americans, contrasting them with traditional European ones. He wrote that the new guides produced for the American traveler since World War II attempt to provide practical guidance for tourists of every sort, but they fail to offer the detailed cultural information of the Baedekers and Guides Bleus. The contemporary approach assumes American travelers simply don't want that kind of information, that they are in Europe to merely be a "consumer of food, drink, lodging, tickets and souvenirs." By contrast, the older type of guide could "lead you through a gallery, show you a city street by street, give you a great deal of historical, geographical and literary background. . . . They treat the tourist like an intelligent and inquisitive human being"—the very kind of human being J. B. Jackson embodied.[1]

USA, 1954, Travel and Field Notes

Jackson took a car trip through Colorado to Kansas in November 1954.[2] He began his travel journal by writing of his visit to an old friend. As the journey progressed, his observations led him to the discovery of the features of railroad towns. He was then three-and-a-half years into publishing the magazine, and on this trip Jackson not only paid attention to changing landscapes; he began writing field notes. He penciled small sketches of the layout of towns, labeling key aspects. As he stopped, he enjoyed listening to the conversation of locals and recorded it. He also wrote thoughts about future issues of *Landscape* and ways to expand its reach. He read about comparable places in other countries and made lists of what to examine and people to contact on future travel.

Jackson began this journal after leaving the Colorado home of Will Haegler, the former Swiss hotel keeper who had become his ranching partner after his return to

New Mexico in 1946.[3] Uncharacteristically he wrote that in leaving the Haeglers to drive east, he dreaded the car trip ahead. It was "hard to set out in the overcast day—like a day when snow comes—and to foresee the growing staleness, physical and mental, the fatigue, the signs of approaching trouble in the car, and to foresee the monotonous miles of Eastern Colorado and Kansas—and still no end in sight by evening" (see color plate 6).

This mood soon dissipated, and he began to write about the physical world around him and those inhabiting it. He summarized what he saw in the "succession of country little villages" he passed: "white one story frame houses, a few Chinese elms, a store, a school, a church, a shipping yard near the RR—and here and there in the folds of the brown landscape, a small farm or ranch house." He liked seeing the "cheerful terribly prosaic but energetic countryside, and I felt sorry for no one in it." He imagined the busy lives lived there, ones so different from his own: "Each house, no matter how forlorn, was probably only a cocoon, full of a bright future, distant or immediate; children coming back from school, radios, trucks driving in at the end of the day—much futile activity no doubt; little of importance thought or said or done during the day, but always hope and a confidence that things can be arranged as they are wanted."

At the Haegler home on the previous night he had been reading Ralph Waldo Emerson and recalled the author's thought that "every man instinctively feels that he is entitled to the best—especially every American." It made Jackson wonder about the future of the country. A reader also of contemporary social criticism, Jackson attempted to probe the American psyche. "How are we ever to trim our sails, nationally speaking, until disaster overtakes us? What parent will have his child walk to school now that he knows of school buses? or forfeit the best medical attention? or have poor roads? I daresay not one of the men or women I saw felt that their present isolation or modest living was anything but temporary."

At Union, Colorado, Jackson stopped for coffee and doughnuts and overheard a conversation between the waitresses and a young man, clearly a favorite. When a young woman came in for a cup of coffee the waitress asked her to deliver a package in town. Jackson noted that the customer "reluctantly confessed she was going to be all day at the beauty parlor and would have no time for anything else before she came home." Jackson wondered if she was on her way to Denver, "a long way to go." He observed as the young man "put a nickel in the juke box on the counter and played 'Junior is a big boy now.' He was wearing the currently stylish low heeled cowboy boots" (see color plate 7).

Changing subjects, he labeled Union as a "T plan town, the first I had wit enough to observe." By "T town," Jackson meant a western town, as found in Colorado and Kansas, formed around a primary intersection at a right angle between the railroad and Main Street. And with that he began to examine the geographical structure of such towns. He had already written "The Almost Perfect Town," as well as much of *Landscape*'s Spring issue on "High Plains Country" (Spring 1954). Now Jackson was seeing something new, and in the back of his mind he was likely plotting a future piece for his magazine.

He flipped his notebook to its reverse side and began to draw. With this move, Jackson's 1954 journal also became field notes. The reverse side holds eleven pages upon which Jackson drew a small layout of each of the towns he was traveling through, typically placing two such drawings on a page. On each he labeled features, such as railroad tracks, schools, parks, grain elevators, highways, and hotels. To the side of each drawing, he noted such information as population, primary crop (wheat or corn), and location (if he could determine it) of a civic center. He meant by this "the gathering place for informal sociability, like a Mexican plaza"; typically, it was a post office or hotel.

On the front side of the notebook Jackson continued to write his observations and reflections: "The country after Union became if anything flatter and more featureless; vast wheat fields on either side." He described the houses he saw with their outbuildings and crops. Turning to the surrounding properties, he observed the occasional "line of small trees; very rarely an attempt at a lawn or garden, and hardly ever a vegetable patch. The yard & grounds were usually littered with farm machinery." He saw cattle in corrals and grazing in fields. Nevertheless, "it was wheat country, almost exclusively, though I daresay on the rougher land there was range."

The road he traveled paralleled the railroad. Turning his attention to the structure of the T towns, he found them "astonishingly alike in form. . . . in fact creatures of the RR." Their main streets intersected "at right angles to the RR (and highway) depot & elevators at one end, school at the other." These towns were not as large as they seemed: "The main street was usual[ly] 3 blocks on both sides of one story builtup houses: with say 2 dozen or more blocks of residences in 3 directions." While the region's smaller towns were fading—"No new retail businesses, cafes & hotels closed, and little life"—the people in them seemed vital. Jackson noted, "active and healthy looking men, many children screaming in the playground of the (consolidated) school, and no sign of defeat."

In the larger towns, Jackson perceived "the beginnings of city features." He wrote,

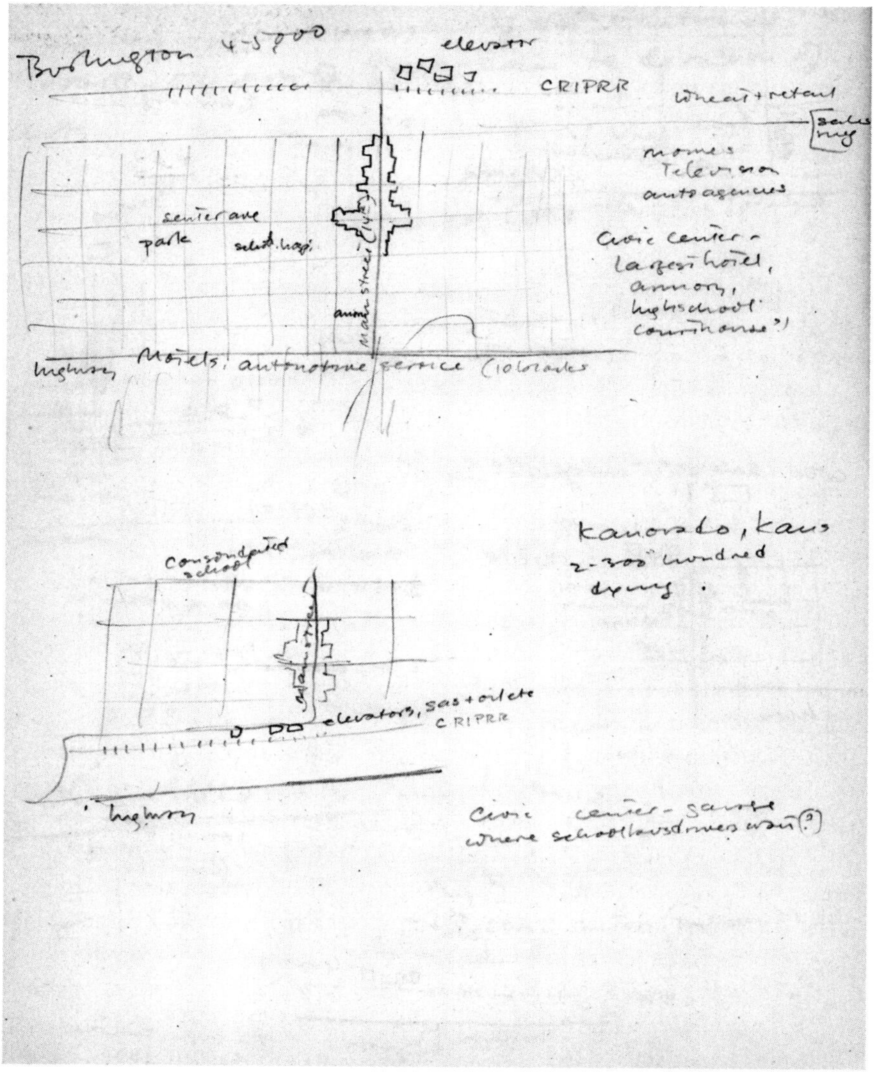

Figure 23. J. B. Jackson, travel journal, Kansas T town sketch map, 1954

"I listed as best I could the civic features—main street, school, park, elevators, heavy goods, and a something I called 'civic center'. . . . The ones I found were certainly inadequate enough for prolonged conviviality—the post office (probably only before & immediately after the mail comes in and is sorted) the garage (where the school buses wait) . . . [or] where farm machinery is repaired, and the lobbies of the larger hotels." Ignoring established meeting places, such as armories, schools, and churches, he chose to look at such "informal gathering places" as probably having "some bearing on the nature of the town."

As he reflected, Jackson thought it "likely" that, despite the similarities of these T towns, they were based on no formal plan. Rather, each town had developed "around the meeting of railroad and country road leading to depot or shipping point." The streets were wide, and when two crossed, there lay the potential for a town center. In one such town, a "wooden war record, with eagle & flag, was fixed to the wall of the bank at such an intersection—as if the crossing were recognized as a kind of center." Typically, the main streets were only "country roads leading nowhere in particular," and this gave them "a back water quality. Trucks stopped in the middle and drivers conversed." This led him to think that "this T plan—main street at right angles to the highway, produces something like a plaza life," but this could evaporate with the increase in truck traffic. Although each town had a park, its distance from the town center kept it from everyday use.

The towns themselves offered little Jackson found charming. "The vegetation was of necessity scanty, the yards poorly tended, and the houses of the poorest construction & design—one story, hip roof structures, white and graceless." Brick construction could be found only on the main street, "one story with a tin roofed porch. . . . venerable—all of 50 years old." No chain stores or outposts of national companies marked the dying towns, although of necessity there were filling stations. In the more lively towns, a good deal of its life was "along the highway, where a whole set of automotive institutions had grown up—Farm equipment stores, motels, drive ins, etc." Perhaps making a note to himself for a future issue of *Landscape,* Jackson wrote, "The economic explanation of the T towns appeared the logical one; but they might have been typical of a certain region and as such worth studying. A good picture would be main street with the depot and elevators at the end."

The next day, after driving through Kansas, he wrote, "The west stopped somewhere around Colby; the wheat west stopped somewhere west of Kanato, where corn began." When he paused for coffee at Phillipsburg, he saw it as "a court house town not yet thoroughly awake." Children were out, however, in the stadium, "practicing band parade formations in the stadium." Jackson noticed he was seeing in the Kansas towns some "sensationally modern schools." Continuing on the road, he found "the country was more & more rolling: the deep, narrow valleys full of oak & cottonwood & willows, with an old house occasionally hidden among the trees."

Kanato seemed to him "a prosperous, semi-eastern town, with obsolete big residences formed into tourist courts, funeral parlors, legion homes etc." When he stopped for coffee, he asked the waitress and two young women, likely sitting at the counter, "What does the town do?" The three "merely laughed embarrassedly. And even the head man was a little at a loss to answer, suggesting the crops of wheat and corn 'and waiting for oil.'"

Jackson seemed to grow less interested in the towns as he drove on, although he noted that "progressively the architecture became more elaborate—and occasionally grotesquely imaginative." After a maddening detour that led to "15 minutes of fury on my part," his jeep had a flat tire in the town of Hiawatha. He stopped for the night in St. Joseph, Kansas, at the Shangri-La court—"very luxurious, $5.50."

His journal writing ended with a reflection on Ray, the contemporary owner of the "Westward Moving House": "Ray's capacity as transformer is actually another version of the service career. The retailer or distributor—anything other than creative in a manual labor sense."

Planning future travel in Europe, Jackson jotted down the name of a hotel in Athens and of a man and locations in Vienna. He listed references and made notes about farms in Germany and settlements in Haiti. He set down quotes from reading and wrote some summaries. One entry conveys his enjoyment of whimsy: "Mr Geker, retired Cigar & candy salesman of Springfield Mo (pop 90,000) keeps a box at the P.O in order to have some place to go when he goes down town."

He thought about *Landscape.* He plotted out an issue on the High Plains that might feature the writing of Baker Brownell, a sociologist then interested in small-town renewal in Montana, and contemplated other issues that would treat the landscapes of Pueblo Indians, Mormons, Mennonites, and Mexican ranches. Perhaps mulling over extending the list of those who might like to receive complimentary copies of the magazine, he wrote down, "Mailing list—Magazine of Art Editorial Board, officers of American Federation of Arts."

He also considered the idea of an issue of *Landscape* devoted to "The birth, growth & influence of a highway." Following this heading, he set down a list of likely topics for articles and other items to fill the magazine's pages: "Effect on land values, new businesses, appearance, communication, traffic problems. Interviews with filling stations, chambers of commerce, highway patrol, highway Department, merchants, farmers, motels. Photographs and map."

Jackson's observations and field notes in this 1954 travel journal establish his growing sense of calling. Since boyhood he had traveled and sketched and, at least since 1937, made entries in travel journals. Practices that once began as a personal record or a novelist's notes became a fundamental part of his work as writer and editor once *Landscape* was underway. Travel and recreation thus pleasingly merged with professional life. From 1951 until he turned over the magazine in 1968, in his own curious way, Jackson was always working, even at moments when he was jotting down a quirky anecdote.

USA, 1955

In early January 1955, traveling with his dog, Jackson drove a new Jeep from Washington, D.C., south to Pensacola, Florida, likely on a journey home to New Mexico after a Christmas visit with his mother in Connecticut.[4] As Jackson traveled south, he seems mainly to have observed from his Jeep's windows. He looked for ways that the South contrasted with New England. Although interested in race and aware of racial discrimination, certain of his observations were disturbing, displaying both ignorance and prejudice. Jackson was moving fast, and this 1955 trip did not inspire deep insights. Nonetheless, his entries convey a sense of what interested him in his less-engaged moments and how he interpreted some of what he saw. Returning to the South two years later, he would take a longer and closer look.

On a cold morning, Jackson left the Potomac Motor Court and, at Arlington, got on the Shirley Highway. A constant critic of the new federal highway system for its destructiveness to existing landscapes, he wrote that this segment was "not an interesting drive, though a quick and easy one." As the highway ended near Quantico, he viewed from a distance the new Iwo Jima Memorial and the many road markers for Civil War sites. He couldn't read them, for "nearsighted as I am I have either to stop dead to see them, or back up—something not to be advised in the midst of fast traffic."[5]

Driving south through Virginia, Jackson noted, "The farm fields had many of them board fences, usually around the pasture for the prize livestock or near the road. The effect is neat and pretty, and peculiarly southern—about the only distinguishable southern item on the landscape most of the time." He listed the types of trees he saw and made a sketch of a house. Writing of the road leading to that house and its surround of trees and lawn, he commented, "It appears shabby, damp, and decaying. and with few refinements of detail or plan; nevertheless very pleasant to see in the midst of the winter trees."

Jackson paid attention to the signs that told of racially segregated facilities, such as those for tourist camps that frequently mentioned "'for colored' or curb service 'for colored.'" He found the southern term *colored* "a clumsy expression but preferable so it would seem to Negro or Aframerican or Black; and perhaps because it suggests that the only difference between White & Negro Americans is a matter of color, not of race—even if the 2 ar[e] much the same. Any how the accommodation 'for Colored' were invariably dirty, primitive and thoroughly obsolete."

He took a bypass around Fredericksburg and then straight through Richmond, where he found the houses offered "a very good cross section of middle class American architecture during say the last 50 years. . . . The latest houses, though undoubtedly the most expensive were the least ambitious, being semi detached for the most part, and with imitation attics which in no case could be used." In the older section he saw (and later sketched) the city's distinctive townhouses: "not the same as Baltimore or Washington or Philadelphia or Boston. 3 stories (brick in almost every case) with a sizeable piazza or verandah on the ground floor." Guessing they were from mid-nineteenth century, he thought that "gave them a different feeling." He considered a possible future project in which he might "analyze and account for the different urban styles in the Eastern USA; there are at least 5 distinct variations. Do they come from local building traditions, or are they adaptations of some prototype?"

One comment offers some insight into the manner in which Jackson often traveled: "I am sure Richmond has a part deserving visiting; but as usual I was rushed; in this case to get gas at the same time the speedometer read 500 miles, and a place where I could chuse [*sic*] the correct road for Durham." Once his mileage gauge passed that marker on his new vehicle, Jackson now had leave to go faster, and was glad he did, for "the country became no more interesting." Looking at roadside signs, he pondered the loss of "Old Dominion," Virginia's earlier nickname. He liked Petersburg, noting the avoidance of both "neon & black granite [likely glass veneer] facades" on the main street.[6] "Colored people everywhere," he remarked, "and since Camp Lee is not far off, many soldiers." He particularly admired Petersburg's courthouse, writing, "A New England courthouse suggested honest public officials: These suggest statesmen." What he couldn't understand was the "Mystery" of the city's mile-long main street. Rather than a grid, its mid-nineteenth-century houses fronted on a single "dusty & noisy road."

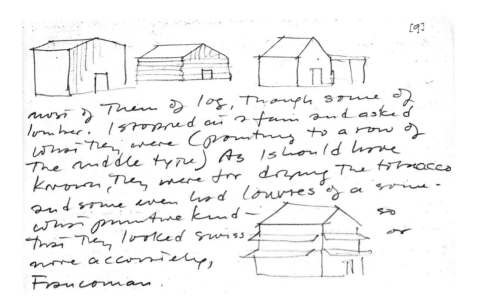

most of them of logs, though some of lumber. I stopped at a farm and asked what they were (pointing to a row of the middle type) As I should have known, they were for drying the tobacco and some even had louvres of a sort—what primitive kind—so that they looked swiss—or more accurately, Franconian.

Somewhere outside of Petersburg, Jackson began to notice "strange little barns on every farm," either of lumber or of logs. He stopped and inquired about their purpose to learn they were the drying barns for the region's tobacco. He was curious about why they were all of the same size; "And some farms may have 6 or more of these structures—each as big as a one family house—in a row." He stopped and spoke to an African American farmer, noticing he had a tractor and cattle in a corral, leading him to comment, "One thing few of us realized: much tobacoo [*sic*] (at least in Virginia) is raised by negro[e]s, and not as the ads would have it, by whites."

Moving into North Carolina, Jackson observed changes of soil and vegetation and again the many structures on each farm. "I remember a Godey's Ladys Book of 1849 or 50 commenting on the same thing: I didn[']t credit it at the time, but it was and remains true a century later—every Southern farm I[']ve seen has enough houses on it to be a village." Reaching Durham, he prided himself on the 250 miles he had driven, and stopped for the night.

The next day as Jackson traveled quickly through a number of North Carolina towns, he looked at agriculture and farm buildings. Focusing on a typical structure from Concord to Charlotte, he made a sketch and then, in words wrapped around the drawing, described it as "a plain gable construction surrounded and

Figure 24. J. B. Jackson, travel journal, Virginia, 1955

almost hidden by porches and sheds: sometimes the center was not a door but a passageway, a dog trot: often the core of the barn was of rough trimmed logs, and not caulked or chinked." He saw some reconstructed tobacco barns, converted to uses such as stables or hay lofts, and in poor shape. He found in them "a good deal of picturesqueness and antiquity—especially when you saw a lanky negro leading a mule into the dark passageway."

As the scenery changed, Jackson liked the aesthetic effect of contour plowing. He noticed haystacks similar to those in Europe, "a heap built around a pole thrust in the field." Moving into the Piedmont, settled by Scotch Irish, he saw fewer fences and shabbier barns. After he traveled through Charlotte on the way to Spartanburg, his stop for the night, he wrote, "The negro slums in Charlotte. . . . The crudest and dirtiest set of uniform houses—all squeezed together—I have ever seen. Before long negroes will find the slums of the big Eastern cities just as good as the slums in the New South."

Pondering the "Automobile Row on a western scale" on the outskirts of Charlotte and Spartanburg, Jackson saw "a mass of filling stations, tire repair places, hubcap

Figure 25. J. B. Jackson travel journal, North Carolina, 1955

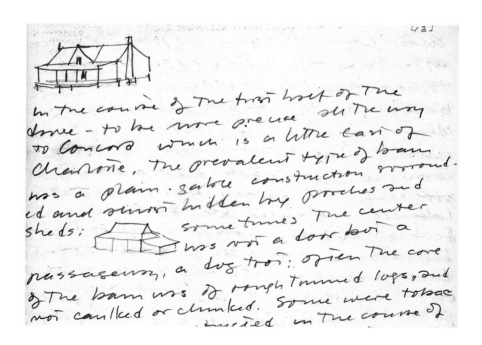

displays, used cars; and with it of course a complete dearth of the traditional human street scene." He considered two possible causes: trucks carrying freight displacing railroads and poorer people with low priced cars leading to "constant trading, constant tinkering." With that, he ended the day's notes with a light touch: "The cashier at the A&P," where he bought dogfood, "kept a peeled tangerine in that compartment of the cash register where silver dollars are usually held. She took a section every time she rang up a sale."

Moving south and west through the cotton landscape of South Carolina, Jackson drew and commented on the houses of African Americans along the road, describing them as "absolutely primitive—without paint, without ornament, without front yards in many cases—merely dull brown constructions scattered along the highway, down lanes and in the fields. . . . the modernist dream turned into a nightmare—functionalism, utilitarianism, style[le]ss-ness at their absolute." Given his distaste for architectural modernism, this pronouncement was a double condemnation.

After commenting again on the beauty of contour farming, he wrote: "The fence now keeps in and has ceased to keep out."[7] He reported "mile after mile of rolling farmland, empty of activity or of crops at this time of year . . . without any kind of barrier. . . . A beautiful and spacious setting: The rows of hills unbroken by peaks or sharp valleys, the views extensive and undramatic, and near at hand the handsomely terraced fields—many lying fallow or reverting to second growth—with here and there a uniform clump of pines; all straight all dark green, all the same height." He also wondered what the rampant growth of kudzu, promoted by the U.S. government as way of preventing erosion, would do to obscure landscape features.

Stopping in Anderson, South Carolina, to have his Jeep serviced, Jackson conversed with a local man about farming. Anderson reminded him of an older South, "shoeshine parlors, pool halls, canopies over the street supported by pipe: tall ceilinged stores poorly lit; many people on the street, wares displayed on the sidewalk, and the sense of good food—the smell of it and the sight of fruits and nuts and heaps of flour sacks." As he went further south he admired the older houses and fine trees. And the quiet: "What was most remarkable was the utter silence of machines etc[.] when I stopped; only the sound of birds, the voices of negroes and the closing of doors."

"The miracle of the South," he commented, "is that anything should die; the miracle of the North is that anything can be reborn. Winter here is in its way more mysterious than it is with us; for what tells the plants it is time to stop growing, time to sleep? The question in the North is what tells them to come to life?" Thinking of the ways this difference played in the minds of northerners and southerners, he wrote, "Landscape must deal with this dimension of the natural world as well as the physical."

In Georgia, Jackson looked with eyes that had seen Europe. Eatonton reminded him of both New England and Italy. "The street was a New England street with lawns and trees and houses far apart. The light, and the softness of the air was Italy, and so was the abundance of children racing about the round fence posts." In Macon, he saw "all this splendor but in good repair . . . a charming and lively city, so Southern in a European sense that I have expected to see the glint of bright blue water down the end of the broad & crowded street. The southern sun is especially kind to hill tops; and every house perched on a hill is invested in these climes with romance & beauty."

At one level Jackson surely knew that, as well as this vision of beauty, Macon held the reality of poverty. But for the moment, he simply chose to enjoy what he called the "magic" of the place. As he headed south and west of Macon, looking at commercial farms growing cotton, rye, and nut-yielding trees, he pronounced them "beautiful, clean, efficient, and even exciting." He praised the loveliness of the camellias blooming in Marshallville, Georgia. But then he paused. "It is ungracious to look for the seamy side of this New South: but still it is sometimes evident: Tenant farmers have been done away with, and instead there develops a rural proletariat." Without evidence, he chose to believe that this class was not only mobile, but also "well paid, not overworked, contented."

Jackson traveled on to Athens, home of the University of Georgia, and then to Americus, a town that interested him. Although it had suffered economically from the loss of the cottonseed oil industry, it retained "a tremendous hotel in Queen Anne XIX century—a blown up version of a Chelsea studio block: very queer." Older houses survived, taking in tourists and boarders, but few new ones had been built. He regarded Americus as "a rather pleasant farmers town," quite different from those in New England. Americus had "stores bursting with pecans and peanuts, negroes yelling at each other, a pompous byzantine bank, and dignified 1870 storefronts." These impressions were, Jackson confessed, written four days afterward, and he seemingly found it "almost impossible to reconstruct the impressions of the Trip, so quickly forgotten are even the most vivid."

After taking a short detour west to Mobile, Alabama, Jackson backtracked east into Florida to view more of the Gulf Coast: "It was there I saw the gulf: dark blue in the bright sun, but with a further line of land a few miles out; this was only an inlet. The Coast is of fine white sand, a narrow beach with the pines & azaleas immediately overhanging it. The undergrowth was a tangle; the soil a deep buff, a warm classical color." He was struck by this shoreline's contrast with those he had seen in Europe. There was "nowhere a sign of civilization—only occasionally a shack on stilts with out buildings, pine trees. Nowhere, furthermore, was there any sign of marine activity: no boats, no piers, no sea industries." A European coast would have had "its own historical & economic character, perhaps because travel by boat would be the safest way" to get access to inland products. Lacking this, "the Florida panhandle might just as well be inland a hundred miles."

In Pensacola, Jackson was pleased to find "some fresh fish for sale—along with heaps of conch shells and pecans." On the way there he had observed that "for a good many miles the coast was lined with resort settlements and hotels, none of the very highest quality perhaps, being untidy, scattered about under the pines, and poorly put together; but with a fine view of the nearby sea or gulf, and having romantic rather than respectable or prestige names—Shalimar, Shangri La; Paradise Inn, Palomar etc. nowhere a Ritz or Waldorf or Astor or Ambassador etc."

While this journal may not allow us to see Jackson at his observational best, it does give a sense of what caught his eye and how he judged the places and people he saw. And his final comment offers some insight into the way his travel impressions crystallized into writings such as "Other-Directed Houses," one of his most important essays. For a quick trip speeding through the Southeast, perhaps this is enough.

Europe, 1955–1956

Jackson's journal of winter 1955–56, when he was traveling in Europe, holds a complex record. In it he developed thoughts on topics that later emerged into some of his most important essays. There are entries of light-hearted humor. And there are, as well, ones of anguish, where Jackson gave unusual expression to some of his darker emotions.

He began writing not with observation but with a meditation on the varied levels of culture expressed in the arts. "Art is divided into two, cut like a pie into innumerable halves—classic, romantic, form and expression, primitive and academic; and to add another dichotomy: popular and formal." But what were popular arts, and what separated them from "folk art"?

"Popular arts," he decided, "are those which the people enjoy . . . not for self expression, or interpretation of the everyday world or insight into the individual—but for gayety, celebration, make believe—variety and recreation." He thought he ought to focus an issue of *Landscape* on popular architecture "as seen in such buildings as roadside restaurants, motels, filling stations, houses and establishments designed to attract the attention of passersby in cars, and to signify their importance, utility, beauty, etc." Explicitly following David Riesman's typology in *The Lonely Crowd* (1950), he decided to call this new phenomenon "Other-Directed architecture." He thus began this journal with the thoughts that ended his preceding one, arising from observations on Florida's coast.

In Hilversum, roughly forty miles from Amsterdam, Jackson began developing another theme. Asking where he might find a leather coat, he was directed toward a broad street with a bus depot, a movie theater, two beer halls, two restaurants, and shops selling sports equipment. Jackson tried to make sense of what he saw: "It occurred to me that certain traditional pleasure places—beerhalls, novelties and so on—are likely to be found in the area associated with outsiders coming into town . . . and that the tie up is roughly popular sports-travel-leisure or holiday entertainments—and crowds." These thoughts matured, and in issues dated

Figure 26. Flamingoes, *Landscape*, vol. 6, no. 2, 1957

1956–57 and 1957 "Other-Directed Houses" and "The Stranger's Path" appeared in *Landscape* (see color plate 8, a photograph from Jackson's collection, evocative of this kind of urban district in the United States).[8]

Perhaps inspired by a couple of Dutch comic books purchased during the trip, Jackson took off in a humorous direction, producing a send-up of folk art written in glossy-magazine style. (To the best of my knowledge, this untitled work remained unpublished. In *Landscape* such pieces typically appeared under the pseudonym Ajax.) Jackson begins by introducing the Loobeys, fictional residents of Santa Fe, "the leading folk family of America. . . . Ari Loobey builds furniture out of the local white pine; Lou his wife practices dancing of the folk to all and sundry." They home-school their three children to protect them from contemporary life. As Mrs. Loobey explains, "None have been taught to read; that way they are spared contact with the comics and the depravity of much current literature." The elder son, however, is not immune to the broader world about him, and his mother sees danger in his increasing interest in cars, fearing it might lead him to study engineering at MIT. Detailing the senior Loobeys' aesthetics, sloppiness, foodways, self-absorption, and opposition to modern life, Jackson takes a swipe at those in Santa Fe at odds with his own values and sense of decorum. He also reveals a bit more evidence of his own political conservatism by placing copies of the *Nation*—then as now, one of the most prominent voices of the American Left—alongside other disliked possessions of the Loobeys.[9]

Jackson's travel observations began on New Year's Day of 1956. After driving through the Netherlands, he wrote a two-page description of the landscape seen from his car window. He then returned to observations on contemporary culture and the ludicrous world of the Loobeys. "It is folk to play the guitar badly," he wrote, "but nevertheless to play it—to consider photography as an art.—to abhor comic books but to look upon Al Capp as a Great American."

When Jackson joined his mother in Germany, his jaunty tone vanished. He began to write about an experience of depression, a subject that was to become a significant theme in subsequent travel journals. Nothing in his earlier extant writing hints at this; nor do I know what evoked this particular episode. It came over him when his mother was visiting with an old friend, Emlen Grosjean, daughter of Joseph E. Davies, a prominent lawyer and diplomat during the early to mid-twentieth century. After riding to Frankfurt with Emlen's businessman husband, Jackson went to a café, where he sat alone, in a low state: "While I was reading, and drinking coffee, a wave of inferiority came over me and stayed throughout the morning, no matter what I did. I couldn't cross the street alone, nor make myself heard when I spoke, and no ideas that came to me were of any worth: I walked accompanied by a dull companion, and everyone around me seemed better adjusted, stronger, happier than I."

Eventually, he walked around Frankfurt into the bombed-out region left by the war. "It had a vaguely popular quality—booths with mill end knitted goods, secondhand books, bars with an Italian or Spanish decor, perhaps the site of a large open air market." He went into an alley and found an *Unterhaltungssalon,* roughly translated as an entertainment salon. This turned out to be "an empty, antiseptic room with slot machines & pin ball machines." He watched the players and had a bratwurst before picking up the car he would drive to Zurich with his mother. In the lobby of the restaurant where he was to meet the Grosjeans and Alice Jackson, he drank a vermouth and read. "I would eventually have achieved a calm, for it was a quiet and stylish lobby; but they all arrived at once—full of their own emotions."

After lunch, he and Alice Jackson set off for Switzerland. The drive there was difficult. During lunch he had become indignant at his mother's naïveté about a business matter. Alone with her in the car, he was out of sorts. "For sometime along the autobahn to Da[r]mstadt we discussed Emlen's way of life, and I was very severe, since I was more interested in my immediate surroundings and the glimpse of Frankfurt than in domestic problems and Mother's passionate involvement in personal matters." But as he wrote this, he confessed his own limitations. "I also felt how little of that I gave her, and how she prefers that kind of talk and thought to my own impersonal speculations." Although he could not change his nature, he could "develop a respect for the human interest side of many people's life." This would, he recognized, require "a very fine judgment and tolerance." Then he shook off this demand on himself by noting, "all too often human interest is merely an excuse for moral indignation—which Malraux calls the favorite bourgeois emotion."

That evening, after dinner at the hotel in Baden Baden where they were staying the night, Jackson read something that provoked him to take up his pen again. "It was an article in [the German Protestant newspaper] Christ und Welt which encouraged me to write a diary—a form of therapy and exercise in relating oneself to oneself, and to the world—that an[d] a remark of Shaw[']s saying write 1000 words a day." What followed was his account of the morning in Baden Baden and afternoon on the road to Zurich, where he bought a book, hoping to use some of it in translated form in *Landscape.*

He returned to low spirits, as he reflected on what he had seen in the countryside. He had hoped for a delight in those surroundings he did not find. The road running through the center of each village was destructive to community life, and the villages themselves were deeply disappointing at close range: "When I stopped just to buy cigarettes the whole forlorn and workaday atmosphere overwhelmed me. . . . A flourishing countryside in summer, but not a very prosperous one. I should say; for who really wants to live in those dark and smelly houses, and work the small fields? and once that question arises, how can one really enjoy the spectacle of the rural landscape—except as an exhibit of an economic & social order now beginning to disintegrate?" With that, "much of my supposed pleasure vanished."

Jackson returned to the question of how to understand present-day popular art. Its importance, he speculated, lay in "the scope it gives to a different feeling for art." He decided there was a distinction between "Snob art" and "Mob art": "Snob art . . . [is] serious, more or less permanent, and involved with self-expression, whereas Mob art is the contemporary equivalent of folk art—dedicated to leisure, celebration and impressing the passerby. . . . Snob art degenerates according to a more or less regular process: from Exhibition to fairs, night clubs, movies & cafes to be imitated broadly as a kind of chic but at the same time new motifs arise from below—The automobile, The zootsuiter, sports enthusiasm and popular leisure time entertainments: and it is also possible that these pop art forms may in time perculate [*sic*] upwards into snob art."

He identified in Europe a third form, "a semi official" art, linked to "history & the national heritage (as opposed to the individual)." Another category that interested him because it was as yet "untouched" by a label or discussion: "such trifles as mascots for cars (many German trucks have bathing beauties etc on the radiators)," items found in home gardens, and "certain elements of mens or boys clothing." He began to probe the "common bond" linking "sports cars & motorcycles & bicycles=pleasure=glamor: certain jackets & caps are inspired by autoculture, and certain parts of town, identified with autos and the center of young life."

A line across the page marks a separation from these thoughts to the entry that followed, for the next day his mother, then age seventy-five, had a serious fall, breaking her hip in complicated ways. Recovery required a two-hour surgery and a long hospital stay. Jackson reacted intensely, thereby revealing his deep ties to his mother. His next entry, written four days after the accident, described his feelings on first seeing his mother after she had been given an anesthetic so her leg could be put in traction. Jackson found her in the emergency room, "very sleepy, but still bright and cheerful with her eternally young interest in experiences. . . . How much I have to unlearn of what she has taught me! How much I have to learn from her still! Her love of life, of mystery for its own sake, of everything fresh and innocent—and new! But what has prevented me, all these years, from acquiring it—or rather what has made me reject it after my first youth."

He gave his mother's surgeon a letter from her home physician. The surgeon then told him of "a slight weakness in mother's heart and . . . the clot in the right leg." Jackson should anticipate, the doctor cautioned him, that she would require a long hospital stay.

Jackson moved to a small hotel nearby, where, alone, his fears for his mother grew. On the day of the surgery, as he awaited the time he could see her, he confessed, "My last 3 days have been a hell of uncertainty, fatigue and apprehension, which every motion and word uttered by mother have increased. . . . I am beside myself with nervousness." The night before, he had realized that his worries, rather than arising from fears about his mother, "were actually self-pity." He understood he needed "someone to talk to; for I live in perpetual self disgust and inadequacy feelings." Turning to thoughts about his mother, he wrote, "Sometime in the future she will go, and I will think of a life ended before it has had all it wanted, that lives on hopes & illusions & love—all of which must cease; and I will be left alone, desiccated and idle and no longer young." He asked himself, "How are these two conditions related—my self-hatred, and my deep love & pity for mother? How will they be resolved?" Thinking back to Wayne's illness, he wondered, "Have I the strength I had for Boo to pull her through if anything goes wrong?"

As Alice Jackson recovered in the Zurich hospital, her son attended to her during visiting hours, sent cables to Wayne, and communicated with those concerned about her. Beyond these duties, he found himself on his own in Zurich. During the many weeks of his mother's convalescence, he had ample leisure to ponder his current state and think about the future. On January 16, 1956, a few days after the surgery, he wrote. "I should resolve never again to write a novel—unless the present one is accepted after rewriting. Instead I should concentrate on building up Landscape not only as a source of prestige but as an outlet for what I have to say."

This statement jumps out from the page. As I read it more than sixty years later, I find it remarkable that during the important early years of *Landscape,* when Jackson was writing much of its copy and working to build its readership, he retained his dream of being a novelist. He thought through his future work in these terms: "The difficulty is to produce a kind of prose—foreign to my experience and by no means general—which deals not only with ideas and events, but which has color and personality—an autobiographical prose with some of the appeal of fiction without its conventions and artifices: travel reactions etc." The magazine, he added, "should always contain something of mine."

Reading this, I initially wondered about what seemed to be Jackson's amnesia. By 1956 he had written four of his most memorable essays: "Chihuahua; As We Might Have Been" (1951), "Ghosts at the Door" (1951), "The Almost Perfect Town" (1952), and "The Westward Moving House" (1953). He had continued to write, but in a more observational mode, producing such pieces as "Pueblo Architecture and Our Own" (Winter 1953–54) and "High Plains Country" (1954). Perhaps he felt his more recent work lacked the imaginative reach and sparkle of the earlier pieces. His Ajax pseudonym may have allowed him to offer a clever sendup of high-style modern domestic architecture in "Living Outdoors with Mrs. Panther" (Winter 1954–55), but possibly that didn't count. Did Jackson sense that, with other writers now submitting their work to *Landscape,* he had begun to relax a bit, and that he now needed to push himself harder to write more creatively under his own name? In any case, his renewed commitment to "color and personality" worked. In the year following this travel journal entry, Jackson produced both "Other-Directed Houses" and "The Stranger's Path."

And in larger terms, his resolve in Zurich was an important moment. Over time, by limiting his focus to writing on landscape and producing his magazine, Jackson moved into a career he never anticipated. He came to lecture widely, write a well-received book, publish new and old essays in many books and periodicals, and teach at two important universities. Out of the many dimensions of his activity— writing, editing, speaking, and teaching—emerged a new awareness of the landscape of everyday America and his own role as its interpreter. If one thinks back over Jackson's real accomplishments, his resolution in 1956 was a critical step that allowed him to sustain the creativity he had unleased with the founding of *Landscape* and find his true calling.

Forays at Home, 1956

Jackson's travel journals offer meaningful insights into his reactions and feelings and occasionally touch on his life in New Mexico; but one of them is unique. It's a journal telling of the traveling he did at home.

In April 1956, Jackson began to explore the larger Santa Fe metropolitan area to discover new experiences and insights. Although he had moved to La Cienega, he was still a part of Santa Fe's social network. This journal, however, shows that he was beginning to search for connection to worlds different from the artistic and elite Santa Fe he had known. Here one meets a seeker, not only of changes of scene, but also of changes in himself.

While these efforts seem to come out of the personal crisis experienced during his January travels in Europe, my sense is that the feelings behind them go back much farther. Despite a lack of evidence, I believe that what becomes fully visible in 1956 had its inception over a decade earlier, during Jackson's service in World War II. One can see glimmers of this possibility in Jackson's 1943 letter to Boyden, when he spoke of sharing his gift of fudge with those in his unit—men from a broad range of backgrounds—and of his hope that he would not be transferred since it would mean leaving his "friends." While there may have been hints in his roughing it as a cowboy before enlistment and in his postwar attempt at ranching, these efforts fit within the established groove of suitable activity for elite boys and men of his era.[10] Following his 1951 move into Santa Fe, however, Jackson's reflections after his return visit to Pojoaque offer a first written appearance of his wish for association with a broader swathe of humanity.

Although the origins are speculative, what is clear from Jackson's 1956 journal is the outcome, a narrative of moments in which he was trying to live more fully in the non-elite world around him. This was not slumming; it was the beginnings of a desire for connection to a rougher world that he believed to be more authentic. It is traced here in three episodes: an enjoyable conversation at a café and gas station about motorcycles; a less-successful meeting with his Hispanic neighbors to discuss recreation; and a curiosity-provoking prayer service at a Pentecostal church. Much later in Jackson's life, such efforts at connection would become clear in his published writings and explicit in his actions.

On April 2, 1956, Jackson wrote down a conversation outside the Shamrock café (likely a place connected to one of the many Shamrock gas stations in the vicinity of Santa Fe). He had gone there for coffee because he was cold. "I had no overcoat," he wrote, and "the left door of the jeep was gone." He began talking to a young motorcycle rider dressed in jeans, boots, a mock leather jacket, and a peaked cap. Although Jackson noticed the motorcycle lacked a front fender, he didn't speak of this. Rather, he asked the youth if he found it cold riding on his motorcycle. The cyclist, who was on his way to Albuquerque, responded with the same question about Jackson's jeep with its missing door. When he turned to talk to a young attendant at the gas station linked to the café, Jackson learned the "motorcycle was for racing: it had cost 850 dollars." "I said that was a lot of money," Jackson wrote. "He said it had been worth it." Talk about the weather and motorcycles ensued, and before the cyclist departed Jackson learned from him that "85 an hour was his speed to Albuquerque."

Conversation about motorcycles continued between Jackson, an older man, and the station attendant. They spoke about the quality of the cycles Sears sold, rough motorcycle use by drivers traveling cross country, the value of chain rather than shaft-driven cycles, and motorcycle clubs. From the others, Jackson learned about a young trick rider who had ridden his cycle upright or while standing on his head, and who had died in the war. Jackson himself spoke of European motorcycles, scooters, and mopeds. It mattered to him that the attendant, "a stern, reserved young man," was friendly and listened. Conversation ultimately stopped when a waitress told the attendant she was out of dimes and needed him to fetch some.

"I enjoyed their talk," Jackson wrote. "It was what I wanted to hear. I was not only interested in motorcycles, I wanted to hear other voices, other points of view. They had facts and experiences. Many people in Santa Fe have neither. Perhaps on a lower level there is another life in Santa Fe. For the first time I feel free to find out."

The next day, April 3, he was on more familiar ground, but nonetheless outside his normal social sphere. He was one of the few non-Hispanics attending an evening meeting to consider recreation facilities in La Cienega.[11] Jackson began with harsh words for the "carload of small Mexican teenagers" brought by the janitor. "They were a pathetically unprepossessing group: dirty, coarse & stupid featured even when young."

After the adults found seats around a table, a young woman from the county extension office told them that the group needed to decide on the kind of recreation equipment to be paid for from a small fund. As various voices discussed what was needed, suggestions came for school equipment, a football field, and a baseball diamond. "I offered the land I own," Jackson related. "Many seemed to think it was too far away, others didn[']t." Debate ensued about parcels of land that might be purchased. "The teenagers giggled louder than ever. When asked what they wanted they didn't reply." However, they did have a clear wish, for they whispered to one of the adults that "they wanted a field house, a place for dances & basketball." When the county representative asked about where the money for this would come from, no one had an answer, but "the suggestion recurred, and was the most popular of all." Nothing was decided, other than that the man who seemed to take the lead in the discussion, Mr. Chavez, "was made chairman & I was made secretary. Chavez volunteered to see 2 people about buying land."

On paper, Jackson vented his discouragement. "What will come of it? Nothing." With this came harsh judgment of the perspectives of those who attended: "I suspect it is all very well to propose democratic procedures. The Spanish Americans are not at home in it. They would unconsciously prefer to be given what they want: working for it doesn't make a thing more valuable to them. It[']s valuable because they like it. Hopes were roused, but when they are dashed no one will understand why. The world will merely have dealt them another raw deal. . . . Chavez bogged down in discussion of football uniforms, yet they could not even volunteer to build goal posts." Clearly, it was going to take time for Jackson to understand and accept the ways his Hispanic neighbors saw the world and to learn how to work effectively with them.

On the following Sunday, April 8, Jackson reported in his journal his third foray into the broader Santa Fe he was seeking to discover: a visit to an Assembly of God church. It was located behind a grocery store on Cerrillos Road, a main route running south from the center of Santa Fe. In describing the church and service, Jackson again tried out the discipline of writing in simple sentences. "The room was large. It was broader by far than it was long. It resembled a classroom or lecture hall. A stage was at the rear. The ceiling was of rough plasterboard. The windows of frosted glass. . . . The minister was a lanky man in his forties. He had a Texas accent, and wore octagonal glasses, a bright green tie and a brown suit." Counting the house, Jackson figured that of the approximately sixty people attending, about half were children, "mostly little girls in starched party dresses, corkscrew curls and small hats covered with buds," who ran around the room.

Jackson had arrived in the middle of the service. A prayer ended, and congregational singing followed, led by "a heavy young woman" in a red dress who stretched out her arms as if in prayer. During the choruses the minister and several in the congregation clapped rhythmically. Prayers were requested for individuals: one sick, one facing medical treatment, one for her husband in the hope his heart be "softened so that he would come to church." The minister began his own prayer, "first in a monotonous loud voice, then in a sing song—frequently interjecting 'Praise the Load!' 'Halleluja!' 'Aymen!' and making a strange little sound like Hem! or Heng! whenever he came to a break in his train of thought. The adults all raised their arms and prayed aloud—each with their own prayer. I could hear 'For Jesus sake!' 'Oh God!' 'Halleluja!' from different people."

After another hymn and the passing of the collection plate, the minister started his sermon. His smile disappeared as he read from the Old Testament and then made a statement about living in "a world of universal stress and uncertainty." He spoke of "the need for perfection which we could only achieve with the Lord's help." He addressed God often, occasioning members of the congregation to add their Amens. Jackson noted that the minister "managed to glance at me with curiosity and shrewdness." The sermon turned to the congregants' need of money, their sickness and loneliness, and the church's mortgage and penury. Jackson seemed to appreciate these practical concerns more than the "blood and thunder." His judgment, however, was guarded: "It was not a coherent sermon, in spite of the decent anglo saxon simplicity of his language: the habit of addressing God, of breaking into prayer was disconcerting."

On returning home Jackson turned to an encyclopedia of religion, read about the denomination, and made notes in this journal. What struck him was "the condition for immediate experience of religion—the absence of any forms, of any hierarchy or even the need for preparation." This led him to consider the larger implications for the United States. His own class of origin placed great importance on education, yet the people he had just witnessed saw no need for such preparation. Jackson saw this as evidence of "the American radicalism which without defiance or self-consciousness abandons ancient forms and meets on a friendly almost domestic basis. The American revolution has already taken place in this class[.] It will in time form the abandonment of many cherished middle class traditions in public & private life—and its impact on education and politics will be most severely felt."

These were the words of a man struggling to understand and expand his social and personal boundaries. In the four decades that followed, this struggle would lead Jackson to venture repeatedly across country on motorcycle, bring him into closer relations with Hispanic neighbors in La Cienega, begin a religious quest that would take him into many churches as he searched for a spiritual home, and write with a feeling of emotional connection about the working-class landscapes surrounding him in La Cienega.

USA, 1956, Continued

On April 11, 1956, Jackson hit the road again, heading south from La Cienega. He had with him the spiral notebook in which he had written of his explorations earlier in the month and seemed as eager as he had been then to see and accept the world around him. He was in a sunny mood on this trip, and everything (or almost everything) pleased him (see color plate 9).

Jackson wrote several mini-essays on what he was seeing, informed by themes he was developing in his *Landscape* pieces. He wrote of man and nature, the meaning and uses of popular art, and architectural and planning choices. His words give evidence of his growing appreciation at a distance of the working class (with accompanying disdain for the middle class) and sympathy with Mexican seasonal laborers. Walking through a market across the Texas border filled him with delight. Lastly, he surveyed the southwestern landscape, remembering his past at Fort Bliss, but then looked at a new town arising near his old army base to cast his lot with the present and the future.

Expressions of pleasure at seeing early signs of spring south of Albuquerque soon gave way to a deeper observation of what he believed to be "one of the beauties of the Southwest . . . the distance between man and nature. There are two totally distinct landscapes . . . the scenery of naked rocks, rocks covered with sand and a little grass and cactus, the valleys eroded and filled with sand—and then the few human installations—a roadside stand, a cluster of mud houses, a tawdry village, or a crew of men working on the highway or on a well drill off in a lonely field. . . . The setting is monumental, permanent, massive. The human affairs are temporary, squalid and without even a pretense of beauty. But the two go well together, and I would not have it otherwise." Jackson then declared he preferred the man-made world, "especially when it seems untouched by any middle class ideas of beauty and suitability."

As he drove, he looked for expressions of popular ideas of beauty. He found little novelty, for "exigencies of space & cost produce the same one story cube almost everywhere, and what actually distinguishes one wayside house from another is some slight indication of its function—a gas pump, a front yard, a show window—and the signs on most of them. The strange shapes & location are pretty much confined to the newer outskirts of towns, along the highways. . . . dedicated to the passing tourist, and not primarily to the citizen with a car. Within the towns themselves the only way a building can distinguish itself is by having signs—as many signs as possible, large, vertical, and when possible lighted up. Signs are thus an essential element of pop architecture—as an appeal to the public and as identification."

Jackson was on his way to Las Cruces, a route he had likely taken many times to visit Adlai Feather at State College. Familiarity, however, did not keep him from close observation. On the drive, he noticed, "The trees along the river are yellow green. The irrigation ditches and tanks are full and reflect the pale sky. Now and then bright patches of new alfalfa like velvet—in neat flat fields bordered by earthworks. The water everywhere floods neatly and in broad sheets. The tractors at work grading the fields, throwing up a cloud of dust, are like people putting the last touch to some perfection."

As evening began to fall, Jackson grew aware of the Mexican workers. While a few were in cars, it was the pedestrians who caught his eye: "Braceros walk along the road from work: different hats, different faces, and what must they think of this country, so like their own with its angular-forked naked red hills all around. The wonderfully flat geometrical fields, the livid new green trees—and yet nowhere the village or the group they want?"

As he approached Las Cruces on a roadway flanked by trees, he was struck by the idea that "the straight line, the geometrical effect is what men like most of all: that is their mark on the landscape, and the first plowman with a bent stick who farmed the soil tried to make a straight line. He has now succeeded, and who can hold it against him? Contour lines, free forms are artificial—even if often better: but the straight line, the flat surface, the perfect symmetry is what we really prefer."

Jackson was continuing to work out his ideas on popular art and the varied ways it functioned in American culture to give shape to structures and signage. Driving around State College he "discovered a further and most important principle of pop art." He photographed two Quonset huts on campus, the first mention of a practice that was to become increasingly important to his work. They had "Southwestern facades stuck on the front." Although possibly designed by architects to blend with the rest of the campus, these structures nevertheless illustrated a key aspect of architectural pop art: "functional & decorative features are distinctly separate, each is allowed to play its part. . . . I foresee the day when more and more pop-art buildings go up with elegant—or playful or representational facades while the rest of the structure is absolutely plain." Las Cruces offered Jackson the inspiration and desire to investigate what he saw as elements of pop art in architecture, "signs, colors, local tradition," all seemingly "an art-generation behind the times." However, as he looked critically at the plan of the college campus, he judged its buildings were too far apart, thereby creating no composition.

After making personal visits—one with a young Hispanic man he knew, there to study accounting; others with old friends, including Adlai Feather—he headed for El Paso. His mood turned melancholy, and taking a novelistic turn, he imagined the lives of those living along the road. "The day is over and there's been no change: the mountains become inaccessible, dark & lonely & finally invisible. Nothing has been done, and men & women stand around in what is left of the sunlight in their shabby work clothes in the barren yard with the watered tree & the tractor waiting to begin work early the next morning—and the cars stream by with their lights on the road, saying I told you so: it[']s only the city where life is."

In El Paso the next morning, Jackson brightened again. Driving into the downtown on those "amazing streets," he saw new prosperity, the "brand new stream lined brick houses with great overhanging roofs and smooth lawns and new cars, all fresh and prosperous and not to be disturbed at that early hour." He walked the streets and again took photographs.

He reflected on the differences between the El Paso of the mid-1950s and the city he knew from 1940, when he was posted at nearby Fort Bliss: "The old Army type stores were pretty well gone. . . . I walked along El Paso street where the whorehouse was[,] where upstairs they shouted down the dumbwaiter '2 gin slings and a dollar blackjack.' And the place where I got my tat[t]oo—both gone; the whorehouse advertised light housekeeping apartments, and a man was shaving at the window." He saw new Chinese restaurants, Mexican boys looking in the window of an army store, a large Mexican restaurant full of customers. Essentially, he decided, "the street is made for soldiers on payday nights."

From El Paso Jackson drove down to Juarez, Mexico, crossing the bridge for the same two-cent toll he had paid sixteen years before and finding the place much as he remembered it. To the sound of peddlers crying their wares, he walked to the Basilica (with his usual attention to the dress and demeanor of persons around him), peered into the side streets, and surveyed the policemen and soldiers in their barracks—all with interest but little enthusiasm, until he got to the market. There his attention lit on several "sleek headed young men (with a trace of anxiety in their eye: when were they next to eat?) crouched on the sidewalk selling shreds of what looked like Eucalyptus bark—a packet for 5 cents—from Chiapas—good for the liver." As he watched them, his first reaction to the market was "ugly buildings, dirty people, vile displays of wares." He thought he'd take a photograph, but he stopped himself. "I realized that it would come out something squalid: yet while I looked at it I thought I had never seen anything more refreshing & reinvigorating."

And with that, he took the measure of what he once had been and was becoming. "The day is long past when I looked for certain things—saddlery shops, etc., or a sign of the 'genuine' and primitive. Now it is all the same to me. . . . The wonderful life of the streets in a Latin or warm county: the beautiful variety to the pattern of movement and sound—all reflecting & praising the sun: streets of hardware, of secondhand iron & metal findings; of toys, clothes, furniture: loud signs on the dilapidated blue & green & pink facades, a few trucks edging through, but people owning the street in a way they never can in America." He believed his new appreciation came from the "freedom" generated by his speculations on pop art. "It makes no difference what the artistic or ethnological quality of the show: I can still like it for something more fundamental." He could now see that all persons "are always in fancy dress, always acting a part—even if the part may have somewhat changed." Thus to him the morning in Juarez proved as "beautiful and bewilderingly varied as any oriental market place might have been—even though I knew quite well that the old 'color' has gone forever."

His next stop was Fort Bliss. He found the place where he had once trained for the Cavalry "utterly transformed by a tremendous tourist highway, bordered by motels, shopping centers, service stations, with convertible standing next to bright blue swimming pools." It was "a new and enthusiastic landscape," he wrote; one without memory of its past and doomed in time to "grow old and change gladly."[12] "What I saw there, 16 years ago, was the last of the West—for me and for the whole Southwest. . . . If it were still there I would be sick to recover it again and to try to play a part in it; but it is gone." Although the present West was "without heroism or vigor or traditional style," he could nevertheless be part of the new with its "easier, richer way of life: new cars, motorcycles, public resorts and spectacular growth. . . . I hope I shall never entirely forget that revelation: the eclipse of my old west, and the rise of a brand new one in its way as stimulating as the old—and like the old democratic and unbourgeois."

As Jackson explored the nearby bedroom communities of Logan Heights and Mountain View, he saw "street after street of one story, almost identical houses with bright lawns, a car in the driveway, children coming back from school, and sometimes an old father in farm clothes sitting idly on the small front porch." As he thought about this, he understood that while it was "all too new to have any character," such places could "only be judged in the most limited manner: are the utilities adequate? Are the houses well built? Is the[re] room for growth and change?" Any more lasting judgment would have to await the passage of time, but "in the meanwhile why should we not wonder at the vitality and enterprise which created them, at the wonderful ease with which Americans establish their comfortable way of life almost overnight, and how fortunate we are to be able to start at scratch over and over again."

After casting his lot with the present, Jackson drove to Alamogordo to see an exhibit of high school science projects.

Europe, 1956

In 1957, on the occasion of the twenty-fifth reunion of the Harvard class of 1932, Jackson wrote the only entry he ever made in any of its many reunion books. He listed his service on the Harvard Tercentenary Committee, his move to New Mexico "to ranch," his war service, and his current position as publisher of a "magazine devoted to human geography." He added, "I am still engaged in the undertaking, which has the merit of allowing me to travel abroad a portion of each year."[13]

Was he bragging to his former classmates about his freedom in contrast to their confinement in legal or banking offices, or was he merely stating what was important to him? The statement appeared in 1957, after a year of significant travels. There is no way to know if 1956 was unusual; the survival of three journals—two of trips in Europe—from that year may simply be a matter of chance.

In late May 1956, Jackson drove from Zurich through the Alps to Austria. Returning to the region offered the chance to resume the trip forestalled in January by his mother's accident and surgery. Now, traveling alone, he filled his journal of seventy-two pages (averaging about two hundred words to a page) with observations. He wrote of the natural landscape, the region's villages and towns, museums, and local customs, and he considered the impact of tourism on a world he had known before the war. He seemed to have enjoyed this trip. The journal contains no attempts to understand his mental state. He was mainly content to observe, with only occasional reflections; it was not until the sixty-third page that he stepped back to explore at length ideas about the landscape.

Jackson was preoccupied with changes to the region since his last extended visit—changes particularly brought about by tourism. Following the advice of Baedeker and the Automobile Club Guide as to dining and lodging, Jackson knew that he himself was a tourist. But he likely understood himself as a special one: an observer who wrote and edited a magazine. Tourism held for him few negatives, but once he did comment on the harm it wrought. Visiting Rattenberg in Austria, Jackson noted how "an old world main street, crooked, narrow, lined with tall arcaded buildings each with a wrought iron sign, meant to resound—if to resound at all—to local intermittent sounds and voices," now held an "incessant stream of buses, cars, motorcycles, many of which stopped to allow the passengers to photograph or drink beer or coffee."

For the most part, however, he regarded the tourist-wrought changes as positive, for they created a livelier world—especially for the young, who could now ski and play badminton and enjoy many diversions such as sports events, dances, and television. The influx of tourist money and tourist demands enabled pleasures that previously "the country never could have afforded. . . . I've been struck by the number of small villages or hamlets which have never been able to hold people overnight in the past—and therefore lacked any real tourist industry—which now cater to the transient tourist—either a meal, a drink, a swimming pool[,] a picnic ground etc which likewise helps to break down the barriers between peasant and city."

Jackson was, of course, an unusually observant tourist. After a recent talk I gave about him, a documentary filmmaker commented that Jackson seemed to her a "spy." I think of this as I ponder his journals. His war service gave him firsthand experience in intelligence, and with Wayne in the CIA, Jackson had some familiarity with the world of spies.[14] I now add this to the mix of his engagement with anthropology of the American Southwest and a life lived in many places when I think of Jackson always looking in from the outside.

On occasion, his observations were noticed. Driving through the mountains of the Tyrol, he stopped in a narrow pass for a lunch in the open air. Two couples arrived, "the men in black leather outfits, descended from motorcycles with hard boiled eggs and rolls, and drank beer." One of the two men kept the party entertained with his wit. He was "so pleased with himself that he eyed me surreptitiously to see if I was admiring him. I signified that I was."

Usually, however, Jackson's presence went unnoticed. This was true when he attended, without invitation, a wedding reception in a village near Salzburg and acted as a guest. "A vast collection of motorcycles" parked at an inn, drew his attention. "I got out to take a picture of the motorcycles, then went into the inn." He found the real guests, peasants all, in Salzburger costume. The young newly married couple stood under a sign wishing them good luck. Unsmiling, they received a long line of guests who brought wedding presents.

Knowing Jackson did not write or dictate at the time of observation but from memory, what I find extraordinary is his ability to recall the vast number of details of what he then saw: the site itself, the various groups of people, the dress, the activity, the décor of the room, the gestures of the wedding couple. This same recall is apparent throughout his journal writings: he commented on the weather, the signs of spring, the colors, the light. He described the road, mentioning its quality, the traffic, delays, the workmen making repairs. He wrote of the mountains and valleys, fields, farm workers, and animals. He considered the specifics of each town along the route, the nature of the houses and shops and churches. He often suggested the dates when they might have been built and pronounced aesthetic judgments. Wherever he stopped to take photographs or to sketch, he made note of it, and he recalled as well where and when he bought cigarettes or had a cup of coffee or a meal. At such times he normally not only reported what he ate, but also described those around him and how they behaved. As I transcribed this journal, with its descriptive passages running on for pages, I could easily imagine him as the narrator of a travel film putting in words what the motion picture camera recorded.

Jackson was attentive to details. Once, stopping to watch ceremonies in a small town in the Tyrol, he looked at boys and men marching around in costumes, accompanied by a brass band. His shrewd eye noticed their uniforms. "The boys (who came to attention when I took a picture of them) had long green open coats with flat silver buttons: the whole effect could not have been more stylish: the only thing was, all the costumes were new."

In the Tyrol, he paid a personal visit, well planned in advance, to the writer Geoffrey Stone and his family, now living there.[15] Stone had been an editor of and frequent contributor to the *American Review,* the deeply conservative magazine that in the mid-1930s had published Jackson's "Prussianism and Hitlerism" and his review of a book on architectural modernism. In 1956 the Stones and their three teenage children had recently moved into a new, unfinished house. As usual, Jackson pronounced judgment on the house, the children, and the (badly cooked) meal. But most of all he took the measure of how his own politics had evolved. A Catholic couple was visiting as well, a Count Hallstein and his wife. Jackson was struck by the conversation, which apparently included only the men. Talk turned to the question of economic inequality. "We discussed whether it was right for some men to be very rich—taking a General Motors executive with an income of 500,000 as an example." Jackson alone held that "there were healthy limits to wealth as to poverty at the other end." Stone and Hallstein argued that great wealth was an "incentive to others" and, using the example of the Medici, that it had broader benefits. They maintained that "we would always have rich & poor, that the state had no business interfering and that there were after all worse sins than greed for material possessions." To Jackson, this "expressed a reactionary social philosophy which they were determined to believe in," revealing that his politics in the mid-1950s did not include a full embrace of unlimited market capitalism.

Jackson saw Geoffrey Stone as removing himself from the contemporary world to that of "conservative Catholicism." Not only was Stone no longer writing; he read little. Jackson ended his report on the evening with the comment that "at 11 I went back to the hotel, having had too much to drink, and having seen all of the Stones I wanted to for the time being."

A visit to Braunau in Austria gave Jackson the opportunity to ponder Hitler's birthplace. He stayed overnight and walked at length through the town, checking out its known attractions. "If Hitler had not left Braunau so soon," he mused, "if he had managed to be happy here; but he is not the only one who has rebelled against provincial life as a poor young man, and the same poison must attack many others of his class throughout Central Europe—for all the amenities available." At the local history museum, Jackson mischievously asked its custodian "whether there were other famous Braunauers aside from Hitler." This turned what Jackson had intended as a short stop into a long tour during which the man explained every item in the museum. Jackson felt trapped at the time; nonetheless, after listing what he saw, he remarked, "However tiresome the sequence of rooms and displays might have been it was nonetheless an impressive & exhaustive collection." The museum gave him "a birdseye view of the history & economy of the region I could not have got in any other way."

What Jackson saw in the museum led him to question the manner in which Santa Fe's new folk art museum presented its collection.[16] He described a display in Braunau illustrating the range of superstitions "involved in almost every aspect of daily life" that particularly caught his eye: "a small scale model of kitchen, bedroom, barn displayed under it the amulets, charms etc involved in the activities of the rooms—a tremendous collection—particularly in the barns, with prayers for sick animals, charms to protect the building and ornaments for door and eaves." The specifics that followed were likely written to present to the Santa Fe museum on his return.

Jackson noted that although he was able to learn its location, he "omitted to see Hitler's birthplace." I've often wondered what Hitler meant to him. Unlike many others in his generation of Americans, Jackson was never ignorant of the rise of fascism: he observed it firsthand in Munich as early as 1932, when he attended a Nazi rally; he caught a glimpse of Hitler while traveling in southern Bavaria; he wrote about fascism directly and through fictional characters in the 1930s. In 1938, the Anschluss upended the lives of people he knew. Serving in the army during World War II, he was no longer an observer but a man of action who worked to defeat Hitler's Germany. In the 1950s, however, and especially when he was in Braunau, Jackson seemed to treat Hitler and Austria's past lightly. For example, after describing his day of touring in Braunau, his next journal entry recounted humorous episodes garnered from newspapers. Trying to understand a turn that to me seems incomprehensible, my only thought is, given his long associations with Austria, Jackson chose not to let Hitler's ghost spoil his pleasure.

Driving from Branau to Eferding and Linz, he wrote a remarkable statement that probed the language of growth as applied to human settlements. "I think much of the whole problem of appropriateness in architecture—the relationship between building & setting—stems from a misuse or misunderstanding of the concept of growth. A town does not grow; it never is part of its environment until it is part of its history: every house was once new and disturbing in the natural picture, and every[ ]one was built in violence—in the destruction of the natural site and natural materials." Europeans thought of older villages and towns as part of the "setting," when "actually the setting was destroyed when the first house was built."

Jackson was not proposing acceptance of all new buildings, but rather considering appropriate justifications for protest. As he put it, "there are unsuitable functions and sizes" in cityscapes, but the grounds for opposition should be "hygienic & economic . . . and of course concern for zoning and density. . . . What I mean to say is, we cannot speak of a town growing in an organic sense unless we have some notion of its final form, and we have no such notion. Each change, each addition represents a violent alteration, and only when it has finally stopped changing can we begin to talk of a control of growth."

He also tried to understand what made certain landscapes, such as the one then before his eyes, appeal to him. Not willing to accept simply that he liked what he saw, he decided a landscape's attraction was based significantly on association, in this case the way houses and their surrounds suggest an identity with their human inhabitants. "A large part of the appeal of the countryside lay in the traditional bourgeois qualities of the settlements." Because he shared with others like himself a sense that peasants and farmers were "sturdy yeomanry, the basis of our present society . . . the more or less traditional village features . . . [implied] a local autonomy—These things are instinctively congenial: we love them because they appear to justify our present world & its values." For Jackson, they created the illusion (or possibly demonstrated the reality) that he "was among like thinking, like feeling, like working, acting people. Certainly when this scattered settlement pattern vanished my interest & affection for the countryside diminished at once." I find this passage remarkable. All I might simply accept, looking out a car window, Jackson questioned and attempted to answer.

Driving on to Freistadt, he continued to take delight in its old town "surrounded by a wall and a moat, a jumble of narrow streets in the midst of which was an enormous square" with fountain and statue. Surrounding the square were colored houses and an onion-shaped tower. "The effect was the usual happy one of age, brightness, self respect and rural charm. . . . The atmosphere was that of backwoods New England. There never were such enchanting little valleys with streams rushing down out of the pine trees into green meadows, the roading [*sic*] crossing to hide among the trees then reaching out far above among more meadows."

Stopping at Schloss Rosenau, a castle in the forest district in the northwest of Lower Austria that had seen better times, he conversed with its custodian, who asked Jackson to give publicity to the surrounding region: "'Please make a little propaganda for the Waldviertel,' he begged." Jackson said that he would, "but the Waldviertel was too simple for tourists—Austrian or foreign—no hotels, no food: he said he knew: they ate no vegetables, only cabbage."

Jackson likely had a wry smile on his face as he ended his account of traveling in Austria with this unsentimental flourish.

USA and the Yucatan, 1957

In January and February 1957, Jackson took a long trip with his mother through the American South, with a detour to the Yucatan.[17] This journal allows us to experience a different Jackson, confident and professional. One year after his epiphany in Zurich, he is a man with standing and a calling, presenting himself to strangers as the editor of a serious magazine. He visits universities and interviews scholars. He analyzes the southern landscape and discusses and charts its towns. After work, there is play, and he allows himself to take time off to enjoy a Mexican resort. On resuming his road trip through the South, he continues his study of towns and devises new, unique methods of gaining information.

Because he related conversations and wrote down curious observations, this travel journal allows access to many facets of Jackson's personality and growing sense of his work. This record has four distinct parts: a professional call; a car trip from Connecticut to New Orleans; time in the Yucatan; and a car trip to return his mother to her home and begin his own way back to New Mexico.

PROFESSIONAL CALL

Before setting off on the first leg of actual travels, Jackson assumed his new professional persona in a visit to Henry Wallace in South Salem, New York. It was New Year's Day, and Jackson drove to South Salem from his mother's home in suburban Connecticut. Wallace—once a controversial vice president under Franklin Roosevelt and then a presidential candidate of the Progressive Party in 1948—was, at the time of Jackson's visit, living quietly on his working farm.

It was not Wallace's political career that brought Jackson to his doorstep, but rather his work as a statistician, businessman, writer, and Iowa newspaper man. After assessing Wallace's property and fine house, Jackson took the measure of the man: "He met me when I rang, commented on my promptness and on my leather coat. He was sniffing (sinus trouble) a large grey haired man, heavy tan, small embarrassed eyes—bursting out of his clothes like a farmer on Sunday."

Jackson had likely been encouraged to make this visit by Edgar Anderson, one of *Landscape* magazine's first and most significant contributors. Leading Jackson into his study, Wallace got down to business right away by relating that, when he had asked Anderson "what he did with his free time, he said he liked writing for a thing called landscape." Jackson responded that Anderson had been "very helpful." Wallace then asked, "Did I want names of helpers? I told him I wanted people with broad interests like Anderson. . . . 'The[re]'re not many like Edgar' he said."

Jackson tried to get Wallace to write an article for *Landscape,* but got only his agreement to do a book review. In suggesting others Jackson might seek out, Wallace read to him a list of names of geneticists and botanists from a catalog of the American Philosophical Society. When Wallace went upstairs to get more information, Jackson examined the catalog, "wishing I had it." Wallace came downstairs loaded with rare books to show and reprints of articles he had written that he gave Jackson permission to republish.[18]

Jackson reported that Wallace said "he had never felt entirely at home in Iowa because as a child he had read Eastern children's books with references to plants & animals he never saw out west; so when he came East he felt he was returning to where he belonged." The two men discussed Anderson's statements in a *Landscape* piece, particularly one about the causes of isolation among farmers. Talk turned to maps, and then Wallace showed Jackson some slides. "Wallace never looked me in the eye wil[l]ingly," Jackson observed, "and when I looked at him, he always changed the subject. His helpfulness & friendliness was all in deeds not words or gestures. . . . In[ ]spite of his countrified appearance he has the approach & authority of a scholar, and some of his judgments were ueqviral [unequivocal?]."

THE DRIVE SOUTH

On the first leg of the journey south, Jackson's writings offer documentation of his growing ambitions for *Landscape* and sense of calling. He was seeking new contacts and potential contributors. In addition—and in contrast with his 1955 car trip through the region—Jackson was on a serious mission to see firsthand and attempt to understand the landscape of the American South. On January 4, 1957, he began the trip with his mother. After a stopover allowing her to visit briefly with one of her friends, the two began the journey to New Orleans. Although his mother was in the car, for much of this trip she doesn't figure in Jackson's account, giving the general impression that he was traveling solo.[19]

As he reached Pennsylvania, Jackson began serious writing in the journal with a dense description of the various strands of settlement on the land: "Rolling country, trees on hilltops after King of Prussia—merely a name on the turnpike it abruptly becomes suburban road—fine old stone farm houses covered with ivy with white fenced paddocks, stables, meadows, avenues of trees." Driving through a valley, he found that the view opened up to farming country. As the road "wandered on narrow winding rows between unfenced fields. Barns, houses all white. a springlike quiet and haze to Eagle where there was an old fashioned inn. Many villages here are named for old inns: White Horse, Blue Ball, King of Prussia."

Characteristically, Jackson tried over many pages to write down everything he noticed: the colors of the soil, housing types, and how well all was being cared for. He noticed small details, such as bells on porches to call in field workers. Relics from the past interested him, as did contemporary changes. After viewing what today might be called strip malls south of Washington, D.C., he wrote, "The fate of the shopping center—to remain physically intact & handsome, but to have cheaper & cheaper stores—and even empty ones." Wondering where the rust-red soil had begun, he described seeing from the road "the bottom 2 feet of white painted houses . . . splashed red everywhere." Then in Virginia: "Bull Run & Manassas—divided highway. Historic events gives dignity to the landscape—not empty but emptied."

Reaching Culpeper, Virginia, Jackson drew a diagrammatic map, somewhat like those of the T towns of his trip through Colorado and Kansas in 1954. Beyond the enigmatic word "pop," it contained no written information, but in the journal he noted, "I drew a sketch map: the civic center was merely a group of buildings on a side street—no square or common or monument that I could see. . . . In the country—progressively poorer. game cocks and hens ran across the road. A bench on the sagging front porch; shacks instead of barns; snake fences. Negroes emerging from sideroads leading into the woods; dressed up to hitchhike into town."

Jackson's second such map was of Charlottesville, where he and his mother stayed overnight. It offered some documentation: "better houses on heights"; "Negroes & factories in hollows." It was at this point that Jackson began to write of those he respectfully called "Negroes" (a word he used forty-seven times in this journal), sometimes called "colored" (seven uses) and—disrespectfully—"Coons" (five uses). Curious about how African Americans lived, he seemed to find their world strange, perhaps even exotic. He discussed their poverty and physical isolation in the segregated cities and towns of the South. On the one hand, he viewed them sympathetically; on the other, he remained deeply prejudiced. Knowing that, during the last decade of his life, Jackson frequently claimed he himself had "Negro blood," his steadily growing fascination during this 1957 trip through the South may hold special significance.[20]

Jackson's chronicle of Charlottesville gives some sense of how he filled his time when he was not driving. At dinner in his hotel, he allowed his mother's presence to come into his journal for the first time. "In Chippendale dining room (1926 with pink lamps on tables) negro head waiter in brown suit and spectacles kept hitching up his pants and paying no attention to public. As mother said[,] we know the South is sloppy but we don[']t know the form its slopp[i]ness takes." Afterward, the two watched television in a public room for a time. "TV is not yet the magic of movies," Jackson observed. "The setting is too domestic or everyday[,] The screen too small, the programs too short or unreal to create another world; so people come & go, change programs talk." Jackson then took himself alone to a "Square & Round Dance" at the National Guard Armory, where he danced the "Paul Jones" with a "Pretty blond." He looked in at a roller skating rink in a nearby recreation building and noticed that, as with the dance at the armory, there were no African Americans in attendance. Jackson seemed to be trying out new sides of himself. This did not lessen his investigative energies, however. The next day he drove alone around Charlottesville, stopping to walk through the university. Curiously, his primary focus there seemed to be the bonding of the bricks in the older buildings,

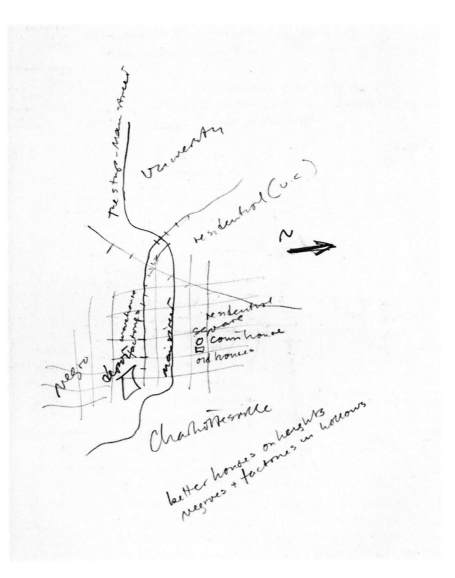

Figure 27. J. B. Jackson, travel journal, Charlottesville sketch map, 1957

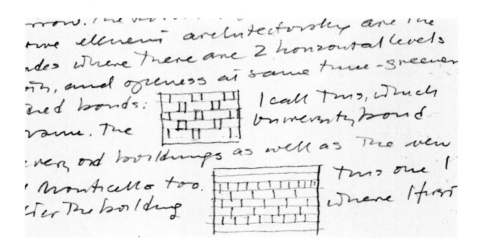

Figure 28. J. B. Jackson, travel journal, University of Virginia, brick detail, 1957

which he discussed at some length. He followed his visit to the university with a drive, "along upper Main street & into negro section."

By the time Jackson got to Chapel Hill, North Carolina, he was focused on understanding the American small town, which he defined as having a population under fifty thousand. On arrival, he went straight to the University of North Carolina. Having only Jackson's extant journals to work with, I can't be certain, but his effort to make contacts without prior introductions or appointments seems to have been new, for he gave himself these directions in this journal: "The procedure is as follows: go to information office in administration, get map of campus & directory of professors—Then set out for Geography or Planning or Architecture or whatever." (Months later, when Jackson made a comparable excursion to Berkeley, it became a visit that led to changes both in his magazine and in his professional life.[21])

Prompted by the suggestion of Gerald W. Breese, a sociologist then the director of Princeton's Bureau of Urban Research, Jackson first went to see Gordon Blackwell, head of UNC's Institute for Research in Social Science. Jackson was casually dismissive of the group's project: "They are analyzing very slowly a crescent of towns between Winston Salem & Charlotte, which are becoming industrialized, but are evidently going about it so deliberately that I don't see how their information can ever be up to date." He learned that his subject had not been examined—or rather, that "nothing has been written on the small town as such—merely on specific small towns and usually with the idea of plan[n]ing changes."

Blackwell sent Jackson to Stuart Chapin, who "though more talkative still had nothing to offer—except the surveys the student had made of several small towns in the state—again with plan[n]ing in mind." Jackson moved on to Huntington Hobbs, "old fashioned, slow spoken and somehow isolated by his prosaic interests in North Carolina & its economy—said he dealt only with rural sociology. . . . From him I got little except a sense that he & his interest & knowledge had little in common with the dynamic Eastern inspired social study going on downstairs." Meeting a young teacher of geography who worked on Latin America, Jackson asked him to review books in his specialty. John Albert Parker, a professor of city planning, gave Jackson names of potentially interested persons and "asked a great many questions about Landscape [magazine]. He admitted that as far as he knew little had been done on the small American town, and agreed with me that interdisciplinary cooperation was often lacking." He introduced Jackson to a student whose dissertation was on North Carolina small towns. "We agreed that I could see his thesis when it was done."

Jackson found two conversations particularly productive. Finding Parker "friendly & helpful and enthusiastic about Landscape when he understood what I was trying to do," Jackson discussed small towns with him. In Jackson's final campus visit, he met S. T. Emory in the geography department, "a very intelligent and attractive southern gentleman who at once understood what I wanted, and talked at great length about the changing morphology of the American town. His conversation and his point of view was the most congenial of them all, for he was less concerned with change & improvement and more with trying to understand what existed." At the end of his report, as Jackson summarized his potential new contributors to *Landscape,* setting down their names and topics, he was now clearly a professional editor.

The drive to the Myrtle Beach on the South Carolina shore proved to Jackson once again that "you see little or nothing of the country travelling on the new Federal highways which cut through hills and swamps and avoid the old winding traces where the farms and villages are." The stay in Myrtle Beach, off season, was likely a concession to his mother, as were perhaps many other features of the trip mentioned in this journal. Uncharacteristic of his solo car travels were meals in hotel restaurants (frequently described as versions of "dreadful"), followed by television in the lobby.

So was the tour of Charleston, South Carolina, taken in a horse-drawn victoria, during which he was forced to listen to the spiel of its Viennese driver. He characterized a typical "old historic house" that had become "a Tea room by Southern ladies with antiques and a legend of Pirates or Revolutionary events or Colonial high living on the menu, and local specialties—shrimp pie in Charleston." Taking a swipe at Santa Fe's Fonda Bar, Jackson included it with the "Rampart room (restaurant) in Charleston . . . with prints[,] pictures, locally inspired drinks—either that or exoticism of the rankest sort—other directedness with a vengeance." Each such room was "so dark you can hardly see the furniture." Such places had "a purple or red or blue light, organ music . . . and small weak expensive drinks."

In Savannah, he found and listed "motel signs, occasional tourist trap souvenir place with Florida pennants, alligator bags[,] pralines (pronounced 'Pray lines')." After exploring Savannah, at least partly on foot, Jackson inserted a sketch map in his journal and wrote in an almost stream-of-consciousness fashion: "Over a high narrow bridge into Savannah—paper mill spewing out yellow smoke smelling of rotting cabbage[,] Negro slums at foot of bridge & housing development—monotonous but not bad." At the "spacious old fashioned hotel" where he and his mother stayed, there were "mobs of colored porters & doormen eager for tips everywhere." With a population of about 120,000, he judged Savannah to be "not very prosperous . . . hotel on edge of business district & near old residential area—now going down hill."

Savannah was aging in its own unique way, he noted. "Old houses are not made over & restored because there isn[']t enough money or interest; not torn down because city is growing elsewhere: solid 4 story brick victorian residents [residences], their faces buried in tulip & sycamores & live oak & magnolia trees along the edge of the street, high stoops, become doctors' offices (There's a medical school nearby) institutions, apartment houses, semi slum boarding houses." Excepting the "vile" alleys containing stables, "the city is pretty clean though shabby. Fine wrought & cast iron, good heavy regency & Victorian Gothic."

Observing the city's many churches and historical markers, he wrote of their touting such antiquities as "American's 'First novelist' 'Oldest church' (Presbyterian)." The parks, however "ill kept," were of "Regency design . . . with fine trees & shrubbery and monument in middle." Jackson explored the end of the historic area that gave way to the "slum business area (with gaudy main street) negro area and 1880 middle class free standing houses. . . . [and, further along] a series of unpaved blind alleys with unpainted 1[-]story frame houses." It reminded him of the broad streets of "Naples or Mexico—crowded with small stores with big signs—movie houses, bars audible a block away." He noticed the African American community's local weekly paper, the *Tribune* and picked it up, discovering it to be "full of society news and adds [ads] for dy[e]ing & straightening hair & success stories." Seeming to find Savannah's "Negroes . . . sullen & ill mannered," he sought an explanation at a candy store, from "a Southern Jewess named Krauss . . . [who] said they had better houses & better jobs, hard to get domestics; often showed resentment of whites in buses which are not segregated. No professional negroes yet. They are called Mr or Mrs now." Following his quotes from Ms. Krauss, he noted, "many Jew firms, and evidently Greek orthodox too: Bishop of Cyprus is in town."

Jackson went to the movies in Savannah with his mother and saw two recently released films: *Anastasia* and *Giant*. The audience's reaction to "remarks on treatment of Mexicans [in *Giant* were] greeted with knowing laughter." Observing the Saturday afternoon crowd on the main street, Jackson wrote, "Teenagers in black slacks, sport shirts, girls in tights & red socks, negresses likewise. Motorcyclists with studs on soles of boots & white visored caps, coons making their tires scream." Although Jackson labeled Savannah "a dull city," he admitted that "the old part has great charm," adding, "I'd like to know someone here."

After Savannah, Jackson began to pay more attention to Jews. Arriving in Athens, Georgia, he observed in the hotel a "Jewish group, somehow connected with synagogue, holding banquet in ballroom—not like NY Jews—dignified, much jewelry and fur & makeup & coiffure. but not fashionable dress." Much later—during the third phase of the trip, when he was in Natchez—he noticed the "Jew Names" on its small stores. The reverse side of the journal, where he tried to write more systematically about the characteristics of "Small Towns," contains this observation: "New & remodeled stores destroy old unity by flashy facades hiding upper story—more than do signs or lights—no local feeling—merely the appeal of the bizarre & exotic—Foreign names—Jewish, Italian, Syrian—among doctors, merchants (clothing & fashions) French & English among hardware, banks etc." It is significant that Jackson saw Jews—some of whom had been in North America as long as the Brinckerhoffs, of whose name he was immensely proud—as carrying "foreign" names.

As he continued his drive through Georgia, Jackson seemed to become increasingly curious about African Americans and sought to learn more about their conditions and life in the South. After stopping for lunch in Wrightsville, he wrote, "Houses with much jigsaw work from here on. Negro cottages: The porch room probably for storage: I stopped at one & talked to children—Willy, and his brother Willy B. in rags stood on porch. no father, mother at work in nearby farm." Jackson spoke to an African American porter at his hotel, who told him "race conditions worse in small towns than in cities where negroes could keep to themselves. Said teaching level was higher among negroes because college graduates had no other place to find work." Once again, Jackson was able to talk to strangers, here across the color line.

At the University of Georgia in Athens, Jackson paid calls, reporting without comment on those he visited. He drove to Atlanta and visited Georgia Tech, where he got a few names from a faculty member who offered "information like a recorded voice on the Telephone—not interested in me, but in doing a service—or in showing his knowledge."

Such a visit and a rude awakening at 4 AM likely by a manager's "voice telling me my door wasn't locked" cast a pall, and Jackson took a "miserable exit of Atlanta." He drove to Newman, a small town roughly forty miles away, stopping for lunch. Here he made two small sketches devoted to one of his enduring fascinations, the courthouse square. "Courthouse in square—post 1830 plan. Squares here are actually a block taken out of the middle: not the way they sometimes are in Texas—the center of a design."

Once across Georgia's western border, Jackson perked up, seeing Alabama as "almost at once prettier than Georgia." He stopped to visit Tuskegee Institute and went to the Carver Museum, where a "Negro freshman in ROTC uniform" showed him around. Boredom was setting in, however. After stopping overnight in Troy, Jackson wrote, "Hotel small, quiet, old & depressing; a few drummers. The usual gathering in the semi darkness to watch television—like a clan[d]estine sect." He described the small coffee shop as "miserable," and his room as having "things broken & missing & rusty." That night he and his mother went to see the movie *Baby Doll,* where he observed "colored public in balcony." He noted they also saw "a degenerate animated cartoon—fairy & vulgar voices & gestures & attitudes."[22]

After ten days of driving through the South, Jackson attempted to pin down some of the region's distinctive characteristics.[23] He drew up a list of eight categories: FOOD, DRINK, ACCENT, CLIMATE, SOUTHERN STYLE, NEGROES, DEFICIENCIES, AND VIRTUES. Many of the elements within the categories summarized his earlier observations, but several held new information or strengthened impressions.

Here animus rather than affection for the South came through. Under "DRINK" he wrote of the ubiquitous presence of Coca Cola advertising: "Coca cola every where—even on official signs over post offices & on courthouse lawns." Under

"ACCENT," came his difficulties in communication. He recorded that one sixteen-year-old fellow seemed at first to be "subnormal—without a palate perhaps. often couldn[']t understand negroes."

As elsewhere along the route, Jackson displayed a fascination with seeing where African Americans lived and how they dressed and acted. Under the rubric "NEGROES," he repeated what he had often been told by southern whites: "We get along fine: we leave each other alone." He continued with the observation, hardly unusual during this time of early desegregation, "Many Southerners hate negroes—perhaps have worked near them." He quoted a University of Georgia professor, who told him he discovered when he sent his (white) students out to take surveys that "'negroes don[']t exist to these young people: they never take them into account.'" At one hotel, he saw only whites working there, "no negro help at all." The local papers, he found, were "full of integration news. a few editorials abusing negro leaders."

When Jackson turned to "DEFICIENCIES" he had a great deal to say: "poor & sloppy villages & houses, cows grazing on right of way, inadequate zoning." He included slums and deficient service in hotels and restaurants. He remarked upon southerners' "eagerness for business—factories etc." Rather than viewing this aspect favorably, he put it down to "materialism without thought of consequences." He also complained that there was "too much Confederacy. Jefferson Davis' pew in church draped with Confederate flag, Confederate flag flying on hotel in Mobile, such & such a high school 'best in Confederacy.'"

"VIRTUES" allowed a return of some of his positive feelings. In this telling list, he included winter weather, varied landscapes, detailed historical markers, and low prices. He remarked on the politeness and friendliness he'd encountered among whites, and the lack of rush. To this he added—backhandedly—"Willingness to admit ignorance or helplessness. . . . Simplicity & indifference to 'smartness.'"

At this point in his journey, Jackson paused in his efforts to understand the South for a trip of a different nature, a luxury excursion to Mexico.

THE YUCATAN

New Orleans served as the point of departure for the one-week trip to the Yucatan Jackson took with his mother. The flight to Mexico offered him a great feeling of release: "contact with larger nature—The only contact mobile man can enjoy—weather, sky, sea, wide impersonal landscape—and unknown forces: the old intimacy is dead, but the new one can & will come. I felt better to be away from the human landscape."

The two arrived in Merida at four in the afternoon and were driven eighty miles to a resort hotel at Chichén Itzá. En route Jackson set down the type of impressions found in his journals of travel in Europe. He attempted here in a rush of words to capture everything he could see, hear, and smell. "Shoeshine boys slapping their boxes, a bell ringing in the university 10 minutes before the hour. Traffic policemen whistling all the time. . . . Smell of oranges being peeled by rotary machine leaving long yellow strings of peel: frying bread & candy: leather in sad[d]ler's shops." He noted trees, church towers, signs, giving brief details, such as "colored houses, wild facades, shabby exuberant gardens." As ever, he was interested in local people, observing, "faces all familiar in their strangeness. as if you had seen each one before & had wondered at its peculiarities. few coarse features—Taxi driver (Jewish-Spanish) said perhaps 10% Spanish blood; identified different stock in passersby."

Jackson was now forty-seven, traveling not—as in 1937—with two male companions and roughing it, but with his mother on a luxury trip, chauffeured to and guided around several primary Mayan sites. Jackson in 1957 seemed to enjoy staying at the resort hotel, going on excursions with Alice, and meeting other travelers. He was no less observant and curious, however. In the midst of the manicured hotel garden, for example, he noted, "All neat & beautiful. Then a glimpse of furious ant activity swarming over a piece of wood—large black ants in a writhing heap." And he retained pleasure in social contact with locals: "Indian-Mayas in white come plodding through ruins on way to village. One with family told me the name of the priest in his village, & where he was going—departing he said 'Felicitaciones, señor.'"

During this visit, Jackson had little chance to see life outside tourist spots, but when he did, he tried to capture what he saw. At a fiesta in the town of Valladolid, he found "magic lighting on houses, faces, amusement stands, slow crowds of men & women in white, blue looking until they come within aura of booths." Fascinated by the activity around him, he seemed particularly to enjoy viewing the Vaqueria, a dance that gathered a "long line of girls—60 or 70 . . . all in costume, all sober, eyes downcast, not talking[,] hair ribbons, good filigree jewelry, embroidered [']junpil' or gown." As the musicians began to play, a "Master of ceremonies led 4 men at a time to face 4 girls. Then they danced until he brought 4 more [men]." The dancers "never touched. . . . No smiles."

Because visits to Yucatan sites included guided excursions with others, Jackson had a chance to observe and reflect on tourist ways: "Tourists conversation usually tourist maintenance—price & quality of hotels, itineraries, food." He watched as others around him took pictures of themselves, listened as they tested an echo, and sang. A friendly couple told him that they "had travelled everywhere." Quoting, "I like to see the simple people & get off the beaten path, but like luxury too: only the best of food," Jackson concluded, "All demand best when it is available: all think of themselves as tourists, loyal to tourist interests."

Jackson also pondered the great Mayan ruins of Chichén Itzá, as if seeing them for the first time.[24] Of one structure, he asked, "What use did it serve? What artistic laws did it obey? What do its ornaments mean?" More generally, he wondered, "Why were they abandoned?" He assessed their visual power: "We gaze at geometrical forms in 3 dimensions and respond as to an incomprehensible piece of sculpture. They *seem* to be oriented to have more facade than interior or side treatment: a horizontality. Little or no emphasis on the various axes or bays. . . . They have a classic muteness & simplicity."

RETURN JOURNEY

When the week in the Yucatan ended, Jackson and his mother returned by air to New Orleans. He had been decidedly uncurious about the city before leaving for Mexico, writing only that it was "another big city, strangling its original character[,] its center in traffic. Trying to keep it alive by making it tourist bait." Although he noticed the nineteenth-century houses and found the fashionable St. Charles Street area "very attractive," he judged the city "synthetic, ugly, confused, out of control." Thus, the two travelers were quickly back on the road, now heading north.

At this point Jackson split his travel journal into two parts. He continued his narrative of his trip in the usual way, from the front of the notebook to the back; but he also began to write, from the back to the front, in an effort to set down and analyze the characteristics of small towns. This attempt to look, research, and record in a more systematic way suggests that, after a week's vacation, Jackson was eager to get back to work.

The most interesting elements on the reverse sides came under the heading "Sources." These reveal something of Jackson's developing method. He listed first the most accessible and obvious source, the yellow pages of local phone books. He wrote, "*Classified directory*—New Iberia shows pages of 'oil'—machinery, drillers, companies etc. But only 1 'salt' a big business here, & 1 sauce—the relish comes from here—and little sugar." Then, an aside to himself: "Check ratio of Drs, Beauticians, restaurants, churches."

He abided by this in three instances:

Greenville   72 filling stations
               36 beauty parlors
               40 churches
N. Iberia   18 beauty parlors
               16 churches
Chattanooga—132 beauty parlors
               162 churches

Jackson next turned to another common resource, local street maps, and posed to himself a series of questions:

Questions with map—where do negroes (or other minority groups) live
Which is the most prosperous residential quarter?

Where is town growing?
Where is idle time spent—in town & for longer periods?
Where is professional area?
" " " governmental area?
Where is parking problem acute?
Where is vice?
Is there a local verschönerung herem? [perhaps he meant a beautifying district, such as an historic one]

What is zoning doing?
Roughly E, W, S, N—characteristics?
Industries
Where do most people go to work?
(direction & distance more than industry)
Chamber of Commerce.

Traveling from New Orleans to Baton Rouge, Jackson didn't choose the shortest distance between them, but detoured to observe a number of towns—New Iberia, St. Martinville, Lafayette, and Opelousas, the area in Louisiana often called Cajun country. In a stream-of-consciousness mode, he produced a long riff on what he heard and saw in an unnamed town, a reminder that he was once a writer of fiction: "Early early morning sound of sparrows, newspapers in bundles outside of drugs. Town is silent by 10 PM. houses on main street are lighted pale pink, pale green from neon lights. Store display windows dark. Young boys in big cars tearing around making tires squeak, turning around in silent filling station drive ways. Sounds come from Pool & Domino parlor. Throngs & crash of slot machines, billiard balls knocking against each other—a cool sound like white ivory. A few voices exclaiming[,] jingle of coins & bells in slot machines. In empty bars 2 men sit looking out open door into street, talking to bartender. Elderly woman in movie ticket window talking to friend." Abandoning sound for sight, he watched customers at a magazine stand, reading but not buying; those wandering into the hotel lobby to view television; men on the steps of city hall just sitting. All this told him he was in a town "abandoned by architects or civic planners; left to cocktail lounge or coffee shop or Bar."

Combining the two sides of the journal gives what Jackson noticed: the bayou, the shrimp restaurants, the use of French by African Americans as well as whites, trailer encampments, special products sold, and industries, with "oil most distinctive and active element in landscape." At one point he stopped to sketch.

In Baton Rouge, Jackson went to visit Fred Kniffen, a well-known Louisiana State University geographer, but made no comment about him in the journal.[25] From his hotel he heard "the yells of young boys & men in the night streets, their gaffows [guffaws]." He described these as "the shrillest an[i]mal sounds ever produced—man the an[i]mal with the most preening & loudest voice."

On February 2, he drove from Baton Rouge to Natchez, Mississippi, a small town that had once, before the Civil War, exemplified southern grandeur. He visited one of the plantation houses, proclaiming it "most beautiful," and also admired its magnolia trees, azaleas, holly, iron fences, and ornate white columns. Nevertheless, most of his writing in Natchez dealt with the town's poverty, and he characterized it as "a dingy, smelly (pulp) damp. unprosperous town."

Jackson was training himself to be an even closer observer. He set forth "rules of slum streets—walk them, not ride through them to realize how all encompassing slum area is, even if only 6 square blocks." On an early morning, he found "chickens crowing in slum backyards. dogs & cats prowling. Shanties painted white on facade only. Few signs of care for gardens; heaps of litter on empty lots & in ravines[,] no sidewalks outside of city center[;] at 8 children in fresh clothes holding new unsharpened pencils on way to school." As elsewhere in the South, he commented on the "usual wild noisy driving around corners," the "retail street that caters to Negroes," and "Jew Names." He saw "slums—black & white all around town" and noticed a "vile smell everywhere."

Jackson's report reveals prejudices normally covered by an understanding of polite speech. The importance of Jewish merchants in southern towns became "Jew Names." On the approach to Natchez via Woodville, he saw "coons sitting outside stores—often bus depots, loitering on street corners." Jackson's use here of this derogatory term for African Americans as well as his reference to "Jew Names" reveals that he was still in bigotry's clutches.

Jackson continued north to Greenville, Mississippi, and, after visiting the Chamber of Commerce, spoke with Hodding Carter. Greenville's courageous newspaper editor was known as a fighter against intolerance of all kinds, including his town's recently formed branch of the White Citizens' Council. It is curious that, as with Kniffen, Jackson did not comment substantively on his meeting with Carter, but only on their conversation about the controversial movie *Baby Doll*, largely filmed in or near Greenville. Since Jackson and his mother had seen it, they, like others, wanted to know if it was accurate in its portrayal of Mississippi life. Carter said that it was not.[26]

From Greenville, Jackson drove to Memphis, his one reported "culture" stop on this leg of the trip. He visited the Brooks Museum, where he admired some of the paintings, and afterward went to lunch at "a vast new shopping center," Poplar Plaza. Driving on, he caught a glimpse of Savannah, Tennessee, and the Tennessee river "in flood." In Chattanooga, faithfully consulting one of his established "sources," he counted the number of beauty parlors and churches listed in the phone book.

After a drive on the following day to Asheville, North Carolina, Jackson wrote in a different and more florid prose: "left, again in rain, and at once ascended in clouds through mountains alongside artificial lake & river feeding into it, clouds woven among pine trees like Chinese water color of water & mountain. river raced down steplike red rocks in narrow wooded valley." As he continued in this vein, I decided he must be using this notebook to try out a range of voices. This particular effort ended with a jolt, as Jackson described coming into Asheville: "a violently ugly, dejected, frantic place, a mass of motels & filling stations & slums around a city of 53,000 on several hills in the midst of beautiful sub alpine scenery."

The next day, he went to the Chamber of Commerce in Asheville and talked to "a Mr Koontz, cigar stub in his mouth," to learn a string of negatives. Asheville, said Mr. Koontz, was a convention city with a labor surplus; the hills of the town should have been leveled; its tourist trade only benefited a small number. Jackson also learned that the "Negro section [was] near tracks on S side of town." After this chat, he and his mother took a tour of Biltmore. Here Jackson was uncritical, judging the Vanderbilt estate to have "all the virtues & none of the faults of wealth on display." The tour must have been short, however, for they drove to Marion for lunch in its "small clean old fashioned hotel" and had "a semi decent meal of homecooked food."

Jackson, who enjoyed conversing with strangers and frequently tried to capture something of the sounds of their language, described the entertainment during lunch—"a woman in a dreadful lightbrown felt wig played the piano haltingly." He reported that the pianist told him, "Since I rescued my family from a burning house & lost all my hair . . . and am waiting for it to grow back, and since I tripped on a rollarskate [roller skate] and broke all my front teeth I didn[']t want to [get] teeth yet while; and people get tired of music interrupted by announcements & com[m]ercials."

Jackson returned to New Canaan and may have lingered there with his mother for a while. Whatever the reason, he stopped writing in his journal for almost two weeks. February 23 found him in Herkimer, New York, and from this point on many of his comments seem perfunctory. One observation stands out, however. After driving along a hilly road through upstate New York, he stated, "Tourists can never see & realize the injustices done by dividing fields in highway construction, or destruction of houses & villages." It was similar to judging "the injustices of a city & its makeup by looking at it"—coincidentally, something he himself had been doing for the past many weeks. Such judgments were either "faulty (without a moral factor) or . . . purely esthetic—in which case the less we know the better." Was Jackson scolding himself?

In any case, he was now back in professional mode, working for his magazine and making contacts. He set down his plan for a forthcoming farm issue of *Landscape* in which he planned to treat "ironically" a statement that he apparently disliked, made by the assistant secretary of agriculture. Driving on to Clinton, New York, he paid a visit to the Hamilton College librarian, whom he found "very kind & welcoming, but all somehow depressing—familiar with no mystery." From there he went to Syracuse to visit a professor of geography at Syracuse University who specialized in China. In a kind of shorthand, Jackson described him as "whitehaired, gentle, shrewd. Kierkegaard, Christian Century, Sartre on the table." Jackson continued regarding their conversation, which focused on "his writing about Turkey: he is particularly eager to have his Kodac[h]romes published—that is the appeal."

Jackson approved of what he saw between Syracuse and Rochester, especially "Palmyra in splendid rolling country: a fine broad street bordered by uniform bondings—at one end 4 church towers (on 4 corners) at the other a classical facade: a more satisfactory main street difficult to find." He was pleased by the "extraordinary topographical variety within short range in New York State." In Rochester, after visiting with friends, he observed "elms everywhere—little undergrowth: houses high on foundations & wineglass elms." With the comment that "elm country" consisted of "Western NY State, Ontario, Michigan. Strangely, few or comparatively few S & W of Michigan," Jackson ended the journal. It is likely Jackson then continued on to New Mexico, a route driven quickly and one perhaps too familiar to offer discoveries for his journal.

Earlier, while still in New York State, he wrote an entry that captures something of his mischievousness. He had gone to a drugstore for lunch and had this exchange with the woman behind the counter: "'Can I have a toasted peanut butter sandwich?' 'No!' 'What do you mean, no? No sandwiches? no peanut butter, or no toast?' 'I'll go find out.' She came back to say it was OK."

Europe, 1958

In January 1958, Jackson began a lengthy trip overseas that lasted until early March.[27] It was a rich and complicated journey. He traveled alone to Munich and through Eastern Europe to Turkey. From there he took a plane to Greece and Crete, where he was joined by his mother. The two of them later flew to Vienna for an extended stay.

Along the way Jackson wrote in two travel journals. I found transcribing these difficult, especially one, a European notebook with closely spaced horizontal and vertical lines. Jackson wrote in a small hand on every horizontal line, allowing almost no margins. A single page could contain as many as 514 words. As I struggled through the transcription, I found I learned much from it and its companion journal—so much so that this essay is broken into sections, each covering a leg of Jackson's trip.

MUNICH

Jackson's first stop was Munich. At the time of his arrival, the city was still celebrating the December birth of its millionth citizen, heralded as a sign of its recovery from World War II. He knew Munich well, and that enabled him to reflect on what remained from before the war and changes in the city since his last visit. His initial impression was of its scars. Munich had been severely damaged in the war, and despite much rebuilding, its wounds were still visible both in buildings and in the loss of trees. Among the new structures he discovered "so many holes in every skyline still, hidden or half hidden behind the new plaster facades: the street surfaces patched & repatched from bomb[ ]splinters like a Mexican innertube—puddles & mud in them all."

Jackson found Munich's many new buildings striking. "Whenever a new building has gone up" he wrote, "they are flat of façade, large of window, delicately cheerful in color and detail: a sort of neo-biedemeier simplicity, an implied criticism of the old . . . style which persisted (with Nazi infusion) until 1940. The new style pretends to say nothing: I am a house, an office building, nothing more—though on either side stands one of the older kind with heavily significant ornament, ponderous reminiscence of Baroque or Italian or Renaissance." With its new buildings, "cheerfully Latin in their clarity and elegance," Munich seemed to be repudiating its past.

Jackson believed a key element of the new architecture's intention was "to say as little as possible, to communicate or suggest no emotion—merely to *be*." He continued, "That is what these contemporary houses strive for: that is what unites 'good' and 'bad' contemporary architecture—a reluctance to communicate[.] Better or worse than the old? I can[']t say: but different: and by contrast—merely by contrast—the old seems dramatized and false."

With fighting the Nazis now more than a decade behind him, many of his memories were tinged with his former curiosity about, perhaps even youthful appreciation of, Nazism during his boyhood. Back then he had seen "wild looking men in lederhosen pass out leaflets with the French cock. Helmet & spurs—violating the Ruhr: a swastika is somewhere in the design. For many years I saved it," meaning one the leaflets. He recalled that earlier Munich was a place of "empty tree shaded streets—a city beautiful & somehow countrified compared to Vienna, but with the same atmosphere of romantic countryside, romantic history come to an abrupt & tragic end."

On his first trip to the city, summer of 1923, he arrived in Munich with his mother, later to be joined by Wayne and Betty. He remembered the décor of the vast single room in the pension where he and Alice Jackson had initially stayed, and his first experience of the city with its "streets sleepy & hot, and the mediterranean South in the air." Here he witnessed the early stirrings of fascism. Talk was of the runaway inflation: Jackson remembered the millions of marks it took to buy a scarf.

Of his second visit, Jackson recalled only an opera; however, his third, in 1933, came with all his postgraduate mixed emotions about Harvard and the privilege of his wealthy former classmates. Meeting with friends, he stayed at a pension near the Englischer Garten and took German lessons. He remembered that at a supper, he had "despised & envied the genteel atmosphere—a prolongation of Harvard niceness and culture." One of his classmates had a Packard automobile and was staying with his family "in style at the Continental. . . . They dressed stylishly in lederhosen, went off for weekends to Garmisch & elsewhere, spoke idiomatic German, knew titled people." Moving into the present, Jackson wrote (with some satisfaction) that the same fellow currently "runs a dairy in the Berkshires, married to a girl called Hogner."

Of Munich in the era of Hitler, Jackson claimed only a vague recollection. In his mind's eye, he saw the city as "an apotheosis of the Heimatsefühl [home feeling]—flags & uniforms & Blut und Boden [Blood and Soil] and neo-classic revival." He did, however, remember the many Munich cultural institutions he visited in the years immediately before World War II, and recalled conversations about such matters as "Bavarian versus Austrian manners, . . . Wagner & Bayreuth."

During the war years, Jackson had, of course, entered Munich not as a tourist but as an officer in army intelligence. Thirteen years later, he thought back to 1945, when he was driving in a jeep through "Ruins, . . . streets bulldozed through headhigh rubble: not dead, but slowly creeping among its ruins like an animal looking for a place to die." He had stayed for the night at the military airport. "Already USA taking over 'Culture,' with Willem van Loon somewhat in charge, and Bill Hale too."

In 1952, he had returned to Munich, staying in "shabby comfort" in a hotel where Hitler was said to have taken tea in the tearoom, and the orchestra continued to play the Führer's favorite music. There was little traffic then, and tractors pulled trailers laden with rubble. The sidewalks were muddy, and he saw "men & women rubbing bricks together to get the mortar off on the dark side streets." New building had not yet begun, merely "makeshift repairs and demolition." Stores, however, were crowded and filled with goods, for "better times of course were well on their way by then." The old Bavarian feeling still remained, leading the city to what Jackson considered its "strenuous" and "irrational attempts to restore" its landmarks. For example, "the neo-Baroque Parliament, neither a handsome nor a conspicuous building, was getting fresh gelt and reconstruction—though houses to live in were woefully short." An acquaintance in the city told him that "they all preferred the homes without plumbing—aesthetically speaking. . . . There were warm public rooms in public buildings for those who had no heat."

Jackson reported no memories of his brief visit in 1956, for he was only there for two days, and he had in his care his mother, still convalescing after her fall and surgery in Zurich.

Returning to the present, Jackson revealed his true reason for coming to Munich: he wanted to buy a BMW motorcycle at the source. On the morning following his arrival, he awoke "sick & feverish," but chose to ignore it and "reluctantly and fearfully, wishing for some sign to prevent my going near the BMW factory . . . took the 8 streetcar out to the works." It was snowing, and the roads were slushy; Jackson walked the half mile from the suburban stop to the factory. But it was a Saturday; the factory was closed. Told to come back on Monday, he returned to the center of town, "greatly relieved, still feverish & sleepy & weak & middle-aged."

Pursuing culture instead, he took himself to the Städtische Galerie and viewed an exhibit of the early paintings of Wassily Kandinsky. Jackson wrote that they were "very Jugendstil in design, subject and color portraits, landscapes, illustrations— the nature studies—the best—a breaking away from geomet[r]ical & aerial perspective—until the final breakaway from objective reality into abstraction." Jackson also viewed a number of paintings by Paul Klee, but found them largely uninteresting. He seems to have been more taken by the section of the museum holding earlier works of art, musing, "Who looks at the dark intensive wil[l]fully meaningful portraits now, I wonder?"

He was distracted by a group of about twenty teenage schoolboys entering the museum, leading him to ponder fashion, generational differences, and the possible reemergence of fascism. Looking at the boys, "bareheaded, wearing duffle coats, tight trousers," he pronounced them a generation with its own "particular style: a V profile: delicate Italian shoes or loafers (the girls too: ballet slippers at times) narrow trousers beginning above the ankle, and then—then the duffle coat with hood." The girls wore immense "ill fitting pullovers with vast knitted turtlenecks" and on top had "great heads of hair." He saw the boys' inspiration as "Jean Cocteau—in his 70s," and for the girls, "Audrey Hepburn & a dozen other young stars." The result was "lightfooted delicate refinement—accented at times by carefully sheathed umbrellas: as if they wished to have little contact with the earth." Noting the relation of dress to young people's choice of motorcycles, he reflected that "along with this delicacy goes the moped—easily mounted, informal and not without elegance." After recalling a newspaper report on their dancing preferences,

Jackson described German youth as "graceful, free, distinctly of its own time . . . totally unlike the heavy footed, booted, earnest, political minded youth I remember: unemployed, aching for guidance & acceptance, ready for inspiration."

He continued in this vein, only to begin to question: "This present generation is so completely in keeping with the modest, unpretentious, delicate, uncommunicative art (and architecture) of the period you might almost suppose they had been designed by one and the same artist: freshness of line & color, but carefully refraining from suggesting any point of view or tradition. . . . But teutonicism must still be somewhere latent. . . . On the news[s]tands there are military magazines & military pulp literature . . . [that] speaks of the old Hitler vocabulary—in its affirmative boisterous aspects—persisting in the new army." On the basis of his observations of Munich youth, Jackson remarked, "No rowdy tough dress suggestive of paramilitary ambitions: but rowdy conduct—yelling across the street, calling out to girls, walking 3 or 4 abreast and much arrogant loitering at busy corners." In concluding, Jackson wondered if commentators' assertions—that young people in Germany lacked prejudice, believed in democracy, held wide cultural interests, and were helpful—offered "an accurate analysis."

In these observations and reflections, we see something of Jackson's perceptive eye, his interest in fashion, and his efforts to link what he sees to larger meanings. Style carried content, and he offered his own take on what the style of the young told about their generation. Yet he ultimately asked himself if his impressions and reading were leading him to make a faulty interpretation.

Although his fever remained, Jackson spent his remaining time in Munich as a culture-seeking tourist—looking at paintings in museums, browsing in bookstores, walking the streets, and visiting important sites. While he seems to have been a lone wanderer, he does mention conversations with two men. At the Frauenkirche, he met an expert, who told him about the use of brick in Munich buildings.[28] The other person, identified only as Gus, may have been a friend, for in addition to conversing with him about stained glass windows, Jackson promised to show him his sketches.

The record of his second late afternoon or evening is hard to follow, perhaps because some time had elapsed before he set down his impressions: "now 3 days later," he wrote, "and a great many miles and emotions away." A passage in heavy brackets, however, suggests meaningful considerations on his mind: "If one aspect of the modern 2d half 20th Century world is the reconciling of opposites, the elimination of old dichotomies—good & evil, negative positive, matter & spirit etc, then the dualism town-country in its cultural ramifications is certainly on its way out—a further effect or merely an instance? Or did the dichotomy ever really exist? At all events we must work to eliminate it: to think of the entire human landscape as one, and . . . of the human & natural as one."

Jackson's last day in Munich, a Sunday, was fully given to art appreciation. Leaving his hotel, "sketch book in hand," he went to a service at the newly constructed Lutheran Church, seemingly not to pray but to see its building. Afterward he walked to the Schackgalerie across the river, a museum known for its Romantic-era paintings. In viewing them, he thought about the sequence of Romanticism in terms of the seasons of the year, likely recalling Spengler: "Sunny, motionless & young to begin with, dark & ominous at the end." After a visit to the Pinakothek and lunch, he went to the Odeonsplatz to sketch. There he drew the Theatine church, "somewhat to my dispar [sic] . . . instantly as if in my sleep—so familiar and sympathetic are Baroque proportions, features & plan."

Jackson's final entry in Munich described eating supper alone and reading a book in German, whose title loosely translated is "Transformations of the 20th Century."[29] Describing it as a demonstration of how science is affecting contemporary thought, Jackson commented that while "excellent in intention and in the earlier parts . . . the general conclusion—that Science is overcoming dualism, conquering the concept of time—a little overdone: surely there must be complications and contradictions." He ended his report on Munich with the confession, "But I've lost the book & must buy it again."

EASTERN EUROPE

A second travel journal begins in mystery: "To continue where I was rudely interrupted by the customs at Svelingrad." Jackson wrote this after being detained overnight at this Bulgarian city on the border of Turkey and Greece. He had previously been writing in a German notebook bound in thick black paper, such as a student might use in school. The second one is similar, but the binding is purple.

In the black-bound notebook, in addition to entries during his time in Munich, are drafts of many essays, written in Vienna at the end of his multilegged trip through Eastern Europe to Turkey, then to Greece, and finally to Vienna. Recalling leaving Munich, he first mentioned a layover in Vienna and then announced, "Mar 4. Now, the first few flakes, as the Balkan Express leaves Vienna." It signaled the beginning of a journey by train through Eastern Europe to Turkey. Collectively, these drafts tell of experiences in Belgrade, then the capital of Yugoslavia, and of other key moments as he traveled through Eastern Europe. (Curiously, the cities do not include Sofia, although he visited there.) In revised form, they appeared in *Landscape*'s Spring 1958 issue.[30]

Both notebooks offer interesting insights into Jackson the traveler. Aware of the political culture of Eastern Europe, he wrote about the sights and sounds of propaganda and the erasure of elements of history. Typically, he was eager to learn about the conditions of ordinary people beyond the "Iron Curtain." He constantly engaged strangers in conversation and accepted their company. In his openness, he proved naive, for he failed to recognize that he was under surveillance.

The purple-bound journal records the many ways Jackson, traveling alone and curious about Eastern-bloc countries and their peoples, reached out to others, especially outsiders. He began the narrative with his time in the (mysteriously named and possibly misspelled) Trorovow, during an evening of music in a room "warm from stove with beech wood." He invited the "orchestra leader[,] a gypsy with a strange wandering eye . . . to the table for a glass of wine, asked him to play Bulgarian music." The man seemed "flattered & uneasy, constantly looking around." Jackson had been told by friends he should "never refer to gypsies as such in their presence. Always recognizable by voice—complexion, expression."

The next morning, Jackson ("unshaven, no breakfast") went to a museum: "2 friends waiting to show me around—not to be shaken off." (Later, he likely understood that these "friends" were engaged in surveilling him.) Once at their destination, they were escorted by a museum official and were shown ancient relics and historical objects. It struck Jackson that in the exhibit of the 1873 Revolution, there was "no mention of English & French aid." The rest of the museum seemed to him to be politically inspired: "Partizan & antifascist room, then Chamber of com[m]erce type display . . . bust of Stalin & Dimitrov—passed by in silence."

Still accompanied, Jackson returned to the hotel for coffee and tea and then a walk around the city with the two men. "Many greetings—across bridge, school children, singing in groups, being shepardad [*sic*] up hill," he observed. "In school court yard below children being drilled in chorus of 'Greetings & good health, dear Teacher.' Wonderful view down into canyon & town—Turkish section, gypsy section—factories—Albanian village on horizon, almost Mediterranean vegetation, on ruins—not being restored, simply excavated." He and his "friends" parted company at the town hall.

In the afternoon, Jackson roamed alone and sketched. His journal reflects his interest in what he heard and saw. "Loudspeakers in every likely square blaring music from radio, and speeches." He walked beside the river and drew. Returning to town, he found the "Turkish quarter," where he observed that there were "few turks left, a few dirty gypsies lying around at bridgehead, eating bread. Man—hair dresser—came & watched me sketch. . . . Woman selling sunflower seeds."

Unexpectedly, he saw the morning companion he nicknamed "Blond," who gave him a folder of postcards. Jackson had asked both men to join him for drinks at his hotel: "At 6.30," he wrote, "dining room filling up for evening show; they arrived, dressed 'officially' for corso. . . . Blonde brought pretty wife. She drank a chocolate liqueur. Later they signed postcards in Bulgarian, French Esperanto—['a mod- est gift to our American friend with best wishes to the American people' warm farewell."

Jackson left early the following morning, by train for Plovdiv, a city with ancient roots. Along the way he observed from the train window "isolated villages, stone wall fields, rushing river, beech forests." At a stop in Stara Zagora, Jackson got out briefly to encounter a crowd at the station. He went into a park: "folkmusic be- ing broadcast; insistent gypsies bootblacks." Back at the station, he found waiting "phaetons with white linen covers & bright bridles." He walked into town and back to the train station, where he started up a conversation with "dark eyed young man," an actor hoping to study in Germany, who asked Jackson to mail a letter for him. Returning to the train, Jackson found others in his compartment, including a law- yer with a child and an officer "snoring full length." As the train was starting, the ac- tor reappeared to give Jackson his address and asked him to "write him from Amer- ica." During the trip Jackson chatted with the lawyer, who told him that, working as a lawyer in a collective, there was "'no exploitation'—made 20,000 a year. Went to Black sea in summer. Never been out of Bulgaria."

Alighting from the train in Plovdiv, Jackson's first impressions were of a "large central square & park. Outside Post office stand for parades—Red Square style— an ad for subscriptions to Pravda[.] Monday afternoon corso in progress." He se- cured a room for the night at the "Trimontium—enormous Moscow style hotel, 2 years old" and found its comforts satisfactory. In the city, "Lenin, Stalin, Dimitrov everywhere—red crepe paper. Along main street, crowded with corso, up into old town—Greekity old houses, cobblestones, walled gardens; asked man where Eth- nographic Museum was; he led me silently for 10 minutes to old restored mansion (1850) with walled garden."

Once at the museum, Jackson expressed an interest in Orpheus, who was reputed to have founded the city. The "elderly agreeable director" told him, "Orpheus was only a legend, no spot [i.e., trace] left. He called Archeological museum, made an appointment for me." A bust of Stalin was in the office of the director, who remarked (according to Jackson), "We all want peace etc. The world would breathe freely if Dulles resigned." At parting, Jackson told the director, "Orpheus was the first citizen of Plovdiv."

The next day Jackson went to the Archeological museum where again, there was no knowledge of Orpheus, even with the help of French and Soviet encyclopedias. After Jackson referred them to Hugh Hencken, the Harvard archeologist who directed the university's Peabody Museum, they responded that they "wanted 'Archeology' & 'exchange.'" During such meetings, Jackson and Eastern Europeans relied on French as a common language.

Jackson noted sights in Plovdiv and wrote about conversations from which he learned of Bulgarians' sense of isolation from the West and young people's curiosity about rock and roll. He heard political speech blaring from loudspeakers and began to experience the distinct feeling that he was being watched. On returning to his hotel the second day, he was met by a "policeman, young, polite, neat," accompanied by a German woman serving as interpreter. "Examined my papers," wrote Jackson. "Why had I not reported to police? Never told to. Danger of attack by Hooligans. I said I had no fear of Bulgarians. Call made to HQ: waited for follow up. . . . Telephone call for further delay. . . . At last telephone call came releasing me." Jackson rushed to the station and caught a train for Svelingrad.

During the journey, Jackson filled his journal as usual with observations made along the way and with fragments of his conversations with passengers, including one he had with a young woman geologist in which he learned a good deal about her work, background, struggles, and aspirations. "As she got out passport control came, examined her papers & took my pass[port]: in 10 minutes we were in Svelingrad."

And it was here that Jackson's travails began. He "was led to [the] customs house. Official in shabby overcoat went roughly & hastily through my belongings, took money slips, then dismissed me." He went to the station's buffet, a dirty and noisy place, where he drank some slivovitz. When called back to face the head of customs and an army captain, the customs head "officiously & roughly started once again to go through bags, item by item. How many films of Bulgaria?" When Jackson said four, he seized "4 unused rolls & thought they were the ones, scornfully tossing the exposed ones back into the bag." He took all Jackson's papers "including letters of introduction & folder of postcards." "Where is the notebook you always write in?"

the official demanded. Jackson turned it over, now aware that "evidently word had got back of my writing." He grew angry, stating that, as a "tourist I had been allowed to take pictures and go where I liked. They were evidently acting on instructions to find out what contact with the outside world I had had." With that, "they promised to return 'examined' material at end of 3 hours."

Jackson returned to the buffet and had another slivovitz. When the customs official reappeared, Jackson quoted his own words: "This is 3^d time." They returned Jackson's books to him but retained the postcards, films, and a notebook—and, of course, his passport. "Alone in room I tore out last 7 pages of notebook & returned it to briefcase," a furious Jackson wrote. He went back once more to the buffet, where he had something to eat and a soda while worrying "about film being discovered new, about missing pages, about names & addresses in it, about passport still in their possession." He read a German novel, Verner Bergengruen's *Der Tod von Reval,* until the buffet closed at midnight. Then he was taken to a "2 story dormitory for RR workers across tracks" for the night. He was awakened at 4 AM, in time to get the train for Edirne. The authorities handed back his passport to his "great relief."

At this point Jackson was fully aware of the surveillance he had been under as he traveled through Eastern Europe. It was the Cold War era, and as an American, he was suspect. What he did not know was that he had also been under surveillance in his home country, with the FBI tracking his movements through Washington, D.C., as he visited the diplomatic outposts of several Eastern European countries to prepare for future travel there. As an American speaking about Yugoslavia and traveling to countries in the Communist bloc, Jackson was suspect both at home and abroad.

At the end of the purple-bound journal, Jackson wrote a reminder to himself about future writing from the trip: "*For Balkan notes*—evidences of the archetypal city—The corso: The routes in the city as contrasted with zones—merchants: housewives, strangers path; groups of minority dwellings (painted different colors in Istanbul) The new com[m]unist Path—Red Square." He hoped to send the *New Yorker* a "factual account of 10 days observation," in which he would emphasize the good points (for which he listed only "friendliness") as well as the bad, "isolation from west. police control. propaganda—absence of respect for remoter past (Orpheus)."

Either the *New Yorker* rejected the piece or Jackson lost his nerve and never submitted it. Fortunately, he had his own publication, and thus a place for his observations. When they appeared as "Southeast to Turkey" in the Spring 1958 issue, Jackson chose to keep his difficulties at the Bulgarian border to himself.

TURKEY

After his ordeal at the Bulgarian-Turkish border, Jackson was clearly tired and out of sorts. Early the next morning, he arrived in Edirne, his first destination in Turkey. His initial look at this small city of forty thousand, close to the Bulgarian border, revealed a "shabby awakening town." The taxi driver, he wrote, drove him to an "abject hotel; I refused to get out: Baedeker had said Hotel im Ban (1956) where was new hotel? He drove me to another equally ugly & dirty & lifeless."

Jackson balked and took himself to the Tük-American Kültür, a small center promoting cross-cultural understanding and instruction in the English language. As it didn't open until 9 AM, he ventured into a place "next door. full of quiet dirty men drinking tea at small tables. I ordered one: in small glass—strong, hot, plenty of sugar. absolutely delicious, a miracle drug: I forgot troubles of day before & fatigue: had another." Restored, he walked around, eating "incredibly good cheese pastry" and taking in the market. Once the doors of the center opened, its director, Mrs. Hirziglar, had a young male assistant take him to what turned out to be yet another shabby hotel. She suggested Jackson return to the center in the early afternoon.

Once Jackson got out on the street, ate the food, and explored the town, he made no more complaints. What kicked in was his fascination in what he saw. When he returned to the Kültür center, he was met by the director's husband, a "nice looking grave young man, athletic director of high school," presently on vacation, who served as his guide on a walk around the town.

Seeing and learning about the mosque that provided music therapy for the mentally ill inspired Jackson's most memorable moment in Erdine. The building, he observed, had "classical proportions & composition—golden stone, very simple in detail: deserted. interior all planks & fallen plaster." He was fascinated by the "therapy center—octagonal room (dome) with 8 alcoves for patients to be in, center platform for musicians. Harmony evidently the therapy, in architecture & sounds." He was taken by the large flock of pigeons at the base of the dome. A clapping of hands led them to "fly up into opening at top of dome out into blue sky & sun—like a mass resurrection in a baroque ceiling."

In the evening, Jackson returned to the Kültür center and spoke briefly about New Mexico to an English class, answering such questions as "Did they have death penalty in N.M.? What was relationship between governor & mayor?" The following day, he returned there to write letters and phone his mother in Vienna before going out to sketch. After a walk with the obliging Hirziglars taking him to the famous mosques of the town, Jackson went to a have a Turkish bath in an abandoned mosque. He described it as "most exhilarating—when have I ever been so clean?" Regarding Edirne, Jackson concluded, there was "nothing here between the finest—the mosques—and the meanest."

The next day he was off by bus to Istanbul. Upon arriving, Jackson took himself to a second-class hotel, noting, "those with lobbies full of people I avoided." Because "Istanbul" was the subject of a memorable essay bearing its name in the collection "Southeast to Turkey," reading his journal about his visit there came as a surprise.[31] He stayed in Istanbul for only a day and a half, and much of his time was spent in tasks at American Express. He read the *Herald Tribune* over tea in a "vast formal dark coffee house[,] very old fashioned elegance." Returning to his hotel, he watched the sun set over the old city, had a drink, and ate a hurried restaurant meal.

The next morning, after a visit to the American consulate's office, he strolled through the various districts of the city: "Shoe street & leather street. . . . wholesale Textile, retail Textile . . . small steep streets—to large area around university buildings." He sketched a mosque and then found his way to the "American military attaché." Jackson reported that the man he met there "asked usual G-2 [i.e., military intelligence] questions—shoulder tabs, armoured units. radar & military installations. Russian troops etc. Could give him little."

This consultation does call for a pause to remember the surveillance of Jackson in the United States and Bulgaria. The question his travel had raised for the FBI was whether he posed a security risk.[32] Ironically, he'd offered American military intelligence in Istanbul any information he could stemming from his observations in countries under Soviet influence and control. The FBI had it wrong; Bulgarians authorities had it (at least partially) right.

During the rest of the day, after completing tasks related to future travel, he took a walk into the "Sefardic quarter, bought 2 Spanish-Jewish papers. At water's edge sketched old city with clouds of smoke: then took rowboat across Golden Horn." Following the rituals of travel, he bought postcards and stamps and in the evening after dinner went to back to his hotel "to write PCs and bed."

The next day he ventured to Bursa by boat and bus. Night had fallen when he arrived in Bursa, and he walked up what he had come to label the "Stranger's

Path." There he found "many small dirty hotels. strings of pack donkeys. phoetons [phaetons] etc. tried to find hotel on main street but no luck: heavy corso." He ended up taking a taxi to an "old fashioned (1927 type) newly built palace resort hotel," where, despite having no language in common with the desk manager, he checked in.

Entering the hotel's vast colonnaded dining room, he found two musicians offering "songs all played from memory & wrong." Jackson belittled every element of what followed; but, at the same time, picking up meaningful signs and connecting them, he saw these defects in a different light. He wrote, "That is what is charming about there [their] imitations of European grandeur—not only out of date but every detail strange—toothpicks on table, . . . children watching musicians, cloakroom girl goes home at 9. waiters look like hospital orderlies, food lukewarm. . . . A miserable pseudo European meal."

The next morning in Bursa Jackson again walked the "stranger's path[.] Then along saddlers, harness & stable alley. Into mosque. up into heights where there was a beautiful view of city & snow capped mountains—mosques everywhere." He stopped to sketch at a couple of points. (One of these sketches still exists.) At the Great Mosque, his drawing presented a new challenge: Jackson found it "impossible to grasp intuitively [the] proportions and layout of Moslem architecture. I can do a whole Baroque church at one glance: a mosque I have to inspect over & over."

As the day went on, he found a companion: at lunch, "Young Lt (instructor in French at military preparatory school) came and sat with me. Had learned (good) French in school; first said he was instructor in Turkish literature. Married 2 months. Liked hunting rabbits & quail in mts, had motorcycle for coming into town." For much of the day, the young man drove Jackson to mosques, watched while he sketched, and provided information. When they parted, Jackson offered to send the lieutenant a crash helmet and expressed the wish that they would meet again.

From Bursa, Jackson traveled by bus to Izmir. His journal records some of what he saw along the way: "an occasional tractor, large USA road building equipment making straighter wider road through mts. one story villages. women in trousers, geese, common. Up through brushy rocky mts. wooden plows, going straight up hill. men had heads wrapped in cloth. never a pretentious or larger house." Jackson's destination was the Aegean coast and the airport from which, on the following day, he would fly to Athens to begin another leg of the journey. In departing, he wrote simply, "sorry to leave Turkey."

Color plate 1. J. B. Jackson illustration, Dunster House, Harvard, 1931

Color plate 2. J. B. Jackson illustration, Ybbs an der Donau, Austria, 1932

Color plate 3. J. B. Jackson illustration, "Spanish Type Cattle Ranch," northern New Mexico, 1952

On reverse: "The proximity of the corrals and working space to the house, typical of the older colonial stock farm, has been carried over into the Spanish ranch. Although driven wells are now becoming common, many such ranches still depend on streams for their water supply. The surrounding range is likely to be undivided into pastures. (Examples to be found in the Chama Valley, Comor, Ojo Caliente, and region south of Las Vegas.)"

Color plate 4. J. B. Jackson illustration, trees in front of Jackson's house, La Cienega, New Mexico, 1994

Color plate 5. J. B. Jackson's house in action, La Cienega

Color plate 6. J. B. Jackson illustration, Pueblo, Colorado, 1970

Color plate 7. J. B. Jackson illustration, Hooper, Colorado, 1984

Color plate 8. J. B. Jackson photograph, Rex Club

1979

Color plate 10.
J. B. Jackson on
motorcycle

Color plate 9. J. B.
Jackson illustration,
road, 1979

Color plate 11. J. B.
Jackson illustration,
Berkeley, 1968

Color plate 12.
Drawing of J. B.
Jackson sketching by
Nell Sinton

Color plate 13. Mantel, dining room, J. B. Jackson's house, La Cienega

Color plate 14. J. B. Jackson illustration, Navaho hogan, 1980

Color plate 15. J. B.
Jackson illustration,
"Telephone Poles,"
1947

Color plate 16. J. B.
Jackson photograph,
flags on the Strip

Jackson's enthusiasm for travel was low as he approached Athens, where he was to meet his mother. As he logged the petty details of getting out of the airport and settled in his hotel, small matters annoyed him. Nevertheless, he commented: "Greek alphabet quite different from Cyrillic. . . . A lively growing dusty city. . . . older buildings 'Greek revival' never an arch—ingenious variety considering how few motives they use. . . . Still Balkan despite metropolitan atmosphere."

The next morning he made arrangements at American Express for travel to Crete and a hotel in Heraklion. Then he walked through the various commercial districts and sketched a mosque and the Acropolis. Writing sometime afterward, he asked himself, "What makes Athens better than Sofia or Belgrade?" and answered, "Better dressed people, better shops, more cars & small enterprises: more buildings, less evidence of state & propaganda." Later, he added, "perhaps I see it all from a class point of view: a cononist [communist] from East Europe would see propaganda for capitalism & evidence of capitalist domination."

On the following day, Alice Jackson, who had been in Vienna, flew to Athens; from that point on, her son attended to her, unless she was otherwise engaged. During such a break, Jackson had the chance to visit Constantinos Doxiadis, a visionary planner and architect. Jackson found him a "middle aged, serious affable man." When asked whether he had changed his mind regarding ideas recently published in an article, Doxiadis stated he had not only confirmed them but now wanted to write a book on the subject. He believed the "Capitol in Rome was laid out by Mich[el]angelo with optical perspective in mind, and other Renaissance sites as well." Responding to a question Jackson must have asked regarding Moslems and mosques, Doxiadis stated, "The scheme was evident wherever Greeks had been working. (Sinan [the architect under Suleiman the Magnificent] was a Greek, he said.)"

In turn, Doxiadis queried Jackson about the magazine: "'How was Landscape going? Was I German or Austrian to be interested in theories?'" Jackson did not make note of his answers, but the second question, suggesting that it was unusual for an American have such an interest, probably pleased him. Doxiadis told Jackson of his lectures at M.I.T and Harvard and that "He and Prof. Jan Tryhwitt (?) Cambridge Mass turn out a reference periodical on construction and housing called Edlogics of something of the sort. he will send me copies he says [.]" The magazine's actual name was *Ekistics*. It began in 1957 and is still in existence at the time of this writing.

Jackson and Doxiadis thus shared a mutual interest in the human shaping of the natural world that could have led to closer collaboration, but Jackson did not seem to seek this. Nor did he accept Doxiadis's invitation to dine at a taverna that evening. He did, however, appreciate the other man's courtesy, noting that Doxiadis accompanied him to the elevator when Jackson departed.

While Alice Jackson took a bus tour of Athens, her son walked the city, checked on arrangements, and sketched. The next morning he visited the Archeological museum. As he "sketched across street[,] man came out to watch, brought me into his office to show 'portrait' by Romanian artist showing man's face with woman's cunt as eye." No further comment by Jackson followed.

In the afternoon, mother and son took a short flight to Heraklion on the island of Crete. They were met by their American Express guide, whose advice and instruction Jackson frequently quoted in his journal, as for example: "Guide told us in hoarse intense voice in good self-learned English—'But we thought of Zeus as a nature god, dying each year[,]' pointed out Venetian walls, museum, told us where to eat." The guide continued to instruct them on the following day, while a chauffeur drove them around the island.

Jackson reported much of the description that followed in a flat, matter-of-fact tone; but at one point, his questioning voice broke through: "saw ruins—same old story vague hypothetical reconstruction of architecture & history. . . . How much is missed not knowing language or literature of current Greece. Who would guess political sentiments, economy, interest, etc by looking? . . . But something comes that way just the same." Jackson also noted the presence of a "USAF band of 19 in town—to play for Greek West Point outside town then for 'secret' US installation. . . . Looked well in uniforms."

The next day, a Sunday, Jackson was on his own for much of the day. After a quick glance into a church, he wrote in his journal and went on what likely was a solitary walk through the town. These were the festival days before Lent, and he observed a Corso in motion, "dressier than before[,] small children in disguise & flying kites." Later he observed "children still in disguise, going around to speak to people & greet them—a disguise even if you don't know the person is always exciting & mysterious."

After a visit to a new museum of artifacts, he noted, "So much restored, you wonder how accurate it is." In midafternoon the guide returned to take Jackson and his mother to Knossos. "Wandered at will," he recounted, "streets & houses labelled.

But where is the original of the strange inverted column? Of the chrome yellow wall paint?" Later, Jackson set out on foot, "trying to find harbor—saw many ruins near water front & a street of old Turkish-style houses."

Returning to Athens, the two hovered around Floca, a café that served them most of their meals. Alice Jackson, still at heart a buyer and seller of antiques, spent much of her time in the city exploring the bazaar and shops and purchasing gifts, accompanied by her middle-aged son. At one point he remarked on having seen "many fine victorian things & oriental too." Later, they went on a guided bus excursion to coastal Sounion to view the columns of a temple dedicated to Poseidon.

As they waited at the airport for their flight to Vienna, Jackson made an observation in his journal that almost broke my heart. He often commented on Jews in ways demonstrating, whether in the United States or in Europe, his sense of them as a separate people. Sometimes it was a simple historic reference, as the loss in Edirne of population "when Jews went to Palestine," or a simple identifier, as when a "young Spanish jew in newspaper shop" led him to a destination he was seeking. But his lack of human sympathy, his sense of "otherness" regarding the Jews that he saw in the airport in Athens felt like something else.

"There trooped through waiting room some 40 Jews—men[,] women & children—all poor, Eastern European dress and baggage—on way to Israel . . . never saw such repellent individuals: ugly, dirty, shabby, sullen faced, many with bad eyes or skin diseases." He talked to several. A man, who offered him a cigarette, held a "pale baby in red dress." He was "cross eyed, glasses, protruding ears, unshaven, hideous, modest and respectful." He had "been waiting for months" to leave Russia." Others, Jackson learned, were from Estonia and Latvia. Of them, he wrote disparagingly, "pathetic—hardly the same species as the neat well fed tall young blonde KLM officers—but they are." His final observation: "Their departure is a further defeat of German culture in Eastern Europe."

Many of my distant relatives and those of my husband, caught in Europe in the 1930s and 1940s, were not as fortunate as these travelers in the Athens airport who escaped the Holocaust. But the bodies of these Jewish Eastern Europeans immigrating to Israel bore the scars of their terrible lives in Russia and its satellites. They had experienced none of the economic and political privileges of the blonde airplane officials, nor of Jackson himself. His cruel view of them as "hardly the same species" reminds me of his prewar self—the self that accepted much of Germany's Nazi regime. Jackson may have been trying to reach out beyond the world of his social origins, but in 1958, it remained a limited reach. It included neither Jews nor African Americans. Whatever his last comment means, it is well to note its focus on German culture, not human beings.

As Jackson prepared to board the plane, he commented, "how little Bulgaria means except recurrent nightmares of not being able to get out!" Embedded within the mundane details of travel and purchases and descriptions of other travelers, this sole mention of the impact on his state of mind following his difficulties at the Bulgarian/Turkish border is telling. Jackson wasn't one to dwell on traumatic experiences, but they could come back to haunt him.

VIENNA

Traveling with his mother, Jackson arrived in Vienna on February 26, 1958. It was not a city to discover, but a familiar place, a city to remind him of his past. On this trip, however, Vienna became a different place altogether—one in which he would be pushed to confront his present. Jackson's life had a number of turning points, and this was one of the most critical.

On March 2, when he again picked up his travel journal, he and his mother were settled in the Imperial Hotel. Alice Jackson enjoyed spending her days shopping, doing errands, and visiting with friends. Her son accompanied her on some of these trips, escorted her to operas and plays in the evening, and scouted for their tickets. At moments, especially when Alice was seeking items of interest only to herself— such as a long-playing record of folk music or a cookbook—Jackson's sense of tedium was palpable.

On his own, Jackson haunted bookstores and bought books, and also accomplished a number of tasks related to *Landscape.* He drafted the pieces on Eastern Europe and Turkey that, in finished form, would appear in its Spring 1958 issue; sought out "a suitable print for the outside of Landscape—oriental—Turkish, and got one for 60 schillings"; and had his photographs from the trip processed. Here he was disappointed: "I looked at photos. most of them good, but few [of] human interest and only 3 of Sophia." He thought he might be able to include some of what remained by enlarging and cropping them. Disappointed in his search at a book store for more images, he noted, "Few books with possible illustrations: I shall have to make many of my own. I fear."

Jackson seemed to find Vienna too familiar to analyze or comment on and had only a few insights he wished to record. At one point, after dining with his mother at Gôsserkeller, he recalled being there decades before. "It was there [I] used to go:

hoarse voiced man came in every evening growling 'Völkisher Brobacher' (Hitler's paper) which was particularly popular in beerkeller circles." On another occasion, he examined a theater building after a performance and found "another instance of how style reconstructions show their date after a ½ century or more—for its rococo is barely recognizable—it would seem straight Victorian—the free & fantastic asymmetry of rococo is here congested and arabesque-like, the lines striving always for a rectangular effect."

A semi-commercial exhibition of present-day Austrian folk art did prove of real interest, for it reinforced his theory that "folk art is a holiday matter—especially religious & festive: that is why it fits well into tourist mentality—costumes, souvneirs [sic] etc." Aware that what he was viewing was no spontaneous creation, he commented that Austrian folk art was likely subject to "careful supervision & stylizing—particularly of course in costumes." Finally, well into his stay, he exclaimed, "How I love & increasingly love the shabbiness of the older part of Vienna!" What he saw was "not an expression of defeat or disillusionment, but of age & experience: The same charm in their sloppy accent, their shabby elegance, and the new is tolerated only because it may perhaps become shabby in its time."

City planning and politics were on Jackson's mind, and at one dinner, he conversed about them with others at his table. He saw an exhibit dealing with city planning in Vienna but was critical of its focus on "isolated buildings [or] streets or sequences." He judged that this outlook put "too much emphasis on esthetics, too little on the social aspects of the city plan."

Normally, however, when Jackson was with others, they were his mother's friends, and his primary role was that of accommodating son. He tried to attend to Alice's every wish regarding companions, theater, opera, and meals. Understanding her great pleasure at being in Vienna and with old friends, he sat through endless meals in their company. He was aware she was no longer as strong as she had been, Once, after a lunch with her, he noted "her feet hurting, her pace slower, her enthusiasm unslackened." At another point when he returned to their hotel, he saw her "tearful at having to go home."

Despite his sympathy for his mother and sense of obligation to her, Jackson became restless in Vienna and, at times, out of sorts. Early on he wrote crossly, "Each day Mother (and as consequence I) go to the Kamtnerstrasse & Graben around noon and return, exhausted and penniless at 4. Mother finds countless little errands to do, and each errand necessitates returning once more—glasses, hat, cookbook, bookbinder." Yet, at the same time, he didn't want the trip to end. "The days go by, entertaining, tiring, futile, always with the depressing thought of returning to the USA."

Emerging from the welter of detail in this travel journal is a unique mention of money. Near the end of his time in Vienna, he pondered his financial situation: "I wish I had a great deal of money for new clothes, many of them, a new car, easy travel & much buying of useless things: I can do none of these things now." It is well to remember that Jackson never had to earn a living. He had the means to create a magazine and sustain it. He could travel abroad for two months at a time. But wealth is relative, and in 1958 he was feeling strapped.

There was one moment—contemplating the contrast between his present and his past—that gave him some self-satisfaction. "So much at least has happened to me: I no longer feel the necessity for protective coloring: on my own & in my own society I command the place I want—a modest, but respected one. Perhaps the beginning of a belated independence & freedom from a desire to be thought one of the group."

As his time in Vienna was coming to a close, however, quite a different story begins to emerge from the journal, revealing that, once again Jackson was floundering. On March 7, he detailed a conversation with his mother in which he "told her I hoped to take at least 6 months off to explore ancient cities. and I explained a little [of] my theory of the Urstadt. But what must be undertaken in these next months—is work or rewriting (lightly) the novel: learn Turkish & Greek & Slav: become a mechanic, a skilled sketcher, and a firm program of what I intend to do: finally find other outlets—Harpers. New Yorker etc." Jackson was forty-eight. He had a draft of a novel. He longed for broader outlets for his writing. And, once again, everything was up for grabs.

Yet, at a different level, something else was stirring—something perhaps related to these ambitions. When Jackson first arrived in Munich in January, ill though he was, he nonetheless found himself compelled to travel by bus and on foot to the BMW factory outside the city. When he found it closed for the weekend, for the moment, he put aside what he called "the motorcycle complex." In the subsequent journal entries of that trip, begun as he passed into Turkey, however, he mentioned motorcycles eleven times. Clearly the coveted BMW was still on his mind, and in Vienna came the search for leather pants to wear when riding it. On his own in the city, he visited a number of leather stores and made inquiries about color, cost, fittings, and time required for a pair made to order. "Black is 'mode,'" he wrote, "and shows fewer spots than brown—much depends on boots, they all said." At one point he declared himself exhausted by the pursuit of leather.

Then, abruptly, on March 8, the focus of his journal shifted away from his experiences in Vienna and inward upon himself. Jackson now wrote to try and understand something bewildering to him. Why, he asked, did he return to the leather shops almost against his will? What was the meaning of this urgent desire to own a pair of leather breeches?

He began by writing of his uneasiness regarding their unsuitability. While most would consider the purchase simply one made for convenience or pleasure, and without experiencing either "excitement or guilt, I have to think of how ugly I will look, how inappropriate to my education; formerly I was too young to wear them, now I am too old." He labeled his problem "an inferiority complex—combined with an exaggerated sense of class," asking himself if it could be overcome. Its source, he decided, lay in "too much society of women, uneasiness in the society of men and a lack of common interests with them," which had resulted in "the fem[in]ine point of view in matters of appearance and public behavior."

Jackson then turned to what masculinity meant to him. So much of his past life had been dominated by the desire to identify himself "with the masculine element," and this had often led him to "misunderstand the masculine point of view—its roughness, venturesomeness, boldness: so that to be a man I too must be rough and tough." He understood this element clearly, but there remained the more important question: "How to overcome the timidity & sense of inferiority? By adventure itself? By surrendering to these powerful, at time irresistible drives, or by sublimating them until age dissipates them? Or by changing my way of life completely?" He realized that such efforts had consumed much of his creative energy. "This urge has so far been the uppermost motive in my existence: literary & artistic & intellectual talents have been neglected or lain undeveloped because always I have wanted to keep an escape to the masculine world." The day before, in a conversation with his mother, he had told of his ambition to reach a wider audience and his hopes to take off half a year for exploration. Now he seemed to be probing to discover what might be holding him back.

Jackson reflected on his wartime service, which had taught him that his image of manhood was quite different from the reality. There he saw men "weak, timid, dependant and . . . far from noble or enviable," and learned by contrast, "I could assume leadership and excel the average in bravery and endurance & maturity." Yet this awareness soon dissipated, and after a year or so he found himself again envious of other men.

What that envy meant had changed over time. In the present, "physical manhood—beauty of form & face—no longer seems important or desirable, and young manhood holds no appeal or envy." The masculinity Jackson felt he was now seeking involved "freedom from convention and responsibility . . . not a sense of solidarity—except in a very vague sense—so much as a sense of freedom."

What Jackson was actually facing at that moment in Vienna was a specific decision, one seemingly minor, but imbued with larger meaning: whether or not to purchase black leather breeches. They were to him "a highly desirable symbol of freedom." But what, he asked himself, did "possession of the symbol mean" to him? "Possession or enjoyment of the reality? and freedom *from* most eventually means freedom *to do something:* and what freedom of that kind do I need?" Possibly, "freedom to see the world—the social world—more objectively perhaps to return as an obedient member of the family, perhaps to reach unsuspected revelations. . . . This much seems to be clear: my urge to identify myself with the disinherited mass of men is inspired not by a pathological, homosexual disease, but by a (no doubt) false assumption that that class and sex are free from the restrictions which bother me—middle class respectability, puritanism, matriarchy. . . . How deep, how long this urge has been with me, I dare not even calculate—for more than 30 years— without so far a satisfactory outlet. And sparse as this confession is, it is the first time I have ever tried it. Perhaps that is of some importance. I am much in the dark, and where guidance comes from I do not know."

He continued, "I suspect that as long as mother is alive I will not enjoy freedom; I suspect my contribution will be entsagung [resignation] rather than affirmation. . . . I do not know whether drives are to be given a free rein, or analyzed & sublimated out of existence. If it were an evil one I would know that; if it were one generally recognized as desirable—sexual excess, creativity, religious experience I would know that and have no trouble. But it is clear that either the urge must be annihilated, or it must at last be given free rein—and if it is to be given free rein it must justify itself in my own happiness and creativity."

At this point, Jackson digressed to name the streets he had walked and to report a lunch with his mother and one of her female friends, before returning to his main topic.

"Why leather? why black? why breeches? All 3 are evidently essential to the disease." Jackson clearly was aware of homosexual leather culture. He was also a learned man, who had read both Freud and Jung. He began to free associate, probing his early experiences as if on a psychiatrist's couch. "I remember as a child of 5 or 6—one of my earliest memories—playing with father[']s puttees [strips of leather or cloth that men, particularly soldiers, wrapped around their calves for support]—he wore them often, and his discovery [of] me and making me put one on—punishment? play? I don[']t know, but the symptoms date back to earliest childhood."

This led him to ponder a darker side of memory. "Likewise this other drive—to masochism—self degradation—is tied up with another childhood dream—to be a horse—a work horse with heavy harness; I imagined myself concealed inside a horse with full harness. The harness was important. Finally, Allan the colored man [a servant in the household of Jackson's first years] had served in the navy during the Spanish American war: he told me how he had been flogged: I was entranced to hear about it. Much later—when I was 8 or 9, at Riverdale we played cops & robbers—a boy called Wilson—who said his father was connected with the police—could give him a pair of handcuffs, and we all wanted to wear them, I as much as the rest."

Jackson then veered into another direction, his first sight of a man in leather breeches. It came, he wrote, in 1933, when he was on a train trip and, in Salzburg, looked out a window. "A worker on the RR was wearing a pair and I was at once excited, and dreamt—daydreamt—thereafter of owning a pair, but"

The entry ends there, at least for the reader. On the following page, Jackson wrote perhaps sixteen additional lines, but only tiny, indecipherable bits of words remain. The page is torn from the notebook, I presume by Jackson himself.

This intimate exploration, unique in his writing as far as I know, forces the question I have frequently been asked: What was Jackson's sexuality? The query is generally posed as a statement: "You *know* that Brinck was gay?"[33] I've never been able to respond with certainty, and, as suggestive as is this journal passage, regarding homosexual and masochistic urges, it doesn't provide an irrefutable answer.

Admittedly, there were times when I assumed Jackson was homosexual—at some point and in some way—but naturally I never asked him directly (or indirectly). The closest the two of us ever came to discussing same-sex relationships was a letter Brinck wrote to me in the early 1980s. By then he had read about the treatment (in the manuscript for my book *Alma Mater*) of "smashes" in women's colleges—

female crushes on other girls. He suggested I mention the similar phenomenon in all-male schools.[34]

In my private conversations with others regarding Jackson's sexuality, a response of one of Jackson's most important younger friends alerted me to the cultural shift between the years of Jackson's maturity and the present: "No," this friend commented, "Jackson wasn't gay, but he may have been homosexual." This was a reminder that Brinck came to maturity in an age quite different from the time of my writing today, a time of the closet, when the out gay culture of the present didn't exist. When Jackson was a student at Harvard, for example, the 1920 expulsions of homosexual undergraduates and the wrecking of their promising careers were almost certainly part of the buzz of college life, making it clear that homosexual behavior among students had to be hidden.[35] (Jackson was likely to have been aware at the same time of the homosexual orientation of his faculty adviser, F. O. Matthiessen, and that of other Harvard professors.) In 1958, the McCarthy era had only recently ended, with its witch hunts against homosexuals in the State Department and diplomatic service. In this 1958 journal, Jackson himself labeled homosexuality a "pathological . . . disease"—one to which black, leather, and breeches were "essential."

Beyond his musings in Vienna, the only other reference to homosexuality in Jackson's private writings is oblique: his statement in 1951 regarding *Finistère,* the novel by Fritz Peters. As discussed previously, Jackson judged the book negatively in part because its theme of homosexuality required either sensationalism or "great psychological insight," suggesting that Jackson himself had likely mused about the latter.

In what follows, I have no intention of denying that Jackson was either an active homosexual or had homosexual yearnings, only that two additional, perhaps related, concerns were on his mind in 1958 as he continued writing: his desire to break with the "feminine point of view in matters of appearance and public behavior," springing from "too much society of women"; and his wish to identify with "the disinherited mass of men." In my mind, these words demand reflection on the complicated relationships between social class and gender presentation, both likely linked in his mind with sexuality.

When Jackson recalled seeing a leather-clad working man from the train in 1933, he connected this memory with freedom, seeming to suggest leather pants meant to him the psychological freedom of a male manual laborer. Then a middle-aged man, he was again engaging his long struggle to move beyond his origins, a most uneven process, as these travel journals reveal. I have come to interpret his reference to the "worker on the RR" as linked to both inner freedom and his desire to identify more fully with ordinary people.

The gendered part I have come to call Jackson's "masculinity project." Thinking of his efforts to be manly puts him in a different light. Two facts are clear: J. B. Jackson never got over his pain at being abandoned by his father; and, by the 1950s, Jackson—despite his love for his mother—had come to have conflicted feelings about living within the world of women.

What did it mean to him to be a man? How were manliness and social class connected? Specifically, how did Jackson's "masculinity project" relate to the class position his mother sought to maintain (or aspired to) in her own life? For a span of almost six years, life in the military had resolved this question for Jackson. But as he himself reflected in this entry, within a short time his insecurities regarding his manliness returned. Looking back with regret on many of his earlier efforts to prove himself manly and connect with others beyond the limited world of his upbringing, Jackson failed to recall his recent attempts, documented in his 1956 journal of his forays at home, when he spoke about motorcycles outside a café and visited an evangelical church.

I believe that during Jackson's time abroad in the winter of 1958, he was seeking to take these efforts a step further. In Munich, he made a trip to the BMW factory in pursuit of his "motorcycle complex." In Vienna, he searched for the black leather pants to wear when riding the cycle. This was a turning point when he set out on a determined path to assert his masculinity and shake off his inherited status, along with its associated prejudices.

Why did his efforts to be manly take this specific form? By 1958, Jackson had likely seen many images of masculinity associated with motorcycles in movies and magazines, including those featuring the recently deceased James Dean. Moreover, it was a time when the Hells Angels were coming to national attention with their outlaw machismo. Jackson may have been relatively small in size and almost fifty, but when dressed in black leather and perched on his motorcycle, he could identify with these other, more romantic (or infamous) riders, even when he rode solo.

His experiences with speed had already proven exhilarating. In "The Abstract World of the Hot-Rodder," published at this same time in *Landscape* (Winter 1957–58), Jackson rhapsodized over the pleasures of what he called "abstract travel." "One feature of the familiar world after another is left behind," he wrote, "and the sportsman enters a world of his own, new and at the same time intensely personal; a world of flowing movement, blurred lights, rushing wind or water; he feels the surface beneath him, hears the sound of his progress, and has a tense rapport with his vehicle."[36]

Later in his life, teaching at Harvard and Berkeley in alternate seasons, Jackson was known to ride his motorcycle from Santa Fe to one or the other university and back (see color plate 10). Harvard legend has him driving up the ramp at the university's Carpenter Center, and even riding his cycle onto the Harvard stage from which he lectured. By the time I and my family came to visit him in the early 1980s, a BMW tattoo was visible on his upper arm, and his motorcycle was parked in his driveway. I, however, never saw him ride it.

In early 1984, I learned that Jackson was off on a new trajectory, working as a manual laborer. He was to hold a succession of jobs, first painting and roofing, then cleaning up trailer courts and using his truck to haul great amounts of trash to the dump, and finally working as an employee in a garage mopping up after the Hispanic mechanics. He came to attend an evangelical church. Late in life, Jackson declared himself African American, insisting he had "black blood." The labor was real; the racial identification more questionable. But the source was the same as what he had written in 1958 in Vienna: the drive to confirm his masculinity and connect with the disinherited mass of men. Elsewhere in this book, I write of Jackson's efforts in his final decade to affirm—in his writings as well as his actions—his connection with others. In the list of goals in this journal that Jackson related to his mother on March 7, the day before writing the above long entry, one is almost hidden: "become a mechanic." Along with the motorcycle and leather pants, I read this as the words of an anguished man imagining a new beginning. Although many of the goals expressed that day vaporized—he didn't publish a novel, he didn't learn "Turkish & Greek & Slav," and the specific outlets he set for his writing eluded him—Jackson did expand his powers of expression and ways of acting in the world. With this emerged opportunities he could not then have imagined.

These efforts affected me personally. As he became more and more receptive to different kinds of people, Jackson widened his circle of friends to include Hispanics, African Americans, and Jews. This made my close friendship with him possible.

And ultimately, he did learn mechanics. In 1980, during a semester when he taught at the University of Texas in Austin, he took a course in town in auto mechanics. As he wrote to me at the time, he was "learning another way of thinking, and another class of American: young Blacks and Chicanos very eager to acquire training, and very bright in the world of autos." Perhaps he wore his black leather breeches to those classes.

Mora, New Mexico, 1960

Over the Labor Day weekend in 1960, Jackson traveled to the small community of Mora, New Mexico, a little under a hundred miles northeast of Santa Fe. He now had the motorcycle he desired, likely a BMW, and in some ways he experienced this trip as a personal test of his ability to ride it. Returning to a place familiar to him from his prewar days, he sought ways to make contact with people other than those in his social circle in New Mexico and the writers, planners, and academics he was coming to know through *Landscape*. The trip was thus an exercise in trying out the kind of masculinity he imagined for himself in Vienna.

As Jackson started out from Santa Fe on Friday noon, September 2, the beginning was a bit rough: "I wanted to turn back, and went slow: stones flew up and cut me in the face." He pushed on. Stopping for lunch, he seemed to gather courage, writing, "Put on helmet & goggles: gravel ceased—but no lust for speed. beautiful breezy clear weather. Stopped beyond Rome for cigarette." He obviously was in no hurry.

The trip would take him in a somewhat roundabout way to Mora. His destination was familiar territory: his uncle Percy Jackson had once owned a guest ranch in Wagon Mound, and Mora was close by. As a boy, Jackson had visited his uncle there and, during the prewar years, had worked in the same region as a ranch hand.

He began going southeast, however, to pay a visit in San Miguel to a friend he identified only as Brother John and to present him with a bottle of Scotch. The house was in disarray, for Brother John had been ill. From Jackson's statements in the journal, it appears they had probably become friends when Brother John was living in or near Santa Fe, and that his reposting by the archbishop was recent. Jackson found Brother John "not happy, but laughing as usual." Although there were many difficulties in his new assignment to serve seven missions, one aspect of his situation pleased him: "he won't have to set the example."

Though invited to stay the night, Jackson left and rode on for about twenty-five miles to Las Vegas, New Mexico, a small town divided by a river into a Hispanic and an Anglo side. This trip was to be the antithesis of those when he stayed with his mother in genteel hotels in Virginia and Austria. He was clearly seeking to live out the self he had identified in Vienna as freer and more masculine. Jackson thus chose a rooming house run by the American Legion and took his dinner in a Spanish restaurant. He went to see *The Angry Red Planet,* a popular science fiction film about the return of astronauts from Mars, commenting that it was "a poor movie but I enjoyed it." Afterward, he had a beer in "a would be Hawaiian bar" where he heard young men telling elaborate dirty jokes in a combination of English and Spanish. Back in his hotel room he wrote out a long synopsis of the movie he had seen and pronounced his judgment: "Corny lines, corny situation, poor setting, but at least an attempt to create a situation new to the public, and to be scientifically logical."

On Saturday, Jackson pushed on to Mora. From Las Vegas he went north to Guadalupita, a distance of about forty-two miles. As he continued toward Eagle Nest, he experienced some rough terrain, proudly writing, "Crossed small stream 16 times, boulders, ruts, sharp curves, stumps roots: never touched foot to ground.... Never lost motor: frightful road." Along the way he noted the beautiful scenery, writing that one spot was "like an Alpine town—big trees, meadows, steep roofs." More frequently, however, he commented on the seeming deadness of the towns he passed.

He stopped in one place to see if a trucker needed assistance and later "helped 2 boys from Chacon (no English) push pickup around." As he got closer to his destination, he stopped again to chat with men eating their lunch along the side of the road. He ate a lunch of canned beans in a café at Eagle Nest, noting "forest rangers at tables. Tourists coming in on horses, much yanking on reins." He was now in familiar territory. He saw the "Heck place ... half deserted. I worked there 2 weeks putting up hay, milking cows, bringing in fire wood; Mexican hand in bunk house with me."

After negotiating the Red River Pass, finding it "not at all scary," he came to the town of Red River (which, he observed, was filled with Texans) and stopped for a cup of coffee. On the next leg of the journey, he stopped twice to sketch. Somewhat out of sequence, he mentioned being in Taos and talking with a man with a BMW69. He also wrote, "Read indignant letters in Crepusculo about reprinting of Fulton Lewis radio talk on local Cooperative figure. usual liberal cant about McCarthy, reaction, fossil ideas etc."[37]

In the early 1980s when I got to know Jackson well, and Ronald Reagan was president, Brinck occasionally expressed ideas tending toward the conservative side, but in my presence these were likely muted. Working through his traces and finding this reaction to "indignant letters" tell me that in 1960, Jackson was a full-fledged political conservative.

When he arrived in Mora, Jackson clearly felt at home. He went straight to a hotel over the Hanosh general store, run by a Syrian family, where he got a room for $2.50.[38] There he found Mrs. Hanosh, "frying pistachios imported from Syria," who told him to leave his cycle in the yard and said he'd find many others inside buying drinks because relief checks had just arrived. In his clean room, he looked at the written signs for guests: "lock door, turn out light, don't shave in bathroom etc." He had a good meal at a familiar restaurant, and, sitting alone, eavesdropped on the banal conversation around him, speculating that "perhaps people don[']t have much to say to each other or can[']t say what is deepest & most intimate." He went to another bar for a beer and described its noisy and disorderly scene. He took in another movie, this time the Mexican film *Sordo,* the story of a deaf "carver of religious figures," a character Jackson saw as a "a cliché for harmless-poetic nature." Once again, Jackson classed it as a "poor picture," but that didn't keep him from writing out a full synopsis of its plot.

After the movie, Jackson went back to the bar, likely planning to meet Jo Garcia, the driver of the stalled truck whom Jackson tried to assist. He had seen him before the movie in that bar, already "half drunk," and learned he would be spending the evening in Mora. Jackson described the bar as being a "large empty dirty hall, [with] fluorescent light, beer ad." A teenaged band was playing music—"horribly loud & metallic and exaggerated rhythm"—and two teenaged couples were dancing. Jackson described seeing an "older man clutching his balls and dancing by himself." While sitting next to Garcia, Jackson reported that a "large very black nigger with protruding eyes" approached, "wanted to give me a drink." Perhaps to insult him, Jackson "asked for orange pop: he never reappeared."

This journal entry offers a unblinking look inside a part of Jackson's world never previously revealed so directly. In autumn 1957, Jackson had brought the rough world into *Landscape* in one of his most important essays, "The Stranger's Path." He referred to its title several times his travel journals, always as an urban district observed as he walked through a European city. Here we have an inside look at a comparable spot in a small New Mexican town, where Jackson was not an observer but a participant. And, in the context of an unwelcome overture, his casual use of the *N* word, written in his journal, revealed the racism that he continued to harbor.

Jackson did not immediately begin the return trip home the next day. It was Sunday, the sun was bright and the weather pleasant. After breakfast he rode out into the country and sketched. He also took some photographs. He observed the countryside and the decayed towns, chatted with locals, bought cigarettes, enjoyed seeing the beautiful churches, took more photographs, and then began his homeward journey.

Trouble began soon after, on the "dirt road (35 miles) to Roy. 20 miles out had flat." He discovered that his tire tube had a leak, but he had brought no patches with him. He replaced the tire with his spare, only to puncture that. He found some boys who proved to be of no assistance, so he set off again. By then it was early evening. "Slowleak somewhere—not so slow. pumped every mile. Then pump gave out. Full moon. didn't dare use bright light for fear of using up battery. Down dirt road into Red River Canyon: small bonfire in valley: paved road. up other side. Then tire gave out."

Getting off his cycle, he was able, after half an hour, to hail a truck. He left his motorcycle under a tree and got into the "pickup with highway constructor & wife." The couple took him to a filling station, where he was directed to the house of Mr. Basi, described by Jackson as "a wrecker." Basi promised help, but only after he finished his supper. Jackson returned to the filling station where, at after a long delay, Basi appeared with his grandson. They "tied MC on truck[.] Then back to [the town of] Roy. Mrs Basi gave me salami, bread, coleslaw, water."

The night's lodging offered a relaxed contrast to the bar scene of the night before. "Small hotel, all men," he wrote, "doors all open down cor[r]idor—men sprawling on beds, talking, smoking: construction workers I suppose. Glad to be resting: read a little, listened to faint radio music bright moonlight on bed. slept cold." Reviewing the help he had received, he commented, "Pleasant brief contacts—knowing not personalities but (in this case) a piece of mechanism, imediste [immediate?] rapport & basis for argument. Good people—all willing to offer help: but Mexicans strangely enough, usually give it."

Coda

These extant travel journals, dating from 1954 to 1960, reveal much about J. B. Jackson during a critical period of his life. They provide a window into his remarkable observational powers and prodigious memory. They document what intrigued him, the questions he asked, the people he sought out, his deep learning, his appreciation of art, his power to connect disparate elements of cultures, and his ability to interpret the varied landscapes he saw and think about the people living in them.

The journals also testify to some of his practices as a writer on landscape and as the editor/publisher of the magazine by that name. On certain of his travels, Jackson chose to meet people who might contribute to *Landscape* or who had already written for it. Significantly, by 1956 he had also begun taking photographs. As Jackson wrote about his travels, he pondered the meaning of what he saw and experienced. His journals reveal creative moments that sparked important essays, as well as clever writing that never made it into published form. The existence in these journals of draft essays—cross-outs and all—offer interesting insight into some of his writing practices.

Occasionally Jackson revealed his ambitions and his frustrations as he lived out the job he had given himself and the life he had chosen. He wrote of his struggle to become the person he wanted to be. As his friend, I know that his restlessness continued long after 1960. He never tasted the full fruits of contentment, carrying some discontent and feelings of failure as long as he lived. But he did go a long way toward resolving what he thought it meant to be a man, fighting against his prejudices, and connecting with others.

The journals also reveal Jackson's continuing limitations in this period, despite his efforts to reach beyond his upbringing and his social circle. Yes, he widened his acquaintances to let in Hispanics and those in the working class who were white and Christian. But certain of his words bear witness to old prejudices, especially toward those who bore scars of society's treatment of them.

Jackson's acquisition of a motorcycle, the leather attire for riding it, and even the BMW tattoo that came to adorn his arm were important steps in his reaching out to the world immediately around him. I write this without admiring Jackson's vision of masculinity. As a woman who was a teenager in the American South in the 1950s, I have long rejected all that vision stood for in favor of a nurturing masculinity, such as I found in my life's partner. But Jackson, a man of contrasts, had this masculinity, too—it was what enabled me to become his friend. I only suggest that the persona he took on and tried to live out on his motorcycle was useful to him at this time in his life and helped him move forward.

In 1960, as Jackson traveled to Mora, he was just learning to ride his cycle. He was living in La Cienega but had not yet built the house there that he would move into in 1965. He had not begun university teaching, his essays had not yet found their way into books, many invitations to lecture were yet to come. But *Landscape* was well established, he had his motorcycle, and, as he approached his fifty-first birthday, he was on his way.

6

AT THE PODIUM

Teaching the Everyday Landscape

In the 1960s J. B. Jackson became a professor, first at Berkeley and then at Harvard. He had no formal graduate education as a credential. What he did have was the authority that came with creating a magazine that offered a new way of seeing the physical world as shaped by the cultures of its inhabitants.

As Jackson worked to cultivate a broad and significant group of contributors to *Landscape,* he reached out to many who were university professors, beginning with geographers. The journal he kept as he traveled through the American South in 1957 records his efforts to find professors and doctoral candidates willing to talk to him about their work. Later that same year, Jackson went to the University of California at Berkeley, this time by invitation. Carl Sauer, chair of the geography department, invited Jackson to visit and welcomed him at a party where he met the entire department.

Important consequences followed. Jackson needed good articles for *Landscape;* the Berkeley geographers saw opportunity in Jackson's magazine for publishing their work. From that point on, Jackson was in Berkeley's orbit and connected to planners, architects, and landscape architects. He was welcomed at the university and attended classes. Before long, he was himself giving informal talks and seminars.[1] Beginning in 1964–65, he was listed in the Berkeley catalog as a lecturer in landscape architecture in the College of Environmental Design.[2]

In 1966–67, Jackson began teaching formal courses to undergraduates, initially offering a research seminar in cultural geography, a course he continued for the following four years (see color plate 11). He added a lecture course, History of the Environment (Environmental Design 169). As described in the university's 1968–69 catalog, it consisted of "three 1-hour lectures per week" during the ten-week winter quarter, with the content: "Evolution of the American landscape, 1865 to present, with particular emphasis on highways, recreation, conservation, the agricultural landscape, and new forms of collective settlements."[3] Paul Groth, his long-time teaching assistant, later stated that Jackson "reviewed and memorized the lectures before each class, and had the text for the lecture in front of him on the lectern—although he only referred to the text when he wanted to read an exact quotation from a source." He typically showed and commented on five to nine slides in the final ten minutes of the session.[4]

In 1972–73, moving up an academic notch at Berkeley, Jackson was listed in landscape architecture among the assistant professors as an adjunct. The following year, he rose to the rank of professor. (As someone coming from outside academia, was he pleased by this, or merely amused?) Over the years, the description of Environmental Design 169 remained the same, but in 1974–75, it became an upper-level hour course of lecture and discussion, with enrollment limited and requiring the permission of the instructor. Jackson gave it a new title, History of the Man-Made Environment, teaching it through 1978.

Marc Treib, longtime Berkeley professor and prolific author on landscape architecture and design, audited Jackson's class at Berkeley in the late 1970s. Treib later reported that in dealing with American places and spaces, Jackson focused on "generalizable ideas about streets and their agglomeration as farms, towns, and cities" with an emphasis on "what we share, what we have in common." Treib recalled being "astounded by the concision of Jackson's ideas, and the simplicity and ease of his delivery" in the classroom "as if in a fireside chat." Treib relished his memory of certain details, such as "his explanation of how the ecology of the roadside differed markedly from that of the surrounding fields."[5]

No doubt aware of Jackson's success at Berkeley, Harvard sought him out, and Jackson began teaching there at the end of the 1960s. By this point, he had given up his editing and publishing role in *Landscape,* taking the helm a final time in the Spring 1968 issue. His life assumed a new migratory pattern. Each autumn he left La Cienega to travel to Cambridge, Massachusetts. At Harvard he stayed (at least during some fall semesters) in Eliot House, where four decades earlier he had lived

Figure 29. J. B.
Jackson as teacher

as a college student. For the winter quarter, he was back in Berkeley. In between teaching stints, when he wasn't lecturing around the country or taking trips abroad, he lived in La Cienega.

Harvard course catalogs and the annual *Confi Guide*—Harvard students' chatty critique of courses offered during the previous year—make it possible to track Jackson's courses at Harvard.[6] He first appeared in the 1969–70 catalog, when his course Studies of the American Environment was offered for the fall semester. Its focus was upon "the evolution of the man-made environment in the United States, as exemplified by the spatial organization of houses, farms, institutions, cities, and regions."[7] The course was nested under visual and environmental studies, a new major for Harvard undergraduates, and also a popular choice for students in the Graduate School of Design. At least until its last year or so, it was essentially the same course Jackson taught at Berkeley.[8] For close to a decade Jackson held the position at Harvard of "Lecturer on Environmental Studies and Landscape Architecture."

In the 1973 *Confi Guide,* Jackson was labeled "the Motorcycle Maniac." He offered many slides taken on summer travels, so—one student cautioned—"Do not expect to find glorious twilight panoramas of the Golden Gate or the Empire State Building. Jackson typically comes with heavy doses of the farm, the strip, the factory and the working class house—all basic features in spatial organization." While the guide praised Jackson for his delivery as well as his slides, it also revealed that he demanded little work outside the classroom, beyond the project each student turned in toward the end of the semester.[9]

One member of the Harvard graduating class of 1973 recalls being "struck by Professor Jackson's remarkably engaging, low-key delivery. Yet his speech and appearance were rather formal (perhaps 'reserved' would be a better word) and a bit unexpected, given his well-known connections with the Far West and, especially, his celebrated cross-country solo motorcycle trips." The former student recalled the reading list for the course as "far and away the most eclectic and enjoyable one I ever encountered at Harvard."[10]

For the fall term, 1973, the title of Jackson's course was changed to Studies of the Man-made American Environment since the Civil War. Undergraduates nicknamed it "Gas Stations," and students flocked to it. It was during this semester that I met Jackson.

At that time I had no knowledge of the important turning point Jackson was reaching in his teaching career. During that term, he was offered a more desirable position at the university. Because Harvard's administrative records on Jackson remain sealed, I cannot learn the exact terms of the offer, but in the first letter he ever wrote to me, he described it this way: "There was a question of my taking on a full year appointment at Harvard, and giving 2 courses—or the same course extended."[11]

A letter written by his brother, Wayne, conveys some sense of what was on Jackson's mind in 1973 regarding Harvard and Berkeley.[12] Just after he returned from a conversation with the dean and the offer of a full-year teaching position, Brinck phoned Wayne, who replied immediately afterward by letter.[13] Wayne described Harvard's offer in elevated terms: it would no longer be a temporary lecturer's position, but a professorship. (As a person aware of the precise distinctions of academic titles, I am not certain that this is so.)

A word about Wayne's likely state of mind in 1973. By that time, he had retired from the CIA. In his last years at the agency, he had, as a member of the CIA

Figure 30. Cartoon of J. B. Jackson in *Confi Guide*, Harvard, 1974

historical staff, written a five-volume biography of Allen Dulles. The manuscript rested in the shadows, however, for it was classified and thus buried from public view.[14] By contrast, Brinck had an ever-growing public reputation. My sense is that Wayne, aware of the different trajectories of their careers, and conscious of Harvard's prestige, was both proud of his brother and wished to shine in his reflected light.

Wayne wanted Brinck to accept the dean's offer, writing that it represented the highest accolade imaginable for his younger brother's achievements. "You have single-handedly created a field of study, combining the intellectual, artistic, philosophical and historical which obviously appeals to young minds in their most flexible and receptive years, the field has been formally recognized by the leading university in the US and will become an established discipline. . . . So many strands in your life have come together to create what you launched in landscape and what has culminated in a professorship at Harvard."

Wayne believed the offer should have made Brinck happy, but he found from their phone conversation that his brother was depressed by the prospect. There seemed to be two factors involved. The first, as Wayne put it, was "that you feel that your independence is mortgaged, that the time and energy to pursue more ramifications of your work seem prejudiced." To Wayne, this seemed an obstacle likely to be overcome by the "help promised" and "the encouragement of colleagues" he would receive in this more established position. In pushing against Brinck's fear that the Harvard position would tame him, Wayne likely echoed a phrase of his brother: "there is no reason for your eliminating more pioneer work—it may take something of a different form but I can't believe the potentiality doesn't exist."

The second factor was Brinck's "distress" at finding his university "contemporaries seeming old and played out." This was a worry more difficult for the older brother, born in 1905, to quell. Finding himself aging, Wayne tried to nudge both himself and his younger brother into accepting their advancing years. "There's no backing away from aging," he wrote, "and neither of us has aged substantially in the sense of losing interest. Mother, until the very last years, always kept her curiosity and sense of concern and we both have some of that, you probably more than I—certainly in different fields."

In closing, Wayne acknowledged that spending two semesters at Harvard would mean giving up "Berkeley and the stimulation that part of the world gives you," and would also result in Brinck's having less time in La Cienega. But for Wayne, these losses were worth it; simply "the price you have to pay for the startling success you have achieved."

The price, however, was too high for Brinck Jackson, and he turned down Harvard's offer. Writing to me from Berkeley on February 22, 1974, he explained, "It is foolish to give a course and expect real student commitment when there is no follow up—no advanced work in the subject; and Harvard expected me to do the entire thing. The chances here [at Berkeley] for an extended course are better." Of course, this was likely only the piece of the story Jackson wanted to convey to me at that time.

Jackson continued to teach the single semester at Harvard, offering the course in post–Civil War Man-made American Environment. By then, some of his views were getting pushback from Harvard students on the left. However, as noted in the *Confi Guide,* a strong positive remained: "While some students may have been attracted by the course's gut reputation, . . . [it] more likely enjoys its immense popularity due to the actual content and presentation."[15] In 1976, the guide's report put its praise in different words. Jackson was "a professor who really seems to care about his students. . . . While a lot of people take 'Gas Stations' because it is easy, many discover along the way that it is not the flaming gut they expected. It is a testament to Jackson that they end up enjoying it nonetheless."[16]

Fall 1976 was the final semester Jackson taught at Harvard. He remained at Berkeley a little longer, teaching his last course there in winter quarter 1978.[17] Nonetheless, his work as teacher lived on through Jackson's profound effect on many of his students and younger colleagues. His courses lived on, as well, under professors he helped train. In 1977, John R. Stilgoe began teaching the Harvard course Jackson inaugurated; at the present moment he is still writing and offering instruction to the university's students. In the spring semester of 1978, Paul Groth, Jackson's teaching assistant at Berkeley, began almost four decades of teaching and expanding the courses Jackson initiated there. Looking beyond these two institutions, a significant number of Jackson's former students and acolytes have claimed his heritage directly as they went on to important careers as writers, teachers, and practitioners in architecture, landscape architecture, planning, American history, and American studies. These women and men have not only carried the spark of Jackson's vision; they have broadened and reshaped the field of landscape studies he created, bringing to it their new approaches and perspectives.

Lecturing on the Everyday Landscape

With *Landscape* magazine, Jackson achieved his goal of becoming a published writer, but he did not anticipate what followed. He emerged as a highly sought-after lecturer whose spoken words became another instrument enabling others to see what was before their eyes. Judging from their titles, a number of these lectures became early drafts for some of Jackson's most important essays. By the time I met him in 1973, Jackson was receiving constant invitations to speak; our correspondence is peppered with descriptions of the travels these lectures occasioned.

The origins of Jackson's lecturing life began locally in the 1950s, in Santa Fe, with his civic involvement, commitment to internationalism, and interest in planning. As he began to establish connections with geographers at Berkeley and elsewhere, he came to learn about groups concerned with various facets of landscape—such as land use, resources, conservation, urban issues, and transportation—attended their meetings, and contributed to the discussions. Over time such contacts led to a substantial number of invitations to speak. Invitations were also augmented by Jackson's effort to cultivate contributors to *Landscape,* through correspondence and contacts at various universities. In these ways, Jackson built a network of alliances and supporters. He was good on his feet—smart, articulate, and witty. He spoke in a resonant voice and in an appealing manner. He had important ideas and approaches to impart, and he found receptive audiences for them.

Although Jackson's university teaching can be fully documented, the record of his lectures has proven somewhat elusive. In searching for his traces, however, I've been fortunate enough to receive copies of letters written by Jackson to important urbanists, geographers, and intelligent observers. Although these materials don't give much information about the lectures themselves, they offer examples of the groundwork Jackson laid in making the kinds of professional connections that could lead to lecture invitations.[18]

For example, in the fall of 1958, Jackson attended a conference on Urban Design Criticism, financed by the Rockefeller Foundation and organized by David Crane of the Institute for Urban Studies at the University of Pennsylvania. Upon his return to La Cienega, Jackson wrote a long letter to Crane thanking him for the excellent conference and praising his "brilliant working paper." Jackson went on to criticize the lack of geographers in attendance, and he offered a list of names of potential invitees for future conferences and titles of publications supplying even more. Over the next two pages, he specified important issues that he felt needed to be addressed. In a postscript, he invited Crane to create and edit a regularly occurring department in *Landscape.* The letter's combination of generosity, tough love, and invitation demonstrates how Jackson made allies.

One set of letters makes the connection between cultivation and lecturing particularly clear. Over many years, Jackson corresponded with Patrick Horsbrugh, a British professor who had a long career teaching architecture and its environmental implications in successive universities in the United States. The first letter from Jackson that Horsbrugh retained came in spring 1958, after the two met at the University of Illinois. In this dictated and typewritten letter, Jackson asked Horsbrugh to illustrate a forthcoming article on fences in *Landscape.* Horsbrugh declined but instead sent his piece on barns, illustrated with his sketches, ultimately receiving a small check for the contribution. Following the lead of a mutual friend who gave him a gift subscription to *Landscape,* Horsbrugh over the years sent money for gift subscriptions to others.

Letters continued over the years, punctuated by occasional meetings. In 1963, Horsbrugh was teaching at the University of Texas, and in response to the White House Conference on Natural Beauty, he organized a 1965 conference dealing with the environmental crisis. He invited Jackson to speak and appear on a panel. Jackson's talk, "Various Aspects of Landscape Analysis," was implicitly critical of Lady Bird Johnson's highway beautification efforts. (The First Lady attended the conference, at least long enough to have her photograph taken.) Jackson's talk was published in the proceedings, and ultimately he received $625 from the state of Texas for serving as a consultant to the conference.[19]

By the 1970s, Jackson's lecturing commitments were taking him to locales far and wide across North America. At one point, likely around 1990, he had an assistant or typist compile a table of contents of his lecture file. The list is topical, not chronological, but dates are attached to many titles, running from the mid-1970s until the late-1980s.[20] The list, however, is incomplete.[21]

One useful source of information comes from the set of letters that Jackson wrote between 1974 and 1995 to Nell Sinton, a noted artist from San Francisco and Jackson's dear friend (see color plate 12).[22] In 1979, seeking to find his way after retiring from university teaching, Jackson corresponded with her frequently, and his letters provide a useful year-long record of his lecturing. In early January, Jackson told Sinton he had "9 lectures to prepare" before leaving for Berkeley and Fort Worth. Three of these he delivered to an audience at the Amon Carter Museum in Fort Worth (later published as *The Southern Landscape Tradition in Texas*).[23]

After his return, Jackson expressed his pleasure in the museum's public exhibit of twenty of his sketches "beautifully mounted and framed." He reported venturing to the University of Arkansas to speak, offering a talk in March in Chicago, and considering a week of lectures at the University of Pennsylvania. He added, "The lecturing as such doesn't bother me: I talk as if in a trance: it is the people you meet *afterwards* that are hard to take!"

Sinton must have replied in helpful ways, because Jackson responded in turn, "Perhaps you are right: we were brought up to be modest and to be embarrassed by praise." He mentioned planning to lecture at Georgia Tech at the end of April. In a letter in July—written after he had returned, exhausted, from a trip east—he let Sinton know he had resolved to attend no more conferences. Feeling that he had been expected to predict the future, Jackson complained, "I can[']t possibly participate in discussions of 1990 when I[']m uncertain as to what December 1979 holds for me." In the fall of 1979, he went east again, to lecture at the Smithsonian and Harvard. He found the Harvard experience ironic, commenting that he "was given an heroic welcome," then added wryly that after he left his teaching position there, "now all of a sudden they want to make a film of me and my lectures!" Giving lectures, however desirable in the abstract, were beginning to wear him down. Nonetheless, Jackson carried on, and my sense is that he did so out of a desire to keep himself a player in the public world.

What the letters to Sinton don't relate is that at the same time, I imposed on him another lecture at another conference, this time to the American Studies Association in the fall of 1979. My intention—realized fully in both the panel of speakers and the large audience—was to introduce Jackson to American studies scholars. I'm not certain how Jackson felt about the session, as our lunch afterward focused on his grief following Wayne's recent death and his deep anger that Wayne, by not mentioning him in his will—"not even by five dollars"—had denied avowing their relationship.

Jackson didn't stop during his seventies: his lecture file lists twenty-four lectures during that ten-year period. He also taught for a semester at the University of Texas in 1980; in 1983, he enjoyed a residency of several months at the American Academy in Rome; in 1986, he was a visiting professor at Rice University in Houston.

Interests close to home, however, came to engage him, and as he entered his eighties, Jackson lectured and traveled less. The last public talk I heard him give—his response at the 1995 ceremony at which he was awarded the PEN Prize for the

Art of the Essay—was brief but eloquent. I include it here, near the close of this volume.

Researching the Everyday Landscape

The writer sets out to attain his objective, but he goes in a general direction, not along a familiar path: and his objective is a target of opportunity. In short his is a movable, unpredictable goal, not necessary ever to be in the same place. His shot is on impulse: the goal is a sudden insight or flash. Consequently, the procedure cannot be handed on to others, it is a private success or insight: all that he can suggest is being open to inspiration and guesses. Truth is unpredictable, but it has to be searched for.

—J. B. Jackson, Road Notes, Box 3, folder 1 [8], J. B. Jackson Papers

In a manila folder of reading notes on "Roads" dated 1989, J. B. Jackson wrote these words and gave them the title "Ideas." In their articulation of his method and creative process, they are unique. Jackson was likely writing one of his very last essays, "Roads Belong in the Landscape." Among its notable elements is Jackson's metaphoric use of the word *road,* suggesting that working on it prompted this statement of how he researched, discovered, and wrote.

Here Jackson sees his work as writer as a lone journey, imagined perhaps as a hunt. He sets off in a general direction, but on an unknown path. His quarry—truth—is elusive and ever-moving. He searches without knowing the outcome. He hunts alone, hoping for a sudden flash of insight. He cannot direct others but only suggest that in their own searches, they remain open to inspiration and guesses.

With these words before me, I felt that in my search for traces of the writer J. B. Jackson, I caught a glimpse of my quarry at the end of the path. Jackson tells me that his great gift had two elements—willingness to go on an unpredictable search and trust in his powers of insight.

Jackson believed strongly in his own powers. Although this belief was shaken at certain moments of his life, his mind was a resource to which he could generally return. During his boyhood, his schoolmasters complained that his mother believed he was a genius. Although these educators had to deal with what they perceived as the negative results of this belief, essentially, they agreed with it. Frank Boyden, the headmaster of Deerfield Academy, recommended him to college in 1928 with these words, "He is a very unusual boy, of very keen intellect and real genius."

Deerfield's history teacher remarked more comprehensively that "his mind is quick but undisciplined. He receives ideas readily and interprets them understandingly. In other words, he shows a marked capacity for absorbing knowledge through reading and discussion. On the other hand, he shows incapacity for orderly, systematic, careful work. In History, the mechanics of making an outline and analyzing text come hard for him."[24]

Landscape magazine offered Jackson a field of inquiry and a place to publish essays where his writing skill and broad understanding—achieved through reading, observation, and curiosity—could have free rein. He continued to read widely and from many unconventional sources, but, in addition, he developed self-discipline. His papers in the CSWR at the University of New Mexico hold traces of his hard work—in his own unique ways—to satisfy his inquiring mind and find written evidence that would lead to insights.

In October 2015, I spent time at the CSWR, examining his papers, a collection I played a part in organizing and establishing. After Jackson's death, in my limited role as his literary executor, I boxed up the professional materials in his study and sent them to my temporary sabbatical office in the Schlesinger Library. There I sorted Jackson's papers and created a preliminary archival finding aid. I decided that the papers and the literary executorship should reside at the CSWR. Now, almost twenty years later, I came to revisit them.

As I researched the J. B. Jackson Papers in their archival home, I found them beautifully reorganized and significantly augmented. With little memory of what I had passed on, I approached going through them as a researcher facing a new collection and immediately became fascinated by what the papers had to teach. Of particular interest were the working papers of Jackson's later years, containing materials he had gathered and notes he had taken for the purposes of imagined or future essays and lectures.

Someone had compiled a sixty-four-page, single-spaced, typewritten list of the approximately 2,460 books in his library. Reviewing this record was interesting for the glimpse it offered of a learned man's library, combining as it did the complete works of Thomas Carlyle and Honoré de Balzac with contemporary works of literature by such respected writers as Saul Bellow. Among these books one would find those of Lewis Mumford, along with works of social criticism from the 1950s on. Many volumes reflected the primary interests of Jackson's later years—religious and philosophical works of such writers as C. S. Lewis and Benjamin Whorf. And finally, there was exactly what I knew to expect: an abundance of books on American history, architecture, and landscape, along with a unique collection of sources gathered to satisfy his curiosity. This included such works as Edith Kunhardt's *All Kinds of Trucks* (designed for children), the legal study *Regulating the Automobile* by Lester Lave, and many U.S. government reports.

My guess is that most of this library was acquired from the 1950s on, for Jackson had no stable residence before then. Some of the older works may have come from his mother's house, but I know he also loved to pick up secondhand books. (His eyes would light up when he spoke of the bookstalls along the Seine in Paris.) I am aware of what is missing from the list, too, such as an entire bound set of *Fortune Magazine,* for which I had to find a home after his death; and a collection of Baedeker guidebooks from the early 1900s, now in the Mortimer Rare Book Collection of Smith College.

The papers also hold gleanings from university libraries, many gathered during his teaching years. These consist of papers, articles photocopied from library materials, and also some torn from journals he owned, the lot covering a wide range of dates and topics.

There are notes in his handwriting, typically quotes rather than outlines, summaries, or evaluations. Jackson wrote down information in a variety of ways. I've not seen but have learned of the voluminous file of notecards on which he jotted information he intended to use in teaching. They were initially passed on to Paul Groth, who found their order "idiosyncratic. . . . He [Jackson] changed his categories frequently, and often had cards with different headings re-grouped into a new category," without, however, changing the card's labels. Groth counted 151 categories.[25]

In Jackson's papers at the CSWR, his notes were not written on cards. Some are in spiral or bound notebooks and thus topics appear in the chronological order in which he wrote them. At one point, Jackson tried writing on loose-leaf paper that he organized under letters of the alphabet in ringed notebooks of varying sizes. In the 1970s he created a file system, with manila folders holding notes on eight-and-a-half-by-eleven-inch paper, arranged alphabetically.

Each folder had its own printed letter, and on the front cover Jackson listed categories. For example, under *M* are headings Mass Transportation, Music, Monuments, Motels, Mobility, Movies, and McKay. Venturing into it, I found evidence of Jackson's curiosity, wide-ranging interests, and use of unusual sources, including trade journals. The entry for "Mass Transportation" holds a two-page quotation from a July 1920 issue of *American City* regarding the proliferation of houses at the edges of towns serviced by jitneys rather than street railroads. "Music" took its quote from the *Berkeley Monthly,* March 1976, decrying the lack of silence in contemporary popular music and connecting this to its origin in automotive and machine sounds. "Motels" drew its information from *Motel/Motor Inn Journal,* August 1974, offering news that some motels were starting to have movies on demand and chaplains on call, while others were incorporating resort features including tall trees and spa features under a great dome. "Mobile Homes" gave the yearly number of trailers built by different manufacturers (totaling 600,000) gleaned from *Professional Builder,* July 1973.

The earliest citation was simply the title of articles from *Harpers* in 1872–73 regarding various means of transportation under "Mobility." The quotes in "Movies" came from the medium's early days, with citations from *Literary Digest* in the 1910s, including one from 1913 reporting worry by the *Daily Mail* that American movie subtitles were corrupting the English language with words such as *hoodlum, tough, hobo,* and *deadbeat.* Perhaps my favorite is "Monument," drawn from the "Monitor" (likely the *Christian Science Monitor*), March 9, 1975: "A 15 foot monument of a prairie chicken will be unveiled on April 24 along a highway in northern Minnesota—erected by the Minnesota Prairie Chicken society. Payment for the . . . statue in Rothsay will come strictly from the pockets of local prairie chicken lovers."[26]

Beyond Jackson's sense of humor, what is striking here is the wide range of sources, confirmed by entries under other letters of the alphabet. The thick folder *A* shows that, in addition to the above sources, Jackson looked for material in such diverse periodicals as *World's Work* (1903+), *Studies in the Twentieth Century* (1970), *Yale Review* (1909), *Oneida Historical Society* (1885), *Architectural Record* (1893+), *Better Homes and Gardens* (1937+), *Craftsman* (1907), *Architecture and Builders Magazine,* (1899–1900), *Practical Builder* (1967), and *Traffic Quarterly* (1971), among others. Along with back issues of professional journals and government documents, Jackson read popular magazines, including advertisements. He also kept up with serious periodicals, such as the *Atlantic* and *Harper's,* local newspapers, and the *Christian Science Monitor.* Yes, J. B. Jackson was an indefatigable searcher.

He thought of himself as a "man of letters," not as an academic scholar. Entering the public world in the 1950s as a landscape essayist, he aspired to join the league of writers such as Lewis Mumford and Vance Packard who imagined their audience as outside of academia. In Jackson's era, such public intellectuals could publish their work in major magazines with intellectual aspirations and in books issued by commercial houses. They were respected and at times revered by a significant reading public. In creating *Landscape* magazine in 1951, Jackson reached for their ranks.

Yet beginning in the mid-1960s, he also worked within two great universities. His various ways of organizing notes show him attempting the type of research discipline the academy encouraged. But how did he retrieve the material he had found during his searches? How could he pull together the disparate threads of chronological notes in spiral and bound notebooks, folders organization by alphabet, and 151 categories of notecards. What was Jackson's system of organization? How did he, the lone hunter, lay himself open to the flash of insight?

My own sense is Jackson's system lay elsewhere—in his prodigious memory, insight, and, for lack of a better word, chutzpah. Whatever he was in personal relations, in his landscape lecturing and writing Jackson was audacious. As he prepared his classes, thought through his lectures, and wrote his essays, he trusted his genius. He searched, relied on his recall, and hoped for flashes of insight. Fortunately, such flashes often came.

7

THE MAN I KNEW

Jackson's Letters, I

It has taken me time and several false starts to think how I might include my correspondence with J. B. Jackson. I treasure his letters as his side of what was for me a singular correspondence, but I am aware Jackson wrote to many others. Living alone, he valued his friendships. Letters were a particularly good way for him to keep in touch with those he cared for and those he felt might help spread his ideas. It is likely that with each letter he gave thought to the recipient and shaped some of what he wrote to establish or firm up their relationship. In corresponding, Jackson presented selected facets of his many-sided self. I offer excerpts from his letters to me in the hope others will come forward with their Jackson letters, thus allowing a richer portrait of the man and his work.

For me, receiving each one was an important event. His first letter came in winter 1974, responding quickly to the one I wrote to him roughly half a year after our meeting the previous autumn. At the time, I was a thirty-two-year-old assistant professor at Scripps College, early into the initial semester of my first tenure-track job. He was an established writer of sixty-five, teaching in two great universities. I wrote to him initially as an acolyte and have no idea why he chose to answer me as he did in this initial letter.

"I was delighted to get your letter, forwarded from Harvard to Berkeley," he began. (Meeting him at Harvard, I didn't then know he taught at Berkeley in the winter quarter.) The substance of his letter dealt with his recent decision not to accept a fuller offer from Harvard. He explained that "there was a question of my taking on a full year appointment at Harvard, and giving 2 courses—or the same course extended. But I have decided against it. It is foolish to give a course and expect real student commitment when there is no follow up—no advanced work in the subject; and Harvard expected me to do the entire thing." He believed Berkeley offered a better chance "for an extended course . . . for there are already others interested in 'strip culture', vernacular architecture and contemporary folklore." He added, however, that he found "much of the enthusiasm" there to be "undisciplined and without any underlying philosophy."

Our correspondence continued, and when he came to teach at UCLA in the spring of 1978, we toured gritty industrial Los Angeles and had meals together in our Claremont home and in his temporary one in Santa Monica. In the year that followed, I organized a session to present his work to scholars at the American Studies Association. After I wrote the necessary proposal to the ASA program committee and sent him a copy, he responded, "The flattering tone of your letter to the Committee embarrasses me, for I am very much aware that I am merely one of a growing number interested in the topic, and certainly not the one who can formulate the subject of Landscape Studies. But I am very willing to try, and despite my silence I have been giving the matter much thought." In the letters that followed, we discussed the panelists to speak about him, ultimately Yi Fu Tuan, John William Ward, and Dolores Hayden. A flood of correspondence followed, and imbedded in it is a copy of his one-page c.v., half typewritten, half in ink—a résumé famous in its day for its informality and brevity. Jackson also informed me that the University of Texas had recently asked him to teach for a semester beginning in January 1980. I decided I would try to have his Texas lectures tape-recorded.

On Thanksgiving Day, 1979, Jackson wrote a long response to two of my letters, revealing a good deal about his activities and state of mind at that moment. Regarding the taping of his Texas lectures, he was enthusiastic. "This of course is what I want most of all, and at present I'm trying to write the lectures, in order first of all to organize my thoughts on the subject of landscape (it's about time!) and second, to prepare for the course and all that means in terms of references, bibliographies and so on." He thought that if he had a written text, it would make the transcriptions easier. Then came a flattering statement, one I hardly believed: "I know of no one whom I trust and respect more than you, and your advice and criticism will be appreciated." During that period, he had many demands upon his time. Supported by an NEH grant, a former student of his from Berkeley was coming in two weeks to make a film of him "discussing the highway." At Harvard there was a move to film a lecture, but it was stalled. "In the meantime I suppose the best I can do is write the forthcoming lectures and depend on you for guidance."

I had just read the book edited by Donald Meinig, *The Interpretation of Ordinary Landscapes.* I wrote Jackson regarding its appreciation of him and about his own contribution, "The Order of a Landscape." He replied that he was "naturally pleased with Meinig's book, though it is based entirely on 'Landscape' and since then I've changed and amplified many ideas." I had asked if I could read the manuscript he had mentioned on the origins of the American landscape, and he replied that "it has been so badly cannibalized and dismembered that I doubt if I have a complete copy." He was now convinced his "extensive chronological treatment" was the wrong approach. "As a result I am taking up topic by topic: house, road, garden, forest etc and discussing the changing role of each." (This revised manuscript became *The Necessity for Ruins and Other Topics,* published by the University of Massachusetts Press in 1980.) He ended the letter with "Will you be my editor—promoter? Please!"

From what I can read in my response, this request seems to have troubled rather than flattered me. Even now, looking back and knowing what I know, I have no sense of why he wrote it. If he was serious, I can't understand the confidence he was placing in me, an assistant professor at a small college. He was well established on many fronts, including years of university teaching. I also am now aware that my being both Jewish and female may well have posed some problems for him. Over time, I came to accept that his friendship and confidence in me was simply a gift.

I felt at the time a responsibility to try and help him. I was pained by the manner in which he presented himself as someone buffeted by external forces demanding his labor. My response was to ask him if he wanted to take control over his own work and, if he did, whether he wished my assistance with the projects he chose to pursue.

Jackson's answer on December 1 was long and detailed. "Your kind letter, with the advice and the offer of help made me realize how helpless I am, and how much in need of guidance," he began. He told me he was writing to the person at Harvard regarding "what precisely he had in mind" for the filmed lecture. He was awaiting a visit from the former Berkeley student, who would be coming for several days with a cameraman. He had gotten word from the University of Texas regarding the taping of his lectures and was working on writing them.

"I don't know of other projects; they turn up when I[']ve lectured, and usually lead nowhere," he continued. "You ask what I myself want. I have no desire for publicity as such. I have no ambitions for more exposure or more contacts, and I have no judgment of such matters as TV programs and interviews, where they finally appear and whether they are valuable to the cause. As you suggest, all that I really want is to have some of my lectures appear in print." He added that his only desire was "leisure to write, and opportunities to lecture." He didn't relish the teaching ahead of him in Texas, but had taken it on "because of the money, and the ardors [arduousness] of winter here in Santa Fe."

At present he found himself "overwhelmed by routine work": tending to the wood stoves providing heat for his house, keeping up with his large correspondence, and working on numerous lectures for the coming spring, including a two-week stint at Berkeley. Jackson's letter conveys the tension between his two desires. On the one hand he preferred living quietly, "quite alone, with a large, 5 acre place to take care of, and the company of my Spanish american neighbors." On the other, he had hoped for "disciples, students or teachers who would follow my lead." This now seemed out of reach—"my teachings are too vague for that, and I am now merely one among many who talk about the subject." He had come to realize his appeal was "largely personal," stating that he was "listened to as a 'character' rather than for what I say."

He knew he needed help, but "of what sort"? He asked for suggestions, but at the same time ruled out fellowships: "I have had opportunities before, including a Guggenheim, but I have always felt that having private means I should not accept help of that sort. . . . I am a hopeless case: so to repeat, all that I should want is for my lectures—or some of them—to receive a more or less permanent, public form."

When I replied, I pushed back hard against his assertion that he was only "listened to as a 'character,'" rather than for the content of his work. I wrote that although there were certainly others in the field, he was unique in his command of language, imagination, and wit, and that his special gift lay in his ability to dramatize landscape history and make it come alive.

His return letter did not respond to this comment but told me again of the various demands on his time. He relayed one bit of good news: the Harvard project was moving along. (It would ultimately lead to *Figure in a Landscape: A Conversation with J. B. Jackson* by Janet Mendelsohn and Claire Marino). He had canceled two of his lecture engagements for the spring. At present, snow in Santa Fe was keeping him inside, and his typist was taking her time as usual.

He sent me his Texas lectures before my next letter to him. When I wrote back, I praised them and tried to show him how each worked to lead the reader/listener to a fundamental understanding of landscape transformation. I pointed out the way he began with a detail that emerged as part of a larger issue and then built to a conclusion. Jackson also sent me a proposal, perhaps related to the Harvard project.[1] I suggested he remove from it his expressions of a sense of embattlement against environmentalists and Marxists, arguing that his own approach, supported by examples, was the important element to convey.

His next letter to me, written on February 1, 1980, came from Austin, Texas, and was filled with details of his life there and his work at the university, where he found much to be accomplished. He had about 150 students in his lecture course, and his TAs knew nothing about the subject, thus he had to do all the grading. His seminar on the house (or "dwelling," as he put it) was too large. "Furthermore," he wrote, "there are books to put on reserve, reading to provide, and the establishing of pleasant contacts with students and faculty. I spend much time in the libraries— magnificant [sic] places to work but inevitably lacking in some materials I want." He also was annoyed to learn that he had to remain in Texas until May 15, cutting into his gardening time in New Mexico.

Despite these complaints, he was initially enthusiastic about his new life. He liked what he had seen of Texas thus far. "People are not only friendly but courteous, the countryside is beautiful and except the last two days the weather has been mild." He was living in very small quarters in "an expensive condominium," trying to economize. As a result, "life is much simplified and very refreshing in the total change of habits and contacts and point of view. . . . I feel very happy; I feel at home with Texans for many reasons: 40 years in the Southwest have weened me from New England."

Jackson's time at the University of Texas told me a good deal about him. Letters from him came thick at that time, perhaps because for much of the time he was lonely. Successive ones encouraged Dan and me to come and visit when he returned to Santa Fe.

Toward the end of February, however, Jackson began to write of his disappointments at the university. The transcriptions of his lectures were clearly a bust. "I doubt if they can be read by any editor. They not only indicate my very random kind of delivery, not always intelligible, but also indicate the apparent inability of the transcriber to understand many words. The result is really all but unreadable."

On the brighter side, he thought the lectures were going well, and he was adapting them "to suit a Texas student body." He saw his students as having "a strong rural tradition which I thoroughly appreciate," and that was leading him to learn more about Texas history and landscapes. His reading made him "aware of the great importance of land ownership in the development of house types (temporary for most urban dwellers) and in the organization of rural institutions." He closed with a jaunty, "So off I go in a few minutes to read a Texas County history—one a day."

Jackson's letters during his semester of teaching reported that he was accepting more lecturing invitations, some as far afield as the University of Virginia and Cranbrook Academy in Michigan. While in Texas, he lectured at Rice in Houston on "Dwelling versus House (temporary versus permanent home)," and on "The City Beautiful at the Art Museum." The Harvard project was now stalled, and "the interested parties have not peeped. But then, neither has American Studies here at the University of Texas. They probably don't even remember I[']m here, even though I paid my respects the first day." He ended, however, on a cheery note: "so now over to the Texas Historical Library for another County history—very naïve, very attractive books."

In early March, with a week free, Jackson decided to make the fifteen-hour drive home to start his garden "and touch home base before 6 weeks more of TU." Transcription of the lecture tapes had proved hopeless. He had received the first three but learned "the Architecture School farmed out the transcribing to a local typing firm. . . . The errors are too extensive to correct. . . . I must let the affair take care of itself." And that was the end of that.

To his distress, he recently learned that he had either misinterpreted the invitation to teach or it had been misrepresented to him. In reality he had been hired "to fill a slot left vacant by a sabbatical to teach a standard course on Site Planning." That meant students had no knowledge of what they were taking "and were bewildered by the Land[s]cape course." He had been completely ignored. He then turned upbeat. "This is very good for my ego, and I have benefitted to the extent of becoming interested in Texas, which I find very sympathetic." He was, as a result, "doing much outside reading and speculation on vernacular houses."

Jackson saved the best to last. "My book has appeared: at least one copy—*very* thin, *very* small—has been sent to me." This was *The Necessity for Ruins and Other Topics*. Its evocative exploration of the deep past moving into the present make it my favorite of all his books.[2]

Jackson returned to Austin from his days in Santa Fe with strengthened resolve. His April 1, 1980, letter reported that he had learned his former student and successor in teaching landscape courses at Harvard had completed his own book on the American landscape from 1607 to 1850.³ As a result, Jackson would have to alter his own manuscript to begin after the mid-nineteenth century. This would necessitate "leaving out much of my material and accumulating more. This could certainly be done."

Facing his isolation in Austin again, he wrote, "At the moment I am simply looking forward to getting out of the academic atmosphere; it is not the social neglect that bothers me so much as it is the impossibility of exchanging a single idea with others interested in the field; but it is quite evident that no such interest exists." But then he let me know what he was beginning to enjoy in its stead: a full-time— "5 days a week, 6 hours a day"—course in auto-mechanics. Texas turned out to be a success after all.

The course proved to be important to his future, pointing a way to break out of a life that no longer satisfied him. In Texas, as he learned and practiced alongside "young Blacks and Chicanos very eager to acquire training, and very bright in the world of auto," he experienced the deep satisfaction to be had from ordinary manual labor.

Once back in Santa Fe, Jackson declared himself "through with academia—the *last* term papers, the *last* exam, the *last* of the familiar excuses from students." Responding to my praise of *The Necessity for Ruins and Other Topics,* he demurred: "It isn[']t an exciting production, but it allowed me to dispose of interests from the past, and to turn in other directions."

Jackson may have taken his departure from teaching, but certainly not from lecturing. On May 21, he reported he had just returned from New York, where he gave a talk to members of the Architectural League. He confessed that "for some deep[-]seated, incomprehensible reason" he had "attacked the Olmsted landscape tradition—knowing full well that NYC and its landscape architects worship Central Park." This opposition was not new—Jackson had stated it in *Landscape* from early on. As discussed above, my research into his past has revealed that pleasure in going against the grain was already there in his boyhood. Put simply, Jackson enjoyed being a contrarian.

Facing him at home in New Mexico were many calls for his attention. Because the National Endowment for the Arts was offering $700,000 in grant money for "proposals dealing with the urban landscapes," four television stations, MIT, and the University of California requested his support. "It is largely a matter of using my name, and I[']ve no objection," he wrote. He seemed pleased that the University of Massachusetts Press wanted another book from his hand. All things considered, "I am happy to be home—not much richer, financially speaking, from the 4 months in Texas, but with new ideas, and a new freedom—both from academic constraints, and from many inherited prejudices and tastes—or so I hope."

By July Jackson was thinking about two projects. One, precipitated by a lecture he gave at a teachers' conference in Cranbrook, Michigan, was a "short and informal" book to introduce "intelligent Teachers . . . to landscape studies." It proved, however, difficult to write. He attributed this to an "inability on my part to keep on the subject, to be informal without being condescending, and to present a consistent point of view." He soon dropped it.

His second project engendered more enthusiasm. "I am calling it 'The Coming of Landscape Number Three' . . . the contemporary sensory landscape. I'll tell you more when I've form[u]lated it better." He labeled the first two landscapes as "the European land[s]cape until 1600" and the "scientific enlighted Landscape" lasting until 1920. He was engaged by this subject but hampered by "the physical inability to write more than 3 hours a day."

Jackson laid out a busy fall schedule of lecturing in the east and a winter stint at Rice for two to three weeks. Two people from Harvard were coming to film him in late August. In his October 9 letter he reported, "the video project seems to have reached the funding stage." He was going to Harvard, where he would lecture on "vernacular architecture and the landscape of gastronomy—the Landscape of Milk & Honey versus the Landscape of Bread & Wine: Germanic versus Latin." He planned to follow his time at Harvard with a trip to the University of Massachusetts to lecture on Landscape III and see the editor at the press. After that, he would travel to speak on forests at Piney Barrens State College of New Jersey and at the University of Pennsylvania. The very afternoon of the letter he was giving a talk before a small audience on Santa Fe architecture. Ruefully, he commented, "I won[']t say what I think: that it is affected and much too expensive."

At this point in my life, as much as I was learning from Jackson, I was also trying to develop my own ideas of place and space, linked to my interests in women's history and higher education. I spent the summer of 1980 weaving back and forth from California to women's colleges in the East, gathering research materials for the book that was to become *Alma Mater*. I had my first sabbatical from teaching during the academic year 1980–81, and in the fall I was deep into writing. I hadn't gotten fellowships for support for the year and, with Scripps College's permission, was applying for one for the following year. With some hesitancy, I sent Jackson a draft chapter, "The Design of Smith College," seeking his criticism and insights. His return letter was filled with questions and comments about my work. Reading over them now, I note how carefully he read the manuscript and, with my present knowledge of his years at Deerfield, how much he knew about the region in which Smith is located.

I had written to Jackson many months earlier about Paul Shepard's interest in getting him to speak during the coming winter at Pitzer—like Scripps, one of the Claremont Colleges. By October 10, a date was set for him to speak: February 12, 1981. His visit to Claremont then proved to be a happy occasion. Because several of the principals who brought him to Pitzer were themselves on sabbatical and were keeping a low profile, I was entrusted with a good deal of the hosting. During the weekend following Jackson's lecture, Dan and I took him to the best restaurant we could imagine in Los Angeles, L'Orangerie. The setting, the food, Jackson's presence, and our conversation over the long meal seemed to me magical. What I remember most, however, happened on the approach to the freeway to take us back to Claremont. Spying a Burger King, Jackson quipped to Dan, who was driving, "We should have gone there—you would have saved a lot of money!"

The evening before, Dan and I had taken him to the small Conservative Jewish synagogue in Ontario, California, where we were members. I remember sitting beside him during the service and being amused at the tall cowboy hat he sported, his way of responding to the male custom of covering the head during religious services. In a long letter he wrote to me after the visit, Jackson began: "I think what I like best about my two weeks away from home was the Sabbath service you took me to. I was interested in every detail, and every detail was sympathetic and inspiring." He added that he had recently read a discussion in *Commentary* magazine on "the future of Yiddish."

During his visit I also arranged time with two of my friends who were admirers of him. I took Jackson to the Huntington Library to meet James McGregor, a gardener employed there. On a sunny afternoon, I accompanied them on a long walk through the gardens. Jackson later wrote that he had "got much inspiration and information" from McGregor. My clearest memory is Jackson pointing out, with a wry smile, a plant in the herb garden with hallucinogenic properties, stating that women rubbed its leaves on the broomsticks they "rode" as witches. The second visit was with Vince Healy, an artist with a special interest in architecture and gardens. He came to Claremont to walk with Jackson through the Scripps College buildings and grounds. I remember their learned conversation in one of the college's inner courtyards about the "tuning" of fountains, as we examined and listened to one.

During this period, Jackson was continuing to receive many offers to lecture and was also getting letters from publishers hopeful of weaning him from the University of Massachusetts Press. He wrote that he planned to return to "the serious business of writing consecutively on a book: everyone else seems to turn them out with such ease, and I sweat out a brief lecture with agony."

In the spring of 1981, I published an article in *Landscape,* "Seeing Ourselves through the Bars: A Historical Tour of American Zoos." Jackson, no longer associated with the magazine he founded, read it and wrote to me, "What a delight your piece about zoos was! And it took someone like yourself with imagination and historical background to link the enthusiasm for zoos (in some cases) with turn of the century racialism." His interest emboldened me to send him two additional pieces I had published, one of them dealing with the New York Zoological Park, informally known as the Bronx Zoo. There I had written about the leadership of Madison Grant and Henry Fairfield Osborn at the zoo, describing their work as of a piece with their scientific racism and their efforts at immigration restriction. Jackson's letter of August 4, 1981, written after he had read this article, revealed much about his distaste for the contemporary elite's version of "environmentalism." He wrote, "I trust you realize you are exposing the Sierra Club, at least by implication. The philosophy of that gang was a few years ago precisely that of Grant and Osborn etc." Actually, the only parallel was the presumption of the elite leaders of the two organizations. The content of their efforts—racism on the one hand, and environmentalism on the other, had little to do with each other.

When I sent Jackson the talk I had prepared for a commemoration of the Los Angeles Bicentennial, held at the Huntington Library in mid-July of 1981, Jackson remarked in his return letter that he particularly enjoyed the last section focusing on contemporary Los Angeles. "I[']m keeping it to steal from when, many months hence, I come to the contemporary Western American city." He was then delineating the three landscapes and had just begun with "the Medieval forest" of Landscape I.

After writing to him in regard to a student's request for needed sources for a paper on prefabricated houses, he replied with many suggestions, following his own method: he recommended the magazine *Professional Builder* and catalogs from two construction companies. Turning to his own work, he wrote, "I myself am hung up (quite happily) on the subject of boundaries and frontiers. They were totally different in form and philosophy in the Middle Ages: they produced a very different landscape." He ended with the personal concern that was beginning to haunt him, his sense he had lost his audience: "but does anyone really care?"

In February 1982, he wrote to tell me of his upcoming travels, including a speaking engagement in Virginia to address a group of people concerned about Washington, D.C.'s expansion into their region. He understood this as part of a pattern that was beginning to afflict La Cienega as well. His own "little village" had been "once the turf of sloppy, inefficient Spanish blue-collar citizens" but now was "invaded by craftsmen and artists who all clamor for the prese[r]vation of this supposedly untouched peasant community." Expressing as usual his appreciation of ordinary people and his disdain for pretentious elites, he complained, "I resent craftsmen bitterly: their work is expensive, poorly designed and useless—and yet they are honored by NEA while excellent and ingenuous TV repairmen and mechanics are ignored. Perhaps Reagan can redress this unwholesome balance."

He was then writing "voluminously on Anglo-Saxon landscapes," he said, adding that "as the topic becomes more and more absorbing and revealing I get further and further away from any potential public." He planned nonetheless to "inflict" some of his "erudition" on his audiences in upcoming lectures.

Jackson encouraged me, as he did others, to visit him in La Cienega. After many repeated invitations extended to Dan and me (and our children), I wrote him in early spring 1982 that we planned to come during the summer and asked him to let me know about convenient motels nearby. "Dearest Helen, *Of course* I meant you to come & stay in my house!" he replied. He described its many features, including "a large, 2 bed guest room with bath, and plenty of public or leisure spaces." His activities would keep him engaged. "I lead what would seem to others a dull and solitary life. I write and garden, and see a few people who drop by. I am not a patron of the Santa Fe opera (Thank you just the same) because it is too late in the evening; nor do I patronize Santa Fe restaurants—too expensive and too crowded." He let me know we would be free to come and go without any attention to his "eccentric habits": during our visit, he would be working on a part of his book "which means 3 hours of writing a day, occasional trips to the University library in Albuquerque—and then pottering around outdoors."

I was taken aback by this letter. J. B. Jackson was a bachelor, and Dan and I traveled with our two children in tow. I called Paul Shepard, one of his longtime friends, to ask him what to do, only to have Paul reassure me that Jackson at his age certainly knew his own mind, and if he wanted the four of us to visit in his house, we should enjoy the pleasure of staying there. Jackson's warm welcome and his pleasure in the company of our children proved Paul to be right.

My year of sabbatical was proving productive, and I sent Jackson the full draft of what was to become the book *Alma Mater*. He replied with an eight-page letter that offered extremely helpful suggestions for an introductory chapter, as well as a detailed list of questions, corrections, and challenges. Reading over this letter now, I see how careful he was about language, factual details, and larger themes. His many years as an editor stood me—as likely it did many others—in good stead.

By the time his letter of June 15 had arrived, Jackson had received our travel itinerary, letting him know the day of our arrival in August. He cautioned us to get opera tickets in advance. He told of experiencing a Santa Fe already "jammed with tourists." Since we had now accepted his invitation to stay at his house, he wrote, "You will appreciate this quiet, remote spot after a glimpse of the Paris of the Upper rio Grande."

Jackson's Letters, II

In my memory, that first week-long stay at Jackson's house in August of 1982 is bathed in a golden glow. The four of us had a wonderful time, and while there was no appreciable change in my relationship with Jackson, I think the visit created a greater level of trust between us, and I began to feel comfortable calling him "Brinck." The following month, he sent me "to read (and criticize)" the set of essays he planned to send to Yale University Press.

I took the assignment very seriously. I have in my files the many pages of handwritten notes I wrote on the essays. My reply offered praise, comments, and suggestions regarding the individual essays. From a phone conversation mentioned in my letter to him, I learned he was thinking of turning the essays into a single narrative. I urged him not to do so: "Perhaps years of writing for *Landscape,* perhaps lecturing, perhaps a more subtle relation to form and content has given your prose a certain compression, sense of timing, and intellectual structure that works so beautifully within the form of the essay. . . . They are just right as they are."

Between the time I sent this letter and the time his reply arrived on September 22, I received and conveyed to him the very good news that Knopf was publishing my book on women's colleges, and this is what Brinck first focused on. When he got to my appraisals of his essays, he continued, "I will follow your advice as closely as I can. I still feel that since it is probably my last literary endeavor, I ought to insert as many relevant ideas as I can; and that means much rewriting."

He went on to tell me of some recent trips, including one during which he served as a consultant on an exhibition of Georgia landscapes over the last two hundred years. Focusing on the group planning the exhibit, he wrote, "As you can imagine the Georgia Historical Society is largely composed of white haired ladies, and the omission—benign neglect of Blacks was too marked for me to let stand. Even so I fear the Black contribution will be limited to old photos of Blacks hoeing cotton or sitting on the doorstep of their cabins. . . . It's a hard job bringing the two races together in an historical venture." This statement suggests a change in Jackson's attitudes regarding race. In trying to understand what might have brought this about, there is the external factor—the ways in which the United States was evolving— but, in his case, personal experiences were likely more important. Teaching at universities, he got to know and value African American students and may as well have come to admire his few African American colleagues. (A similar process may also have also been at work in reshaping his attitude toward Jews.)

After relaying some personal news, Jackson closed with "Duffy [his dog] is well, and so am I, and I am trying to wind up the rewriting." In his comic self-deprecating way, he added, "Everyone I know is publishing, and here I sit surrounded by tattered manuscripts and books overdue at the library, getting nowhere."

Our letters were beginning to take on a more personal tone. I was less an acolyte and more a friend; he was more expressive of his own concerns. After a long letter in early December 1983, that largely concerned my own activities and thoughts, Brinck replied (either in jest or out of his own sense of inadequacy at the time), "I see that you are writing and publishing and developing new interests and new ideas. I am consumed by the ugliest kind of envy . . . I have been struggling, day after day, hour after hour, with the MS, revising it, rewriting it, discarding enormous hunks and stealing from other pieces of writing of mine." He feared he wouldn't make the December 15 deadline set by Yale University Press, "so I am beset by pre-mature guilt."

He was working also on a number of lectures on vernacular architecture and finding "every paper I write on vernacular supersedes the previous one—and yet I keep them all in a pile on my desk. I am hopelessly involved in the definition of vernacular, and wish I could pass on to you some of my half-baked ideas." He was thinking of refusing an invitation to a conference in Los Angeles on the subject of arts and crafts. As seen in his send-up of the Loobeys in the mid-1950s, he never had sympathy for that artistic realm and now worried this conference would approach it with "an enthusiastic interest . . . which can be treated amusingly and with a certain chic." He feared it would lead to something he found typical of U.S. conferences: "new ideas are sought after not to be assimilated but to be used in the usual intellectual give-and-take."

During this time, Brinck's own life was beginning to take a new shape. He rented out the small house situated high above the main house, near the entrance to his property. He had as new tenants a preacher and his wife, whom he called "Brother & Sister Mitchell." Brinck wrote that he was fond of them: "good people, very modest, very poor, very kind to me, and I hope very happy." He wanted them to stay, and for him that meant that he had to "learn not only to accept their countrified Texas way of life but to consider them as a kind of substitute family." He now ate his evening meals with them. Regarding their plain food, he commented, "It doesn't hurt me a bit—and in fact it gives me an insight into the vernacular that can be useful."

With Christmas came Brinck's homemade card—as always, handsomely illustrated, this time with a block print of the nativity scene. Inside, under his handwritten greeting, was a note that on the day of mailing he had also sent his manuscript off to Yale. Our Christmas gift to him that year must have included something for his dog, for there followed a sheet of pink paper with an awkwardly scrawl. "Dear Aunt Helen and Uncle Dan Thank you for the Christmas present. It was the only one I got! Your unhappy friend, Duffy." Penned underneath in Brinck's familiar writing was "I can[']t understand the tone of this letter. Duffy is free to find a new home anytime he cares to. I am much hurt, but my conscience is quite clear!"

Brinck found another invitation in Southern California acceptable, a symposium in January 1983 at California State Polytechnic University in which he was to be the keynote speaker. Afterward, he invited Dan and me to a restaurant dinner that he jokingly described as "an elegant, 4 course meal among dressy, well behaved people—if that is not asking too much of L.A." I had the honor of introducing Jackson at the event, and I remember his lecture as brilliant: important ideas expressed in a lucid and captivating manner. That evening, Brinck, Dan, and I made an effort to enjoy the proffered "elegant" dinner in Los Angeles, but the misbehavior of the "dressy" couple seated all too close to us made it difficult to do so. This time around, we indeed seemed to have asked "too much of L.A."

The following day, Brinck departed for Paris before heading to Rome for a two-month stay at the American Academy. On February 12, he wrote from Italy to complain that it had taken him two weeks to adjust. "I[']m afraid I am no longer as adaptable as I once was, and the difference in diet, in language, in routine, and in weather has seemed very difficult." He had a very pleasant apartment and found the "various Fellows, residents, visitors," largely classicists, to be "friendly and often interesting." He continued, "My own interests are beginning to center on seeing more of the countryside, and the Academy has been kind enough to arrange 2 excursions for me in the Academy car to two coastal areas where new towns were established by Mussolini."

Brinck found much to criticize about the "outskirts of Rome"—"a scattering of pretentious high-rise tenements all over the landscape—factories, used car lots, dump heaps, superhighways for miles and miles" making "the urban sprawl of the USA seem modest and orderly." With inclement weather in Rome during the past week, he had been "trying to use the predominantly classicist library" of the academy. If the skies cleared, he planned to "make a conscientious attempt to see a quota of Baroque churches. The contrast between this environment and that of the USA is stimulating and gives me much to think about." He hoped to go out sketching and was also trying to continue to write on "Landscape 3 which is in evidence here."

With Dan's family in New Haven and close friends to house me in New York, I planned a mid-April trip east to hear Brinck give a talk at Yale, meet with Jane Garrett (the Knopf editor of my forthcoming book), and attend a conference on American architecture at Columbia University in which Brinck participated. To me, the conference was interesting, but not to him. In an early May letter to me, he, exclaimed, "Wasn[']t that a *miserable* conference? Not a single new idea!" But his life was full. He blithely reported that he would be going the following week to Washington "to have lunch at the White House!" Unfortunately, I got no description of that event.

In August 1983 we returned as a family for another week-long stay in La Cienega as Brinck's guests. This stop in New Mexico was part of a vacation taken on the long drive to Ann Arbor, where we were to live and work for the coming academic year as visiting professors of history at the University of Michigan. Time at Brinck's house passed much as before, but it now included significant visits with some of his long-time friends, giving Dan and me a taste of the artistic and elite social circles in Santa Fe that still embraced him.

During that 1983 summer visit, Brinck introduced a startling new topic for conversation. One evening, as Dan and I joined him in washing and drying dinner dishes, he told us he had learned he was "Black"—that is, part African American. Our years of learning to take the varied revelations of students in stride stood us in good stead. In this instance, we imagined he was using this declaration to test his friends' level of acceptance of him (and wondering also whether "black" in this case was a metaphor for "homosexual"). We obviously passed the test.

His letter of August 15 was filled with references to our visit and his thanks for "two polar bears," his name for our gift of fur coverings for the front seats of his car, which were meant to keep his back cool during hot summer drives. He sent us a book on life in Michigan in its pioneering days to greet our arrival in Ann Arbor. His November 17 letter told of more travel for lectures in which he was "to say something about vernacular architecture: my ideas get more and more cloudy & xtreme; the artiness of the vernacular in Santa Fe drives me into the arms of mobile homes." His book *Discovering the Vernacular Landscape* was in production at Yale University Press, and he bemoaned the publisher's "rare moments of concern and letter writing" followed by "silence." One lecture invitation allowed him "a most beautiful drive . . . through Oklahoma to St Louis"; another got him to Miami where he was "impressed" by the city "as a post-modern Babylon. Such wealth! Such a hopeless ethnic mixture!"

In conversation I had become aware of his distaste for the extent to which American studies focused on literature (something that, in truth, was already changing). As Brinck discussed a younger scholar's forthcoming book on railroads, he grumbled, "I am tired of hearing Henry James and Thoreau quoted on every subject—but that's American Studies for you!" He continued with the subject introduced during our 1983 summer visit, offering new information: "My Black church [in Albuquerque] continues to absorb my interests and to divert me from random sociability."

The next letter I have from Brinck in my file, dated December 3, 1983, announced that he was taking his final exit from academia. He had proofread his forthcoming book and made its index. "I feel that a real turning point has been reached: no more contact with the Academic world, no more cautious writing for a tiny audience of graduate students, no more bibliographies!" Nonetheless he had plans for a trip to Berkeley, a "round table on vernacular architecture," and one to London for a "small Landscape studies Conference. . . . That won[']t be allowed to interfere with my garden, however."

I've always thought of my correspondence with Brinck as a "Victorian" one in which I tried to put into words many of my important feelings and hopes. As I review our letters now, I see it took time for me to write to him in this way. However, by 1984, I was clearly corresponding with a treasured friend. And he was responding in kind. In a letter dated February 1, 1984, Brinck told me of his writing, of course, but also of his new life as a worker. Brother Mitchell, his "pentecostal minister tenant," had found a way of making money through construction, "roofing and painting inside and out" on some new "low cost houses . . . being built in Santa Fe." Brinck had signed on to be his helper—"first to get him solvent and less of a financial burden to me, but also to revive his self-respect; and finally to get me out of the house, out of reading and writing." Early in this work, Brinck announced, "I enjoy every moment of it: being outdoors in what is often biting cold, being with working people, and also dealing with small scale but important questions such as 'will it work?' 'What will it cost?' 'How long will it take?' As to the last question, the answer seems to be months and months, and I hope I can stay with it all the time. I am proud that I am considered a good worker, and I am even in demand by other contractors."

He went on, "This has kept me entirely out of touch with my pleasant, elderly, liberal, Eastern minded Santa Fe friends. I[']m ashamed to say I miss them not at all." In addition to his construction work, he attended two times a week his "Black church, which is experiencing a new lease on life, thanks to a new preacher—young, eloquent, coal black, charismatic. So my circle has greatly changed." He outlined his lectures coming up, followed by a return "to Construction and total proletarian obscurity and gardening. . . . I am still wedded to country solitude—and construction! Radios playing rock-and-roll instead of Mozart—what a relief!"

In an undated letter from the spring or early summer of 1984, he returned to the subject of his construction work. He saw it as "a wonderful physical, social, moral discipline, and part of my new identity, which strangely enough begins to absorb me and effect many of my attitudes and thoughts. The Black church has become very important, and the change in many relationships though humiliating at first, now seems what I really want—a departure from middle class WASP academic liberal points of view—in favor of what I hope is a wider and more generous approach."

During this time, Dan, our two children, and I were in motion. From Ann Arbor we moved to Chapel Hill, North Carolina—the adult generation to enjoy a fellowship year at the National Humanities Center; the younger to cope with a change of public schools. This led Brinck, in a September letter, to teasingly imagine us as "in the midst of the pine forest, being languid and Southern. You will never be fit again for California; the Shreveport heritage is coming to the surface at last." The letter came from Edgartown, Massachusetts, where Brinck was speaking to designers at a conference. "It is nice to catch a final glimpse of New England, he wrote, somewhat nostalgically, "fresh painted white houses with tidy lawns and gardens, a glimpse of the ocean, and the New England autumn just around the corner." He had recently had a Sunday *New York Times* review, by Jonathan Raban, of *Discovering the Vernacular Landscape*—perhaps the first harsh, unappreciative one he'd ever received.[4] He found the review "disturbing—not so much because of its tone, but because the Times chose someone so ill-informed; but it's going well enough—the book, that is."

My own book, *Alma Mater,* greeted him on his return to his New Mexico home, and he extended kind words of praise. A letter dated November 24 shifted to a sympathetic tone, for I had just undergone minor surgery, but it was filled with his news. He told me that he had recently been to New York City, Montana State University, and Ohio State and found that "flying about the USA has become increasingly strenuous and uncertain and more like what one would expect from the Balkans: delays, cancellations, crowds, and incessant loudspeaker announcements." Once again, he vowed not to travel anymore, and once again he let me know he was about to travel. "I continue to flounder in my attempts to define 'The Vernacular,'" he wrote, but then gave me a list of prestigious periodicals publishing his work on the subject. He also remarked that, aside from the negative Raban review, "I[']ve had favorable criticism, though it surprises and unsettles me to be thought of as a radical critic of the US and an advocate of strip development & strip architecture. I merely recognize their existence."

Brinck had now moved out of his large house and into the small one by the road, which was no longer occupied by his evangelical tenants, the Mitchells. He claimed this was to save money on heating, but it may have been an attempt to live out his assumed working-class identity more fully. His construction work continued to fill much of his days and gave him "many benefits: physical, moral, social and even financial—$5 an hour." He maintained that he did the heavy work "with the greatest of ease," and, returning to the subject of his African American ancestry, added, "I find myself wondering if this mixed heritage of mine doesn't account in part for my physical vigor and my satisfaction in a very different way of life and a very different society. I wish it had come earlier, but I hope it helps formulate some better ideas about landscapes and the people who make them—with pick and shovel, just as I do!"

Brinck's Christmas card showed none of his new working-class leanings, however. It reproduced an image of a hooded and bearded older man walking through a

Baroque landscape carrying a lit candelabrum. Inside the card, after a personal note, he touched briefly upon his efforts to write on the vernacular and to deal with "the critical response to the book . . . that I am endorsing the strip, am a crypto-Marxist, and am a closet theologian."

During Dan's and my busy year in North Carolina, we saw Brinck briefly when we attended a lecture he gave in Raleigh. In his letter of February 26, 1985, he told of his pleasure at seeing us in the audience. He reported that he had also traveled to Charlotte, where he was "given a complete tour of the city—an amazing place! It has stimulated my interest in medium size cities like Albuquerque and El Paso." He added that he was trying to write a long essay for *Design Quarterly* in an issue devoted to him. Facing a pending interview with the editor of *House and Garden,* he wrote, "I dread the distortions which he will produce." I sensed he was responding to the kind of public attention he both desired and shunned. His next letter, which came in early March, amusingly referred to that interview and a slight injury on his construction job, by telling us our gift of chocolates came "*just in time. . . . a transfusion of chocolate was essential. My system did *not* reject it, and now I am myself again, Thanks entirely to your generosity.*" Brinck definitely knew how to write a thank-you note.

During the following summer, on our return drive from North Carolina to California, we visited him once again. This stay was different from the previous ones, however. Brinck remained in his small dwelling by the road. As we talked there in its kitchen, in these changed circumstances I saw a changed man. He was paying little attention to his appearance and seemed depressed. I didn't know at the time whether his altered state was due to aging, the results of his effort to live out the proletarian life, or psychological depression. Whatever the cause, his state of mind and location proved temporary: Brinck regained his equilibrium and, before long, moved back into his spacious home.

During the last decade of his life, Brinck continued to pay thoughtful attention to my writing, and also now to Dan's. When he wrote about himself, it was to take up familiar themes: his ongoing efforts to wrestle with "the vernacular" in his writings; his travel to give lectures, accompanied by the ever-present desire to do so less and less; his satisfactions with life as a laborer and the associations it gave him with working people. At times, he expressed his belief that he had lost his audience, but receiving the PEN/Diamonstein-Spielvogel Award for the Art of the Essay in 1995 gave him a last lift.

His letters during the 1990s also contained much about practical matters. In

1988, Dan and I had taken positions at Smith College and moved with our daughter and young adult son to Northampton, Massachusetts. We didn't see Brinck for a number of years and decided in 1993 to pay him a visit. In its aftermath, I got his permission to tape our conversations. During two working weeks, the first in January 1994 and the second beginning in late May of the same year, Brinck and I sat in his garden as he reminisced about his past and talked about his ideas. I had transcriptions made in the hope he could use these as a basis for writing new essays, a strategy I had found worked at times with other friends. The transcriptions proved worthless to him, for he was a craftsman who carefully composed words on paper. (I was reminded of this when I read his musings in 1959, revealing how he rewrote and rewrote a sentence until he sensed he had it right.) I began to think of a new approach to bring him to a wider public and in 1995 secured his cooperation to put together a new collection of his essays. Subsequently, he appointed me his literary executor.

Work on *Landscape in Sight* was in process at the time of his death on August 28, 1996.

The Sociable Man

I began to learn of Jackson's social nature in the course of our family's initial summer visit to La Cienega in 1982. The four of us (including our children, ages eleven and four) would leave on daily outings to explore the walks and hikes that the region around Santa Fe offered. When we returned, Brinck was always ready to entertain us, not only with drink and snacks and, later, dinner, but also with his conversation. He told us of each day's local visitors, who came to see him in the afternoon.

Jackson's house was designed for sociability as well as privacy. It had a grand entryway, but by the time we visited in the early 1980s, Brinck's primary place for greeting arriving guests was the parking area to the side of the house. He would usher them into the kitchen, which had a small dining table and chairs at its center. It was there that he sat with his neighbors when they came to call. It was also where house guests had breakfast—taken, in my family's case, hours after Jackson had eaten. Toward the end of his life, the kitchen was where Jackson ate supper, either alone or with a few guests.

Beyond the garage was a very small room. (During our family visits, our son stayed there. Later in his life, it was where Jackson kept many of his sketches.)

Brinck's kitchen led directly into the dining room, where our family took the

Figure 31. Kitchen, J. B. Jackson's house, La Cienega, 1982; photograph by Marc Treib

evening meal with him during visits; five were comfortably served, and on festive occasions, the table could accommodate more. The walls of the dining room boasted an antique wallpaper he told me came from his mother. The mantel over its fireplace served as a secular altar on which Jackson kept the many small items given to him, children's drawings, and a crowd of whimsical objects that caught his fancy (see color plate 13). He would not let me touch them and warned me of this whenever I got too close.[5]

On grand occasions, such as the large outdoor parties I never experienced, I imagine guests entered from the portico at the front of the house. They then came into an entry hallway with a table where Jackson kept his guestbook. The hallway led both to the dining room and the living room. Although I knew the dining area well, in all the time I spent in the house, only once did the living room serve as a gathering place for company (though I occasionally chose it as the quiet room in which to read).

To the right of the entry were Brinck's private quarters, consisting of a large study, a small bedroom, and a bath. In his study, whose bookcase-lined walls held a vast array of books, he had a large working desk. The room also contained, in front of a large window to the outside, an ancient small sofa covered in a cloth made

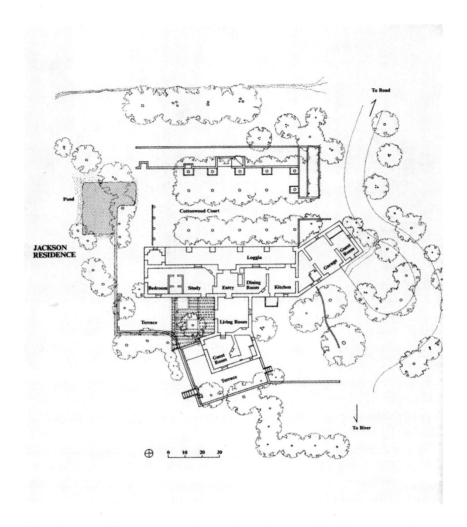

To Road

Pond

JACKSON
RESIDENCE

Cottonwood Court

Loggia

Garage

Guest
Room

Bedroom   Study   Entry   Dining
Room   Kitchen

Terrace

Living Room

Guest
Room

Terrace

To River

0   10   20   30

Figure 32. Site plan of J. B. Jackson's house, La Cienega, drawn by Dorothée Imbert

of horsehair. I seldom came into his study, and I entered his bedroom only once, when, toward the end of his life, the two of us searched its bookcases for the original publications containing his articles to appear in *Landscape in Sight*. The room struck me then as unadorned as a monk's cell.

Other than the kitchen and dining room, the area I knew best was the spacious guest room and bath that lay beyond the living room. Brinck designed the suite

Figure 33. Dining room, J. B. Jackson's house, La Cienega, 1982; photograph by Marc Treib

for his ailing mother in the expectation she would join him once the house was built (he intended the small house close to the road for her nurse). However, Alice Jackson died in July 1965, just before the house was finished. The suite became guest quarters, and Brinck placed on a table near its entrance all sorts of printed information about sites to see in the area.

On our summer visits to him, Brinck seemed most to enjoy an outdoor area, reachable through the living room. Furnished with a coffee table surrounded by chairs and what I remember as an outdoor settee, the setting served as his back porch. Presumably following his usual practice, Brinck would gather our family there around 5 PM for drinks and nibbles. This was no time for him to hurry through, but rather one he prolonged as long as possible. As we unwound and told of our day's adventures, and ultimately our life stories, Jackson enjoyed his stiff drink, all the while making fun of Dan and me as weak persons who drank wine. He kept the children entertained with his "zapper," an electric device that attracted flying insects and electrocuted them on the spot. With each buzz, Brinck would clap his hands and give a hearty laugh. He also tracked the July thunderstorms building in the sky with equal delight.

When we first came to visit, Brinck had two horses on the property, although I never saw them saddled and mounted. By then, according to Marc Treib, he had sold off half his acreage; nonetheless, the grounds seemed generous. Other than strolling about, we spent little time among the cottonwoods at the front of the house. Late in his life, Brinck and I went to converse at the far end of this area by the little stream he was nurturing. As we sat in the shade, he would claim that his affection for this bit of flowing water came from his Dutch heritage.

Recently I was able to read through Jackson's thick guest book.[6] For this purpose a scrapbook, normally the type to hold photos, sufficed. Visitors were asked to sign it and give their addresses. The first entry was made in 1969, the last effectively in 1984 (though there were four entries during the years 1985–86). In the fall and winter of most of the book's first decade, Jackson was away from home teaching; visitors thus came seasonally. In May 1969, most signers were locals with Spanish surnames. By mid-June, Jackson welcomed Marie Armengaud, an old Santa Fe friend and an early contributor to *Landscape*. Soon after came Jay [James E.] Vance, from Berkeley's geography department, and Jean, his wife, both friends. From then on, the guest book reflected Jackson's unique social world, one that combined his neighbors (largely of Hispanic background), old friends, well-known writers and thinkers, and former students.

Sooner or later, everyone I ever met personally in his company or heard him mention, along with many known only to me by their reputations, dropped by and signed. Jackson had a vast acquaintance, and all seem to have come to his door. Most gave only the essential information requested, but some wrote bits of verse or sentiments, occasionally in German, French, Dutch, or other languages. Some came often, signing each time. A few were children, one giving his address as the United States. When there was a large grouping of Hispanic names, it seemed likely that Jackson held a party and asked all those attending to sign.

By the time I read the entries for 1973, I could begin to see some patterns in the names. Visitors from Cambridge came during the summer. Established friends— Blythe and Jim Brennan, Doug Adams, Eugene Cotton Mather, and members of the Haegler family—made repeated visits. There was the continuing presence of Hispanic neighbors. Likely because of Jackson's teaching and lecturing, there emerged an ever-widening stream of newcomers.

Most visitors merely gave their names, with addresses frequently noting only the city or country where they lived. Addresses changed, and occasionally demonstrated a move to New Mexico. A few of those from abroad used the space to write their sentiments in their native languages, sometimes at some length. Hispanic surnames persisted, with some choosing to write notes in Spanish. An exceptional woman proclaimed she was "Mrs. Senior Citizen of New Mexico" visiting Jackson on her "way" (unspecified). Long-lost relatives wrote of their pleasure in making contact. Wayne signed in once, in 1970, although newspaper reports have him visiting many times. The future architect Douglas Adams and his wife Trish, then living in El Paso, Texas, first visited in September 1970, returning for Christmas at the end of the year. Doug returned frequently for the remainder of Jackson's life, to ride motorcycles and sketch with him. Adlai Feather, Jackson's old friend and first contributor to *Landscape,* came with his family. Emlen, the close friend of Jackson's mother, signed twice, and her daughters, Nancy and Mia, visited in 1971.[7]

Among Brinck's visitors were a number of prominent figures whose names I recognize. Some came once, others many times. Listing only the first time each signed Jackson's guestbook, I found visiting him were the previously mentioned geographer Jay [James] Vance (1969), anthropologist Ned [Edward T.] Hall (1969), architectural historians Norma Evenson (1969) and Vincent Scully (1969), artist Gustave Baumann (1970), geographer John Fraser Hart (1975), landscape architect Garrett Eckbo (1977), environmentalist Paul Shepard (1977), artist Nell Sinton (1978), professor of landscape architecture Michael Laurie (1978), architect Charles

Moore (1982), professor of landscape architecture Marc Treib (1981), and landscape architect Larry (Lawrence) Halprin (1981).

I picked up other bits of information from the guestbook. Blythe and Jim Brennan, Brinck's close friends and motorcycling companions whom I came to know, moved to Santa Fe in the mid-1970s. With her visit in 1979, I got confirmation of the identity of his good friend from *Landscape*'s founding days—Miranda Masocco, now married (with Levy her last name) and living in Los Angeles.

Jackson gave numerous fetes at which most of the attendees were his neighbors, including the Romeros, de Bacas, Gonzaleses, and Montoyas. On Friday, August 8, 1975, when he hosted a party "in honor of Mrs. F Baca," he gathered the names of the more than twenty of those attending. On the following day, he was host to a "Cienega Dinner," where the numbers surpassed forty. On August 12, Jackson gave some kind of event for Loraine and Eddy—possibly their wedding—and about thirty-three guests signed in.

Sheila Cudahy Pellegrini, wealthy publisher and translator, first entered her name in the guestbook in 1979. She was then of Millbrook, New York, but soon moved to Santa Fe and became Brinck's close friend. The guest book that year also saw many return visits of old friends. Vera Laski, an anthropologist Jackson had helped decades before, came to visit and wrote, "Your house is the image of Your Self: solid, generous, with wide expanding horizons—and most precious to your friends." Marni Sandweiss, who was to become a historian of photography and the American West, came in mid-September. Janet Mendelsohn, planning to make a Cambridge-based video of Jackson, visited in August 1980 and then returned with her filming partner Claire Marino. In 1981, acknowledging frequent visits, Jackson's neighbors Leonora and George [Yrjö (Y.A.)] Paloheimo signed, as did Nell Sinton, his San Francisco friend. Marc Treib, in the Department of Architecture at Berkeley, wrote, "Always a pleasure!" Also visiting Jackson in these years were his teaching assistants at Harvard and Berkeley, John Stilgoe and Paul Groth; both were later to assume his university courses.

(By the time I reached the entries for 1982, however, it was clear to me that not all guests signed, for the book contains the names of neither Dan, Helen, Ben, nor Sarah Horowitz, who stayed for a full week both that summer and the next.)

In mid-August, 1982, a small party of approximately twelve brought together Jean Vance (Jay's wife) with Jackson's Hispanic neighbors and Reverend and Mrs. Mitchell. In late September, Jackson hosted at his house a meeting of La Sociedad

Folklorica, attended by twenty-two, and did so again in the following year. In 1982 he also hosted a gathering from Kansas State University and, in 1983, the Texas Studio of the University of Houston.

In September 1983, when the Brennans came to visit and celebrate his birthday, Blythe wrote, "Thank you dear Brinck! (John!)"—making it clear that he had asked her to call him by his hitherto ignored first name.

On January 8, 1984, Jackson gave another large party for his Hispanic neighbors—one of the final events listed in his guestbook. Nonetheless, his sociable life continued, as I observed firsthand during my frequent visits in the 1990s, when I would meet guests who had been invited into his home, as well as those who came during his daily afternoon hours of open hospitality.

In 1994, Dan and I and our children, one now an adult, spent Christmas vacation in Santa Fe, visiting Brinck, but not staying at his house. I helped with his Christmas midday dinner, to which he invited not only our family but also close friends of long standing and a young architect and his girlfriend, adding a bit of European glamour to the circle. It was a festive midday meal in the dining room, complete with Christmas paper crowns and noisemakers. Afterward we sat by the living room fire with brandy. It was the only time I can remember when the room was used for something other than a hallway pass-through or a place for solitary reading. Jackson was in fine form and seemed to enjoy the day. However, there was no guestbook to sign; and I am not aware of any after 1984 that records Jackson's generous hospitality.

Separating Fact from Fancy

What is truth and how do we know it? One of its elements is that it is often not as pleasing as fancy. I'll never forget the magical moment when Brinck looked across his dining room table at my five-year-old daughter and asked, "Do you know who George Washington was?" She nodded that she did. "Well, he kissed my grandmother, and my grandmother kissed me." Brinck walked around the table to her place, planted a light kiss on her cheek, and said, "And now I kiss you."[8]

Brinck explained to Dan and me, disbelieving and struggling to do the math, that John Brinckerhoff, his great-grandfather for whom he himself was named, was Washington's aide de camp during the American Revolution. He had a daughter quite late in life and held her in his arms for Washington's kiss. She gave birth to

Brinck's father in the mid-1800s, and he in turn was a considerably older man when Brinck was born. It was a lovely moment. But except for the shared name and his own father's middle age, the story was a complete fiction.

There was indeed a John Brinckerhoff who knew George Washington, but he was not, however, Washington's aide de camp: he was far too old for such service during the Revolution. John Brinckerhoff lived in Fishkill, New York, and when Continental Army forces were stationed there, he and Washington formed a friendship. Washington was known to come to Brinckerhoff's home as a guest.[9]

That John Brinckerhoff, however, was not J. B. Jackson's great-grandfather. Born in 1702, he was too old for it to be possible. He had children, but they were not of an age to be held for a kiss in the war decade that began in 1775.[10] Nor was J. B. Jackson in the genealogical line to have this particular John Brinckerhoff as an ancestor. The Brinckerhoff name came down from Jackson's grandmother on his father's side. Elizabeth Brinckerhoff McNulty, born in 1833, became Mrs. William Jackson, carrying the name "Brinckerhoff" from her own maternal line. Working upward on her genealogical chart, one can find no ancestral John Brinckerhoff living during the years of the Revolutionary War.

What there was in Jackson's heritage, however, was money and the desire to carry on a prestigious name. The 1870 census lists the New Jersey household of Brinck's grandfather, William Jackson. He was at that time a retired lumber merchant, whose real property was evaluated at $60,000 and personal wealth at $20,000; in today's dollars, a total equaling over $1.6 million. William Jackson and his wife christened his eldest son, born in 1856, William Brinckerhoff Jackson. The founding of the Daughters of the American Revolution (DAR) in 1890 likely enhanced the cachet of the Brinckerhoff name. In 1909, Alice and William Brinckerhoff Jackson named their child John Brinckerhoff Jackson.

Interestingly, Brinck Jackson's father seems not to have used his middle name. He was, however, only briefly in the household that included wife, son, and two stepchildren before separating from Alice in 1914. She continued to use her husband's name, and when wanting to make an impression, she was Mrs. William Brinckerhoff Jackson. Perhaps that same impulse toward social ascent led her to call her younger son "Brinck" or "Brincky," rather than John.

If I remember correctly, it was in 1982 that Jackson took all four of us to a cocktail party at the home of Christian Herter Jr., son of the former U.S. secretary of state and Massachusetts governor. There Jackson behaved in a manner I hadn't seen before. As we entered he complimented his host's red tie, remarking in his most elite eastern voice, "Not all reds are appealing, but yours is a handsome red." This seemed to me at the time the way he faced the blue bloods of Santa Fe.

In 1982, I had accepted Jackson's request that I call him "Brinck," and that was the name I knew him by at the time he bestowed the "George Washington" kiss on our daughter. Not long after that visit, however, he asked me to call him "John." And therein lies another story, and another need to separate fact from fancy.

When we visited the following summer, Jackson announced to Dan and me that he was black, based on no evidence that I have been able to unearth. With that, he informed us of the shock of "the establishment" in learning of his blackness: "They have cut me now, completely," he declared with a mixture of amusement, pride, and anger. Preparing to converse with Brinck on tape in 1994, I began a search for evidence of his African American heritage. I've never found any, but negative results are not conclusive. His family had been in this country a long time, and, as we now know, DNA tests have revealed the complex origins of many who have submitted their samples. Although I think of his assertion of African American heritage as one of his fancies, he may well have known more than I have been able to learn.

Nonetheless, it is interesting to think about what "blackness" seems to have meant to him in later life and how defining himself as African American fits into a pattern of reinvention. He had assumed many different roles before the 1980s: college esthete, novelist, ranch worker, soldier, cultivated New Mexican citizen, essayist and magazine publisher, and BMW rider. In 1983, he was developing a new persona as manual laborer. For purposes of this new identity, he asked to be called John. He showed me his business card, which announced, "John Jackson, man of work"—not John Brinckerhoff Jackson, graduate of Harvard College, published by Yale University Press. Earlier in his life—and as late as 1960—he had frequently expressed racist sentiments. Now, in his seventies, the connection he was making to his African American heritage—real or imagined—was the physical strength he associated with his manual labor. As "John," Jackson ascribed his relish for outdoor work and his toughness to what he called his "black blood." (Let it be said that although I adapted to his successive preferred names in his company or in written salutations, when I thought of him or spoke to others about him, it was always as "Mr. Jackson.")

One additional fancy I have uncovered in my research is Jackson's description of how he got into Harvard. In 1994, during one of our taped conversations, Brinck told me that his entry into college was easy. "I got a letter from the president of Yale saying, "Would you like to come to our college?" How did he get to Harvard?:

"You just wrote in and said, 'I want to come to your college.'" However, as his Harvard records clearly show (and as I have described in previous pages), getting accepted into Harvard was no such easy matter for John Brinckerhoff Jackson.

I don't know how many more fancies tinctured Jackson's conversation. However, these few have led me to trust less and less of what he said about the past in our taped conversations. What I am able to accept without question from that time are his evaluations of the lifelong influence books exerted upon him, his reactions to current situations, and his thoughts as they existed in 1994. My growing distrust of his statements about his past helped power my desire to know more and more about it and to seek his traces in letters, documents, and other writings of the time.

But even these can be deceptive. I found on Ancestry.com a record of Jackson's enlistment in the army, dated October 8, 1940, with the location of Santa Fe, New Mexico (see page 63). Jackson gave his residence as Colfax County, New Mexico. He put down that he had "4 years of college," and his occupation was "farm hands, animal and livestock." He anticipated service in the cavalry as a private in the Philippines. All these entries seem accurate. But listed with them is inaccurate information. Jackson gave his birth year as 1911, his birthplace as Massachusetts, and his height as 68 inches. In a letter written soon after enlisting, Jackson stated that he had claimed to be born in Massachusetts rather than in France in order to "avoid complications." Did he also make himself younger by two years because he felt he had a better chance of being accepted into the military if he was in his late twenties rather than in his early thirties? And when he gave his height as sixty-eight inches, a mere half-inch higher than the figure he gave when seeking employment in 1935, did he think this might also be in his favor?[11]

Jackson's effort to join the army was in many ways an admirable one. So what do the white lies on his enlistment record suggest about him? To me they show that his goal was to join the army, and that he was willing to bend the truth in order to do so. But they also warn me to be a bit wary of the biographical "facts" he provided when he was the only source of information about himself. At age sixteen, in response to his mother's suggestion of a way to make himself more disciplined in his schoolwork at Choate, he commented, "Making myself go without tea for a month may be good practice but total abstinence from lying, for a day would be better." I have taken this caution to heart as I have searched for Jackson's true traces throughout his long life.

8

TRACKING THE VERNACULAR

Jackson's writings in his later years mesh with his personal life in the mid-1980s and 1990s, as he began to stay longer periods at home in La Cienega, engage in manual labor, and see himself as African American. In this time, he increasingly rejected his elite status and sought connections with the workaday world about him. He continued to recognize the need to accept present-day technology and automobiles. He had hopes for the Southwest he loved and wanted its communities to grow in healthful ways. Finally, as he aged, he reflected on his life of writing and teaching about the landscape and how he would be remembered.

Much current familiarity with Jackson's work derives from books that anthologized his essays during his lifetime, leaving forgotten many essays of his final years. I have grouped discussion of these lesser-known essays into three common themes that absorbed Jackson in the last decade of his life: automobility, the future of the Southwest, and connection. In addition, although he often denied this, Jackson wanted to be known for his contributions to the creation of landscape studies as a field. This is apparent in his response to a 1991 inquiry regarding the five books that most influenced him. It also informed what was perhaps his last public talk, given in 1995 upon receiving the PEN Award for the Art of the Essay. And, finally, it shaped our communication in the last two months of his life.

Automobility

Anyone who visited Jackson in La Cienega knew of his love of cars, trucks, and motorcycles. When I knew him, the back door of his house, leading to the kitchen, was the normal entrance, and visitors parked alongside whatever vehicles Jackson operated at the time. In 1982, when we arrived for our first visit, our young son saw Jackson's BMW cycle and became instantly convinced that our coming to visit Brinck was the right idea.

The love of motorized travel suffuses much of Jackson's prose from the very beginning of *Landscape* magazine. He celebrated speed in "The Abstract World of the Hot Rodder," and, in season and out, he defended the automobile in myriad ways. Jackson's last years saw no letup.

In "The Vernacular City" published in *Center: A Journal for Architecture in America,* 1985, Jackson examined the urban form reshaped by the rise of the automobile.[1] Taking the rapidly growing Texas city of Lubbock as his example, he demonstrated

Figure 34. J. B. Jackson illustration, "Hot Rodder," 1957–58

how efforts to accommodate cars formed the spine and structure of the new American city. "Lubbock tells us what those new cities look like. In particular, it tells us about how the street, the road, the highway has taken the place of architecture as the basic visual element, the infrastructure of the city."

Jackson explained that a stranger typically goes to a city like Lubbock for a purpose, such as a visit to a shopping center or hospital; but someone choosing to travel there simply to see it finds that, unlike European cities, it is not possible to view much on foot. Lubbock requires a car. Having made this statement, Jackson then took his typical historical turn to discuss the changing urban form that brought the road into such prominence, illustrating this process through changes in Zenith, the fictional city in *Babbitt,* Sinclair Lewis's novel of 1922.[2]

One year later, 1923, came an important town planning conference in Paris that introduced aerial photography as a means "to understand and regulate the city," a tool for landscape discovery that Jackson particularly valued. By then, the automobile had already entered into the thinking of American urban planners. Initially they hoped the car would lead to cleaner and better-paved roadways and reduce the pressures toward urban centralization. In these early days, however, the City Beautiful Movement was maintaining that architecture, especially classic architecture, ought to compose "the essence of the city."[3]

The Sunbelt cities of later decades, however, were based on a different foundation. Sketching their history with a broad brush, Jackson wrote, "The new city grows a web of streets long before houses appear." He described the coming of roads as if they were rivers. "In the beginning, there is nothing more than the Interstate. Suddenly there comes an interchange, like a break in a dam or in a river bank. In no time a flood of artifacts submerges the hitherto flat and empty countryside: swarms of trailers and bulldozers and power poles and storage facilities, the rows of small, identical dwellings, gas stations, churches, used car lots, and a Holiday Inn; and a broad main street with one highrise; more houses, more interchanges." It is thus that a new American city emerges, "which no one, even a hundred miles away, had ever heard of before."[4]

The new streets required new rules. City authorities moved to regulate vehicular flow by putting in traffic lights, outlawing parking, dividing the lanes with a median. Such changes affected the businesses along the route and created the Strip, with its particular form of architecture. Jackson returned to what he had once called "other-directed houses," now renaming the architecture of the Strip "commercial vernacular." Here he redefined vernacular as a "form of building that is temporary, utilitarian, unorthodox in terms of style, and often unorthodox in construction. . . . It is contingent; it responds to environmental influences—social as well as natural—and alters as those influences alter."[5]

Turning briefly to the Strip's opposite development, the new office complexes and towers being built, Jackson recognized "a growing amount of architecture that responds to the power and menace of the street by *turning away* from it . . . But we seldom have time to dwell on these elements in the contemporary city: the street and its traffic calls for all of our attention."[6]

Six years later, Jackson offered a different take on roads in a 1991 essay for the journal *Places*. In "Vernacular Landscape on the Move," he addressed what he saw emerging as the "auto-vernacular landscape"—that is, one in which the automobile had become central, in contrast with the former primacy of the dwelling.[7] Jackson was thinking more and more about the lives of his neighbors in La Cienega, with new insights from his work as a manual laborer. Returning to an earlier era, he considered the upper-middle-class house of the early twentieth century with its clearly defined interior space (never suggesting he had created for himself such a house in La Cienega). There "every space, every hour of the day, imposed its own appropriate behavior. . . . We could control who had access to it and who could be excluded." In this environment "Access" meant hospitality of a formal sort offered in domestic spaces given over to infrequent entertaining. Moreover, the ideal dwelling was isolated from the street "and what it stood for." Drawing on memories of his own childhood, he added, "We had heard of the fascinations of street life and had a highly romanticized image of its wickedness and its freedom, but we rarely ventured into it."[8]

Taking his familiar turn into deep history, Jackson shifted to the very beginning of separate landholdings and dwellings that became in time the "'moral unit'— a permanent territory with a religious and social and economic identity capable of entering into an agreement with the sovereign power." Much of the population, however, was left out, and over time, the numbers of the landless grew. By late eighteenth century they constituted almost half of the population of Europe. The houses of this poorest class, "crudely constructed out of local materials," were merely shelters; the tasks and pleasures of the landless took place outside, in public space.[9] By contrast, a dream from the early days of the United States held sway: the freeholder with a substantial house in a "mythical village of self-sufficient households in a bucolic setting." However, by the early nineteenth century, as house separated from work, this became more myth than reality.

A "new landscape" was now coming into being. It was "based less on territoriality and specialized spaces with restricted access and more on that vernacular liking for mobility and the temporary use of public or semi-public spaces. . . . The space of the street is the heart of the city, not green and spacious parks or the . . . blocks of masonry in which people live and work."[10]

Jackson was at this time stating and restating this narrative in other writings, part of his historical grounding of the mobile home. What was new here was its link with the world of cars and roads, leading him to coin the term "auto-vernacular landscape." "I think," he wrote, "a vernacular house is one that is surrounded by a large number of cars. They are parked on a driveway that leads to the garage, in the back yard, sometimes on the front lawn, and along the curb." He listed the many uses of the car—the husband driving to his job or using his vehicle for the work of "delivering, collecting, hauling, servicing and transporting people and freight"; the wife taking her car to her job; the child being driven to school. "All those automobiles stand for liberation from the constraints imposed by the house: the prospect of easier contact with the surrounding world, the prospect of showing off and the most important prospect of all, achieving privacy."[11]

Jackson established the historical credentials of this new landscape in the long ago. What the contemporary world shares with these times, he asserted, is "its obsessive wandering, its casual attitude toward the house and other traditional institutions, and, above all, its habit of sharing or borrowing public spaces."[12] In mid-twentieth-century America, these spaces included not only gas stations but also parking lots, garages, facilities for transit and storage, and roads themselves—places he accepted and even admired for their "impersonal, empty beauty and attraction." Although he did not equate these spaces with the "moral unit" of house and land in the Middle Ages, nonetheless he understood that it was in such places that "strangers come together and . . . they often turn for help, advice and companionship."[13]

Of the shanties and trailers then congregating on the fringes of American towns and cities, Jackson wrote that they did not stand alone but were attended by businesses providing residents with the necessities of existence and services for their cars and trucks. He offered the glimpse of the day's end: "Driveways and alleys are filled with cars and trucks being worked on, and lowriders or their equivalent with flashy paint jobs roar up and down the street, giving off clouds of blue exhaust. The neighborhood, such as it is, comes to life, and you begin to think this is a world where community and cars belong together, like bread and butter or ham and eggs."[14]

Did Jackson believe this was enough? Perhaps not, for as he concluded, he offered his hopes. "A thousand years ago out of desperation we tried to devise a new arrangement: house and land. After a rough start it took hold, and as we all know, it created a rich and beautiful landscape. Perhaps we can do it again."[15]

Don't Go the Way of Santa Fe

During the 1980s when we visited Brinck, he liked to hear about our adventures when the four of us would return from our various explorations at the end of each day. However, when we went off to the opera in the evenings, he wasn't interested. Although he listened to arias on the radio, he shuddered at any mention of the Santa Fe Opera. As new-style restaurants came to Santa Fe, we considered it a family treat to try them, but Brinck would turn up his nose and refuse any invitation to join us. In the 1990s, during my solo visits, if Jackson and I went out to supper, it was to Luby's Cafeteria.

For many years I took Brinck's choices as efforts to reject his class origins. While this likely played its part, two of the essays he wrote in his last decade suggest more was at stake. In addition to his anti-elite stance, which grew ever stronger over time, what fueled his anger was his belief that Santa Fe and much of New Mexico was neglecting appropriate development in order to chase tourist dollars.

He set this out in a 1991 article in *New Mexico Magazine* called "Our Towns: The Struggle to Survive." Taking the opportunity to reach a broad statewide public, Jackson took an affectionate look at some of the ordinary towns of New Mexico—Clayton, Tucumcari, Clovis, Roswell, Grants, Gallup, and Farmington—as he experienced them before and after World War II. From the perspective of a younger man working on a ranch, the life offered by one of these small towns had many charms including "a freer kind of community." Jackson recalled their "ranching atmosphere—cowboy machismo, horse and rodeo culture, and the social and political rule of important ranch families." Such a town was a place where immigrants could look for jobs. "Main street had its one department store, its one prestigious hardware and ranch supply outlet, its one hotel decorated with longhorns and cattle brands."[16]

By contrast, contemporary tourists had come to see many of these towns simply as places to pass through on their way to the picturesque areas of Santa Fe and Taos. Jackson attributed this to the bad press they received, labeling them "narrow, prejudiced, complacent . . . a cultural desert." Liberal journalists had accused them of being "politically reactionary" and dismissed them as "economically on the verge of extinction." Yet, Jackson insisted, these towns had not gone away. As the economic and social world changed, they remained in place, for they were still needed for jobs, education, and places where one could retire.

Jackson explored two avenues of possible change. One was the path taken by Durango, Colorado, a town turned into tourist destination. "Main street is made over in the image of the Old West," he wrote, "with false fronts and curio shops and expensive restaurants. The results are amusing, not to say cute." However, he found it "painful to witness this masquerading": towns, such as Durango, "for the sake of more money now wear a disguise."

Jackson favored the other path. Rather than dressing up as the "Old West," New Mexico towns needed to embrace change. They should accept the current era with its malls and highway strips, support low-cost housing and places of public recreation, and build "more convenient public buildings, even if it means tearing down the old monumental city hall or courthouse."[17] More importantly, the towns should foster education both in and out of school. Believing local government should provide available information that could be easily understood, Jackson advocated a future in which each town would develop "a high school with first-rate vocational training, a non-intimidating public library," local radio and TV, and a newspaper dealing with "local developments and problems."[18]

Jackson was aware this would "not automatically produce a better community" and solve all problems. These changes might, however, help the town "adjust to the modern world and mitigate its isolation." Imagining the future, he saw such modifications as strengthening the town's "role as center of information, ideas and policies," enabling it to "re-establish its former homogeneity and self-respect, involvement in the development of a more responsible, more sustainable approach to the exploitation of the surrounding landscape, and reinforce a sense of local pride."[19]

Jackson's prescription for change invites some key questions, unasked and unanswered. He had long been committed to addressing issues through local and state efforts rather than national ones; yet, at the same time, he understood his state's relative poverty. How then were developments, requiring a great infusion of money, to be financed? Where was the tax base to pay for the vocational high school, the new public library and city hall? Jackson neither asked these questions nor offered potential answers, for his primary purpose in "Our Towns," it seems, was coaching and cheerleading. Seen in the perspective of his long residence twelve miles south of Santa Fe, Jackson was also offering a back-handed slap not just to Durango but to Santa Fe.

In "Cultures and Regionalism" in *MASS,* a publication for design professionals, Jackson returned the following year to the issue of appropriate development, now for his more typical audience. Here he drew on his knowledge of the Romantic Movement's reaction against the universalism promulgated by the Enlightenment and the French Revolution. Often Romanticism served as his enemy, but in this piece it became his ally as he focused its European-based understanding of culture's vital beginnings in regions sharing a common language and common roots. The United States, given its transient population and what appeared as open spaces, saw no comparable intellectual movement. American regionalism as it emerged in the twentieth century had different origins. Promoted by the federal government, it focused on resources, leading to the creation of "dairy regions, forest resource regions, irrigation and metropolitan transport regions," among others. National parks became "recreation regions." What troubled Jackson was that some regions "operate at the expense of local life-styles and traditions."[20]

As Jackson looked at protected areas such as those inhabited by the Mennonites and Pueblo Indians, he decried the way in which they were "allowed to survive, provided they catered to the taste of tourists and others in search of wilderness recreation." It galled him that those living within these regions were forced into acting against their own better interests and instincts. "As the experience of the Southwest shows, they pay dearly for their protection, obliged to concentrate on producing pre-technological timeless rural charm, whatever the natives might want in the way of change."[21]

Writing in the early 1990s, Jackson was aware of the resurgence of "particularism," defining it as the "violent popular revolt against the universalism of Communist technocrats attempting to suppress ancient regional identities" in Soviet Russia and Eastern Europe. In the United States and Canada, he saw "the re-emergence of the Indian, and in the Southwest, of Hispanic self-awareness." These movements, as he understood them, were not "simply ethnic or racial in inspiration": they involved territory, and their proponents demanded "control over their environment, their own ancestral homeland" (see color plate 14).[22]

Once he articulated this, Jackson gently inserted his long-held desire for resistance against federal government control. He invoked the nation's origins, suggesting the anachronistic possibility that in creating a system of "self-governing states with permanent boundaries and limited dependence on the central government," the Founding Fathers foresaw "the possibility of regional awareness."

In his writing on landscape over the decades, Jackson accepted the impact of technological change, such as that coming from the advent of the automobile. He challenged planners and designers to focus on what people actually wanted rather than proposing changes based on abstractions or aesthetic preferences.

In our conversations, Brinck spoke in general terms of his "conservatism." It was a specific kind of conservatism, however, one directed mainly at the federal government and large-scale planning. As early as his first issue of *Landscape,* he argued against federal projects.[23] Over the four decades between 1951 and 1992, Jackson's stance remained essentially the same. He believed political action was best undertaken at the local or regional level, because decision makers were more likely to listen to ordinary citizens and respect their wishes. He felt he stood for the people of many cultures in the Southwest who were likely to be silenced. He enjoyed the messiness and hurly-burly of American life and therefore distrusted large-scale planning in the belief that its typical aesthetics favored homogenized landscapes.

In his 1992 *MASS* piece, Jackson mentioned one positive sign in the growth of regionalism, the new role played by state universities in becoming "centers of state or regional studies and cultivating themselves as state or regional cultural institutions." (Though, likely with a smirk, he added, "when they are not aspiring to national eminence.")

The people of New Mexico, he continued, "are handicapped by our sense of provincial inferiority. We are rightly ashamed of our backward social services and our illiteracy; we are ashamed of being so poor." He applauded the efforts of many groups who had struggled persistently, including Pueblo Indians, Hispanics, small farmers, and blue-collar workers. They "preserve the basic elements of an authentic regional culture: the small community, the practice of religion, the family, and the freedom to exploit natural resources on a day-by-day domestic scale. What gives our landscape much of its impressiveness is the evidence of that struggle."

Jackson looked forward to a time when this struggle would emerge in a realistic political regionalism appropriate to the needs of its people. Taking another indirect dig at Santa Fe, he stated that what makes a region special are "not the elements of novelty and picturesqueness it introduces," but rather the opportunity "to recreate a culture and a landscape in our own image."[24]

The Search for Connection

With his "retirement" from teaching, Jackson spent more of the year at his home in La Cienega. Over time, as he became increasingly engaged in the worlds of work and church around him, he delved more deeply into the life of his neighbors and became more appreciative of them.

At one point, likely in 1983, I went with him to visit the Mitchells, the evangelical couple who had lived in the small house on Jackson's property but were now ensconced in a mobile home some distance away. As we were shown inside the trailer, Jackson offered compliments to our hosts about everything he saw. Brinck had earlier told me that he attended Reverend Mitchell's services and especially liked the way congregants confessed their weaknesses and wrongdoings. By the time of my visit, Jackson's relation to the pastor was complex: on the one hand, Jackson was his patron who had earlier given him a roof over his head and continued to dole out cash; on the other, Jackson was his employee, working in construction under the preacher's direction.

After the pastor left for other pastures, Brinck continued to work as a manual laborer. I remember most clearly his job cleaning the grounds around dwellings in lower-class neighborhoods. I never got straight his actual working arrangements; I only knew that he left in his truck early in the mornings and came back at midday bragging about the weight of the trash he carried away to the dump. He also complained about the unkindness of some of those who lived in the houses or trailers where he worked. But he liked the physical labor.

As previously mentioned, after declaring himself black, Brinck began attending an African American church in Albuquerque. I never followed him there, but I listened to his reports of going with church members to stand in the late-night hours outside bars (he called them "saloons") to admonish the sinners and attempt to save their souls. He relished his acceptance by members of the church. Some years later, I did agree to go with him to a Sunday morning mass at the Catholic church in La Cienega. This last place of his religious devotions was mainly attended by his Hispanic neighbors.

In these later years Brinck often lamented to me that he was a has-been—nobody was interested anymore in what he had to say. Yes, a certain moment of his celebrity had passed. *Vogue* magazine no longer saw him as one of the people being talked about, and scholarship in cultural geography was moving in new directions, with a new vocabulary and new questions.

Nonetheless, he received many requests from journals to contribute articles during this period, and occasionally he accepted invitations to speak. The year 1985 saw publication of *The Essential Landscape,* the most handsome volume of his work. The book gathered eight of his published essays from *Landscape* (dating from its first issue in 1951 to 1979) and accompanied his writings with stunning photographs of New Mexico places and people. Jackson added to his previously published work the long essay "Looking at New Mexico," describing what he saw throughout the seasons in the various regions of his adopted state, as enriched by his knowledge of archeology and history.

In 1994, he published a new collection of his essays, *A Sense of Place, a Sense of Time,* the book that garnered him the PEN prize for the Art of the Essay. In his acceptance speech in New York in 1995, Jackson uttered a key sentence: "all of us need a territory of our own and also need the company of others." Jackson's effort to find and understand the meaning of "the company of others" in "a territory of our own" gave him an important subject in his final years.

His choice to begin each weekday with hard physical labor was partially driven by his desire to be connected to others. Unlike solitary work as a writer, manual toil joined him directly to his clients, other workers, and his boss. And when his physical work in the morning ended, he stayed connected. On returning home at midday, he walked up to his mailbox on the road to deposit a refrigerated can of Coke for the mailman. In the afternoon, he opened his house to visitors, who normally came between one and three. His Hispanic neighbors came often to call, some to sit and talk over a soft drink, others to combine sociability with a request for money. On Sundays, he attended the churches of his successive choosing—the evangelical church nearby, the African American church in Albuquerque, and finally the Catholic one in his village.

Jackson's writing during these years came to express the importance of such connections. In a 1985 essay published in the *Public Interest,* he dealt with this directly.[25] After considering and dismissing the monumental squares and great parks of an earlier period, Jackson wrote of the importance of the street, which offered the new public space of the present to its fractured public. The street could serve this function because it allowed expression of the particularity of each of the society's varied groups, defined by ethnicity, social class, age, and primary concerns. In the street, the interest of each group with "its own special social forms, its own special language and set of relations, can flourish," because it is "a space which confers a brief visibility on the group."[26]

In the medieval era, he wrote, "the street was the place of work, the place of buying and selling, the place of meeting and negotiating, and the scene of the important religious and civic ceremonies and processions." Now that it had returned to some of these functions, he saw the possibility that it could play "the social role we have long associated with the traditional public square: the place where we exhibit our permanent identity as members of the community."

He quoted the words of Yale philosopher Paul Weiss to affirm that this required participants to observe "a mosaic of accepted customs, conventions, habitual ways of evaluating, responding, and acting." By so doing, those congregating in the street might, in Weiss's words, "be perfected, become social beings. They must act to make the structure of the group an integral part of themselves and a desirable link with others."[27] What underlay Jackson's embrace of the street was his affirmation that the individual does not exist alone. Society holds a deeply moral role in completing the individual as a social being.

At one level this statement reflects one of Jackson's enduring beliefs, which he had expressed in print at least from his college days at Harvard. But toward the end of his life, something else was at work—a growing appreciation for his neighbors' way of life in La Cienega and a desire to feel a part of it. He had long been known as a "patron," but now he sought deeper connection.

Design Quarterly, published by the Walker Art Center in Minneapolis, devoted an entire issue to Jackson's "Urban Circumstances," an essay on vernacular houses, exploring three types: slave dwellings of the American South, the houses of mill workers in New England, and mobile homes in contemporary United States.[28] Although his treatment of slave quarters makes this piece, to my mind, one of the least satisfactory essays in Jackson's large body of work, it offers considerable insight into the man in his later years. Moreover, his key landscape preoccupations at the time remain important: understanding working-class life and its impact on the landscape, in this case, trailer courts and the city as reconfigured by the automobile, roads, and the street.

Once again in this essay Jackson reconsidered the meaning of *vernacular.* He first put a dictionary definition into his own words: "the everyday speech of a class or of a locality or region. . . . A dialect, substandard in terms of the correct literary language of the establishment." The word had expanded into the realm of the arts, including that of architecture. Jackson sought to alter its usage from merely "local" to "departure from a standard form, a form based on tradition or a generally accepted set of rules and conditions." While his reasons for urging this deviation varied, Jackson asserted that there remained an underlying principle: "the vernacular is governed by *circumstances,* by the sum of determining factors beyond our willful control." In contrast, "the establishment is ruled by universally accepted laws." While the establishment sets the "permanent forms and spaces in the community . . . it is the vernacular that in most cases determines how those forms and spaces are used."[29]

Jackson offered the trailer court as the ultimate present-day example of workers' housing. In his frequent writing on the mobile home, he offered various, but typically affectionate, takes on it. In this piece he described how the trailer fit into his conception of the vernacular. "It does not pretend to be a local product, it does not pretend to adjust to the natural setting, it does not acknowledge the existence of a regional style." Rather, the trailer is vernacular because of its temporary possession by its occupant. Despite its name and how it arrived on its plot of land, the mobile home doesn't move once in place; rather, its occupants move because they are forced to be mobile in their jobs. As Jackson put it, "trailers, largely because of their uniformity, change hands almost as easily and as frequently as automobiles." Those who occupy trailers are rejected by the outside community, and "true to their vernacular heritage, [they] form their own community of mutual help and sociability and interdependence."[30]

Jackson demonstrated his liking for both those who lived in trailers and for the functional dwelling itself. He wrote that its occupants aspire to a "real" house, but the trailer suits them for the present. "In the meantime they live in an attractive if congested micro-environment of their own, far more comfortable and convenient than their first home in the house of their parents." They seek to improve their temporary property but never in ways to harm its resale. They do some landscaping of the ground on which their specific trailer sits. While they put "valued family possessions" in storage, they buy another auto for work and chores and recreation. And thus, the road's importance: "Almost every phase of existence depends on mobility and the highway. . . . No matter how satisfactory the trailer may be, it demands too little attention to be the center of existence. The highway leads to a wider world, and is always there . . . [and offers] freedom from bondage to a particular environment and its way of life, freedom from the restraints of a rigid society and an unrewarding job, freedom to move and start out all over again."[31]

"Working at Home," Jackson's final published effort to connect his understanding of working-class life to the landscape, appeared in *Cite* in 1992.[32] This essay was a personal statement. Although it displays elements of his traditional approaches, including the move into deep history, his immediate surroundings in La Cienega served as his primary material. He employed the first person to consider the ways his working-class Hispanic neighbors used their homes as workshops.

"When should we keep the place where we work separate from the place where we live?" he began. Rather than answer his own question, he considered the situations that made many such separations reasonable, such as areas of traffic and heavy industry in large cities. Of his own locale, he observed, "I also have neighbors who operate a laundromat, and others who live above their machine shop. Their front yards are disheveled parking lots. Still, I enjoy doing business with them. They are near at hand and they are friendly."[33]

Putting aside issues of aesthetics and property values, he raised the question of "how we define the home and its role in the community." In an apparent answer, he turned to the proceedings of a 1990 conference, "Home: A Place in the World," and could hardly contain his disgust. Hoping for considerations of the house, Jackson found instead a discussion of the idea of home as "a mental or moral condition." Worse still, consideration was limited to a certain class. Jackson wrote, "So the cat was at last out of the bag! Despite all the discourse about alienation and exile and the grandeur of homelessness (especially for the writer and thinker), home proved to be no more than an academic version of the middle-class American house, dedicated to privacy, leisure, and remoteness from the workaday world."[34]

Throughout European history, Jackson maintained, the home had emphatically not been a secluded place of privacy and leisure. This led him to the real subject of his essay, the historical emergence of the American working-class house as a work place. Jackson traced its roots to the 1930s and the householder's acquisition of an automobile or a truck. To own such an expensive object "involved not only repairs and maintenance but improvements and experimentation, and a new money-making career evolved—always centered on the house—on hauling, and distributing and collecting, and of transporting passengers, usually on a small, local scale." This did not affect the interior of the house, but it altered its surroundings. "The front lawn, the backyard, and the margin of the street were all taken over, to the dismay of neighbors."[35]

In the years following World War II, the attached garage made its appearance. It was "spacious, equipped with light and power, easily accessible, and very visible." It offered "space for work and for keeping tools, and its open door and driveway encouraged neighbors to come by and offer advice." The 1950s saw the introduction of smaller power tools, giving "a remarkable boost to every garage industry and private craftsman."[36]

In looking at the broader working-class areas of Santa Fe, Jackson was no romantic. He found not only houses with trucks and open garages, but also the activities that come in their wake—businesses focused on cars, creating a "scattering of used-car lots and auto junkyards and gas stations, not to mention traffic." As he focused on homes-as-workshops, found in areas such as his La Cienega neighborhood, he wrote that these "do chores and provide services that the modern family has neither the time nor talent to cope with." Jackson's specifics tell of his pleasure in these: "A man on Maple Street will take care of your problem when he gets home from work. You can find him in his garage. . . . A man who can mend furniture or put your power mower in shape . . . a woman who bakes and decorates birthday cakes, or sells medicinal herbs . . . and a man and his son who can repair computers and work on your car radio. All of these helpers request payment in cash to avoid income tax complications."[37]

The services they offer are no longer found in the commercial center of the city or in malls, but in their providers' homes, and are offered only to a selected clientele, those who live in the neighborhood and are in the know. Making use of such helpers "requires knowledge of the worker's car and hours of his day job. To find him one must wait to see his car outside wherever he goes after work hours." In sum, to get whatever you need fixed or the cake you wish baked, "you have to be a member of the community of long standing." With this piece of insider knowledge, Jackson declares himself to be just that.[38]

It was a community Jackson admired, arising unplanned. It "comes into being imperceptibly and naturally, and seems to work surprisingly well." It also led him to think once again about the function of the house. In an early issue of *Landscape* magazine, decades before, Jackson described the contemporary house as a "transformer." He now saw that while this label may have worked for its interior, in that the house provided a "refuge," another image was currently needed for its exterior. In "Working at Home," Jackson found it to be the "extended hand." At the piece's close, he drew on the thinking of his last decade to write, "It is the hand we raise to indicate our presence, the hand that protects and holds what is its own. Like the hand, the house creates its own small world. It is the visible expression of our identity and our intentions; it is the hand that reaches out to establish and confirm relationships. Without it, we are never complete social beings."[39]

The "extended hand" is also a fitting symbol of the vital connection with people and place that Jackson sought to establish in the final years of his life.

The Five Books That Most Influenced Jackson

In 1991, *Landscape Journal* asked a wide range of writers in its field to name the five books that most influenced their work on landscape and to offer commentary regarding their choices. Of the thirty-seven who complied, almost all of them listed books and articles of colleagues. The result was a composite of 195 different publications by 159 different authors.[40]

The works of J. B. Jackson were listed more than any other writer. Several of his later books of essays were mentioned—*The Essential Landscape, The Necessity for Ruins, Discovering the Vernacular Landscape*—but the more prominent place was given to Jackson's magazine, *Landscape,* and its key role in the 1950s and 1960s. Five cited it in its entirety, suggesting it provided a way of seeing and a model of writing.

By contrast, Jackson himself listed no contemporary writer or writing. He began by explaining. "You should take into account that when I read these books, I had no well-developed interest in the landscape, and that in those days there was no well-developed discipline dealing with landscapes as we have now." The five books he was listing "simply gave me a background in certain historical aspects of the man-environment debate." He apologized that he wasn't "able to include any urban books, or books about the USA; but those came later when I had already developed my approach."[41]

What he listed were the works of Charles Dickens, Oswald Spengler's *Decline of the West,* Irving Babbitt's *Rousseau and Romanticism,* Marc Bloch's *French Rural History,* and Samuel Johnson's *Journey to the Western Islands of Scotland.* The first four follow both the chronology of their publication and Jackson's own biography. He began reading Dickens as a boy of eleven and encountered Spengler and Babbitt during his college years. Jackson likely read the work of French historian Marc Bloch after World War II. The odd one out, chronologically, is his fifth choice, a work by the great eighteenth-century British essayist, biographer, and lexicographer Samuel Johnson.

With this statement and unusual list, Jackson was marking his place as the originator of the field of landscape studies. It was these works—all outside the purview of cultural geography, American studies, or urban history—that prepared him for the creation.

Regarded in retrospect, the preparation Dickens offered for writing on the landscape came, as Jackson put it, through the novelist's "deep sympathy for vernacular culture." Dickens had probably also helped fire Jackson's ambition to be a published novelist, an ambition long held but realized only once.

In singling out Spengler, Jackson wrote that he "often re-read large portions of the book, and its ideas and theories are still part of my way of seeing the world." He was introduced to Spengler's work in 1928–29 at the University of Wisconsin's Experimental College. Jackson talked to me at length about Spengler during our 1994 taped conversations, expressing admiration for his bold and vivid characterizations of Europe's seasons of civilization. A primary element of Spengler's appeal was the way he linked all aspects of culture—joining music to landscape architecture and poetry as he considered western civilization's autumn in the nineteenth century. What most engaged Jackson in 1994, however, was the way Spengler considered technology as "the last gasp of our Faustian civilization." In Jackson's mind, Spengler would have us ignore the arts of the twentieth century. Connecting Spengler's work regarding roads and transportation, we should "turn our eyes to the "the marvelous ocean liner . . . suspension bridges, . . . fast trains. . . . And what evolves out of this is a landscape or countryside of enormous cities, skyscrapers, and subways."[42]

In the year following his first reading of Spengler, Jackson transferred to Harvard. There he took a course from Irving Babbitt and read his *Rousseau and Romanticism,* published in 1919. In this important statement of twentieth-century conservative thought, Babbitt opposed Rousseau's sentimentality, his emphasis on natural forces, and the utopian belief he held in human perfectibility. In 1991, Jackson wrote simply that the book "taught me to distrust nature worship." However, it had, in addition, spurred his early 1931 justification for rejecting the modern movement in architecture.[43]

My own guess is Marc Bloch's influence came not just from *French Rural History* but also from his two-volume *Feudal Society.*[44] Both works were published in English by the 1960s, but Jackson may have read them in French beginning with their separate publication in the 1930s and 1940s. Bloch offered Jackson ways of looking into the deep past, excavating the lives of ordinary people, and exploring the reciprocal relationships between people and the land.

To readers of Jackson's work, the choice of Johnson's *Journey to the Western Islands of Scotland* may have seemed less obvious. Jackson justified its presence on his list by the way it "describes and judges landscape in social and economic transition." Jackson quoted from it: "The true state of every nation is the state of common life."

Johnson's book and the man himself likely appealed to Jackson, because of his own blend of conservatism, dislike of Romantic notions of nature, acceptance of technology, and hope for the future. Johnson stood for the Church of England, the scientific arts promoted by the Royal society, enthusiasm for the spread of literacy in his own society, and the belief in progress.[45]

What I think Jackson probably most admired about Johnson was the specificity with which he wrote about aspects of the land he was visiting. Johnson paid attention to the nature of the soils, in particular the means used to fertilize them and the tools for turning and ploughing. He noted and described huts in detail. In one place he visited, he observed that poor women engaged in the daily work of sock knitting.[46] He wrote of the absence of trees, caused by a lack (among the people of Scotland) of the necessary sense of a long future for the land.[47] Jackson was a very curious man, and when he met strangers, he asked questions such as Johnson must have asked.[48]

Finally, Johnson's creed was Jackson's own. In an apparent apology for writing about the nature of the windows observed in Scotland, Johnson wrote, "The true state of every nation is the state of common life. The manners of the people are not to be found in the schools of learning, or the palaces of greatness, where the national character is obscured or obliterated by travel or instruction, by philosophy or vanity; nor is public happiness to be estimated by assemblies of the gay, or the banquets of the rich." Where "the measure of a general prosperity" should be taken is "in the streets, and the villages, in the shops and farms."[49]

In his writings Jackson made references to Samuel Johnson but only once mentioned him to me. In 1994, as I began taping his reminiscences, he criticized my failure to hold up my end of our conversation. I tried to tell him I was only there to allow his ideas to come through. To this, Jackson seemed to agree, but he then added, "I think, whether it's practical or not, that given somebody else's ideas it's best in a give and take. Samuel Johnson talking to Boswell." After I suggested he was saying that if I offered more, the result would be "more interesting than Samuel Johnson all his own," Jackson replied affirmatively.[50] I tried to accommodate, but not aware then about Jackson's 1991 list of important books, I did not know of his deep identification with Samuel Johnson and, regrettably, failed to press him further.

Jackson's Remarks at PEN Award Presentation, 1995

When Jackson was awarded the PEN prize, for *A Sense of Place, a Sense of Time,* I attended the ceremony, along with many others of my generation whose lives and thinking he had influenced. We listened as other authors receiving recognition used their acceptance speeches to treat the moment as if it were the Academy Awards, thanking all who had helped and supported them in their long journeys to become writers. Jackson took a different tack. Speaking in the rich resonant voice of his lectures, he chose to explain instead what he meant by *landscape*.

Here are his remarks.[51]

Several of these so-called essays were actually talks I gave to undergraduates to lure them into signing up for a course in the history of the American landscape.

In those talks I mentioned a number of places in the everyday world of contemporary America: the trailer court, the interstate highway, the front lawn, fields and fences and barns and recreation areas; for I assumed that most students had had contact with them in the course of growing up, and that they might even remember them with something like affection. What I wanted to do was to remind them that each of them had his or her own landscape which was part of the way they related to the wider world.

I always tried to avoid the word "environment." I knew that it was prestigious and politically correct to discuss. But it is, I think, essentially an abstraction: something to read about and talk about, but something never really experienced. Whereas a landscape, no matter how new or small, is really close to us. It is [that] which we use or misuse, modify or even create from scratch, a place with which we have daily contact. Moreover, we are likely to share a landscape with others. And I have come to believe that a landscape is among the oldest and most universal of our collective memories. It is where we learn to live and work and celebrate together. It is where we evolve as social, territorial beings. It is part of our identity—though not all of it: and to me the most disastrous heresy to affect the 20th century has been environmental determinism, which would ascribe to our landscape or environment our total identity—moral, social and physical.

Dr. Johnson once said, more than once, that "men more frequently require to be *reminded* than to be informed." We need to be reminded of what our landscape means to us and has meant to the past, if we are to become responsible inhabitants. My job, as I saw it was simply to encourage students to study their landscape and to remember that all of us need a territory of our own, and also need the company of others.

Those were very simple guidelines. But I am glad to say that landscape studies over the past generation have become more important and thoughtful.

How Jackson Wanted to Be Remembered

In what turned out to be my final visit to Brinck, I traveled to La Cienega to show him the illustrations I proposed to include in the forthcoming *Landscape in Sight*. It gave him a chance to visualize the collection of his essays, and all went pleasantly—that is, until I was about to leave for the airport. He asked me then to send him the lengthy introduction I had written (and sent to the publisher). Once back home, I took a deep breath and complied.

What followed was a phone call to me in my college office. Brinck was furious, this time at me. He disliked the introduction—"hated" would perhaps be a better word. When I asked for specifics, he gave me two: I mentioned that he had gone to Deerfield Academy, and that at Harvard he had written the book for the Hasty Pudding show. I was completely baffled by this. I replied that both details were matters of public record: I had read his published writings in the Deerfield literary magazine, and his Hasty Pudding contribution was in the Harvard University archives.

Why was the inclusion of these two minor elements from his past so infuriating to Jackson? He may have seen the Hasty Pudding discussion as defining his Harvard experience in ways he later rejected—as frivolous or possibly outré, since the actors' performances were in drag. The Deerfield mention is more complicated. I think it is because Deerfield had once been "home," not only due to the fact that Jackson had designated it as his birthplace when he signed up for the army, but also in a more meaningful sense. During Jackson's Deerfield years and war service, Frank Boyden had served, at least to some degree, as a surrogate father. But in 1996 Boyden was long gone, and Jackson didn't like being solicited for contributions to a school he believed had changed. As he had written at the time of one such approach, "The Academy that I knew was a small and unpretentious school," and he wanted to be removed from all lists of "prospective patrons."[52] The passage of time can do many things in a long life. In this case, it made Jackson forget that Deerfield had once been "home."

My discussion with Jackson over the introduction continued with a letter from him, written on a Monday evening early in August 1996. It began, "You would have been dismayed if you had seen the first 40 pages of the document you sent me. Correcting or eliminating the quotations from me proved to be more of an undertaking than I foresaw, and the manuscript was so disfigured by my insertions or deletions that what I am sending is a totally rewritten version." He sweetened this news with a compliment: my introductory essay was "the best specimen I have seen of your writing. It is clear, with a light touch and with great tact and fairness of expression." It was complimented by others as presenting "a very complete picture" of him.

But then came his negative. What I had written—according to others—offered "comparatively little" regarding his "literary attainments." In rereading the introduction, Jackson decided *that* was the problem. "Of course what I want to be remembered for is not my eccentric education or way of life but my contributions to a kind of geographical or cultural approach."

He went over what he desired in an introduction. Following the "formula" of the "19th century," it should be "first an objective, factual impersonal repetition of biographical facts, parents, place of birth, education, choice of a career, and the end or creative work." After that should come "an appraisal and judgment—usually favorable; and finally a systematic list of publications." To aid my rewriting in this vein, he enclosed "a stripped down narrative, eliminating all names and institutions, all family references and listing only those institutions or places or persons which might have influenced my study of landscape." After declaring that he would leave to me the positive and negative appraisal of his contributions, he then proceeded to supply some of the text. It offered praise of his early essays, along with criticisms of his more recent work. As the writer of the introduction, I should state, he continued, that although his "techniques and methods and conclusions about landscapes will soon be outdated," his "writings have the value of expressing humanistic values, and of finding those values among ordinary people in ordinary places."

In closing, he added, "I know the rewriting of your excellent introduction will be a burden; but to repeat: I want much less of me and my picturesque qualities, and more of my (highly moralistic, conservative) humanist-religious convictions." He signed the letter, "Love, B"—a formality, not a sentiment.

I replied on August 9, and our disagreements continued. Brinck's final statement conveys how he wanted to be remembered, and, perhaps more personally, how he thought I should treat him: "What I think I deserve is not praise or analysis, but some recognition that I have tried to teach a fresh and unscholarly approach to the contemporary American landscape, that I have tried to help students and others to explore their surroundings, that I have never sought publicity—particularly personal publicity; and that finally as an old man whose approach is out of date I deserve to be treated with dignity and restraint."

What I did not know (or perhaps did not remember) until 2017, when I read through the unprocessed boxes of Jackson papers recently deposited at the CSWR, was that behind the scenes, our editor at Yale University Press, in working to calm the waters, had written to Jackson that she and I had agreed on a strategy for the introduction in which I would "purge" in its early section "the names of institutions or persons of strictly private experiences."[53] I remained deeply troubled about what seemed to me to be an irreconcilable conflict.

To try and put things right, Dan suggested I write Brinck a personal letter in the vein of our usual correspondence. And so I did, telling him about the life I was leading in Cambridge as I headed into a sabbatical for the coming academic year.

Jackson wrote back to me on August 25 in a similar manner, reporting that he was trying to straighten out his library and clean out what he no longer needed. He offered detailed information about our mutual friends, ending with the visitors he was anticipating. The letter was written and posted three days before he died. I had not received it when I went to his funeral, bereft at the loss of him. The day after I returned to Cambridge from New Mexico, our mailman delivered Jackson's letter with its thoughtful reply to mine, delayed for a week because he had mistakenly sent it to Northampton. It gave me a measure of solace.

9

WHAT LIVES ON

Now, over two decades after J. B. Jackson's death, I look back to think about what lives on. I am not able to speak for cultural geographers, planners, or members of the design professions. As a U.S. cultural historian, I'm in a different field. Nevertheless, my work has been deeply affected by my encounter with Jackson's writing in *Landscape* magazine and in his books. He influenced the way I see and helped me think about places and spaces in the fourth dimension, changing over time. His work shaped the courses I offered to students and influenced much of my writing. The two essays that follow give voice to the intellectual gifts I received from him.

In writing most of what has preceded this final section, I have felt it important to reveal traces of the boy and man as he was (or presented himself) through sources written at the time. Nonetheless, I still value the 1994 oral record because of what it reflects of Jackson's memory and understanding at that time, and in the following essays I feel free to turn to it and my own recollections.

Jackson's Will

In 1995, at our breakfast following the PEN ceremony, the two of us had a very serious conversation. On the previous afternoon, he had learned from his financial adviser that he was wealthier than he had thought, and this caused him to be concerned about the disposition of his estate after his death. He asked me what he should do. I then asked him what was on his mind. He told me he was thinking of making a major bequest to Hospice. When I paused, saying I was reluctant to advise him, he would have none of it. He wanted my advice, he insisted, adding, "I depend upon you." I took a deep breath and stated that, because in the last decades he had demonstrated a strong commitment to young people and education, I thought he should think of giving to the other end of life. We left it at that and went on to talk about his desire to travel once again to Switzerland.

When his will was settled, I learned he listened to my (and perhaps others') advice. He left the bulk of his estate, reported to be $3.1 million, to the University of New Mexico.[1] There it continues to support both higher education and the intellectual work of Jackson's career though the J. B. Jackson Professorship in Cultural Landscape Studies and the Center for Southwest Research.

At an earlier time, during one of our visits, Jackson asked Dan and me if we would accept his house after his death. Our answer was instant: although we wished it were possible, we were not able to do so. Behind this response was our sober understanding of ourselves during this busy time in our lives and of our many personal and financial commitments. I have occasionally regretted this necessity, but no longer, not since learning of its better use by its beneficiary.

Jackson left the proceeds from the sale of his house in La Cienega to the Santa Fe Community Foundation. With the selling of the house, the foundation created the John Brinckerhoff Jackson Endowment Fund. The distribution of its first moneys in 1998 came with this statement: Jackson "really cared about people so that this funding is benefiting youth, the elderly, families, and vocational training."[2] In 2000, a following announcement appeared in the *Santa Fe New Mexican,* under the heading "Imagine a world where the elderly never lost their homes." Underneath came the message: "You don't have to. John Brinckerhoff Jackson imagined such a world. The prominent writer left a bequest of real estate to the Santa Fe Community Foundation to help long-time residents with emergency needs, including property taxes."[3]

Reading this, now over two decades after his death, I think of Jackson in the mid-1990s sitting with his Hispanic neighbors. I saw and heard him listening and responding to their stories of hardship and, on occasion, giving them emergency cash. It makes me deeply gratified that Jackson's house went to the right place. Through his wise bequest, the foundation is able to carry on Jackson's commitment to helping his neighbors in need.

Landscape in the Fourth Dimension

Among J. B. Jackson's legacies, one particularly important to me as a historian, is the way he opened the mind's eye to the possibility of seeing landscapes in the fourth dimension. Normally we view the world around us in three dimensions or, as we look at photographs and paintings, in two, giving the illusion of depth. Jackson's writings add to our view of landscape the fourth dimension—time.

Many of Jackson's most memorable essays deal with the impact of time on the landscape, his word to encompass the evolving physical forms created on the earth by human beings working within their particular cultures. The critical word here is "evolving." Jackson presents his readers, as he once presented those attending his lectures, with description and analysis that make it possible to look at the surrounding world not only with the dimensions of height, width, and depth, but as unfolding over time. He places spaces and structures in the cultures at their moments of creation. But, as time does not stand still, these forms are never constant: they are always in transformation, reshaped by new human desires and technological possibilities. Reading passages where Jackson describes changes on the land remains a great joy, evoking something comparable to the pleasure I took as a child in time-lapse photography that revealed a plant growing or a flower unfurling.

The dimension of time is evident in the very first issue of *Landscape.* Jackson implied it as he considered "Chihuahua; As We Might Have Been," writing about what developed in the aftermath of the Mexican-American War (1846–48), as the great desert of the Southwest, once one piece of the earth, was divided by two nations. With the essay "Ghosts at the Door" in the magazine's second issue, Jackson initiated an intellectual strategy of thinking about American landscapes in terms of their European antecedents. His early essays in *Landscape* offer many examples of this way of thinking and imagining.

Once Jackson began teaching, he developed a desire to go back and explore the past in more thoroughgoing ways, and this led to *American Space: The Centennial Years 1865 to 1876,* his 1972 book tracing the changing landscape of the United States in the decade following the Civil War. In a work filled with descriptive detail, Jackson argued that during those postwar years a new understanding of space emerged that broke traditional boundaries in ways that facilitated orderly flow. The creation of the turnstile was one of its achievements. As Americans began to see with "the eye of the engineer," a new attitude began reshaping the land, one that paid attention to resources and limits. An aesthetic arose that encouraged the development of urban parks and suburbs that would offer greater connection to nature.[4]

After publication of *American Space,* Jackson developed a vast manuscript he titled "The American Landscape: The First 1000 Years." There he took what historians call the *longue durée,* beginning his study in premedieval times and ending it with the early years of European settlement of North America. When I questioned him about the manuscript, he told me he had submitted it to Norton, the publisher of his 1938 novel and of *American Space.* However, Norton sent it to a reader, a traditional American historian, who did not understand Jackson's intention and criticized it harshly.[5] Jackson, with no agent or anyone else to advise him, never tried to revise the work or offer it to other publishers. He did cannibalize parts of "1000 Years" for essays, some of which appeared in *The Necessity for Ruins, and Other Topics.*

In the mid-1990s, I was visiting Jackson at a moment when he—believing his papers to be a burden—was energetically tossing them onto a bonfire. I was able to rescue what remained and sent these materials, including a copy of the "1000 Years" manuscript, to my home in Massachusetts for safekeeping. There I read it and had it scanned for my computer. I saw that despite flaws that might trouble an academic historian, it is an important work. I have come to understand it as a meditation on history offering a transformative view of the evolving landscape of Europe and early U.S. colonial times—landscape in the fourth dimension.[6]

Jackson was a man of letters, not an academic. He had literary gifts to draw readers in and engage them, but his was a special kind of intelligence, a perfect fit perhaps for an earlier era and one still powerful to me and many others. He asked questions both of people and of books. He read prodigiously in English, French, and German and had a remarkable memory. He had a command of many fields and, at least through the 1960s and early 1970s, kept up with developments in philosophy and interpretation. But he had never trained to be a scholar. He had many ways of taking notes, but no consistent way of organizing them. Although he knew how to type, he ceased to use a typewriter himself and came to depend on others and their schedules. Perhaps more dangerous for scholarly readers, he was satisfied to assert speculation as fact, and his footnotes were incomplete at best.

And yet, he left much for this scholar to treasure. To give one example: the "1000 years" manuscript has three chapters on the emergence of the city. These were compressed into an elegant essay called "The Discovery of the Street" that appeared in *The Necessity for Ruins, and Other Topics.* In this essay's ten pages, Jackson demonstrated how the city emerged from a vertical "cluster of towers and bastions and roofs" to a horizontal grid of streets. The shift began with the rise of the marketplace in the eleventh century, a permanent and centrally located territory legally demarcated for merchants and craftsmen. Commonly located at a crossroads, the marketplace was a secular space that, over time, determined the creation of streets (or the restoration of Roman roads). Following this came the dividing of urban space into lots and the emergence of land ownership. Ultimately roads were created to take persons to and from their domains. In many cases, roads leading from the market and beyond were placed at right angles and formed straight perpendicular lines: thus emerged the horizontal grid. In conclusion, Jackson wrote: "The celestial model, never easy to discern in the dark medieval spaces among stone walls and crowded huts, has been at last forgotten; the map, the diagram, the coordinates are what help us make sense of the city."[7]

I cannot judge the accuracy of Jackson's treatment of this long development, but I love its spur to the imagination. In this example, he presented the city as ever-evolving. Here and elsewhere, he invited his readers to witness—without judgment—how past became present, how landscape changed to meet new human needs, technology, and opportunities. Jackson offered a dynamic view of landscape as an arena of human striving, past and present, where societies shaped and re-shaped places and spaces on the face of the earth. He offered the intellectual gift of landscape in the fourth dimension.

Jackson's Discerning Eye

When I think about J. B. Jackson's legacy, what looms large is the way he tried to teach Americans how to see the everyday world around them. To be sure, he had a special eye. Nonetheless, his words and enthusiasm prompted many in his thrall to give his kind of seeing a try.

His special gift was recognized during his lifetime. For example, in a *New York Times* review in April 1996 of "A Sense of Place, a Sense of Time," an exhibition of Jackson's drawings mounted by the Municipal Art Society in New York, the distinguished American architectural critic Herbert Muschamp declared Jackson to be "America's greatest living writer on the cultural forces that have shaped the land this nation occupies." The value of Jackson's drawings lay especially in "the light they shed on his writings. No one familiar with the writings needs further proof that Jackson has an eye."[8]

"Jackson," Muschamp continued, "has always insisted that we look at the environment in other than pictorial terms, and his drawings should not be seen just as pictures of buildings, hills or highways. For Jackson, it seems, drawing is not primarily a way of depicting things. It is a tool for framing things, a technique for fixing or loosening the boundaries around the object on view."

Muschamp gave as an example "Telephone Poles," a drawing dated 1947 (see color plate 15). He saw it as conveying "the futility of bounding the boundless. The two dimensions of the paper frame a road, a sky and telephone lines that recede into infinite space. This is a counter-Renaissance design, the American antithesis of paintings in which fifteenth-century architects visualized the ideal city in terms of the new technique of perspectival space. . . . [Jackson] uses perspectival space to illustrate the mythology of the open road. The frame is made to be escaped."

With these words in mind, I recently looked hard at "Telephone Poles." Yes, I can see what Muschamp saw; but to me, the central contribution of this lovely sketch, drawn on a road trip in his jeep, are the telephone poles. Jackson could see and put front and center what others often choose to avoid, the poles and wires along the road, not just the land and the trees. In a 1988 interview Jackson told Bob Calo, "I see things very clearly, and I rely on what I see. . . . And I see things that other people don't see, and I call their attention to it."[9] Jackson aimed to take in the totality of what was there, not just what he had been taught by landscape paintings to *wish* was there.

This is not to say that Jackson was inexperienced. He had sketched buildings and scenes from childhood, and these sketches served as mementoes of travel.[10] The architect Doug Adams, Jackson's former teaching assistant and his longtime companion on sketching trips, has chronicled how Jackson's military service in World War II shaped his vision, moving it away from perspectives he had gained in formal training in architecture and art history. Sketches that Jackson drew during the war were utilitarian parts of his work in military intelligence, as he sought knowledge of his surroundings to help plan the movement of U.S. troops. Jackson also learned in the army how to read and interpret aerial photographs.[11]

In addition, there were other elements in play. As a freshman at Meiklejohn's Experimental College, Jackson had read Oswald Spengler and imbibed his sweeping vision of civilizations as they rose and fell, following the pattern of the seasons of the year. Over two decades later, living in New Mexico in the early 1950s, Jackson could visualize Spengler's ideas in looking out of an airplane window. As he wrote and interpreted, he declared the importance of the eye of the "human geographer." Jackson brought to his eye, however, not the temperament of the scientific geographer but that of an artist and a citizen. In addition, from childhood on, he developed a unique aesthetic, one with intense likes and dislikes.

When I sat down to interview Jackson in 1994, I discovered he had prepared an agenda. He opened our conversation with his discovery of the meadow at age four. The outbreak of World War I had forced his mother to retreat with her children to her mother's house in Switzerland. As a little boy, he had no interest in war or international events. Eight decades later, what Jackson vividly recalled was his pleasure in seeing mountain meadows for the first time. "It was green and fresh and beautiful," he recalled, "and the cows were grazing, and the water was flowing. . . . It was my first glimpse, or my first awareness of the landscape." What delighted him was "it was open."

Jackson then wondered what difference it would have made if his first awareness had been of the "Adirondacks . . . Canada, . . . or wherever, where there were trees. I would have had a different impression, I think, of what the world should be like." The meadows in Switzerland gave him a place that "was beautiful in the way I wanted it as a little boy." He gave this childhood experience as his reason for his lifetime of "liking of open country."[12]

Looking today at wide range Jackson's sketches and watercolors made beginning at midcentury, I see this liking. There is the love of the road in "Telephone Poles," and many of his images depict open country. Jackson made countless sketches in New Mexico, the place he chose to call home. Here I think that Jackson particularly admired his adopted region's open vistas and the wonderful clarity of its light.

From his youth on, Jackson also had great appreciation for the Baroque, and he repeatedly contrasted it with modernism's sterility. In 1994, he told me of his first view of a modern building at the Paris exposition of Modern Art in the 1920s: "I did not like Le Corbusier, and everybody was kind of making fun of his houses on stilts and saying it was for chickens."[13] Later, as a student at Harvard and eager for culture, he enthused over the Baroque in an undergraduate publication. It was to him the "last vital style which fulfilled its function of interpreting an age," a style that depended "on man for its growth," in an era "when man allowed no factors of environment or primitive peculiarities to deter him from becoming what he considered cultured."[14] In Mexico and Europe he often drew Baroque buildings; in Munich in 1958, he wrote after sketching a church, "I drew instantly as if in my sleep—so familiar and sympathetic are Baroque proportions, features & plan."

As Jackson's ideas developed in the 1950s, he understood that Americans desired more than the modernist credo of form following function. Americans wanted an architecture that helped them "to sell goods, to establish social position, to inspire confidence, to impress or elevate or excite. The result is a carnival of extravagant taste, an architectural idiom partaking more of advertising or theater or landscaping" than the Bauhaus aesthetic allowed. Jackson saw and liked this, too.[15]

Jackson took pleasure in the variety and exuberance of the Strip. He understood and accepted "all those streamlined facades . . . those flamboyant entrances and deliberately bizarre decorative effects, those cheerfully self-assertive masses of color and light and movement." Here he did not try to draw what he saw but captured it with his camera (see color plate 16).[16]

"I'm pro-automobiles," Jackson announced in our interview in 1994 and went on to emphasize the privacy that the automobile gave: "Of course it is there, even if you may have somebody next to you. It's a different ride, it's a wonderful relationship. You're there next to each other with the wind blowing, and I think it's marvelous."[17]

Jackson also loved the sheer speed of the automobile. "When I was a little boy there were so few cars, and nothing was prepared for them," he recalled. "But now we've got a whole landscape prepared for people traveling by car. And we've got different perceptions, I think, of speed. There's this wonderful thing that happens to us when we go fast." To which he added, mischievously, "I don't care whether you run over somebody or not."[18] In such conversations I often offered pushback, challenging his anti-environmentalism, strong at that time, and his unquestioning acceptance of capitalism. Jackson would listen to me and then ignore what I had to say, feeling perhaps as I did, that it was important to keep our political differences from getting in the way of our friendship.

Toward the end of his life Jackson was thinking and writing about the road and about speed, particularly its manifestation in extreme sports. Here, I think, if he had desired to take pictures, he would have needed a video camera, not the still shot.

Over time, living as he did among his less affluent neighbors in La Cienega, Jackson came to return to the value that had prompted his military drawings—utility—and honor it in a different context. He had been educated to love beauty, and he did so throughout his life. One could see this in the graceful way he arranged the flowers and weeds he gathered for his dining table. But increasingly he came to believe that beauty should not rule; or rather that utility had its own rules. This is evident in an early essay on the garage, one of the least lovely appendages of the modern house. To Jackson, the garage had a purpose and a history.[19] Over time, he came to understand and tolerate cars parked on grass outside a house. Ultimately, he accepted the collection of car parts stacked beside a house by those capable of making their own auto repairs. More and more, I think Jackson bent his aesthetics to accept what poorer people had to do to get along.

It was when he accepted house trailers and what he referred to as "traileries," the gatherings of mobile homes normally called trailer parks, that Jackson began to encounter resistance; and this was very much on his mind during our interviews in 1994. He was being challenged by those who saw trailers and other such aspects of American life as eyesores. Try as he might to rise above his critics, their attacks—subtle or open—made him angry. In our conversations he recalled a survey of housing taken by the University of California. "I said to the man who was running it, 'But you've left out trailers.' 'Well, they don't count as houses. We don't count them.' How can you do that? How can you approach the world talking about where people live and exclude perhaps a third or a half of it?"[20]

For Jackson, the answer to those who would deny the trailer had many dimensions. A central tactic was intellectual: to explain the divide between his point of view and that of his opponents as part of the opposition between the vernacular on the one hand and the classic or establishment on the other. To him, he vernacular increasingly became the place where "use" resided.

In my conversations with him in 1994, I spoke about the dynamic way in which he put these and other dichotomies in tension, even conflict. He linked this trait to his training at age eleven and twelve in "perfect French" in Switzerland at Le Rosey. This led him to a learned discussion of the etymology of the word "vernacular" and the conclusion that, in terms of language, vernacular stood in contrast to the correct speech of the upper classes: "The vernacular was always lower class. It was always connected with the sticks."[21]

When the conversation turned from language to consider the vernacular in art, material culture, and landscape, Jackson stated that those in lower classes or living far from capital cities try to imitate the urbane upper class, but do not do it well. "Local materials are being used, and local skills are used, and so you do get vernacular in almost every form of expression." Here again I challenged him, suggesting that he was conflating commercial culture with vernacular culture. The trailer, after all, was made by a company and then sold to its user. He had a quick answer: the trailer was vernacular not in its origin, but in its use. Its end was to satisfy "local needs. So, vernacular has that point of view. I mean it is a useful thing in the local community." What was involved was a different cast of mind. As Jackson put it, "There is a vernacular point of view, a vernacular point of life."

When I asked him if he was talking about use as opposed to beauty, he answered, "'Use' is the prime word. The vernacular point of view is: how do we use a thing? The establishment point of view is: how is it made?" He acknowledged that what he was saying sounded utilitarian, but he did not mean it to do so: "Use means life itself, does it not?" He then clarified that he was talking about "immediate use, not use for your grandchildren, not use next year, but now. . . . If you want permanence, you turn to the establishment."

Jackson recognized his own complexity—that he himself had emerged from an older world. "One cannot, at least I cannot, discard either of them. I have been brought up, and that is my mentality, to feel that the establishment very often has the truth. . . . It has an estate, it has a house, it has a position. . . . I do feel that the old-fashioned establishment point of view of correctness, of probity, or honor, correctness of all sorts, is very much a thing of the past. . . . People are just not interested any more, and this is where the vernacular is seeping up. The vernacular point of view—of doing a thing because it is useful, loving things because they are useful, because it is new, because it is attractive, because other people are doing it—is seeping up throughout culture and eventually is going to take over."[22]

Jackson was a man truly caught between two worlds. I think that this fact of his being underlay much of the creative tension that runs both through his writings and through the photographs he used for illustration. While most of his drawings convey something of the beauty that caught his eye, many of his photographs seem an effort to express an appreciation of the "vernacular." They are quite in keeping with the reverent collection of common objects, given to him or of his own purchase, that he carefully placed on his elegantly constructed mantel.

As Jackson aged among his neighbors in La Cienega, his growing appreciation of the vernacular point of view took on new dimensions. He came to have great empathy for those caught in the lower class. As he spoke of an afternoon visit that ended in his guest's request for money, Jackson understood his place as a kind of *patron;* but he wasn't patronizing. He reflected, "I think vernacular people, again to take my neighbors, are very dependent on others, not only emotionally but in terms of health, in the case of setting an example, getting a job. They are terribly dependent. I think it is a wonderful thing. It is really the way the world should be."[23]

By the time of the interviews, Jackson was thinking of himself in the world in religious terms, and trailers took on deeper, ethical meanings. He remarked, "When I look at the world and try to understand it, and do not succeed in it, I am looking for these symbols because the truth is hidden from us." He mentioned those

symbols that had meant something to him, such as the road or the church steeple, and added, "The trailer is a symbol just as much as any. It is an ugly symbol, but nevertheless it is a symbol. . . . It represents . . . a new kind of a house, a new approach to their environment, a new approach to each other."[24]

Jackson found looking at trailers had humbled him, forcing him to think beyond aesthetic, ecological, or economic terms. "It comes back to this, to human complications of creation and of making ourselves at home in the place, and of trying to improve, always trying to improve." After commenting on the importance of human connectedness, he said that he now saw in the world around him more clearly "elements . . . which are baffling and which are repulsive, and yet they have to be assimilated into God's world. . . . They are part of the picture that we have to see."[25]

Jackson's essays helped me see, as his work has helped many others. In 2015, a conference at the University of New Mexico brought together a group of French and Continental scholars working on Jackson's photographic practices with a group of Americans who continue to draw on and interpret J. B. Jackson and his work. The man himself would have been surprised at this. In 1994, Jackson believed himself to be a has-been. In response to my interest in him and his work that prompted me to assemble the collection of his essays, *Landscape in Sight,* Jackson retorted, "You

Figure 35. Mantel, dining room, J. B. Jackson's house, La Cienega; photograph by Edward T. Hall

make me sound important. Who's going to read this thing? Who's going to read it?" I didn't try to refute this, but merely let him know that didn't matter to me, that I chose to focus on what I cared about, not because any publisher expressed an interest. "Well, all right," he answered, but added, "I've lived long enough and have read enough to see how evanescent reputations are. . . . They just vanish almost overnight."[26] The 2015 conference bore witness to the opposite.

Notes sur l'asphalte, an exhibition in 2017 at the Pavillion Populaire in Montpellier, France, gave Jackson a prominent place in the pantheon of photographers exploring "A Mobile and Precarious America, 1950–1990."[27] The text of its handsome catalog conveys Jackson's pivotal role in stimulating photographers to look at the landscape with unflinching eyes.[28] With a life that began in France, reshaped in the European theater in World War II, and often stimulated by travel abroad, Jackson would likely have been both amused and delighted by this recognition.

A key part of what lies behind the sustaining power of J. B. Jackson's work is his discerning eye. In one of our interviews, he contended, "I think that people just do not look, and this is a part of the decay of our civilization, of being abstract in thought instead of using the evidence of the eyes." He contrasted his own seeing to that of "an aesthete, saying how pretty it is, or an environmentalist who says how awful it is. . . . This I feel about myself—that I have looked. I have not necessarily interpreted the evidence intelligently or rightly, but I have looked and looked and looked."[29]

A Last Word

I cared deeply about J. B. Jackson. I was in my early thirties when I first got to know his work and meet him personally. I learned a great deal from him, and his writings became a part of the way I saw the world, taught, and wrote. His friendship came at an important time in my life. But I have never understood why he chose to encourage my friendship, why we bonded to the degree we did, or why he ultimately chose me as his literary executor.

I embodied many of the elements against which he had stood at a distance for much of his life: I was female, from the mid reaches of the middle class, and Jewish. These elements became the substance of many of our conversations and, all except my religious background, entered into our teasing. "Well, Mrs. Horowitz, that's the Shreveport in you," he would say; or, "You, as a woman, could hardly expect to understand." Without knowing then all of his prejudices, I tended to throw back a "Well, Mr. Jackson" retort in kind. How did our friendship happen? Perhaps one could argue that it was one of his ways of exorcising his past. But it didn't feel that way at all, for Jackson would not then have been able to offer the warmth and affection that accompanied our time together and much of our correspondence. I came to simply accept the friendship he offered as a gift. Or jokingly attributed it to being born and raised in Shreveport, Louisiana.

Jackson's capaciousness and kindness helped shape my life and my relations with others. In some ways these essays are acts of homage, but they are definitely curious ones, for I know that Jackson, were he alive, would be deeply offended by much of what I have written. At the end of his life he asked me to write nothing regarding his personal history, but to limit myself to his work alone. I violated this in my introduction to the 1997 collection of his essays, *Landscape in Sight,* and I violate it again now.

I do this out of my belief that wisdom comes in knowing—in unvarnished and unexpurgated ways—what was and is. In the late 1980s and early 1990s, researching and writing the biography of M. Carey Thomas, I promised myself that I would be true to my craft and present all I found. This turned out to include both her extraordinary achievements and her racial, ethnic, and class prejudices. This same promise holds true for these essays on J. B. Jackson. The first one was easier, for Thomas, famed president of Bryn Mawr College and spokesperson for educated women, died before my birth. Jackson, by contrast, was a living presence in my life for over two decades. Moreover, the differences between the two are striking. She was a subject who, as she grew older, became more prejudiced and attained the power to act in discriminatory ways. As Jackson matured, he became increasingly accepting of those he once demeaned. In short, he grew while she shrank. He worked hard to embrace the contemporary world, not only in its landscapes but also in its changing attitudes. He worked to fight against the prejudices of his origins.

Nonetheless, because Jackson was a friend whose memory I cherish, this commitment to present in these essays all that I've learned has proven hard to keep. I do so because, as a historian, I hold dear the belief that the fuller understanding of a place, time, or person needs to be based on what can be known. To learn about Jackson's origins and struggles, to find the person underneath the persona, and to observe the development of some of his approaches, ideas, and ways of writing is to understand more fully the man and his contributions. He was a superb writer, one who throughout his long life worked hard at his craft. He was also a man of a certain time and place who, in the context of his era and social position, had to confront his own complicated self. And, over time, he changed.

J. B. Jackson had the ambition and manifold gifts to teach us to see everyday America. He was a human being of rare intelligence, great wit, and engaging warmth. I miss him still.

NOTES

ABBREVIATIONS

ARJ	Alice Richardson Jackson
CSWR	Center for Southwest Research, University of New Mexico, Albuquerque
DA	Archives, Deerfield Academy, Deerfield, Massachusetts
FB	Frank Boyden
GCSJ	George C. St. John
HAPS	Harvard Alumni Placement Service, Harvard University, Cambridge, Massachusetts
HLH-JBJ OI	Author's oral interviews with Jackson
HLH-P	Author's possession
HUA	Harvard University Archives, Cambridge, Massachusetts
JBJ	John Brinckerhoff Jackson
JBJ-P	J. B. Jackson Papers, Center for Southwest Research, University of New Mexico, Albuquerque
N-CU-MS	W. W. Norton & Company records, Manuscript Collection, Columbia University, New York
U-JBJ	Unprocessed JBJ Papers, J. B. Jackson Papers, Center for Southwest Research, University of New Mexico, Albuquerque
WBJ	William B. Jackson
WGJ	Wayne G. Jackson
WWN	William Warder Norton

1. JBJ, "A Statement of Policy," *Landscape* 6, no. 1 (Autumn 1956), 3.

2. JBJ, "Forum 1: Landscape Reflects Culture, History," *Centre Daily Times,* State College, PA, October 2, 1975.

3. After the publication of this book, this material, as well as the tapes and transcripts of my 1994 conversations with Jackson, will go to the Center for Southwest Research (CSWR), Zimmerman Library, University of New Mexico, Albuquerque, NM. I have no knowledge of what was lost to the flames.

4. Janet Mendelsohn and Christopher Wilson, eds., *Drawn to Landscape: The Pioneering Work of J. B. Jackson* (Staunton, VA: George F. Thompson, 2015). Other important assessments include Paul Groth and Todd Bressi, eds., *Understanding Ordinary Landscapes* (New Haven: Yale University Press, 1997; Chris Wilson and Paul Groth, eds., *Everyday America: J. B. Jackson and Recent Cultural Landscape Studies* (Berkeley: University of California Press, 2003); *Geographical Review* 88, no. 4 (October 1998), devoted to memories and assessments of J. B. Jackson, especially the particularly memorable article by Paul Starrs, "Brinck Jackson in the Realm of the Everyday," 492–506.

5. *Journal of Interdisciplinary History* 5, no. 2 (Autumn 1974), 336–40.

6. Jackson told me he had a trust fund, courtesy of his grandfather, who did not trust his own son to provide for the next generation: I found no documentation for this, however. It is clear that, although lacking in money at times, JBJ seems never to have had to work for a living.

7. Although Jackson felt he was breaking new ground, he was also following an important tradition of gentlemen cowboys, such as Theodore Roosevelt. See Melissa Bingmann, *Prep School Cowboys: Ranch Schools in the American West* (Albuquerque: University of New Mexico Press, 2015).

8. The Bronze Star is documented by a letter from Louis A. Craig, Major General, U.S.A., Commanding Officer to WGJ, November 24, 1944, in JBJ files, HLH-P. Jackson wrote to Frank Boyden, October 17, 1943, of receiving the Silver Star the day before, DA. The Purple Heart, along with the Silver Star, is incised on Jackson's gravestone.

1. "Acte de Naissance," U-JBJ, CSWR.

2. The British wedding, solemnized at the Kensington Register's Office in London, was dated April 28, 1908, U-JBJ, CSWR.

3. Notations likely by ARJ, U-JBJ, CSWR.

4. WBJ passport, 1914. USM1490_220–0922, Ancestry.com.

5. Gravesite information, Find a Grave, https://www.findagrave.com/memorial/112704821/alice-jackson; ARJ Consular registration certificate 1915- 40457_649063_0494–00726, Ancestry.com.

6. ARJ passenger list, return 1914. Massachusetts passenger and crew 1914. MAT843_228–0386, Ancestry.com.

7. The street number, unclear, may be slightly incorrect. ARJ household. 1920 Census, Ancestry.com.

8. Lt. Col. Ernest P. Bicknell, deputy commissioner, Europe, Red Cross to Lt. Col. WBJ, Paris, France, January 8, 1920, U-JBJ, CSWR.

9. Photograph of WBJ, 1920, U-JBJ, CSWR.

10. FB to Wilmot V. Trevoy, March 31, 1924, DA.

11. Wilmot V. Trevoy to FB, April 2, 1924, DA.

12. No reference has been found to a school of this exact name, but there was an Institut Carriat in Bourg (SW France). The school's "name" comes from Jackson's application to Harvard. Its archives holds a complete file, "JACKSON, JOHN BRINCKERHOFF—A.B. 1932 (33)," spanning his first letter of inquiry, fall of 1928, through graduation. It also includes Alumni Placement Service material. HUA.

13. JBJ to ARJ, undated but early spring 1926, U-JBJ, CSWR.

14. Wardell St. John to FB, June 8, 1926, DA.

15. The quote comes from Richard Sheridan's 1775 play, *The Rivals,* one of Mrs. Malaprop's malapropisms; though "obstinate" here replaces "headstrong" in the original.

16. GCSJ to FB, July 7, 1926, DA.

17. In Jackson's years, girls from Deerfield could still matriculate in the academy, but girls were not accepted as boarding students.

18. John McPhee, *The Headmaster: Frank L. Boyden of Deerfield* (New York: Farrar, Straus and Giroux, 1966); quote, 53.

19. GCSJ to FB, July 7, 1926, DA.

20. FB to GCSJ, July 13, 1926, DA.

21. FB to ARJ, September 30, 1926, DA.

22. FB to ARJ, December 20, 1926, DA.

23. ARJ to FB, undated, but chronological arrangement of letters places it after December 20, 1926, DA.

24. FB to ARJ, January 13, 1927, DA.

25. FB to ARJ., February 3, 1927, DA.

26. JBJ (in this case, "Brincky") to Miss Sweet, Baden-Baden, July 30 [1927], DA.

27. ARJ to FB, October 14 [1927], DA.

28. The unsent letters, kept in FB's files, are dated October 14 [1927] and October 30, 1927. The sent letter: FB to ARJ, November 18, 1927, DA.

29. I am relying here on the tribute McPhee, *Headmaster,* and many helpful communications from John Notz, a Deerfield alumnus from Chicago.

30. Mr. Avirett's report on Brinckerhoff Jackson, DA.

31. FB to Meiklejohn, April 19, 1928. J. B. Jackson had only two years at Deerfield Academy; perhaps FB decided to count his year at Eaglebrook Lodge.

32. Adam R. Nelson, *Education and Democracy: The Meaning of Alexander Meiklejohn, 1872–1964* (Madison: University of Wisconsin Press, 2001), 133–64; re: Amherst College teachers, 145.

33. Alexander Meiklejohn, *The Experimental College* (New York: Harper and Bros., 1932), 34.

34. Paul Groth, "John Brinckerhoff Jackson," American National Biography online, http://www.anb.org/articles/14/14–01151.html.

35. Cynthia Stokes Brown, "The Experimental College Revisited," *Wisconsin Magazine of History* 66, no. 2 (Winter 1982–83), discusses the normal evaluation process, one not followed in Jackson's case, 97–98.

36. For the internal records of Jackson's work at the Experimental College, I am grateful to William H. Tishler, professor emeritus of landscape architecture at University of Wisconsin–Madison, who obtained for me copies of Jackson's papers, evaluations, and final letter to Jackson's mother from files at the University of Wisconsin.

37. HLH-JBJ OI, January 18, 1994.

38. Jackson's initial letter to the "Dean of Freshman" is undated, but the response, "Assistant" to JBJ ("My dear Sir"), carries the date September 27, 1928, carbon copy, HUA.

39. In this instance, JBJ to "Dean of Freshman," undated, HUA.

40. "Assistant" to JBJ ("My dear Sir"), September 27, 1928, carbon copy, HUA.

41. JBJ to "Committee on Admissions," December 9, 1928. The stationery gives JBJ's name as "Brinckerhoff Jackson," and JBJ spells misspells Harvard in his heading ("Havard"). His address is Adams Hall, Madison, Wisconsin, HUA.

42. Unknown sender to JBJ, December 12, 1928, carbon copy, HUA.

43. JBJ to "Committee on Admissions," December 21, 1928. This letter is written on stationery headed by 315 E. 51st Street, New York City, HUA.

44. Henry Pennypacker to JBJ, December 26, 1928, carbon copy, HUA.

45. JBJ to "Committee on Admissions," January 2, 1929; reply, January 3, 1929, carbon copy, HUA.

46. JBJ to "Committee on Admissions," March 10, 1929, HUA.

47. Unsigned to "My dear Sir," March 13, 1929, carbon copy, HUA.

48. *Yale Potpourri, 1873–74,* 120, has a William Brinckerhoff Jackson from Belleview, New Jersey, on its list as a freshman at the Sheffield Scientific School, but there is no evidence he graduated from Yale; the date of his death cannot be determined.

49. This is the only naming of the educational institution Jackson attended in the year between Eaglebrook Lodge and Choate.

50. JBJ, Application to "Committee on Admissions," undated, HUA.

51. All the grade cards are undated, though they carry the semester date. HUA. They and the accompanying notes generally follow in sequence in his folder; the letter to ARJ is dated December 5, 1929, HUA.

52. JBJ to "The Dean of Juniors," August 13, 1930; JBJ telegram, sent September 22, 1930, carried the attached note from the assistant dean of September 23, 1930, HUA.

53. Paul Groth demonstrated the impact of Harvard's professor of geography Derwent Whittlesey on Jackson. The two courses Jackson took focused on agriculture and extractive industries and on manufacturing and transportation. Groth, who as a Berkeley graduate student knew Jackson's teaching at first hand and took over his courses after Jackson's retirement, has written that Jackson "emphasized all of Whittlesey's subjects as axiomatic" (Paul Groth, "Introduction: J. B. Jackson and Geography," *Geographical Review* 88, no. 4, [October 1998] iii–vi).

54. "Application blank for the five houses opening September 1931," HUA.

55. *New York Times,* April 9, 1932.

56. JBJ, HAPS application, January 7, 1935, HUA.

57. Contract, dated April 7, 1938; JBJ to WWN, May 13 [1938], W. W. Norton & Company records [ca. 1923]–1967, Series I, BOX #41, 1928–1934 box: Hi-K, folder: folder "J" General Folder, N-CU-MS.

58. [Dean] A. C. Hanford, to JBJ, July 13, 1932, carbon, HUA; "Harvard Awards Midyear Degrees to 212 Students," *Harvard Crimson,* March 2, 1933. http://www.thecrimson.com/article /1933/3/2/harvard-awards-midyear-degrees-to-212/.

59. JBJ, HAPS application, January 7, 1935, HUA.

60. Jackson stated to me that he attended an art school, designed to train commercial artists, in Vienna during his time abroad (HLH-JBJ OI, January 18, 1994); but I have found nothing to support a period in Austria long enough to include such a course in Vienna.

61. JBJ, HAPS, January 7, 1935, HUA.

62. JBJ to WWN, February 27, 1937, N-CU-MS.

2. EARLY WRITINGS

1. The announcement of Betty Jackson's engagement to be married included attendance at Stuart Hall in Staunton, Virginia, and Washington Cathedral School in Washington, D.C. Interestingly, it gave her mother's address as "315 East Fifty-first Street and Paris" ("Betty Jackson Engaged: Her Betrothal to Dr. Frank Hart Peters Announced," *New York Times,* Sept. 26, 1928). Her gravesite gives her death date as June 26, 1935. (https://cs.billiongraves.com/grave/Betty

-Jackson-Peters/4201492#/). Although Jackson spoke to me a good deal about his brother, he never volunteered any mention of his sister.

2. J. Brinckerhoff Jackson, "Blacksome & Veepings," *Choate Literary Magazine* 12, no. 1 (February 1926), 29–38, quote, 29.

3. "Most Influential Books," *Landscape Journal* 10, no. 2 (Fall 1991), 174.

4. J. Brinckerhoff Jackson, "A Plea for a Little Less Wisdom," *Choate Literary Magazine* 12, no. 12 (May 1926), 21–23.

5. Is the young Jackson here speaking out against the Klan? It is possible, but there are ambiguities in this piece I cannot resolve.

6. J. B. J., "The Heirs of Simon Legree," *Pocumtuck,* November 1926, 7–9.

7. Brinckerhoff Jackson, "A Thibetan Idyll," *Pocumtuck,* May 1927, 15–17.

8. Brinckerhoff Jackson, "The Nightmare before Christmas," *Harvard Advocate* 116, no. 4 (Christmas issue): 22–25, quotes 24, 25.

9. JBJ, "Nightmare before Christmas," 22.

10. Brinckerhoff Jackson, "M'man Potiron" *Harvard Advocate* 117, no. 1 (October, 1930), 10–15, quotes 14, 15.

11. J. Brinckerhoff Jackson, "Strohmeyer," *Harvard Advocate* 117, no. 7 (April 1931), 9–19.

12. JBJ, "Strohmeyer," 19.

13. JBJ, "Strohmeyer," 19.

14. JBJ, "Strohmeyer," 9.

15. *Harvard Advocate* 117, no. 5 (February 1931), 5.

16. Brinckerhoff Jackson, "Our Architects Discover Rousseau," *Harvard Advocate* 117, no. 8 (May 1931): 46–57.

17. JBJ, "Our Architects Discover Rousseau," 47.

18. JBJ, "Our Architects Discover Rousseau," 53–54.

19. JBJ, "Our Architects Discover Rousseau," 47.

20. JBJ, "Our Architects Discover Rousseau," 48.

21. JBJ, "Our Architects Discover Rousseau," 53.

22. JBJ, "Our Architects Discover Rousseau," 54.

23. JBJ, "Our Architects Discover Rousseau," 56.

24. JBJ, "Our Architects Discover Rousseau," 56–57.

25. JBJ, scrapbook for his mother, 1946. It contains sketches: each normally gives geographical location and/or specific setting or building, and, occasionally, commentary. If the dates were from memory, some may have been misremembered. (Scrapbook of J. B. Jackson sketches, 1946, copyright held by CSWR.)

26. The correspondence between JBJ and WWN, N-CU-MS. WWN's letters are office carbon copies, typically dictated.

27. JBJ to WWN, March 30 [1934], N-CU-MS. Jackson's address at this time was 5 Linden St., Cambridge.

28. WWN to JBJ, April 5, 1934, N-CU-MS.

29. WGJ was a graduate of both Haverford College and Yale Law School.

30. WWN to Edward Weeks, Atlantic Monthly, April 28, 1934, N-CU-MS.

31. WWN to JBJ, April 28, 1934, N-CU-MS.

32. These pieces and the novel that followed are discussed in the following essay.

33. Revealed in the application discussed below, as JBJ's only income.

34. HAPS application, January 7, 1935, HUA.

35. Donald H. Moyer, Asst. Director, HAPS, to Conde Nast, January 21, 1935, HUA.

36. Francesca van der Kley to Donald H. Moyer, January 24, 1935; Moyer to JBJ, January 26, 1935; file, March 1, 1935, HUA.

37. ARJ to WWN, Tuesday May 18, [1937], N-CU-MS.

38. WWN to ARJ, May 19, 1937, N-CU-MS.

39. Brinckerhoff Jackson, *Saints in Summertime* (New York: W. W. Norton, 1938).

40. JBJ to WWN, February 27, [1938], N-CU-MS.

41. JBJ to WWN, April 9 [1938]; JBJ to Miss Lincoln, June 16 [1938], N-CU-MS.

42. JBJ to WWN, May 13 [1938], N-CU-MS.

43. JBJ to WWN, undated, stamped by the office November 9, 1937, N-CU-MS.

44. JBJ to Miss Lincoln, June 16 [1938], N-CU-MS. These comments were typed for future use in publicity.

45. Contract, dated April 7, 1938; JBJ to WWN, May 13 [1938] N-CU-MS.

46. *New York Times,* July 21, 1938.

47. JBJ to WWN, May 13 [1938]; WWN to JBJ, May 16, 1938, N-CU-MS.

48. JBJ to WWN, October 15 [1938], N-CU-MS.

49. WWN to JBJ, October 18, 1938, N-CU-MS.

50. JBJ to FB, October 16 [1940]. JBJ's address on the letter is MG Troop, 7th Cavalry, Fort Bliss, Tex., DA.

51. WWN to JBJ, November 18, 1940, N-CU-MS.

52. WWN to JBJ, November 6, 1940. The address of the letter sent by airmail was M.G. Troop, 7th Cavalry, Fort Bliss, Texas, N-CU-MS.

53. Brinckerhoff Jackson, "Art and Housing," review of *From Rameses to Rockefeller* by Charles Harris Whitaker, *American Review*, 1935, 373–76; quote, 376.

54. Brinckerhoff Jackson, "Prussianism or Hitlerism," *American Review,* 1934, 454–71.

55. JBJ, "Prussianism or Hitlerism," 456, 457, 458.

56. JBJ, "Prussianism or Hitlerism," 464–65.

57. JBJ, "Prussianism or Hitlerism," 470–71, quote, 471.

58. JBJ, scrapbook, 1946, CSWR.

59. JBJ, "Prussianism or Hitlerism," 464.

60. In 1994, Jackson told me he based this piece on his own experience in Bidutz, Liechten-

stein, where he got to know a young waiter (aspiring to become a photographer) at the inn in which he stayed.

61. Brinckerhoff Jackson, "A Führer Comes to Liechtenstein," *Harper's Magazine* 170 (February 1935, 298–310.

62. JBJ, *Saints in Summertime.*

63. These travel journals, along with those of 1954–1960 will be deposited in the CSWR following the publication of this book. Jackson did not number their pages.

64. As with most of the journals, this one gives only the days of the month, not the year. In this case, letters to WWN and some internal evidence give the needed information.

65. Soon after landing, V.P. sent a cable to Edna. Two months afterward, in May 1938, Jackson reported to WWN that he was about to travel for a week "through Olde Newe England with Perry and Edna."

3. WARTIME SERVICE

1. HLH-JBJ OI, January 17–21 and May 31–June 2, 1994.

2. HLH-JBJ OI, June 2, 1994.

3. HLH-JBJ OI, January 19, 1994.

4. HLH-JBJ OI, June 2, 1994.

5. John Brinckerhoff Jackson, "Landscape as Seen by the Military," *Discovering the Vernacular Landscape* (New Haven: Yale University Press), 131–37, should be read in conjunction with the treatment on these pages.

6. F. Douglas Adams, "J. B. Jackson: Drawn to Intelligence," in Mendelsohn and Wilson, *Drawn to Landscape,* 32–40.

7. Portfolio A, in Mendelsohn and Wilson, *Drawn to Landscape,* 45, 48–55.

8. Original record in Ancestry.com., "U.S., World War II Army Enlistment Records, 1938–1946," https://www.ancestry.com/search/collections/wwiienlist/.

9. JBJ to FB, October 16 [1940], DA. Jackson's return address was MG Troop, 7th Cavalry, Fort Bliss, Tex.

10. JBJ to FB, October 16 [1940], DA.

11. An ironic statement, given New England's careful recording of births.

12. FB to JBJ, October. 28, 1940, DA.

13. JBJ to FB, May 19 [1943], DA.

14. JBJ to FB, October 17, 1943, DA. Where possible, I have added corrections in brackets for clarity. All other errors or typos are in the original.

15. JBJ to FB, September 5, 1945, DA.

16. JBJ to FB, February 10, [1959], DA.

17. JBJ to FB. October 7, [1964], DA.

18. I am relying on my memory of our personal conversation at breakfast, the morning following the PEN ceremony.

19. "Mrs. B. W. Bellinger Engaged to Be Wed" (*New York Times,* March 8, 1943). The "late" is important, for it gives the first indication of J. B. Jackson's father's death in or before 1943. The mention of only Wayne's mother in his 1937 marriage announcement may have been because of marital separation or Wayne being her son only.

20. Liza Mundy, *Code Girls: The Untold Story of the American Women Code Breakers of World War II* (New York: Hachette Books, 2017), documents epistolary engagements during the war between the American women at home and GIs abroad.

21. JBJ was actually thirty-four. See "Separating Fact from Fancy," in chapter 7.

22. This account of Jackson's ranching prior to military service differs from all known other accounts that have him as a ranch hand.

23. Excerpt from Ernie Pyle, *Brave Men* (New York: Gosset & Dunlap, 1944), 280–81.

24. *Springfield (MA) Republican,* June 30, 1944, 8.

25. J. B. Jackson, "Landscape as Seen by the Military," *Discovering the Vernacular Landscape* (New Haven: Yale University Press, 1984), 131–44. It should be read in conjunction with the treatment on these pages.

4. *LANDSCAPE* YEARS

1. JBJ, "Landscape as Seen by the Military," 131–38.

2. JBJ, "Landscape as Seen by the Military," 133, 134. "Bocage" is defined by the online Merriam Webster dictionary as "countryside or landscape (as of western France) marked by intermingling patches of woodland and heath, small fields, tall hedgerows, and orchards" (https://www.merriam-webster.com/dictionary/bocage).

3. Jackson wrote Huertgen.

4. JBJ, "Landscape as Seen by the Military," 134.

5. JBJ to ARJ [March 20, 1951]. See following note.

6. JBJ, diary entries, February 5–10, 1951, and JBJ, carbon copies of letters to ARJ and WGJ, February-March, 1951, HLH-P. All discussion of the process of creating the first issue of *Landscape* comes from these materials. The letters were saved in no chronological order. Their headings normally give only the day of the week and, with a few exceptions, don't lend themselves easily to exact dates. Two professional letters on March 15 helped in the sorting, as well as the date of Easter in 1951. Reconstruction of dates also relies on internal sequences and WGJ's move to Gaylord, a sanitorium in Wallingford, Connecticut. Obvious typographical errors have been corrected.

7. I have standardizd the title of this piece, as it initially appeared in the table of contents of *Landscape* 1, no. 1 (Spring 1951).

8. Entry on George Adlai Feather, SNAC (Social Networks and Archival Context), http://socialarchive.iath.virginia.edu/ark:/99166/w65n5s3p.

9. Adams, "J. B. Jackson: Drawn to Intelligence," 37.

10. Frank Waters, *Masked Gods: Navaho and Pueblo Ceremonialism* (Albuquerque: University of New Mexico Press, 1950).

11. See Jackson's "Jackson's Remarks at PEN Award Presentation, 1995," in chapter 8.

12. Unless otherwise cited, all quotes from published material come from *Landscape* 1, no. 1, (Spring 1951). Here, [JBJ], "The Need of Being Versed in Country Things," 1–5, quotes, 4, 5.

13. JBJ, "Chihuahua; As We Might Have Been," 16–24, quotes, 16, 22–23.

14. I am grateful to Chris Wilson for helping me see this.

15. A. W. Conway, [Jackson], "Southwestern Colonial Farms," 6–9, quotes, 6, 9. In describing this first issue of *Landscape* to his brother, in the first letter among those surviving from 1951 addressed only to Wayne at Gaylord Farms in Connecticut, Jackson wrote he had an editorial with title from a Frost Poem, then "an illustrated article on a certain house type, for which I wanted your picture of the house at Espanola." Wayne is credited with photographs of Chihuahua rangeland and of an older grand house in Chihuahua, Mexico.

16. Letter, March 19, 1951, HLH-P.

17. [Jackson,] "Maps," 36–37, quotes, 37.

18. P. G. A. [JBJ], review of Frank Waters, *Masked Gods: Navaho and Pueblo Ceremonialism,* 25–28, quote, 25.

19. JBJ to Vera Laski, March 15 [1951], HLH-P.

20. [JBJ], review of Waters, *Masked Gods,* 27–28.

21. J. B. J., review of Dorothy L. Pillsbury, *No High Adobe,* 28–29, quote, 29.

22. A. W. C. [JBJ], review of Trent E. Sanford, *The Architecture of the Southwest,* 29–32, quote, 29.

23. [JBJ], review of Sanford, *Architecture of the Southwest,* 30.

24. [JBJ], review of Sanford, *Architecture of the Southwest,* 31.

25. [JBJ], review of Albert N. Williams, *The Water and the Power,* and Bernard Frank and Anthony Netboy, *Water, Land, and People,* 31–35, quotes, 33–34.

26. [JBJ], review of Williams, *Water and the Power,* and Frank and Netboy, *Water, Land, and People,* 34.

27. [JBJ], review of Williams, *Water and the Power,* and Frank and Netboy, *Water, Land, and People,* 35.

28. Jackson, "Ghosts at the Door," *Landscape* 1, no. 2 (Autumn 1951), 3–9, quote, 3.

29. JBJ, "Ghosts at the Door," 3–4.

30. HLH-JBJ OI, January 18, 1994.

31. Jackson, "Ghosts at the Door," 7.

32. Jackson, "The Almost Perfect Town," *Landscape* 2, no. 1 (Spring 1952), 2–8.

33. JBJ, "Almost Perfect Town," 6.

34. Ajax [JBJ], "Storm Brewing," *Landscape* 2, no. 1 (Spring 1952), 22–23.

35. Michel Perrin, "A Black Guide to Sinistria," translated by M. E. Armengaud, *Landscape* 2, no. 2 (Autumn 1952), 30–31, quote, 31.

36. S. C. Babb, "A Brief Lexicon of Road Words, *Landscape* 2, no. 2 (Autumn 1952), 32–33, quote, 32.

37. P. K. [JBJ], review of Kenneth Clark, *Landscape Painting,* in *Landscape* 1, no. 2 (Autumn 1951), 28–30, quote, 30.

38. P. C. A. [JBJ], review of Laura Thompson, *Culture in Crisis: A Study of the Hopi Indians,* in *Landscape* 1, no. 2 (Autumn 1951), 32–34, quote, 34.

39. "Contents for Spring 1952," *Landscape* 2, no. 1 (Spring 1952), 1.

40. Ajax [JBJ], "A Golden Treasure of Western Prose and Song," *Landscape* 2, no. 1 (Spring 1952), 25–28.

41. [JBJ], "Notes and Comments," *Landscape* 2, no. 1 (Spring 1952), 34–35, quote, 35.

42. H. G. W. [JBJ], review of Pal Kelemen, *Baroque and Rococo in Latin America,* in *Landscape* 2, no. 1 (Spring 1952), 31.

43. [JBJ] "What We Want," *Landscape* 1, no. 3 (Winter 1952), 2–5, quote, 5. Jackson's initial sequence of his three issues was Spring, Autumn, Winter. Vol. 2 sequence was Spring, Autumn [without winter], Spring. Vol. 3 then offered Summer, Winter, and Spring—the pattern JBJ kept for future volumes.

44. J. B. J., "Human, All Too Human Geography," *Landscape* 2, no. 2 (Autumn 1952), 2–8, quote, 7.

45. This collection included photographs, historic descriptions, Soviet press releases, a government plan, and depictions from fiction. A single element, a consideration of collectivized farming, listed Jackson as author.

46. JBJ, "Human, All Too Human Geography," 5, 6.

47. JBJ, "Human, All Too Human Geography," 5, 6.

48. HLH-JBJ OI, January 19, 1994.

49. Pierre Deffontaines, "The Place of Believing," *Landscape* 2, no. 3 (Spring 1953), 22–28, quotes, 22.

50. J. B. Jackson, "The Westward-Moving House," *Landscape* 2, no. 3 (Spring 1953), 8–21.

51. JBJ, "Westward-Moving House," 16.

52. JBJ, "Westward-Moving House," 18, 19.

53. H. G. West [JBJ], "A Change in Plans: Is the Modern House a Victorian Invention?" *Landscape* 1, no. 3 (Winter 1952), 18–26, quote, 26.

54. H. G. West [JBJ], review of Siegfried Giedion, ed., *A Decade of New Architecture,* and Hugh Morrison, *Early American Architecture,* in *Landscape* 2, no. 2 (Autumn 1952), 37–39, quote, 38. In a later issue, Ajax mocked the owners of high Modernist houses in a wickedly

funny sendup in "Living Outdoors with Mrs. Panther," *Landscape* 4, no. 2 (Winter 1954–55), 24–25.

55. West [JBJ], review, 39.

56. J. B. Jackson, "A Statement of Policy," *Landscape* 6, no. 1 (Autumn 1956), 2–5, quotes, 3. I am grateful to Paul Groth for letting me read his excellent unpublished paper from 1978, documenting the growing importance of urbanism during the time of Jackson's editorship of *Landscape*.

57. JBJ, "Statement of Policy," 3, 4. Jackson may have been aware of Jane Jacobs's critiques of urban planning, just beginning to appear in print; the convergence is striking.

58. JBJ, "Statement of Policy," 5.

59. John B. Jackson, letter in "Mr. Citizen," *Santa Fe New Mexican,* February 6, 1946, 4.

60. Jackson always spoke of her as "Miss White." One of their visits was documented in the *Santa Fe New Mexican,* June 1, 1941: "Brinckerhoff Jackson has been spending several days in Santa Fe from Fort Bliss where he is serving in the US army, the houseguest of Miss Amelia Elizabeth White. Mr. Jackson is the nephew of the late Percy Jackson."

61. The personal information in this essay, including quoted material, relies on JBJ, diary entries, February 5–10, 1951, and JBJ, carbon copies of letters to ARJ and WGJ, February-March, 1951, HLH-P. See note 6.

62. John B. Jackson, "The Spanish Pueblo Fallacy," *Southwest Review* 35, no. 1 (Winter 1950), 19–26, quote 16. In 1958 the style was mandated as one of the two to be preserved and fostered within the city.

63. This is belied by a positive review of the book in the *Santa Fe New Mexican.*

64. Mayer was a controversial figure. A Jew by birth, a Quaker by choice, he had been outspoken in his opposition to World War II. As a reporter and longtime columnist for the *Progressive Magazine,* he was identified with the American Left. In 1952, he was in the middle of researching his most important book, *They Thought They Were Free,* a study focused on Germans in Hitler's era.

65. *Albuquerque Journal,* September 28, 1952, 7.

66. *Albuquerque Journal,* May 22, 1955, 15.

67. Under the Freedom of Information Act, I initially secured JBJ's FBI file (FOIPA No. 1098215–600) in 2008. Learning that more pre-1960 material was released, I made a second request in 2016 and received a file containing the information in this and the following paragraphs.

68. WGJ later served on the Board of National Estimates of the CIA. With his retirement in 1969, he wrote under contract as a member of the CIA historical staff, "Allen Welsh Dulles as Director of Central Intelligence," a five-volume work originally classified. (It was declassified in 1994.) I read it in typescript in the mid- to late 1990s at the National Security Archive at George Washington University. Information on Wayne G. Jackson comes from notes taken at that time.

69. The effort was spearheaded by Alma Whittlin, an Austrian émigrée. *Albuquerque Journal,* July 28, 1957.

70. *Albuquerque Journal,* October 12, 1958, 18.

71. Ben Bowen, "In the Alcoves," *Santa Fe New Mexican,* October 28, 1958.

72. *Santa Fe New Mexican,* January 18, 1962.

73. *Santa Fe New Mexican,* June 12, 1963, and April 17, 1963.

74. *Santa Fe New Mexican,* September 25, 1966.

75. *Santa Fe New Mexican,* November 29, 1970. In 1972, a section of this Curtin property— with historic roots as the first overnight stop on the Camino Real from Santa Fe to Mexico City—became an outdoor history museum known as El Rancho de Las Golondrinas.

76. *Santa Fe New Mexican,* July 19, 1954; Marc Treib, "J. B. Jackson's Home Ground," *Landscape Architecture* 78, no. 3 (April-May 1988), 52–57.

77. Interview with Donlyn Lyndon, February 6, 2017.

78. In 1971, for example, it was announced that Jackson "will open his home for the Velorio," the day of the dead celebration, held by the Sociedad Folklorica (*Santa Fe New Mexican,* July 15, 1971).

79. *Santa Fe New Mexican,* August 20, 1959.

80. *Santa Fe New Mexican,* September 2, 1959.

81. *Santa Fe New Mexican,* June 18, 1963.

82. *Santa Fe New Mexican,* June 14, 1964.

83. *Santa Fe New Mexican,* September 26, 1976.

84. These appear in a travel journal but were clearly written at Jackson's rented La Cienega residence.

85. JBJ., "Human, All Too Human Geography," *Landscape* 2, no. 2 (Autumn 1952), 2–8, quote, 6.

5. FORAYS

1. P. G. Anson [JBJ], review of four travel books, *Landscape* 6, no. 1 (Autumn 1956), 39–40.

2. If Jackson dated his entries, it was with the month and the day of the week without the year. I relied on an online table offering a range of years in which the days of the week and month match, using internal evidence in the journal, such as the nature of the journey in relation to Jackson's age, the years since he was last at that place or since World War II, etc. Occasionally, he offered useful clues, such as a just-completed highway or a newly published book (Easy Calculation.com, https://www.easycalculation.com/date-day/same-calendar-years.php).

3. As late as 1994, Jackson spoke kindly of Will and of his continued contact with the Haegler family.

4. It has not been possible to use the online calculator here because the days of the week and

month that Jackson gives prove contradictory. Given what information I have, I tentatively place this trip in 1955.

5. I never saw Jackson in glasses or heard him mention nearsightedness.

6. Likely Vitrolite, a colored glass veneer.

7. Jackson may have been referring to "Southwestern Landscapes as Seen from the Air," in which he considered the absence of fences with the coming of mechanized farming (*Landscape* 1, no. 2 [Autumn 1951], 18).

8. JBJ, "Other-Directed Houses," *Landscape* 6, no. 2 (Winter 1956–57), 29–35; "The Stranger's Path," *Landscape* 7, no. 1 (Autumn 1957), 11–15.

9. Jackson also seemingly mocks Black Mountain College in North Carolina, an innovative school of the arts known for its left-wing faculty.

10. Bingmann, *Prep School Cowboys*.

11. While there is no certainty this meeting was in La Cienega, not Santa Fe, internal evidence points to this.

12. Passages in this journal recalling his military service at Fort Bliss are found elsewhere in this volume.

13. Harvard Class of 1932, *Twenty-Fifth Anniversary Report* (Cambridge, MA: Harvard University Printing office, 1957), 608–9.

14. Although Wayne G. Jackson spent his career after World War II high up in the CIA, in these years he was seemingly on the administrative and diplomatic side in Washington, D.C.

15. In Jackson's 1954 journal, he had listed the Tyrol address and phone number of Dora and Geoffrey Stone.

16. The Museum of International Folk Art in Santa Fe opened in 1953. Founded by Florence Dibell Bartlett, it received many of her objects in 1956. Jackson was then serving on the board of the museum's foundation.

17. JBJ-P, Box 2, folder 1, CSWR.

18. H. A. [Henry] Wallace, "Corn and the Midwestern Farmer," reprinted in *Landscape* 6, no. 3 (Spring 1957), 9–12. He contributed a book review in vol. 7, no. 3 (Spring 1958), 31–32, and wrote an admiring letter for the tenth anniversary issue, vol. 10, no. 1 (Fall 1960), 7.

19. In the entire journal of almost 15,000 words, chronicling all three phases of their travels, JBJ referred to Alice Jackson directly only seven times, used the "we" to include her roughly thirty-nine times and "us" only three times.

20. See "Separating Fact from Fancy" in chapter 7.

21. See "Teaching the Everyday Landscape" in chapter 6.

22. By "fairy," Jackson was likely referring to a cartoon portrayal of a homosexual man.

23. Had Jackson read W. J. Cash's *Mind of the South* (1941)? Given his omnivorous reading and the book's prominence in discussions of the South in the years after World War II, it seems likely.

24. Jackson never mentions he visited Mayan sites either in his boyhood with his uncle, Percy Jackson, or in 1937 with two friends.

25. Likely a missed opportunity, as Kniffen's work on vernacular architecture, especially regarding houses, had much to offer Jackson.

26. This comment gives information that Alice Jackson was also on the car trip north.

27. No year is given in this journal. It is 1958 because Munich reached a population of one million on December 15, 1957, and when Jackson arrived in January, celebration of this milestone was still in evidence.

28. Dr. Dagobert Frey, someone noted in an earlier journal, as a contact. He is notorious as responsible for the theft of art from Nazi-occupied Poland.

29. "Wandlung dis 20 Johrhondens," likely *Wandlung des 20 Jahrhondens.*

30. Southeast to Turkey," *Landscape* 7, no. 3 (Spring 1958): 17–22.

31. "Istanbul" in "Southeast to Turkey," *Landscape* 7, no. 3 (Spring 1958): 21–22.

32. See essay "Life in Santa Fe in the Landscape Years," chapter 4.

33. To which my response typically begins, "Do you know this by direct knowledge?"

34. We never, however, discussed this suggestion in person.

35. See William Wright, *Harvard's Secret Court: The Savage 1920 Purge of Campus Homosexuals* (New York: St. Martin's Press, 2005).

36. *Landscape* 7, no. 2 (Winter 1957–58), 22–27.

37. Likely *El crepúsculo de la libertad,* published by Edward C. Cabot.

38. The Hanosh family from Syria and their store in Mora are documented in Monika Ghattas, *Los Árabes of New Mexico: Compadres from a Distant Land* (Santa Fe, NM: Sunstone Press, 2012).

6. AT THE PODIUM

1. Paul Groth, "J. B. Jackson and Geography," *Geographical Review* 88, no. 4 (October 1998), iii–vi.

2. *Bulletin: General Catalogue* 58, no. 16 (Berkeley: University of California, Berkeley 1964), 407.

3. *UC Berkeley, General Catalogue,* 1968–69, 62, no. 10, 305.

4. Paul Groth, "Index of materials," 1, December 18, 2004 (Courtesy Pal Groth).

5. Marc Treib, "The Measure of Wisdom: John Brinckerhoff Jackson (1909–1996)," *Journal of the Society of Architectural Historians* 55, no. 4 (December 1996), 380–81, 490–91, quotes, 490.

6. *The Confidential Guide,* the publication's official name, was inaugurated in 1934 and grew out of an annual review of courses by the *Harvard Crimson* (http://www.thecrimson.com /article/1934/9/1/the-confidential-guide-pthe-publication-of/).

7. Visual and Environmental Studies 127, *Courses of Instruction,* Harvard and Radcliffe, Faculty of Arts and Sciences, 1969–70, 503.

8. "In a phone conversation with Paul Groth on January 13, 1979, John Stilgoe of Harvard stated that in 1976, JBJ changed the course dramatically." Groth, "Index of materials," 1.

9. *Confidential Guide,* 1973, 117.

10. Jeffrey Flemming, personal communication, September 3, 2017.

11. JBJ to HLH, February 22 [1974].

12. WGJ to JBJ, December 20 [1973], HLH-P.

13. Whether the Harvard dean in question was of the Faculty of Arts and Sciences or of the Graduate School of Design is unknown.

14. WGJ, "Allen Welsh Dulles as Director of Central Intelligence."

15. *Confidential Guide,* 1974, 119.

16. *Confidential Guide,* 1976, last page (unpaged).

17. After Jackson's "retirement" from teaching, he taught single terms at UCLA in spring 1978 and at the University of Texas in the second semester of the academic year 1979–80. (Although I attended several of Jackson's UCLA lectures, I was close to giving birth and thus too distracted to have adequate memory of their content or to recollect who gave me outlines of the lectures in my files.)

18. The letters were prompted by Grady Clay, the journalist and editor of *Landscape Architecture Magazine.* Assuming I would write Jackson's biography after his death, Clay contacted persons in his own network to send to me copies of their correspondence with Jackson.

19. J. B. Jackson, "Various Aspects of Landscape Analysis," *Texas Conference on Our Environmental Crisis* (Austin: School of Architecture, University of Texas, 1966), 150–57. In a frontispiece, Lady Bird Johnson is pictured with the chairman of the Texas Board of Regents and another dignitary "during one of the conference sessions."

20. "Lecture File, Table of Contents," typescript, HLH-P. Some entries lack a date, some lack a definite location, and some items listed are publications rather than talks.

21. For example, early entries track initial Berkeley lectures, but his later ones do not necessarily appear. Paul Groth has documented that after retiring from teaching Jackson returned to give a lecture at Berkeley almost every year until 1990 (Paul Groth, typescript, December 18, 2004, courtesy of Paul Groth).

22. Copies of these letters were kindly sent to me by her son, John Sinton.

23. John Brinckerhoff Jackson, *The Southern Landscape Tradition in Texas* (Fort Worth: Amon Carter Museum of Western Art, 1980).

24. See chapter 1, "School," above.

25. Paul Groth to Reuben Rainey, July 10, 1979 (copy, courtesy Paul Groth).

26. The Wikipedia entry for Rothsay states this statue remains one of the town's "major tourist attractions."

7. THE MAN I KNEW

1. It is missing from my files, so I likely returned it to Jackson.

2. Fuller discussion can be found in the essay "Landscape in the Fourth Dimension" in the final chapter of this book.

3. See my review, "Towards a New History of the Landscape and Built Environment," *Reviews in American History* 13, no. 4 (December 1985), 487–93.

4. Jonathan Raban, "From John Winthrop to Mister Softee," *New York Times,* August 12, 1984. By contrast, however, the daily *New York Times* review by Anatole Broyard, July 20, 1984, had offered unstinted praise.

5. The mantel items, originally left to me, now reside at the CSWR.

6. JBJ-U, CSWR. Jackson did not always have guests sign in. Certain persons who wrote for the first time suggested they had visited often.

7. When, in 1977, she signed as Emlen Evers, I was able to place the Emlen of travel journals (see "Europe 1955–1956" in chapter 5) as the former Emlen Grosjean.

8. Jackson left Sarah Horowitz, our daughter, that grandmother's china pieces.

9. Anthony P. Musso, "George Washington a Frequent Guest at Brinckerhoff Home," *Poughkeepsie Journal,* November 15, 2016, http://www.poughkeepsiejournal.com/story/news/local/2016/11/15/dateline-local-history-john-brinckerhoff-house/93912486/.

10. A story in a teacher's magazine may have served as a false memory: "Washington's Visit to Betty," *Primary Education*, February. 1916, 122, 124.

11. By the time I met Jackson in 1973, when he was sixty-four and I thirty-one, I, at 66 inches, was considerably taller than he. While as he aged he may have lost some height, it is unlikely that by then he had lost 4 inches.

8. TRACKING THE VERNACULAR

1. J. B. Jackson, "The Vernacular City," *Center: A Journal for Architecture in America* 1 (1985): 26–43.

2. Jackson mistakenly put the publication year of *Babbitt* as 1923.

3. JBJ, "Vernacular City," 29.

4. JBJ, "Vernacular City," 38.

5. JBJ, "Vernacular City," 41–42.

6. JBJ, "Vernacular City," 43.

7. J. B. Jackson, "Vernacular Landscape on the Move," *Places* 7, no. 3 (1991), 24–35.

8. JBJ, "Vernacular Landscape on the Move," 24.

9. JBJ, "Vernacular Landscape on the Move," 26.

10. JBJ, "Vernacular Landscape on the Move," 28, 33.

11. JBJ, "Vernacular Landscape on the Move," 34.

12. JBJ, "Vernacular Landscape on the Move," 34.

13. JBJ, "Vernacular Landscape on the Move," 34–35.

14. JBJ, "Vernacular Landscape on the Move," 35.

15. JBJ, "Vernacular Landscape on the Move," 35.

16. J. B. Jackson, "Our Towns: The Struggle to Survive," *New Mexico Magazine,* February 1991, 34–42, quotes, 38.

17. JBJ, "Our Towns," 42. This is a significant concession given Jackson's earlier embrace of the older "monumental" structures.

18. JBJ, "Our Towns," 42.

19. JBJ, "Our Towns," 42. The word "homogeneity" is an odd choice here, given the high value Jackson placed on New Mexico's diverse population.

20. J. B. Jackson, "Cultures and Regionalism," originally published in *MASS,* Spring 1992, 12–13 (later reprinted in *Designer/Builder*, 1996), quotes, 12.

21. JBJ, "Cultures and Regionalism," 12.

22. JBJ, "Cultures and Regionalism," 13.

23. See "The First Issue of Landscape" in chapter 4, pages 86–87.

24. JBJ, "Cultures and Regionalism," 13.

25. J. B. Jackson, "The American Public Space," *Public Interest,* winter 1985, 52–65 (a neoconservative journal, 1965–2005).

26. JBJ, "American Public Space," 62–63.

27. JBJ, "American Public Space," 65.

28. J. B. Jackson, "Urban Circumstances," *Design Quarterly,* Walker Art Center, 5–31 (Cambridge: MIT Press, 1985).

29. JBJ, "Urban Circumstances," quotes, 9, continued 12 (photos, 10–11).

30. JBJ, "Urban Circumstances," 30.

31. JBJ, "Urban Circumstances," 30–31.

32. J. B. Jackson, "Working at Home," *Cite: The Architecture + Design Review of Houston* 28 (Spring 1992), 13–15.

33. JBJ, "Working at Home," 13.

34. JBJ, "Working at Home," 13.

35. JBJ, "Working at Home," 14.

36. JBJ, "Working at Home," 14.

37. JBJ, "Working at Home," 14, 15.

38. JBJ, "Working at Home," 15.

39. JBJ, "Working at Home," 15.

40. "Most Influential Books," *Landscape Journal* 10, no. 2 (Fall 1991), 173–86.

41. "Most Influential Books," 174.

42. HLH-JBJ OI, January 21, 1994.

43. See discussion of "Our Architects Discover Rousseau," in chapter 2.

44. And perhaps even more significantly the body of work of the French Annales School.

45. Howard D. Weinbrot, "'Tis Well an Old Age Is Out': Johnson, Swift, and His Generation," in *Samuel Johnson: New Contexts for a New Century,* ed. Howard D. Weinbrot, 50–51 (San Marino, CA: Huntington Library, 2014); also in the same volume is James Engell, "Johnson and Scott, England and Scotland, Boswell, Lockhart, and Croker," 313–42, esp. 317–24.

46. Samuel Johnson, *A Journey to the Western Islands of Scotland* (1775), with Introduction and Notes by J. D. Fleeman (Oxford: Clarendon Press, 1985), 32–33, 10.

47. Johnson, *Journey to the Western Islands,* 116–17.

48. Jackson's approach to conversation with strangers is best documented in Bob Calo, *J. B. Jackson and the Love of Everyday Places* (San Francisco: KQED-TV, 1989).

49. Johnson, *Journey to the Western Islands,* 16–17.

50. HLH-JBJ OI, January 17, 1994.

51. JBJ, JBJ-P, CSWR, Box 1, Folder 6. Jackson ended with complimentary words for the new book of Simon Schama.

52. When Jackson spoke to me about this he conveyed his extreme distaste for the highly personal tone alumni callers took when soliciting contributions from him. Quotes from JBJ to Mr. McClellan, June 26, [mid-1990s], DA.

53. Judy Metro to JBJ, August 21, 1996, U-JBJ, CSWR. After Jackson's death in 1996, the executor of his estate required the excision of mention of Hasty Pudding and Deerfield Academy in my essay.

9. WHAT LIVES ON

1. Megan Kamerick, "This Gift Continues to Give," *Business First,* Albuquerque, October 9, 2005, https://www.bizjournals.com/albuquerque/stories/2005/10/10/focus1.html.

2. *Santa Fe New Mexican,* October 7, 1998.

3. *Santa Fe New Mexican,* March 19, 2000.

4. Helen L. Horowitz and Daniel Horowitz, review of J. B. Jackson, *American Space: The Centennial Years, 1865–1876,* in *Journal of Interdisciplinary History* 5, no. 2 (Autumn 1974), 336–40.

5. Jackson mentioned the reading for Norton was by a Yale historian.

6. Copies of the manuscript are in JBJ-P, CSWR.

7. J. B. Jackson, "The Discovery of the Street," *The Necessity for Ruins and Other Topics* (Amherst: University of Massachusetts Press, 1980), 55–66, quote, 66.

8. Herbert Muschamp, "Eloquent Champion of the Vernacular Landscape," *New York Times,* April 21, 1996, 36; here and in the quotes that follow. "A Sense of Place, a Sense of Time" was

curated by Eleanor M. McPeck. After it closed in New York, it traveled to the Rhode Island School of Design for the month of May 1996.

9. Interview transcripts of J. B. Jackson talking with Bob Calo, c. 1988, 10, JBJ files, HLH-P.

10. The earliest extant drawing dates from 1926, Scrapbook of J. B. Jackson sketches, 1946.

11. F. Douglas Adams, "J. B. Jackson: Drawn to Intelligence," in Mendelsohn and Wilson, *Drawn to Landscape,* 32–40.

12. HLH-JBJ OI, January 17, 1994.

13. HLH-JBJ OI, June 1, 1994.

14. See discussion of Jackson's writings at Harvard in chapter 2.

15. Quote from "Hail and Farewell" (Notes and Comments), *Landscape* 3, no. 2 (Winter 1953–54), 5–6, quote, 6.

16. "Other-Directed Houses," *Landscape* 6, no. 2 (Winter 1956–57), 29–35.

17. HLH-JBJ OI, January 20, 1994.

18. HLH-JBJ OI, January 20, 1994.

19. J. B. Jackson, "The Domestication of the Garage," *Landscape* 20, no. 2 (Winter 1976), 10–19.

20. HLH-JBJ OI, January 19, 1994.

21. HLH-JBJ OI, June 2, 1994.

22. HLH-JBJ OI, January 18, 1994.

23. HLH-JBJ OI, January 18, 1994.

24. HLH-JBJ OI, January 19, 1994.

25. HLH-JBJ OI, January 19, 1994.

26. HLH-JBJ OI, May 31, 1994.

27. Along with Jackson's photographs, the show and catalog featured the work of Donald Appleyard, Allan Jacobs, Chester Liebs, Richard Longstreth, and David Lowenthal.

28. Jordi Ballesta and Camille Fallet, *Notes sur l'asphalte: Une Amérique mobile et précaire, 1950–1990* (Montpellier: Éditions Hazan, 2018).

29. HLH-JBJ OI, January 19, 1994.

ILLUSTRATION CREDITS

Author's collection: *figures 15, 18, 19, 23, 24, 25, 30, 35; color plates 1, 3, 4, 5, 6, 7, 8, 9, 10, 11, 13, 14, 15, 16*

J. B. Jackson Papers, Center for Southwest Research at the University of New Mexico (CSWR): *figures 1, 2, 3, 4, 5, 6, 7, 8, 9, 12, 14, 16, 17, 27, 28*

Deerfield Archives: *figure 10*

Harvard University Archives: *figures 11* (student folder of John Brinckerhoff Jackson; UAIII 15.88.10 1890-1968, Box 2419), *13* (*Harvard Class Album of 1932;* HUD 332.04 [page 248]), *29* (51st *Annual Crimson Confidential Guide to Courses,* 1976; HUK 305.14 [1976-VES 107]; © 2018 The Harvard Crimson, Inc.; All rights reserved; Reprinted with permission)

Landscape Magazine: *figures 20, 21, 34*

John Sinton: *color plates 2, 12*

Paul Starrs: *figure 26*

Marc Treib: *figures 22, 31, 32, 33*

INDEX

Italicized page numbers refer to illustrations, and CP followed by a number denotes plates in the color gallery following page 178. The initials "JBJ" denote John Brinckerhoff Jackson.

Midcentury: Architecture, Landscape, Urbanism, and Design